Miriam's Tambourine

Jewish Folktales
from Around the World

By Howard Schwartz

Poetry

Vessels

Gathering the Sparks

Fiction

A Blessing Over Ashes

Midrashim: Collected Jewish Parables

The Captive Soul of the Messiah: New Tales About Reb Nachman

Rooms of the Soul

Editor

Imperial Messages: One Hundred Modern Parables

Voices Within the Ark: The Modern Jewish Poets

Gates to the New City: A Treasury of Modern Jewish Tales

Elijah's Violin & Other Jewish Fairy Tales

Lilith's Cave: Jewish Tales of the Supernatural

Miriam's Tambourine: Jewish Folktales from Around the World

"But on the eve of the Sabbath, I take the powder made from these
leaves and cast it into the wind . . ."

MIRIAM'S TAMBOURINE

Jewish Folktales from Around the World

Selected and Retold by
HOWARD SCHWARTZ

Illustrated by
Lloyd Bloom

with a Foreword by
Dov Noy

SETH PRESS

Distributed By
THE FREE PRESS
A Division of Macmillan, Inc.
NEW YORK

Seth Press
Distributed by
The Free Press
A Division of Macmillan, Inc.
866 Third Avenue, New York, N. Y. 10022

Collier Macmillan Canada, Inc.

Printed in the United States of America

printing number

1   2   3   4   5   6   7   8   9   10

Some of these tales have previously appeared in *The B'nai Brith International Jewish Monthly, Four Worlds Journal, Keeping Posted, The Melton Journal, Midstream, New Traditions, The Reconstructionist, The St. Louis Jewish Light,* and *Young Judaean.*

"A Garment for the Moon" and "The Palace Beneath the Sea" are reprinted from *The Captive Soul of the Messiah* by Howard Schwartz by permission of Schocken Books Inc. Copyright © 1980, 1981, 1982, 1983 by Howard Schwartz. All Rights Reserved.

Library of Congress Cataloging-in-Publication Data

Schwartz, Howard, 1945–
  Miriam's tambourine.

  Bibliography: p.
  1. Jews—Folklore.   2. Jewish folk literature.
3. Legends, Jewish.   4. Hasidim—Legends.   I. Title.
GR98.S345 1986   398.2'089924   86-15505
ISBN 0-02-929260-3 (Free Press)

For Miriam

And Miriam the Prophetess, the sister of Aaron, took a tambourine in her hand, and all the women went out after her with tambourines and with dances. And Miriam sang unto them.

—Exodus 15: 20–21

Contents

Contents

Acknowledgments

The editor wishes to acknowledge and thank those who assisted in the editing of this book. Foremost among these are Harold Rabinowitz, whose long-term interest in this project provided great support; Ellen Levine, whose patience and encouragement has proven invaluable; Arielle North Olson, whose comments on these tales were insightful and inspiring; and my wife, Tsila Schwartz, whose help and support was the most important of all. Also of great value was the research assistance of Evelyn Abel and Jeremy Garber. Without the dedicated work of the scholars of the Israel Folktale Archives, a book such as this would not be possible. I gratefully thank the directors of the Archives, Dov Noy, Aliza Shenhar and Edna Cheichel, as well as the individual collectors and tellers of the tales included here. Many thanks to the people of The Free Press division of Macmillan: to Erwin Glikes, Laura Wolff, Bill Weiss, George Rowland, and Karen Strauss. Thanks are also due to June Hilliard and Joan Lorson who typed the manuscript, and to those who were kind enough to assist at various stages of this project: Dina Abramovitch of YIVO, Marc Bregman, Marcia Dalbey, Joseph Dan, Nissim Binyamin Gamlieli, Barry Holtz, Thomas W. Jones, the Khanem family, William Novak, Tamar Noy, Mary Rapert, Barbara Rush, Peninnah Schram, Byron Sherwin, Eliot Spack, and Eli Yassif. I also wish to acknowledge the University of Missouri–St. Louis, which provided a research leave during which much of this work was completed.

Foreword
by Dov Noy

What Is Jewish About the Jewish Folktale?

The so-called complex tale or folktale (also known as "Märchen," and including the fairy tale as one of its subcategories, but distinguished from the simple legend and folk belief) is regarded by folk-narrative scholars as the crown of folk culture. Its elaborate motifs and images, its contents and structures have perennially had strong appeal to audiences all over the world. Wherever storytelling is alive—and there is hardly a society which does not have some forms of oral literature even in our technological age—gifted raconteurs continue to enchant listeners of all ages and backgrounds with their many variations of the folktale.

The main elements of the folktale and of the narrative genres related to it (such as the Saint's legend, the demon-tale, etc.) consist of supernatural and magical motifs of one sort or another. In fact, *all* oral narratives transmitted in a society from generation to generation by oral tradition have some extraordinary elements which testify to the creative imagination of the society and to its craving for the unusual, the remote, and for escape from the "grey" of daily life. In the folktale, however, these elements are central to the narrative plot. Any demythologization or defolklorization of a narrative, for the sake of giving it a more contemporary or realistic character, say, also drains it of its soul. Unlike other forms of literature, the folktale's fantastic elements are not corroborated by our limited human experience and knowledge, yet it is they that keep the narrative alive and the listener suspended.

Through the careful and systematic study of folktales and folktale types, scholars have come to regard specific story motifs as belonging to the universal folk-literary heritage of many societies. Their life-histories prove that they have traveled great distances from their place of origin to the place of their present life. Using the historic-geographic (also called the "Finnish" or "comparative") method of folk-narrative research, which makes extensive use of type- and motif-indexing, parallel analysis, and comparison of as many versions of the same tale as are available, it becomes possible to classify virtually all folktales into several motif types and tale-families (tales of demonic adversaries; superhuman tasks; magical objects; etc.), forming a kind of creative web that binds and connects the psychical lives of mankind's many societies. In the early stages of the discipline's modern period, attention focused on the collection of material for study and comprehensive analysis of individual tales and motifs. Most monographs were devoted to single tales, their life-histories, functions, messages, structures and contents. In recent years, however, much attention has been paid to the local and ethnic aspects and components of individual tales. Although its many versions, narrated and collected all over the world, clearly belong to the same tale-type, specific folktales are imbedded in the context of a specific society. They live and breathe in particular cultural environments, are narrated in and informed by different languages, and in all likelihood carry highly characteristic messages.

The problem currently engaging researchers is: What are the factors which shape the local version—the so-called oicotype—of the folktale? Wherein (aside from language of transmission) lies the ethnic uniqueness of the local version? Given the universal appeal of certain motifs and images, why (and how) are the travels of tale-types almost never instances of wholesale transmission?

To apply these questions to the enormous body of Jewish folk-narrative complicates the investigation further. For never did the Jews create or narrate in a hermetically sealed environment. There was always some form of cultural interchange with non-Jewish neighbors—friends and foes alike. The orally transmitted folktales and literary legends of the Jews contain many elements that are no less part of the cultural heritage of Christian, Islamic, Byzantine, and a host of other traditions. What then is uniquely Jewish about the Jewish versions of these tales?

When the fine Jewish folklorist Y.L. Cahan published the first annotated collection of genuine Jewish folktales from Eastern Europe over half a century ago (*Yiddishe Folkmayses*; Vilna, 1931), the collection was vehemently attacked by Jewish writers and critics. They claimed that except for language, there was nothing particularly Jewish about the collection. The most vituperative criticism was directed at the universality of the tales' supernatural motifs and the "superstitions underlying them." The predominant Jewish viewpoint at the time was the *Haskalah*, or Enlightenment movement, spawned in the latter half of the 18th century and shared by the overwhelming majority of the Jewish intelligentsia by the mid-19th century. This view extolled the realistic approach to life as one of the distinctive criteria of Jewish behavior and mentality. Accordingly, it was asserted, Jews have a "natural" aversion to the mystical and fantastic. The minority (among whom was Cahan) who represented fantasy literature as normative to Jewish culture were harmful, even dangerous, insofar as such literature represented Jews as irrational and superstitious people to the outside world. Cahan's work, as well as many others it inspired, was suppressed well into this century.

The progress of anthropological, folkloristic and ethnological studies in recent decades, combined with the great influx of new immigrants into the State of Israel, and the advent of objective field study of Jewish folk-traditions, devoid of apologetic motivation, have completely refuted this elitist attitude. It has been proven in different ways by scholars of varied backgrounds and ideologies, that Jewish pluralism has strongly influenced Jewish attitudes and folkways alike. The multi-dimensional creativity of the Jewish people as an integral cultural factor is now an accepted assumption in the realm of Jewish humanistic and social studies.

A milestone in the history of this overthrowing of the conservative elitist view was the establishment some thirty years ago of the Israel Folklore Archives and the initiation (in 1954) of the folktale collecting projects which continue to this day. The reliable, objective and quantitative data assembled in the IFA, where over 16,000 folktales collected from authenticated sources are registered, bears witness to the commonality of motifs, story lines, images and characters of Jewish and non-Jewish folklore. Stories borrowing heavily from the surrounding culture (in some instances retrieving material that originated in the indigenous Jewish culture, or else imported from other Jewish centers) have time and again been embellished and narrated by Jewish raconteurs in the East and the West in various Jewish languages, and enthusiastically received and enjoyed by Jewish audiences.

Yet, in spite of this commonality, there do indeed exist differences, very often quite significant, between the Jewish and non-Jewish versions of the same tale. Instead of (as some have feared) vitiating the Jewishness of the traditional Jewish folktale, the universality of themes and content has given us the opportunity of looking beneath the universally shared fabric of the tale and discerning the unique ethnic component that makes the story a Jewish one.

The study of thousands of Jewish folktales collected in the Israel Folktale Archives, and comparison with similar stories of other cultures, leads to one conclusion: The Jewish character of a Jewish folktale derives from the identity of the narrator and his audience and the setting in which the tale is told. It is the nuances, details, moods and the emotional component inherent in the storytelling art—more than the specific plots, characters and large-scale images—that define the identity of the story as a Jewish folktale. The allusion to Biblical or Jewish characters and events is less critical to defining the Jewish character of a story than the fact that the story is being told (or imagined by the listener as being told) by a Jewish storyteller to a Jewish audience in a Jewish setting at a meaningful time in the chronology of Jewish living—and for what can only be called a Jewish purpose, namely, to edify and convey a message.

To be more precise, our study of the wealth of Jewish folktales thus far collected suggests what might be called a model of the

Jewish folktale, revolving not so much around the content and story-line of the story, for as we have seen time and again, there is not a twist or detail of plot that is not found in many variations throughout world folk literature, but around the storytelling act, that is, the context in which the story is told, be it in reality or just in the listener's imagination. The model consists of four main elements which characterize the uniquely Jewish aspects of the Jewish folktale. They are:

1. The Time;
2. The Place;
3. The Acting Characters;
4. The Message.

The stories of this collection—many from the IFA collection—are a sample of the vast number of stories on which this model is based, so that the following analysis can be applied to virtually every tale. (Some of these issues are elaborated in my essay, "The Jewish Versions of the 'Animal Languages' Folktale—AT 670G: A Typological-Structural Study" in *Scripta Hierosolymitana*, Jerusalem, 1971; pp. 171–208.)

1. *The Jewish Time.* The time of the respective story is closely connected with the Jewish year cycle and/or with the Jewish life cycle. Much, even most of the Jewish narrating was performed during the relevant "passages" within the realm of the Jewish calendar: Sabbath and festivals during the year; family celebrations occasioned by the "rites of passage" in an individual member's life. There is therefore little wonder that stories related to the dark of the pre-*havdalah* synagogue or home, told in the waning, darkening moments of *Shaleshudes* (the late Sabbath afternoon meal) referred ofttimes to events dark and mysterious, and somehow connected with the Sabbath. The same holds true for stories narrated during the *Shiva* period (the seven days of sequestered mourning observed after the passing of a close relative). These stories show a preoccupation with death, the Angel of Death, rejuvenation, reincarnation, return from the other world, God's justice, theodicy, and the power of the dead to plead on behalf of surviving relatives and the Jewish

People before the heavenly court. These stories—told originally, perhaps, to occupy the children or as a permissible way of passing the time—found their way into the standard repertoire of Jewish folktales.

The title tale of this collection, "Miriam's Tambourine," is a prime example of the *Shaleshudes* tale: the passages through darkness; the Matriarch Sarah crushing the leaves which give the Sabbath its special essence; even the banging of the tambourine seem to evoke the banging on the table that so often accompanied the *zemirot*—the singing that was central to this particular (somewhat ritual) meal. A tale such as "The Prince of Coucy," dealing as it does with a lost brother who finds his fortune in a far-off land and ultimately returns to his home, may very well have originated in a *shiva* home. "The Maiden in the Tree"—a tale of the extraordinary lengths to which God's plan will go to unite man and wife—was a tale associated in all likelihood with the festive meals in the week following a wedding (the *sheva-brachos*), at which delicacies such as those brought to the lovers by the story's magical bird were no doubt very present.

2. *The Jewish Place.* The locale for Jewish storytelling was also identifiably Jewish, either because of the special events and ceremonies which took place there—foremost among which being the Synagogue—or because of a special attitude in Jewish thought toward that place—such as the home, which was considered a holy place, or the Land of Israel, the very soil of which was considered imbued with holiness. Many Jewish folktales emanated from the sermon—the *derasha*—delivered in the synagogue during a hiatus in the morning service, or at greater length and in a more leisurely and hence creatively freer atmosphere on Sabbath afternoon. The *derasha* was by far one of the most popular Jewish folk-activities (certainly in Europe) and was no doubt the source of many folktales.

As one might expect, rabbis—their wisdom and resourcefulness; their erudition and secret knowledge; their goodness and concern for the welfare of the Nation Israel—play a central role in these tales. It is not hard to imagine the tale "The Black Monk and the Master of the Name" being narrated in the context of a Sabbath (or in this particular case, a Shavuoth) *derasha*, associated as it is with the origins of Rabbi Meir Baal ha-Nes, and with its thinly veiled references to the persecutions of the Jews by a cleric endowed with mystical powers.

The classroom was yet another place where Jewish storytelling played an important role, and many of the folktales of the Jews portray a young man accepting admonition or guidance from an older tutor-like man. These tales were an important part of a young person's education, and their rendering in this volume captures, it seems to me, the original setting of the venerable *melamed* (teacher) and his attentive charges.

3. *The Jewish Acting Characters.* The hero of the Jewish folktale is often a historical figure, mainly post-Biblical, but sometimes of Biblical origin. Many of the "ethnic" folktales which derive from specific Jewish culture-areas (the Hasidic tale; the Yemenite tale; etc.) have as their protagonist a local Rabbi, usually widely known and venerated, upon whose sacred grave miracles occur. The characters, even non-Jewish and those adopted from other folk-traditions and "proselytized," as it were, behave as Jews and show many identifiable Jewish qualities as understood by the particular Jewish society in which the tale flourished.

It is important here to realize that the types of hero with which an audience could identify was determined very much by the general socio-economic situation of the Jews in their land. In good times, tales of the exploits of such as Alexander held a fascination; in hard times stories of poor people suddenly finding a great treasure (as in the tale, "Miraculous Dust") were popular.

The most frequent and favorite Jewish folk hero is certainly Elijah the Prophet. Elijah wends his way through Jewish history assuming all sorts of disguises and playing the guardian angel to people in all sorts of predicaments. But never does he act in the context of his own Biblical story. There is not in all the annals of Jewish folk-literature a single story of the prophet moving on his own Biblical landscape in contention with the false prophets of Baal, King Ahab or Queen Jezebel. This is concrete proof that the storytellers used the character of Elijah as an all-purpose hero that could be molded to the needs of the time and with whom their particular audience could identify. In the tale, "The Three Tasks of Elijah," the prophet sells himself into slavery and must toil in his mystical ways to be free. In "The Staff of Elijah," a once wealthy man finds his way to the Land of Israel and a happy, contented life with the help of the prophet's staff. The two tales, though about the same Biblical character, clearly depict different attitudes toward life and toward the status of Jews. Significantly, the former tale originates in the hostile environment of Tunisia; the latter in the more insulated and proto-Zionist environs of Moldavia.

4. *The Jewish Message.* Probably the most characteristically Jewish element of the folktale is the introduction of a moral or lesson. The universal folktale most often had as its purpose the entertainment of the listener and providing relief from the troubles of day-to-day living. The Jewish folktale has as its clear and manifest *raison d'être* a lesson—sometimes about life, but more often about man's duty to God, to his fellow man and to his people. The ubiquitous instructional element of literally *all* Jewish folktales (even if at times unstated and remote from the main thread of the story) distinguishes the Jewish storyteller from all others. The storyteller is cast in the role of teacher—and indeed the tales of Rabbi Nachman were overtly used to instruct—and the audience is the class, the students.

This penchant of Jewish folk literature to invest any tale with a moral or religious message explains a difference that will become apparent to the reader of this collection. Whereas the universal folktale appeals to the present psychological state of the listener, delighting him with a pat resolution in a formulistic happy ending, the Jewish folktale is future-oriented, urging the listener to adopt an ideal or goal as yet unrealized, to improve his ways and change his attitudes.

This model of the Jewish folktale asks much of the reader, for it calls upon him to contribute his own imaginative faculties in reconstructing the context in which the tale may have been told and retold. Toward this end, Howard Schwartz has assisted by recasting the tales in a form that captures the mood of the story-teller, weaving his web in the spontaneous and extemporaneous style that is his hallmark. For this, as well as for his illuminating comments and notations, we—reader and researcher alike—owe him a debt of gratitude.

—Jerusalem

Introduction:
The World of the Jewish Folktale

The Jewish folktale tradition contains a remarkable constellation of figures, both heros and villains. There are rabbis, for example, for whom the secrets of the universe are an open book, and whose skill as sages of the Kabbalah, the body of Jewish mysticism, has opened up unlimited powers for them—which they, of course, use only for the good. Among these are Rabbi Judah Loew, creator of the Golem, the being made out of clay and brought to life with the power of God's Name; Rabbi Adam, a medieval Jewish sorcerer and master of illusion; and Israel ben Eliezer, better known as the Baal Shem Tov, a man capable of prying the best-kept secrets out of heaven and accomplishing virtually anything except for journeying to the Holy Land, which Heaven has forbidden, since it would force the coming of the Messiah and the End of Days.

So too do we find an extraordinary variety of enemies: giants, demons, witches, fallen angels, priests and evil vizers, each one obsessed with bringing destruction upon the head of the Jews. And it is only by the urgent efforts of such wise rabbis that these figures bent on evil are defeated, often at the last moment. And sometimes, when there are no sages or heaven-sent figures, such as Elijah the prophet, to save the Jews, the battle is taken up by dauntless young Jewish men or women.

One such tale is "The Sword of Moses," where three determined but naive young men set out for the mountains of Northern Kurdistan to seek out the legendary sword of Moses, said to have been hidden there. The evidence for this sword is found in a brief biblical passage where Moses speaks of *the shield of thy help and the sword of thy excellence* (Deut. 34:29), referring, it is all too apparent, to the powers of the Lord. The reader is well aware that the young men have set out on a quest to find an object that may not exist. But because of their determination and the rightness of their quest, they end up discovering something equally powerful, the true pronounciation of God's most sacred Name, that known as the Tetragrammaton—another kind of sword that can be wielded to protect their people against any enemies. And although they do not return with a literal sword, they have the satisfaction of knowing their quest has still succeeded, while the reader (especially the young one) comes to recognize that on occasion a symbolic sword can be quite as effective as a literal one.

In a remarkably large number of these stories it is this very secret Name of God that lies at the crux of the tale, lending its power, which is none other than that of God, to protect and defend against the enemies of Israel. Tradition holds that the true pronounciation of this Name is revealed only to the greatest sage of any given generation. So it is that its power is drawn on by Rabbi Adam in one generation, Rabbi Judah Loew in another, and the Baal Shem Tov in still another, but only when the need to use it is compelling.

In general, these tales are filled with the miraculous, with magical dust that turns into the finest weapons, a wooden horse that comes to life, and flax that takes root upon a table from which a rabbi magically pulls out a witch by her hair. Magical transformations are often encountered: a bewitched prince becomes an eagle when the moon is full, a princess sometimes becomes a stork, and an unfortunate rabbi's daughter is born with the head of a donkey. These tales inevitably revolve about the breaking of these spells and the return of the heros and heroines to the blessed state of being normal. In this they are, of course, metaphors for psychic afflications from which none of us are spared, and in their magic remedies they hold out for us the hope of recovery and release.

Such miraculous cures are also represented by a variety of magical herbs and potent waters. Not only the healing waters, in the story of the same title, but also the waters of eternal life, after which so many have sought. In this later tale it is none other than Alexander the Great, an unlikely but indisputable hero of the Jews, who seeks and finds those fabled waters—and then declines to partake of them because he cannot bear to trade his wanderings for a life of peace.

Further guideposts to recovery and resolution are found in dreams, through which the beneficent messages of heaven are delivered. In one tale, "The Treasure," attributed to Rabbi Nachman of Bratslav, a man dreams of a vast treasure buried beneath a bridge. With great effort he makes his way there and discovers, instead of the treasure, a guard who directs him to the true location of the treasure—his own backyard. Here the moral intent of the tale is apparent: the Hasid seeks the treasure of self-knowledge from the Rebbe, and the Rebbe shows the Hasid how it may be found in himself.

So it is that these tales are poised in the realm between the fantastic and the enlightening. In every one an implicit moral is present, as well as a reaffirmation of faith. At the same time these tales do not gloss over the occasional convulsions in our lives that reveal a hidden evil with which we must grapple. Yet there always remains faith that the demons with whom we struggle can eventually be made to take flight, while those we permit to hold sway are never likely to release their grip on our lives.

This doubtless explains the compelling power of such tales, especially among children, who recognize instinctively that they are not only relevant but true to their own lives, each in its own way. For in a manner of speaking all children share the fate of the young Abraham in "The Boy in the Cave" in that they exist on their own no matter how much warmth is lavished upon them. So too do they recognize in the trials of Romana, the Egyptian Snow

White, the temporal fears instilled by an angry parent or a jealous sibling, and the longing that safety be found somewhere, if not in the family circle.

The rabbis or storytellers who preserved these tales by retelling them generation after generation recognized their inherent power and did not require the kind of overt moral we expect to find in the parable or fable. Sometimes, such as in the adventures of the talmudic sage Rabbah bar bar Hannah (which are nothing less than the accounts of a Jewish Sindbad), it is the tale itself that justifies its existence, with its fantastic depiction of another world existing alongside the one that is so familiar.

At the same time these tales reflect to a remarkable extent the lands out of which they emerged, and it is here that their universal and Jewish natures are clothed in a native garb. It is not surprising, for example, that the one tale from India included here, "The Eagle's Treasure," concerns a poverty so extreme that the hero does not have enough funds even to purchase rice seeds to plant. This very same theme is echoed in the tale from Morocco, another barren land, "The Wise Old Woman of the Forest." In both cases the flight into fantasy seems to hold out the only hint of hope, suggesting the dire conditions experienced by the tellers of these tales.

It hardly seems a coincidence that both tales from Tunisia concern the practice of selling oneself into slavery as an act of desperate preservation. In the case of "The Three Trials of Elijah," it is the mysterious prophet who volunteers to sell himself in order to help a poor Jew. But in the other tale, "The Disguised Princess," it is none other than a princess who undertakes this dangerous path and still manages to recover her freedom, not once but three times. No doubt some unfortunate individuals were driven to sell themselves in this fashion when faced with starvation. And the deep seated fear of this terrifying prospect was likely to be found even among those apparently safe from such dangers.

Equally revealing is one of the tales from Afghanistan, still another harsh land. "The Tale of the Magic Horse" begins with seemingly unlimited optimism, as the prince who possesses the magic flying horse has secret trysts with the princess imprisoned by her father in a tower, in yet another variant of the Rapunzel motif. But their lives are suddenly brought down to earth in the most literal sense when the magic amulet that animates the magic horse burns and the prince is stranded in the barren desert far from his beloved. In this tale can be seen the hopefulness with which young lovers view life and the harsh realities awaiting them in the real world, especially in a land such as Afghanistan. In fact, their separation and suffering are so extreme that even their eventual reuniting cannot cause it to be forgotten, while in the tales of less desperate lands, the period of struggle serves more often to strengthen character and the ending still holds out the prospect of living happily ever after.

So too does the fact that Romana comes to the house of forty thieves rather than Snow White's seven dwarves ring true in this Egyptian tale, as does the existence of caves filled with murderous thieves in "The Weaving that Saved the Prince." Even in the Eastern European tales there are strong indications of a harsh world out of which the fantasy has emerged. Certainly the threat of the blood libel hanging over the Jewish community of Prague, in which Jews were accused of seeking Christian blood as part of their Passover preparations, often provoking the most vicious attacks on the Jewish ghetto, gave birth to the epic of the Golem. This clay being, created out of Rabbi Judah Loew's esoteric knowledge and the power of the Divine Name, succeeds in doing what no man can do—tracing the murder of a Christian child to its perpetrator, the evil Thaddeus, who had sought to provoke yet another pogrom.

Over and over these tales reflect the Jewish community as a whole being brought to the brink of disaster by the whim of a ruler or the actions of an insidious enemy. Such dangers were an inherent part of Jewish life in the Middle Ages, and these tales reflect an intense longing for some assured form of salvation. Faced with innumerable enemies, the Jews imagined all kinds of miraculous events in which their lost power was restored. The Golem incarnates such a wish, as do the wonders of Rabbi Adam and the miracles of Elijah.

Thus these tales can be seen as reflections of both the inner and outer worlds. In this way they manage to be both simple and complex at the same time, filled with both faith and doubt, and true to life even while serving as fantasies. In most cases they were preserved orally for many, many generations before they were finally written down, evolving in the process into more embellished narratives, with many variants.

The telling of folktales, found among all peoples, is astonishing in that it is the product of centuries of this group process of retelling. Each storyteller leaves his mark, albeit anonymously. Certain basic types of tales are consistently found in virtually every culture—among them fables, nursery tales, and, of course, fairy tales. The earliest tales that can be identified as Jewish folk tales are found in the Talmud, and more are found scattered in the Midrash. But it is in the Middle Ages that the genre attained its fullest expression. Here, long and elaborate narratives blending elements of the traditional folk tale were not only retold as part of the oral tradition, but written down and published, especially in Constantinople, in the 16th Century.

The tales preserved in this fashion almost inevitably contain a strong Jewish element. It was this religious dimension that brought about their preservation, for they closely resembled the kind of sacred tale that the rabbis had been collecting for so many centuries. Less attention was paid to the universal fairy tale, which takes place in an enchanted and unidentified kingdom. Many such tales were lost amid the upheavals and exiles that were standard fare for the various Jewish communities of both Eastern Europe and the Middle East. It has only been in this century that an effort has been made to collect the surviving oral tales of this type, first by collectors in Eastern Europe such as S. Ansky and Y. L. Cahan, and later by the organized efforts of the Israel Folktale Archives, under the direction of Professor Dov Noy of Hebrew University.

In virtually all other folklores it is impossible to follow such a well-preserved written history of the folktale. In general, folktales evolve until they are written down, and those written versions become the authentic text, not subject to major changes. But many of the tales preserved in the the early Jewish texts continued to be told among the people as well. And this kind of oral tradition kept the tale alive, so that, remarkably enough, the tale often evolves from one century to another, and then is recorded anew. In the Middle Ages especially, the tales were embellished, lengthened and interwoven with additional Jewish subject matter and explicitly drawn morals.

All Jewish literature is built upon the primacy of the Bible, and this is true of Jewish folklore as much as it is of the rabbinical literature. While full-fledged Jewish folktales cannot be found in the Bible (with the possible exception of the Book of Esther), the kinds of supernatural motifs that are so central to folktales are quite common. The staff of Moses serves him as a magical rod, transforming into a snake in Pharoah's court, and later used by Moses to strike the rock in the wilderness, which gave forth water. Similar motifs can be found in the tale of the speaking snake in the Garden of Eden who provokes the Fall, as well as in that of the two enchanted trees in the garden, the Tree of Life and the Tree of the Knowledge of Good and Evil. There is also the speaking ass of Baalam, as well as the giant fish in which Jonah lived. In the later rabbinic literature these elements were considerably elaborated, using as justification the Oral Law that Moses was also said to have received at Mount Sinai, along with the Torah, or Written Law. For all these tales were simply attributed to the portion of the Oral Law known as the Aggadah. And in a sense it is true, since in most cases they are based on the existing rabbinic folklore. So too were a great many rabbinic elements retained in the later folklore, even as the form of the tale evolved out of the midrashic mold. This makes possible the fusion of the rabbinic tale with the universal folktale as it is uniquely found in Jewish literature, especially that of the late Middle Ages.

These, then, are the key phases of Jewish folklore in which folktales are found: in the Apocrypha, in the Talmud and Midrash, in medieval Jewish folklore, scattered among the vast number of Hasidic tales, and in the compilations of modern collectors. Among the fairy tales included here, all of these periods are represented. "Daniel and the Dragon" comes from the Apocrypha, from the Additions to Daniel. The tales drawn from the

Babylonian Talmud are "Miraculous Dust" and "A Voyage to the Ends of the Earth," while "Rabbi Joshua and the Witch" comes from the Jerusalem Talmud. Both Talmuds, the earliest rabbinic commentaries on Jewish law and legend, were codified in the 5th Century.

"Miraculous Dust" is an early example of an Elijah tale, which later became a major sub-genre in itself, found in considerable quantities in every period. Other Elijah tales here are "The Three Tasks of Elijah," "The Staff of Elijah," and "The Donkey Girl," in which Elijah makes a brief but important appearance. In "Miraculous Dust" Elijah intercedes to save Nachum Ish Gam-Zu and the Jews from the fury of Caesar by turning a trunk filled with dust into a magic powder that can be transformed into potent weapons. Such divinely inspired intervention is one of the most common themes in all of the types of tales found in the Aggadah.

The tales drawn from the Midrash, the post-Talmudic compilations of rabbinic commentary and legend, include "The Boy in the Cave," "The Princess Who Became the Morning Star," and "The Golden Amulet." Versions of these tales are found in seminal midrashic collections such as *Pirqe deRabbi Eliezer* and *Yalkut Shimoni*. While the former is generally dated from around the 8th century, and the latter from the 11th century, it is virtually certain that they are both based on earlier rabbinic sources. These tales embellish the legendary history of Abraham and the fall of the Sons of God and the daughters of men, and provide the midrashic history of Joseph's wife Asenath, identifying her as Jacob's granddaughter.

In "The Princess Who Became the Morning Star," the maiden Istahar wrenches the secret prounciation of God's Name from the angel Shemhazai, who is trying to compel her to marry him. When she pronounces the Name she ascends beyond his grasp and is rewarded by heaven by being transformed into the morning star. Here God's Name is used as the ultimate source of power, replacing more common magical devices, such as the enchanted sword. And even when one of these devices is used—the magic ring of King Solomon, for example, on which the Name was engraved—its power is described as being derived from God.

At the same time, "The Princess Who Became the Morning Star" is a tale with a clear-cut moral: by resisting the evil angel, Istahar not only preserves her virtue, but also prevents the world from being destroyed. This story has its basis in the brief and enigmatic biblical tale (Gen. 6:1–4) about angels who descend to earth and take for wives the daughters of men. This myth is expanded in the Midrash, where both the angels, the Sons of God, and the daughters of men are identified, the angels as Shemhazai and Azazel, and the daughters as Istahar and Naamah. It is here that Istahar's transformation into a star is first told, which also serves as the origin myth of the morning star.

The two angels are punished for their sin. Shemhazai is hung upside down between heaven and earth, becoming identified with a constellation, while Azazel is hung in the same fashion in a great canyon. It is here, upside-down, that he plots his revenge and is foiled in the tale "The Secrets of Azazel." In time his identity became fused with that of Satan, and this is the origin on the phrase *"Lech le Azazel"* or "Go to Azazel," meaning "Go to the Devil," that is still used in modern Israel. This is the starting point of the folk legend told in "The Wise Old Woman of the Forest," a tale which is found in a large number of variants, all from Middle Eastern sources. The poor man sets out to search for Azazel, but instead finds his way to the wise old woman who not only changes his fortune, but also supplies answers to all the riddles he has brought with him.

From one of the earliest collections of Jewish folktales, dating from 11th century Tunisia, comes "The Three Tasks of Elijah." Tales drawn from later medieval collections include "A Plague of Ravens," "The Waters of Eternal Life," "The Secrets of Azazel," and "The Enchanted Well." And from collections of folklore as recent as the 19th century (although doubtless based on earlier sources) comes our title tale, "Miriam's Tambourine," as well as "The Maiden in the Tree," "The Prince of Coucy," "The Donkey Girl," "The Golem," "David's Harp," and the tales of the Baal Shem Tou.

The lines of evolution leading from the Bible to the latest phases of Jewish folklore can clearly be recognized in the tale of

"Miriam's Tambourine." Rabbinic legend attributes to the virtues of Miriam, sister of Moses, the presence of an enchanted well that was said to have followed the Israelites in the wilderness, coming to rest opposite the Ark of the Tabernacle, so that the people always had fresh water to draw upon. Once such a supernatural motif enters the tradition, it is certain to be utilized by later generations. In "Miriam's Tambourine" the rabbi and his son not only rediscover the long lost well, but Miriam herself, who is equally eternal. Furthermore, the well is to be found in a garden closely resembling the Garden of Eden, which is linked by a cave to the Red Sea, where Miriam makes her home. With the aid of her enchanted tambourine, they succeed in casting out the serpents that have come to infest the well, thus restoring its primordial purity.

The implicit moral of the tale is that Judaism, with its rich religious and literary tradition, cannot retain its potency if it falls into disuse, for then it is prey to the forces of evil, i.e., the serpents. Only by drawing upon the ancient ways can we expel these evil forces and create a great renewal. Historically, it is possible to read in this tale, as well as in "The Sword of Moses," many of the beliefs that led to the desire to reestablish the State of Israel, with all that it stands for, as a reality in the world.

The tales drawn from 18th and 19th century Hasidic sources include two of those about the Jewish sorcerer Rabbi Adam ("The Enchanted Palace" and "The King Descended from Haman"), the tales about the Baal Shem Tov, founder of Hasidism ("The Demon in the Jug," "The Princess and the Baal Shem Tov' and "The Demon and the Baal Shem Tov") plus those tales told by Rabbi Nachman of Bratslav and recorded by his scribe, Rabbi Nathan of Nemirov ("A Garment for the Moon," "The Treasure," "The Prince and the Slave," "The Enchanted Tree," and "The Palace Beneath the Sea").

Unique among the tales collected here are those of Rabbi Nachman of Bratslav, in that they are the sole tales that can be traced to a single teller. Rabbi Nachman chose to tell his own tales to his Hasidim as teaching stories in which his profoundly mystical vision could find expression. For this reason the tales, with the exception of "The Treasure," are quite intricate and complex in their symbolism. The garment that the tailor Yankel longs to weave for the moon is clearly linked to the kabbalistic tradition of the robe of the *Shekhinah*, the mystical Bride of God. Like the robe to be woven out of light, that of the *Shekhinah* is both diaphanous and durable. The moon's garment is clearly a metaphor for its aura, while the robe of the *Shekhinah* is a metaphor for the divine presence.

So too is there a kabbalistic basis to "The Palace Beneath the Sea," in which kabbalistic symbols are used to transmit the secret of how to open the door to the mysteries waiting to be revealed. Likewise many symbols found in "The Enchanted Tree" are likely connected to the kabbalistic Tree of Life and to the ten emanations, known as *Sefirot*, linked to it. This is an undeniably obscure cosmology, yet Nachman's tales, which grow out of such mystical traditions, also succeed ably in illuminating psychic states while still managing to sustain the fascination of the folktale. This can be seen most clearly in the tale of "The Prince and the Slave," a retelling of the story of Jacob and Esau, where both prince and slave, whose roles become reversed and then righted, share a related fate from the very moment of their birth. Both can be viewed without difficulty as the projection of a single self, light and dark sides, whose struggle is that of everyone who seeks the path of righteousness. In these tales, Rabbi Nachman manages to fuse the sacred and secular into a completely unique creation.

Virtually all of the other tales included here have been drawn from oral sources. These include both the "universal" tales, without specific Jewish elements, and the tales reflecting a Jewish context. Two of these tales, "The Wishing Ring" and "The Man Who Escaped Misfortune," are from Y. L. Cahan's seminal early collections of Yiddish folklore, while all of the others have been drawn from the vast collections of the Israel Folktale Archives.

Yet despite these diverse sources, separated by as much as fourteen centuries, it should be readily apparent that there is a great continuity found among these tales. This continuity pervades all of post-biblical Jewish literature, sacred and secular, simply because each generation built directly upon the traditions of earlier generations. This process was initiated by the awe in which the biblical texts were held by all subsequent generations, who directed their efforts at creating a literature derived from biblical sources and models.

In much of this literature, especially that drawn from the talmudic and midrashic sources, the central concern is to resolve the often incomplete biblical narratives. For example, nothing is told in the Bible of Abraham's childhood and youth. The rabbis felt a strong need to know about this period of the Patriarch's life, because the clue to his recognition of the one God might be found there. This, then, is supplied in a tale, "The Boy in the Cave," which takes as its model the biblical account of the childhood of Moses. Like Moses, the child Abraham is born under the threat of the death of all firstborn male infants, brought about because of a prophecy that the ruler would be overthrown by such a child.

The glowing stone worn by Abraham is itself commonly found in Jewish folklore, and is an example of how rabbinic legends often came to form a chain. Such legends are known, in fact, as chain midrashim. This stone, called the *Tzohar*, contains the last remanent of the light created on the first day, known as the primodial light. According to the legend, the stone first belonged to Adam, later came into the possession of Noah, who hung it from the mast of the ark in order to have light during the forty days of darkness brought on by the Flood, and from there was passed on to Abraham, who wore it around his neck as a healing stone. Its history after Abraham is also recounted in the Midrash and later folklore. The very same stone reappears in the story "The Man Who Escaped Misfortune," miraculously found once the man's bad luck changes to good. So too does the motif of this stone appear in other tales, including "The Golden Amulet," "The Magic Lamp of Rabbi Adam," "The Palace Beneath the Sea," and "A Plague of Ravens," where the illuminating stone is linked to the *Ner Tamid*, the Eternal Light that burns next to the Ark.

In ways such as these, Jewish folktales, like the other seminal forms of Jewish folklore, reflect not only the archetypal themes of the Bible that are their source and inspiration, but also the desires and aspirations of the later generations which retold them. This blend of the past and present endows them with a sense of timelessness, making them as illuminating and eternal as the glowing stone of Abraham, and as appropriate for our age as the ones in which they were first told.

—H.S.

Miriam's Tambourine

Jewish Folktales
from Around the World

Miriam's Tambourine

Long ago, in the land of Babylon, there lived a rabbi and his son who made their home in a small hut deep in the forest, where they spent their days in the study of the mysteries of the Torah. During the day they read from the sacred texts, and at night they peered into the stars and read in them as clearly as in any book. And they were the purest souls to be found in that land.

In those days the Jews of Babylon led lives of peace, for since the days of Daniel there had always been a Jewish adviser to the king, who had protected the interests of his people. There was a remarkable tradition connected to the appointment of this minister. For since the time of Daniel each king had kept a golden chest beside the throne, and in that chest was a precious Book. And that Book could be opened only by the one man in each generation who was destined to serve as the king's minister. In the past, this one man had always been found among the Jews of Babylon, and now, it was time once again to seek out the one who would advise the King.

But this time, none of those who journeyed to the palace

from every city in Babylon was able to open the Book. The Jews of Babylon began to worry, for the longer they went without a Jewish minister, the more dangerous it was, since there was no one to look out for them. So they sent out messengers on horseback to inform all those Jews living in small towns of how important it was to come to the palace and try to open the Book in the presence of the king. Many came, but none succeeded.

The messengers were sent out again, this time to seek those living in the most remote villages and in the forest. In this way a messenger learned of the rabbi and his son living alone deep in the woods, and he sought them out. Now the rabbi and his son were happy to welcome the messenger, for few visitors ever came to their door. And when they learned of his mission, they agreed at once to journey to the palace and attempt to open the Book. Then the messenger took his leave and rode off to search for any others who might have been missed, and the rabbi and his son set off on foot to reach the capital.

While they walked, the rabbi and his son spoke of that mysterious Book, the Book only one man in each generation could open. It had been delivered (so the legend went) to Daniel by an angel while he sat inside the lion's den. He had read it while he waited there, in the presence of the lions. And from it he had learned that he was the first mortal to open that Book, and that only one man in each generation after him would be able to do so. It was said that the secrets in that Book were so deep that they had not been revealed even to the angels. Both the rabbi and his son longed to read that Book and share in those mysteries.

So involved did the rabbi and his son become in their contemplation of this mysterious Book, that for four days and nights they did not even know if it was light and dark. And when at last they stopped walking and looked around, they found themselves in a strange place, which they did not recognize at all. For they had paid no attention to the path on which they were walking, and had become totally lost. Yet they did not become frightened; they had complete faith that God would not lead them astray.

They walked on, and in the distance they saw a beautiful palace, which shone as if it were made of pearl. Around it was a high wall, and when they reached the wall they found the gate locked. They peered through the gate, and marveled at the beauty of the palace in the distance. Their hearts were drawn to it, and they longed to enter there. Yet how could they pass through the gate? It was then that the first miracle occured, for that gate opened only once every hundred years, and then only for the briefest instant. Fate had seen to it that the rabbi and his son had arrived there at exactly the moment it was set to fly open. And when it did open, they did not hesitate. Without a word, they both hurried through the gate before it slammed shut.

Now when the rabbi and his son found themselves standing inside that garden, before that splendid palace, they were filled with joy. They hurried to the door of the palace, and found in it a golden key. They turned the key and entered. Inside the palace they found an old woman with beautiful wise eyes. She was taking leaves out of a silver basket and crushing them between her fingers, into fine powder which she let fall into a golden basket at her side. When the rabbi and his son entered, she looked up; she did not seem surprised to see them. They approached her and the rabbi said, "Peace be with you." "Peace be with you," she said. Then the rabbi asked her what she was doing. "I have children everywhere who suffer from one Sabbath to the next," she said. "But on the eve of the Sabbath, I take the powder made from these leaves and cast it into the wind. And the wind carries it to the four corners of the earth, so that all those who breathe in even the smallest speck have a taste of Paradise, and the Sabbath is filled with joy for them."

The rabbi and his son marveled at this, for they had known the peace and joy of Sabbath many times, and now they knew why. By then they were both very curious to know who the old woman was, and the rabbi asked her her name, and she replied that it was Sarah. Then he asked her what was her husband's name, and she told them that it was Abraham. And when he heard this, the rabbi wondered if she might not be the same Sarah and her husband the same Abraham who are the mother and father of every Jew. The woman just nodded that it was true. Then they asked her where Abraham was, and she told them that he had gone into the Garden of Eden to fetch freshly fallen leaves for her.

It was then that the rabbi's son (who had not yet reached his Bar Mitzvah) saw the hand of fate in their coming to that place. He told Sarah of the journey they had set out on, to attempt to open the Book that had once belonged to Daniel. She nodded as the young boy spoke, and then she said, "That Book can be opened only by one who has the purest soul. And while both of your souls are very pure, still they are not pure enough to open the Book." The rabbi and his son were very sorry to hear that, for they had hoped that at least one of them might be able to succeed. The rabbi said, "But tell us, Sarah, is there any way that we can purify our souls enough so we may open the Book?" And Sarah replied, "Yes, there is one way. You must descend into Miriam's Well, and purify yourselves in those sacred waters."

Now both the rabbi and his son had heard of Miriam's Well. That was the Well that had followed the children of Israel in their desert wanderings, the well God had given them in honor of the righteousness of Miriam, sister of Moses and Aaron. But that well had not been seen since the days of the wandering in the wilderness. Yet, if it were possible for them to find Sarah, perhaps it was also possible to find Miriam's Well. The rabbi asked Sarah where the well could be found, and she told them that they would come to it if they followed the path outside the palace. But she also told them that it would be futile to go there, for the Evil One had placed serpents all around the entrance to the Well. No one could enter there and purify themselves. This bad news greatly saddened both the rabbi and his son, for they had felt so near their goal, and now again it seemed impossible to reach. With a sad voice the boy asked Sarah if there were any way to get past the serpents. Sarah smiled and said, "Yes, but only with the help of Miriam's tambourine."

Once again, hope burned in their hearts, and they wondered where they might find Miriam's tambourine, and if it were the same one that she had played after the Israelities had crossed the Red Sea. So they asked Sarah about this, and she told them that it was indeed the very same tambourine which the maidens of Israel had played as they danced at the Red Sea. And when they asked her where they might find it, she said simply, "Why, with Miriam." And when they asked where Miriam could be found, Sarah told them that if they went through that palace, into the garden, and passed through a hollow tree, they would find the entrance to a cave. And if they traveled through that cave, they would reach the shore of the Red Sea. And there, at the shore of the Red Sea, they would find Miriam, for that is where she made her home.

Of course all this was much more than the rabbi and his son had expected. Yet they did not hesitate, but each thanked Sarah with all his heart and they set off at once to find that cave. Before long, after passing through the most beautiful garden they had ever seen, they reached a magnificent tree that turned out to be hollow, just as Sarah had said. And when they stepped into the hollow trunk, they found the entrance to a cave. They crawled through that long cave, mysteriously illuminated with a pale light, until they reached the shore of the sea. There they found a beautiful young woman, sitting on a rock beside the shore and playing a tambourine, with schools of fish crowded around her, and dolphins doing turns in the air. And as soon as they heard the wonderful rhythm of that tambourine, both the rabbi and his son were spellbound, and began to dance. They danced with the greatest joy they had ever known, for they were feeling the same joy the Israelities had felt after they had escaped the clutches of the Egyptians by passing through the parted waters of the Red Sea.

Now they might have danced there forever had the young woman not put down the tambourine. When she did, their feet came to rest, and they knew they had indeed found Miriam the Prophetess, and that the tambourine she played must be the very one they were seeking. The rabbi and his son introduced themselves to Miriam, and told her of their quest. She hesitated not a moment but handed them the tambourine, and said, "Go, and, God willing, you will expel the serpents nesting there. For know that none of us who inhabit this place can accomplish that, only mortals such as yourselves, who have found your way here. Meanwhile I will wait here for you to return, for this is my home, beside the sea. Know that the sound of this tambourine has great power; it causes those with pure souls to be filled with joy, and evil creatures to cringe and flee as fast as they can. Now please hurry, for if I go as long as a day without hearing the music of my tambourine, my eternal life will come to an end."

The rabbi and his son knew that if Miriam were willing to trust them with her miraculous tambourine, their quest must be very precious in her eyes indeed. The rabbi gratefully accepted the tambourine from her, and held it with great care, as he and his son took their leave and hurried back to the cave. They passed through the cave, and then the tree, until they found their way into the garden and onto the path before the palace. At last they came to the very well they had been seeking. It was set deep within the earth, surrounded by stones that had long ago fused together. Somehow that miraculous well, with its living waters, had followed the Israelites as they wandered from place to place, and had given them fresh water to drink. But now, the rabbi and his son both saw, a multitude of serpents were nesting at its entrance, depriving the world of its wonderful powers.

Then they approached the well, and knew that they had reached the most solemn moment of their lives. When they stood there all the serpents raised their heads, as if to strike, but they paid them no heed. The rabbi handed the tambourine to his son and told him to start to play. Then the boy struck the tambourine for the first time, and as soon as he did, a wonderful, spell-binding music emerged from it, with a strong, insistent rhythm. This time the rabbi and his son were not compelled to dance, for Miriam was not playing; instead the sounds made all of the serpents writhe in agony, and they began at once to slither and crawl away from there as fast as they could go. They headed directly for the garden gate, and slipped beneath it, never to return, and the purity of the Well and the garden were restored at last.

Then, while his son continued to play that tambourine, the rabbi found that the wonderful music gave him the strength to climb down the stones on the inside of the well. When he reached the water and immersed himself, he felt his soul purified to its very kernel. So it was that when the rabbi climbed out of the well, he took the tambourine from his son, and played its wonderful music once again as his son descended into those life-giving waters, and likewise purified his soul. And when they departed from that place, they found that their eyes had been opened, and that all manner of angels and spirits that had flocked around that garden now became apparent to them. Then they hurried back to the hollow tree and passed through the cave, for they wanted to take the tambourine back to Miriam as soon as possible. It was not long before they stood before her shining beauty, and when they returned the tambourine she blessed them both and told them that their wonderful deed would always be remembered.

After that the rabbi and his son hurried back to the gate of the garden, and took their leave, and followed the path they found running outside it. And lo and behold, by morning they found themselves standing before the palace of the king. There they were given an audience, and like so many who had come before them, they approached the Book that had been sealed so long. The rabbi had only to touch the cover of the Book lightly, and it opened to him, and all who surrounded him cheered, for the new minister of the king had finally been found.

Thus it came to pass that the rabbi became the king's trusted adviser and served him for many years, referring to the Book for every important decision, and making certain that his fellow Jews were spared any persecution. And when the rabbi took his leave of this world, they did not have to look far to find the one who would take his place. For his son, who had also immersed himself in Miriam's Well and had been cleansed as fully as his father, had no difficulty in opening the Book and understanding its wisdom. He too served as the king's minister for many years, and that was a time of abundance for the Jews of that land.

Eastern Europe: c. Nineteenth Century

A Plague of Ravens

T here once was a pious man and his wife, who longed, above all else, to be parents, but had been denied this blessing. At last this man grew desperate, and after fasting for two days and three nights he went to the cemetery, wearing his *tallis* and *tefillin*. There he sought out the grave of a holy sage who had been known for his miracles. When he found it, the pious man fell on his face, wept bitterly and begged for help from the soul of the sage.

Suddenly, the ground shook and the earth opened. Much to the amazement of the pious man, ten men—a *minyan*—all wrapped in prayer-shawls, emerged from inside the earth. Their leader was the very holy sage at whose grave the man had come to pray. For that sage had been made the rabbi of a synagogue beneath the earth, in which the most righteous souls buried in that cemetery prayed. The holy man approached the pious man, who trembled in fear before such a congregation. And the holy man said to him, "Why do you weep so bitterly?" "Because I have no children," the man replied. "Do not weep," said the holy man, "for we will make a covenant with you. We will pray on your behalf that you and your wife be blessed with a child. In return, you must make a covenant with us to bring your son here on his eighth day for the *bris*. The man accepted this covenant, and swore to bring his son there to be circumcised. Before he returned to the earth, the holy man said, "Within a year your wife shall bear you a son."

And so it came to pass just as the holy sage had promised—the man and his wife became the parents of a fine son. And on the eighth day he took his son to the tomb of the holy man, just as he had sworn to do, and stood there praying. And all at once the earth opened up as before, and the men of the synagogue beneath the earth emerged once more. They led the father and his son down stairs until they reached their synagogue. The pious man could barely believe that such a thing was possible—a synagogue under the earth! But there it was, no different from any synagogue he had ever seen, with a *beth midrash*, a house of study, as well. Only it was mysteriously lit, by a remarkable light which shone there. This light came forth from the small *ner tamid*, the eternal light which burned before the ark. That light was sufficient to illuminate everything in the place.

It was there that a joyous *bris* was celebrated, and the young son was initiated into the Covenant of the Jews and their Creator. And the pious father realized that he was in the presence of the finest Jewish souls, whose prayers had brought him the great blessing of a child. When the ceremony was over, the father prepared to take his leave. But before he did, the holy man said, "Your son bears a very holy soul, for that is the soul we prayed for him to receive. And this soul will best be nourished in the words of the Torah. Now if you wish, we would be willing to serve as your son's teachers. But if you agree to this, you must leave him with us for six years. Then you may take him back with you in peace."

Now the father was reluctant to leave his son, for whom he had yearned these many years. But he also recognized that what the holy man had said was surely true; the miracle of that synagogue made that clear. And he did not doubt that in this way his son could become one of the wisest of men and a blessing to his people. Therefore he agreed to leave his son for six years, and took his leave alone.

Now when the man returned without their son, his wife was very alarmed. But the man told her everything that had happened, and since she already knew of the wondrous synagogue from the covenant her husband had made with its worshippers, she knew that her husband was telling the truth. Hard as it was, she too resolved to wait six years for the return of her child.

At the end of the six years, the father returned to the tomb of the holy man, wrapped in his prayer garments. He prayed until the earth again opened and the ten men emerged with his son. The face of the boy glowed as if he were an angel of God. Imagine how happy the father was to see him, and to learn that his son knew well the Torah, the Talmud and every science of man. He was about to depart with him when the holy sage spoke: "The decision is entirely yours, but if you agree to let your son remain with us for one more year, we will also teach him the seventy languages of the birds and beasts, and after that you may take him and go in peace." And the father reluctantly agreed to this, for he recognized how well such knowledge might serve his son in this world. Again he told his wife what had happened, and again she agreed it was for the best.

A year later the father returned and met the men of the underground synagogue. This time, after many fond farewells, his son departed with him, and they started to make their way home.

Along the way, father and son came to a river, where they quenched their thirst. As they rested there, the wise child overheard a conversation among some ravens speaking in a nearby tree, for he could understand the language of the birds. And when the boy heard what they said, he first laughed and then he cried. His father was very confused by this and asked him to explain. The boy replied, "I laughed because I heard the ravens say that in the future I would become a king, and I cried because the ravens also said that before that, I would be separated from you for another seven years."

No sooner did the boy finish saying this, than a strong wind came and picked him up and cast him into the water. His father came running after him, but the boy was carried swiftly downstream by the currents, until he was far away. His poor father could not believe such a terrible thing had happened—after all the years he had waited for his son. He grieved because he feared that his son had surely drowned. Thus he returned home in great distress, and when he told his wife what had happened, she too was broken-hearted.

Meanwhile the son had been carried by the currents of the river all the way to the sea. Now it happened that a great fish that God had sent there swallowed the boy and carried him to another kingdom, where he spit him out on the shore. While the boy sat there on the sand, still trying to get his bearings, a man who happened to be the royal shepherd of that kingdom came up to him. The shepherd said, "My son, where do you come from and what brought you to this land?" And although the boy was afraid that the man would not believe he had been cast ashore by a great fish, still, he told him all that had taken place. Now the kindhearted sheperd wondered at this, but still he told the boy that he might make his home with his family, and could assist him in tending the sheep. The boy gladly agreed, and the shepherd became like a father to him. The boy lived there in peace, and soon became a skilled shepherd trusted with the king's most prized flock.

For seven years the boy lived with the shepherd's family, and their fortunes flourished. Then one morning a remarkable thing happened at the palace of the king. An immense flock of ravens descended upon the palace, covering not only the roof, but all the windows and doors as well. It was impossible to go in or out, making the king a prisoner in his own palace. Nothing the guards tried to do helped, for as soon as they drove off a few of the ravens, others flew to take their place. The king recognized that this must be a sign of some kind, and that its meaning must be discovered very soon, or the king would starve in his own palace.

So the king called together his ministers, wise men and soothsayers, and asked them to find the true meaning of the sign and to make the ravens depart, and the one who did would receive half the kingdom as his reward. Of course they all did their best to discover the meaning, and all announced their own interpretations. Some said that it was a sign of coming famine or war, while others said it was a sign that the king would give birth to a son whom he would also bury. But all of these interpretations meant nothing, since they did nothing to drive the ravens away. Already the palace cook had been forced to cut the size of the meals in half, and supplies were running out. The king grew angry and told the wise men that their provisions would be the first to be cut off. If, on the other hand, anyone could end the plague, not only would half the kingdom be his, but the hand of the princess as well.

Now when the young man who lived with the shepherd overheard two sparrows discussing the king's predicament and the reward he had offered, he was certain he could help resolve the matter—for did he not understood the language of the ravens? So he went with the shepherd to the palace and spoke with the ravens in their own language, asking them to let him pass so that he could give their message to the king. Without hesitation the birds cleared a path for him to enter. The king was surprised to see that the young man had been able to come inside, since no one else had been able to go in or out, and he was even more surprised when he learned that the boy was claiming he could end the plague of ravens. But the king was so desperate that he gave the boy his blessings and told him to do his best. Then the boy left the palace and listened to the conversations of the ravens, and found that they all were talking about the two ravens who sat apart from the others in the center of the roof. The boy, who could speak every language as well as understand it, asked the ravens nearby to tell the ones sitting apart from the others to come to the doorway of the palace.

The message was delivered, and before long these very two ravens arrived at the palace door and flew inside. In the presence of the king, with the young boy interpreting, the ravens told their sad tale: They bore the souls of two Jews who had been travelling together in the wilderness when they had been attacked by robbers and slain. But they had recognized these robbers—they were among the king's servants. Now their wives were suffering because, according to the Law, they could not remarry, since no one was certain their husbands were dead. They wanted the king to give them justice and to see to it that their wives would no longer be *agunahs*.

The young man delivered the message of the ravens to the king, and the king ordered that all of his servants come into the palace hall and arrange themselves in a circle. The two ravens flew into the hall and circled above the servants. Then each one landed on the head of one of the killers. The king so terrified these men that they both confessed and were hanged, in full view of the birds. The king then sent a messenger to the town of the widows, with a letter from the king announcing the deaths of their husbands, which would free them to remarry. And as soon as this messenger was dispatched, all at once the ravens flocked skyward and were gone, and light shone into the palace for the first time since they had arrived.

Now when the king saw how the wisdom of the young man had saved them, he was deeply impressed and invited him to live in the palace and to serve as the king's advisor. Before very long the king came to depend on this advisor and this one alone, for his wisdom greatly surpassed that of the others. So too was a great wedding held, to which all the people in the realm were invited, for it was the most joyous day in the history of the kingdom.

Now among those who came to that wedding were the wise young man's parents, who had become wanderers ever since they had lost their son. He recognized them at once, but they did not recognize him, since they believed that he had drowned. He had them brought before him. They could not help but wonder what such a great prince would want with them. He asked them if they were happy on the day of his wedding, and they replied that they wished him and his bride every blessings, but that they themselves had never known a happy day since their son had been lost in a river. And when he heard this, the young prince cried out, "I am your son!" And when his parents saw the birthmark he bore on his chest, they knew it was truly he and could be no other. Then their joy knew no bounds, and that wedding day was the happiest day in all their lives. And they all lived together in peace for many years to come.

Persia: c. Sixteenth Century

Daniel and the Dragon

Long ago, when Cyrus was the king of Babylon, the people worshipped two gods. One of these was an idol whose name was Bel, and the other was a dragon, which made its home in the caves on a nearby island. Now Bel and the dragon were worshipped by all of the king's advisers except for one, Daniel, who was a Jew. Every day the Babylonians made an offering to Bel of eighteen bushels of fine wheat flour and fifty gallons of wine. And once a year the dragon received a living sacrifice in order to appease it.

Since the king recognized Daniel's wisdom, he wondered why he did not worship these two gods. One day he asked him, and Daniel said, "I worship the Lord God who created the heaven and the earth." Then the king asked: "Have you ever seen this God of yours?" Daniel replied, "I have not seen the face of the Creator, but I have seen His Creation, so that I know full well that He exists." And the king said, "Does your God demonstrate his wisdom?" Daniel replied, "He works His will in mysterious ways."

The king's chest swelled with pride. "Our gods Bel and the

dragon are not so mysterious. Every year the dragon consumes one of our maidens, and every day Bel consumes the many offerings we give it, as you know." To this Daniel replied, "This I have heard, your majesty, and yet, to be honest, I find it hard to believe. Permit me to suggest a test to see if Bel is as powerful as it appears. For if Bel does indeed consume these offerings, then its power will be demonstrated. And if not, at least you will know the truth."

The king decided to have such a test, but he wondered how it could be done. He asked Daniel, who replied, "Let us go ourselves to the temple and be present when the offerings are made. And let us take with us a bag full of ashes, for that is all we will need." So it was that Daniel and the king went to the temple, where the whole enormous offering was set out in front of the idol as usual. Now Daniel took ashes from that bag and scattered them all around the temple floor. Then the king had the temple doors sealed with the royal seal, and he and Daniel returned to the palace.

The next morning, Daniel and the king hurried to the temple, they saw that the seals had not been touched. And when they broke them and entered, they saw at once that every single bit of flour and every drop of wine was gone, and the baskets and wineskins were empty. The king smiled with delight and said to Daniel, "Now are you convinced of the power of Bel?" But Daniel did not answer, instead he bent over and pointed to the floor. The king looked down to see what Daniel was showing him, and he saw many footprints running everywhere around the room. The king was so astounded he was speechless. Daniel followed the footprints and discovered a secret entrance behind the idol. He entered, and went down a long passage to an enormous cavern beneath the temple, the king following just a few steps behind. There in the cavern were stored the offerings of many years past; as much as in the king's own graineries. And the king realized that the priests had been taking those offerings for years, so that Bel would appear to be more than just a lifeless idol.

In his fury the king ordered that the priests be arrested and put to death. He rewarded Daniel for his wisdom by giving him the great stores of food they had gathered, which Daniel shared with all the Jewish people. And that was a time of great blessings for them.

But soon the time came when another maiden would have to be offered to the dragon. Daniel could not bear the thought of a life so wasted, so he rose and declared that he would try to kill the dragon. The king was astonished by this, since the dragon was held in such great awe. He told Daniel that the dragon would surely kill him first, but that if he were so willing to risk his life, no one would stop him from trying. If the dragon were truly a god, the king reasoned, it would easily defeat Daniel. And if Daniel were to defeat it, then surely it was not a true god after all.

So it was that Daniel made preparations to go to Dragon's Island, and he asked the king and his court to accompany him there, so that they could witness all that took place. Then Daniel set about to deceive the dragon. He cooked pitch and lard and wax together and from that he sculptured a waxen maiden, on which he put a wig of long black hair. Then he put the wax maiden inside a sack, and took it with him as his only weapon.

After that Daniel, accompanied by the king and his court, sailed to Dragon's Island, where the dragon made its home. It was a terrible, fire-breathing dragon of the most dangerous type. All knew that if the dragon's anger were provoked, it could destroy the entire capital with its fiery breath. It had been pacified for many generations only by the offering of a maiden at harvest time. In case Daniel should fail to kill the dragon, the king had brought along a living maiden and was prepared to sacrifice her in order to be spared the dragon's anger. Daniel knew this, and it made him twice as determined to defeat the dragon for good.

Now Dragon's Island was round, with the entrance to a cave in its center. This cave was itself in the shape of a sea-shell, running in circles beneath the island. It was there that the dragon made its home, sleeping for many months at a time, so that it was very hungry when it awoke. Each year it arose on the night the harvest moon was full, and it was then that the sacrifice of the maidens took place.

The entrance to the cave was surrounded by a deep forest on

all sides. The king and the members of the court who had come with him hid in trees around the entrance, where they could see but not be seen. Meanwhile, Daniel carried the sack near the entrance of the cave, and took out the wax maiden. He then carried the waxen statue to a tree in front of the cave to which the maidens were always chained. Then he hid himself nearby, and waited for the dragon to emerge.

Just as the full moon rose, the terrible dragon appeared at the entrance of the cave. In the light of the moon, the wax maiden looked very much alive, and the dragon pounced on it and swallowed it in a single gulp. But almost immediately the dragon realized it had been tricked. It had not swallowed a human, but something else, something very terrible. And all at once the fire inside the dragon set the waxen lump to burning. And as it burned in that fire, the lump began to swell, and the dragon swelled with it. And suddenly, as Daniel and the king and all the court watched in fascination and disbelief, the dragon blew up, breaking into a thousand pieces that flew all over that island.

The larger pieces of the dragon became frightful serpents that slithered about. And the smaller pieces became scorpions that landed in the trees and all over the ground. And the smallest pieces became poisonous spiders that crept and crawled everywhere. So it was that the king and his court not only saw the dragon destroyed, much to their surprise, since they had thought it immortal, but also were suddenly surrounded by these horrible little beasts—snakes, scorpions and spiders. They turned and ran as fast as they could to get off that island and back on their ships.

As for Daniel, he was overjoyed. He felt so safe in the shelter of the Holy One, blessed be He, that he walked among those poisonous creatures without fear, nor did they approach him. They ran away, for they sensed that it was he who had defeated the dragon.

And the maiden whose life had been saved also gave thanks to the God of Daniel, whom she now recognized as the true God.

From then on it was no longer known as Dragon's Island, but as Serpent's Island, and no one went anywhere near it.

Soon after they had returned to the palace, the king appointed Daniel to govern all of Babylon in his name, and this Daniel did very well, much as Joseph had done in Egypt in the name of Pharoah.

And all of this came to pass because Daniel put his complete faith and trust in the Holy One, blessed be He.

Babylon: c. Second Century B.C.E.

Miraculous Dust

The people of Israel once decided to send a gift to the Roman emperor, as a sign of their loyalty. They wondered whom they might send on this mission, and at last they agreed that the best one to go would be Nachum Ish Gam-Zu, for he had experienced miracles. So they gathered together a box full of precious stones, and sent Nachum Ish Gam-Zu on his way with many blessings and good wishes.

When night was about to fall, Nachum reached an inn, where he stayed overnight. The innkeeper and his wife noticed the box he carried with him and wondered what it contained. So that night, while Nachum slept, they crept into his room and took the box. They carried it to their own room, and when they opened it they were astounded to find that it was filled with precious jewels. They decided at once to steal them, but to prevent Nachum from discovering the theft right away, they filled the box with dust, so that it weighed the same as before. Then they carried the box back to his room and left it there while he was still asleep.

In the morning Nachum went on his way, not suspecting anything at all. For he was the trusting sort, who expected people to be good rather than evil. And whatever happened no matter how terrible it seemed, he would always say: "This too is for the best."

When Nachum reached the court of Caesar, he announced that he had come to deliver a gift to the Emperor from the people of Israel. So he was quickly given an audience with the emperor, who opened the box in his presence. When Caesar saw that the box was filled with dust, he was enraged. He began to shout that the Jews were mocking him, and made threats to destroy them all. Yet despite this catastrophe, Nachum remained calm, and kept repeating: "This too is for the best."

It was then that a miracle occured. Elijah the Prophet, who appears when he is most needed to protect the lives of his beloved people, appeared in disguise as one of the members of Caesar's court. He approached the emperor and said, "Perhaps there is more to this than meets the eye. For surely the Jews are too wise to insult Caesar in such a fashion. Who knows, perhaps this is some kind of magic dust. Why, it might even be the dust left to them by their father Abraham. For it is said that when Abraham threw dust, it turned into weapons of every kind, bows and arrows, spears and the strongest swords, with which he defeated his enemies. Perhaps the Jews have given you this precious magical dust. Before you condemn them, why don't you test it to see if this is the case?"

Caesar considered these words, and agreed that they were reasonable. So he took a pinch of the dust and threw it, and lo and behold, the dust turned into a multitude of swords, spears, bows and arrows. And all who tested them agreed that they were the finest weapons anyone had ever seen, and that whoever used those weapons would surely conquer any enemy.

Then Caesar realized that the Jews had given him a most precious gift, far more precious than any jewels or gold. For that dust could be carried in a little sack, and when the soldiers reached the place of battle they only had to toss it into the air, and it would turn into powerful weapons, with which they could win an easy victory. Caesar was deeply grateful to have such a priceless gift, and he commanded that Nachum Ish Gam-Zu be taken to the emperor's treasury and that his box be filled with precious stones and pearls, as a sign of the emperor's gratitude.

So it was that Nachum Ish Gam-Zu left the court of the emperor, and they bid him farewell with great honor. When he arrived at the same inn where he had stayed overnight on his way to Rome, he once again took lodging there. The innkeeper and his wife, who had not expected to see him again, were completely amazed at the rewards he had received, and they said, "What did you take with you that was so pleasing to Caesar?" Nachum replied, "What I took from here I brought there." Then they said to themselves, "That dust he brought was our own. It must be wonderfully precious. We too will reap a great reward from it."

So the very next day the innkeeper and his wife demolished their entire inn and carried many trunks filled with its dust to the court of the emperor. When they arrived there they were given an audience, and they told Caesar that the dust Nachum Ish Gam-Zu had brought had been their own. But when Caesar threw a pinch of it into the air, nothing happened, for of course the dust was not miraculous. He grew very angry and commanded that the evil innkeeper and his wife be killed.

Meanwhile, Nachum Ish Gam-Zu reached home, and showed the people the wonderful jewels he had received from the emperor in thanks for their gift. And when the people heard the tale of the miraculous dust, they gave thanks to the Holy One, blessed be He, for protecting them in their time of danger and seeing that all went well. And that was a happy time in their lives, for Caesar treated the Jews with honor and respect, and permitted them to worship the Lord as they saw fit.

Babylon: c. Fifth Century

A Voyage to the
Ends of the Earth

Among the sages of old, there was one who was a great traveller. His name was Rabbah bar bar Hannah, and his journeys were well known, for he brought back reports of things never seen before. Yet despite all his journeys, Rabbah always wished to take another voyage or travel on another caravan. And when he was asked where he wanted to go, he would always reply, "To the very ends of the earth."

Once it happened that Rabbah departed for a voyage and was not heard from for several years. He had never been gone that long before, so the rabbis began to worry about him, and finally, when he had not returned for seven years, they began to give up hope of ever seeing him again. Then one day a ship came into port, and a report reached the rabbis that among the passengers there was a man of immense wealth, a pious Jew. The rabbis wondered who this might be, and then a messenger arrived from the very wealthy man, requesting that all of the rabbis join him for dinner that very evening.

Now the rabbis did not turn down this invitation, but one and all they attended that dinner. When they were introduced to this wealthy man, the rabbis discovered to their amazement that it was none other than Rabbah bar bar Hannah. The rabbis embraced and kissed him and gave thanks that he was still among the living. Then they asked him where he had been, and Rabbah replied, "To the ends of the earth." The rabbis were astonished to hear this, and they begged him to tell them of his adventures. Rabbah smiled and agreed to share with them all that had happened, for he had looked forward to seeing them for a very long time. But first, he suggested, it would be proper to eat their dinner, and afterward he would tell them the tales of his long voyage.

Delighted at this prospect, the rabbis sat down at the long table, fourteen of them in all, including Rabbah. No sooner were they seated than a servant brought in a beautiful goose which had been roasted to perfection. The odor of it was almost too wonderful—all of them felt their appetites whetted. They did not taste such fine food very often. Then Rabbah stood up before the goose, and the others assumed he was going to carve it. But instead Rabbah touched it with the stone of the ring he wore—a large stone, of exceptional beauty. And no sooner had he done this, than the goose twitched as if it were alive, and the rabbis jumped back in amazement. A second later it raised its wings and began to fly around the room. And when it perched on the chandelier, the rabbis saw that it had regained its coat of white feathers. They were so stunned they could not believe their eyes. And Rabbah said; "Forgive me for this surprise. And fear not, this was not the only goose that I had prepared." And a moment later the servant brought in another goose, just as luscious as the other, and without hesitation Rabbah carved it and served it to his guests. And he promised to tell them everything once they had eaten.

Now the rabbis were so curious to know how Rabbah had performed that miracle, that they almost wished for the dinner to be over. Yet at the same time it was so delicious they could not help but savor it. And when the last dish had been taken away, they turned with undivided attention to their beloved colleague, to hear all that he would say.

Rabbah began thus: "As you know, I set sail seven years ago on a voyage to the East, to obtain spices from the Orient. I had sailed on that same voyage twice in the past, and the journeys were uneventful. But this journey was not like the others. After we had been at sea a few months, we sighted land for the first time since our departure. Wishing to stretch our legs once more, we landed on that island, First we explored it, and found that nothing grew on its smooth, grey surface. Then we sat down and built a fire with which to cook a meal. But soon after the fire had been lit, the land shifted, and we discovered, to our horror, that we were in fact on the back of a giant whale.

"Before there was time to rush back to the ship, the whale dived under water to put out the fire on its back. As it did, its tail whipped against the ship, and smashed it into pieces, while all of us who had been on the 'island' were cast into the sea. That was a terrible event, in which many a fine man lost his life. In fact, all were drowned except for me. And I survived because, as luck had it, a sturdy piece of the ship's mast floated directly by me, and I was able to grab hold of it.

"In that way I was carried for a great distance, until at last the currents brought me to an island. That island was as dense as a jungle, with fruit trees and flowers of immense size. I thought I might be in Paradise at first, because I had never seen anything so beautiful. But later I discovered that the island was inhabited by demons. It was there that they made their home during the day, and at night they flew away to invade the homes of good men and women and turn their lives upside-down.

"At first I could not see the demons, or even hear them. But little by little, as I drank the water from a spring on that island, I began to hear them speak. At first it sounded like they were whispering, then their words became clear to my ears. I was surprised to hear them speaking Hebrew, the holy tongue. And at last, when I had been on that island several days, the demons became clear to my eyes.

"When I had learned from their conversation that they were not flesh and blood beings, but demons, I became terrified, and feared that my life was as good as lost. I hid myself in the underbush, and only came out to pick fruit to sustain myself. I strained my ears to overhear their conversations whenever I could, so that I could learn if they were speaking about me. At first they gave no sign of having seen me, but in time I caught them whispering about me, and looking in my direction.

"One morning a group of fierce looking demons surrounded my hiding place, and when I saw their demeanor I was so frightened that I did not resist but went with them. They took me to their leader, Ahriman, the son of Lilith. He asked me to sit down to a meal with him, and I noticed that he recited the blessing like any good Jew. This amazed me, and I told him that I too was a Jew. The demon king told me that all the demons on that island were Jewish, and that I would be welcome to remain there among them. Then I told him that it was my intention to return home, where I could continue my studies. But when Ahriman learned that I was the colleague of such honored sages, he was more determined than ever to have me remain there with him.

"When I saw that the demon king had no intention of letting me return, I pretended to cooperate with him and agreed to live there among them. Ahriman clapped his hands when he heard this, and told me that the marriage would take place shortly. 'What marriage?' I asked. Ahriman replied, 'In order to live among us, everyone must be wed. Therefore let us celebrate your marriage!' Naturally, I was terrified to hear this, for I had no intention of being wed to a demon. But to have resisted might have cost me my life. And the fierce demons saw to it that I accompanied them to the place where the marriage was to take place.

"All of the demons of that island had gathered there, and it was a terrible sight indeed. The bride they had chosen for me might have been considered beautiful among them, but for me she was terrible and repulsive. According to their custom, the king had to perform for them before the wedding took place. That is what Ahriman did. He had two mules, saddled and placing one mule a great distance from the other, he leaped from one mule to the other while holding two cups and pouring wine from one to the other without spilling a drop on the ground. Yet, remarkable as this feat was, I paid little attention to it. Instead, I looked around desperately for some way to escape. Suddenly my eyes beheld a giant bird flying across the sky, so huge that it blotted out the sun and covered the entire island with its dark shadow. The demons suddenly became terrified, and scrambled off in every direction; I alone was left standing in the open. Suddenly the giant bird swooped down, grabbed me by the hair and carried me off in its claws.

"In complete terror I found myself suspended from a great height, as I saw the world pass below me. Not until the bird finally flew over the top of a high mountain did I find myself close enough to earth to tear myself free from its grip and leap to the ground below. I landed roughly, and found myself tumbling down the slope of that steep mountain. Once again my life was in danger, but things had happened so quickly that I had not even had time to catch my breath.

"Suddenly I reached the base of the mountain, and was able to stand up again at last. I gave thanks to the Holy One, blessed be He, who had seen fit to preserve my life through such danger, and I sought to discover where I was. I noticed that the earth I stood on seemed strangely warm, and the grass growing there looked more like fur. All at once the earth began to move, and it was all I could do to keep my balance. That is when I discovered that I had not tumbled down a mountain, nor was I standing on land. Rather, I had leaped from the mighty bird onto the horn of an enormous animal, whose size cannot be expressed. I had fallen down that horn until I had landed on the animal's head. And now that animal was moving, and it did not even seem to have noticed me on it. Once again my life was in danger, and I clung with all my strength to the base of that mighty horn, wondering where I might be taken. The animal continued walking all day, and only as darkness fell did it come to rest. Then, after grazing at an oasis, it lay down to sleep.

"Even then, with that giant animal lying down, it was a great distance for me to descend until I reached the ground. But I did not intend to spend another day riding upon it, no matter what. So I closed my eyes and leaped from that great height, and luckily

/27/

I landed in a pile of soft sand, which broke my fall. Then I ran away as fast as I could, and after running all night through a desert, I turned to look back as the sun arose. And even there, many miles away, I could see the clear outline of that mighty animal, and it was then that I recognized it for the first time. It was a Re'em, which the sages speak of, although no one, as far as I know, claims to have seen one. It was like a giant goat, with two horns, each reaching high into the heavens. And I realized how high the bird must have been flying when I jumped from it onto the horn of the Re'em. I could barely believe I had escaped such terrible danger, and I continued through that desert, thankful to be alive.

"After two days alone, with no water to drink, I began to fear I was lost for good, far away from all human habitation. But on the third day, as luck would have it, I saw an approaching caravan in the distance. It passed there just in time, for I did not even have the strength to run towards it, but had to remain lying there until the caravan reached me.

"Now the leader of that caravan was a kindly man, and he ordered his servants to give me water at once, and they waited until I recovered enough to speak. Then they asked me how I had come to be in that desolate place, and I told them my tale. They were truly astounded when they heard it, and saw to it that I was treated with every kindness. I ate in the tent of the leader, who never tired of asking me about the marvels I had seen.

"In that caravan, there was a remarkable figure, an Arab who never revealed his name. This Arab was revered by the leader of the caravan because of his uncanny abilities. He could tell, by smelling that earth, which was the way to this place or that. And whenever they needed to know how far they were from water, this Arab would reply 'Give me a handful of the sand on which you are standing.' And when they did this, he would smell it, and then point and say 'eight miles,' or however many it was, to the nearest water. And he never proved wrong. Thus he was invaluable to that caravan, for his wisdom always led them to the next oasis.

"I myself stood in awe of the Arab, for on two occasions I had switched sand from one place to another, but he always knew which sand was which.

"I spent much time in the company of this Arab, since I rode behind the leader, and the Arab followed me. One day when the caravan was encamped, the Arab came to me and said, 'I know the desert like the palm of my hand. So I know that not far from here there is something that you, a pious Jew, would not want to miss.' I agreed at once to come with him, and he took me a considerable distance until we reached a place where the remains of a once proud people lie scattered, but perfectly preserved. I came closer and studied their garments and saw that they were wearing prayer-shawls. This amazed me, but even more amazing was that among the fringes of their prayer-shawls were strands that were dyed blue. This could only mean that they were from the Generation of the Wilderness, whom Moses guided for forty years. For the secret of how to make that dye had been lost ever since that generation.

"The idea of having found the actual bodies of the Israelites who had died during that long wandering was overwhelming. And there, before my eyes, were true prayer-shawls whose fringes were dyed as the Torah commands. I knew the rabbis of the Yeshivah would be forever grateful to know that exact shade of blue, so I took out a knife and cut off one of those blue fringes, but when I tried to put it in my pocket, I found, to my horror, that my body was frozen, and that I could not move away from that place.

"The Arab saw my distress and asked if I might have taken anything from those dead in the desert. I confessed that I had cut off a single fringe, because the secret of its color had long been lost. But the Arab told me that it was known that whoever took anything from that place, from any of those sacred dead, would come under a spell that would keep them frozen in place until they gave it back. This is what had happened to me, and the instant I resolved to return the fringe, my body was set free from that spell, much to my relief.

"Next the Arab led me to a place where there was a huge crack in the earth, as if from an earthquake. There was smoke rising up from that abyss. While I watched, the Arab took a ball of wool, dipped it in water, and thrust it onto his lance. He held it in the abyss for a moment, and when he pulled it back it was singed.

"Then the Arab told me not to come any closer, lest I be burned by the smoke, but to listen carefully and see if I could hear any voices. This I did, and soon I began to make out distant cries. They were repeating over and over: 'Moses is true and his Torah is true.' I wondered greatly who they were, and the Arab told me that every thirty days the wheel of Gehenna returns to that place and brings them back there, where they repeat those words. For they were cursed to endure this punishment for all time. By then I had guessed who they must be, and so was not surprised when the Arab said that it was Korah and his followers, who had rebelled against Moses, and are still being punished to this very day.

"By this time it seemed as if I had returned to the past, to the time of Moses our teacher, whose presence I felt all around me. And I was never prouder to be a Jew. Then the Arab asked me if I wished to see one more miracle. Of course I agreed, and then he took me to the place where the earth and sky meet. There the horizon comes to an end, and my heart leaped. For I realized that I had finally accomplished my goal of reaching the ends of the earth. I prayed there and gave thanks to the Holy One, blessed be He, for permitting me to complete that quest which had haunted me all my days. And from that moment on I felt that my life was complete.

"We arrived there early in the morning, and I was carrying our provisions with us in a basket. I had put it down there when we came to that place, but when I reached for it, it was gone. I knew that the Arab had not taken it, and I asked him if there were thieves about. He told me that there were not, but that I had placed the basket upon the window of heaven. I need not worry, though, for the wheel of heaven turns one circuit daily, and in the morning the basket would be returned.

"So we spent the day there, and it is a day I will never forget. For that day I felt as if I were bathed in the light of the Divine Presence, and that my life had fulfilled its purpose. And I turned to the Arab who had made all this possible and asked him who he was, who had brought such blessings into my life. For a while he was silent, then he spoke and said, 'Elijah is my name.' And a chill went up and down my spine, for I realized that none other than the prophet Elijah had been my companion and guide.

"I had closed my eyes for an instant when Elijah spoke his name, and when I opened them, I found that he was gone. Then I deeply regretted having asked who he was, for if I had not, he might still be with me. For once Elijah has been recognized, he always disappears. Then, exactly at dawn, just as Elijah had said, the wheel of heaven arrived once again at the ends of the earth, and brought my basket with it. I picked it up and found the food in it untouched. Then I hurried back to where I had left the caravan.

"When I arrived there I found, to my horror, that the caravan had departed. And I did not even know how long we had been gone. Suddenly I was stranded alone in the wilderness. In despair I sat down in that barren place, knowing that my life was as good as lost. Just then, I thought I saw the glint of something in the sand. An object was buried there, and I greatly wondered what it was. I hurried to dig it out, and found that it was a marvelous golden dove, immensely precious, set about with all sorts of precious jewels.

"I stared at that golden dove, which I thought must surely be one of the supreme treasures on earth, and I realized that my luck had not abandoned me, even if Elijah had left me stranded in that place. Still, I did not know how I would ever find my way out of that wilderness. I held the golden dove in my hands while I was thinking about my plight. And when I wished I were back with the caravan, all at once I found myself riding behind the leader, as always—although the Arab who was really Elijah was no longer riding behind me, and was nowhere to be seen. Nor did the leader seem to find it strange that I should be there. In this way I discovered some of the wonderful powers of that golden dove, but I decided at the same time that such powers must be used very sparingly, or else one might become seduced by them.

"With the golden dove hidden in my bags I stayed with the caravan until it reached its goal, the port city nearest the ends of the earth. There I thanked the caravan leader with all my heart for his generosity, and sought to give him one of the jewels from the golden dove. To prove to him that I did indeed wish to make this gift, I took out the jewel so that I could show it to him. But no sooner had I done so than I saw, to my complete amazement, that another jewel took its place. At that moment I realized that the treasure I had come upon was in itself an endless treasure chest, which would never fail me as long as I kept it in my possession.

"When I reached that port city I sold just one of the diamonds and received a purse filled with gold. With it I purchased clothes worthy of a wealthy man and hired a servant to accompany me. After that I was able to find passage on a ship for return to this land, having fulfilled my goal in reaching the ends of the earth. I set sail from there one year ago, some six years having passed since my ship had been wrecked by the whale.

"On this journey home I also saw many miraculous things. Once, while we were sailing on the ship, we observed a jewel-box of immense size floating in the water. The captain immediately steered the ship toward it, and the sailors attempted to catch it in their nets. But the jewel-box always slipped out. Then the captain sent a diver after it, for he was not about to abandon such a treasure. However a shark guarded that jewel-box, and it attacked the diver, who beat a hasty retreat. Then, out of nowhere, we heard a great voice that said, 'What right have you to seek the jewel-box that belongs to the wife of Rabbi Hanina ben Dosa? It is reserved for her in the World to Come, that she may store in it fabric that has been dyed the color of blue that the Torah commands be worn on the fringes of the prayer-shawl.'

"Not long after this we passed within a few miles of a bird standing in the sea, where the water only reached to its ankles. This bird was so large that the one that had carried me away from the island of the demons was tiny by comparison. Thinking that the water was shallow, we desired to go in and cool ourselves. But a heavenly voice called out: 'Do not attempt to go in, for a woodcutter dropped his axe here seven years ago, and it has not yet reached the bottom.' And from the immense size of that bird I knew it could only be the Ziz of which the rabbis speak, which was created on the fifth day, along with Leviathan.

"While we were sailing we passed an enormous fish swimming in the opposite direction from us, and it took three days and three nights to sail the length of it. So too did we pass close enough to land to observe a remarkable sight: we saw a snake that swallowed a frog the size of a city. And a great raven came and swallowed the snake, and then flew up to the branches at the top of a tree. Now, think of the extraordinary size of that tree! If I had not seen it myself, I would not have believed it.

"One night, after we had been sailing for several months, we saw two bright lights in the distance. We could not imagine what they were, and it was not until we approached closer to them that we discovered that those lights were the eyes of an enormous fish, which had lifted its head out of the sea. Those eyes glowed like two full moons, and it blew water out of its nostrils like two fountains.

"But most amazing of all, perhaps, was what we saw shortly after that—a sea-dragon, of immense size. That sea-dragon had coiled itself up tightly around a precious jewel. When the sea-dragon saw us, it tried to swallow the ship, and for a time I thought that my luck had run out at last. But just as the sea-dragon was about to swallow us, an immense raven came and bit off its head. Just then another sea-dragon appeared with a precious stone in its mouth, and it touched the slaughtered sea-dragon with it. All at once, the headless dragon grew a new head and was as alive as before, and tried once again to swallow the ship. Again the raven came and bit off its head. But this time the precious jewel fell into the ship. I managed to catch it in my hand, and I immediately put it away in my sack, so that no one would try to take it from me. Suddenly, however, there was something moving in my sack, and in my confusion I opened it to see what it was. I found that when the jewel had landed upon the golden dove—as soon as it had touched it the dove was brought to life. And as I opened the sack, the golden dove took flight, and soon vanished on the horizon. And in its place I had the precious jewel, which is the one I have had set in my ring, and with which I touched the goose when we were about to sup. And the truth is that I do not feel bad about losing the golden dove, for it was through me that it had been granted life. And I suddenly realized that the dove had been served by me as much as it had served. For it had been my destiny to bring it to that place, that it might be touched by that blessed gem. Nor, God willing, do I ever have to fear being poor, since I still possess the bag filled with gold that I received for the one jewel that I sold. All in all, I believe that I have been greatly blessed . . . and that, my dear friends, is the end of my tale."

And when the rabbis had heard Rabbah's tale, they understood that his soul was blessed indeed, for otherwise the Holy One would never have permitted him to experience such a wealth of miracles. And they gave thanks that he had been permitted to return safely to them from the ends of the earth in order to bring these glad tidings, for they reassured them most mightily that the path they had taken was true, and that their trust in the Almighty was well placed. And Rabbah flourished in his home city for the rest of his days, nor did he set out on a sea voyage ever again. But to the last he shared the vivid memories of all that he had witnessed during that remarkable journey.

Babylon: c. Fifth Century

Rabbi Joshua
and the Witch

In their travels through Babylon, Rabbi Joshua ben Hanania and Rabbi Eliezer ben Hyrcanus arrived at a town in which there was to be found but a handful of Jewish families. It had been years since these Jews had contact with their brethren. Still, they were true to their tradition, and the fathers taught their sons all that they had been taught. So it was that when Rabbi Joshua and Rabbi Eliezer happened to pass two of these Jewish children playing in the street, they saw them making piles of sand, and one of them set one pile aside and said, "This one shall be for the tithe."

Now when they heard this, the two sages knew at once that the children must be Jewish, and they were very surprised that there were any Jews in that city. They asked one of the children to lead them to the Jewish quarter, and when they got there the rabbis knocked on the door of the first house they saw. When the family living there found that fellow Jews had come to visit them, they were overjoyed, and they welcomed the rabbis to stay as their guests.

That evening the rabbis joined their hosts for dinner. The

meal was quite delicious, but the rabbis observed that before any dish was served to them, the host would first carry it into a nearby room. Rabbi Eliezer became suspicious about this and asked why it was done. Then the host told them that his old father was in that room, and that he had vowed not to leave there until rabbis should return to that city.

Now since both visitors were rabbis, they told the host to invite his old father to join them, and he gladly went to do so. When the old man came, his eyes filled with tears at the sight of rabbis in the city again at last. Then Rabbi Joshua asked him why he had made such a strange vow to remain in his room. And the old man replied, "I am growing old, and I want to know that my son will be a father before I depart from this world. But my son is childless, and I vowed to remain in that room until sages arrived who could pray that God bless him with a son."

Both rabbis were moved at the old man's explanation, and Rabbi Eliezer asked Rabbi Joshua to try to help him if he could. Rabbi Joshua agreed to do his best, and he asked their host, the old man's son, to bring him some flaxseed. When the seed was brought, Rabbi Joshua spread it upon the table. Then he took some drops of waters in his fingers and scattered them upon the seeds. All at once, much to the amazement of everyone who was watching, the seeds began to grow.

In the space of a moment the flax was fully grown, as if it had taken root in the table top. Then, while all watched in wonder, Rabbi Joshua reached deep into the flax and grabbed a bunch in his hand. And as he raised his hand up from out of the flax he pulled out, first the locks of hair of a witch, then her head, and finally her whole body. Everyone in the room stared at that witch with complete astonishment. But Rabbi Joshua continued to hold her by the hair, and he stared in her eyes and said: "I order you to break the spell you have cast over this man, so that he may have a child of his own." And the witch trembled with fear before Rabbi Joshua's anger, and confessed that she had indeed made a charm and cast such a spell, but she pleaded that she could not break the spell, since she had cast the bewitched charm into the depths of the sea. Then Rabbi Joshua said to her, "In that case, you will

remain imprisoned in this wooden table until the spell is broken!"
And he let go of the witch's hair, so that she sank back into the
table, beneath the sprouted flax—which suddenly withered, so
that only the seeds were to be seen, scattered on the table as they
had been in the first place.

Then everyone knew that the old man's son had indeed been
the victim of the witch's spell and mourned because the spell could
not be broken. But Rabbi Joshua did not abandon hope. Instead
he asked the childless man to take them to the shore of the sea in
that city. And when the man did so, Rabbi Joshua stood there and
invoked the presence of Rahab, the Prince of the Sea. And he
called upon Rahab to recover the lost charm at once, so that the
spell could be broken. And lo and behold, suddenly the charm
rose to the surface of the water and floated to shore, directly at
Rabbi Joshua's feet. He opened it, took out the parchment on
which the spell was written, and burned it, and the spell was
broken once and for all. At that very same instant, the witch
imprisoned in the table was set free, and went running out of that
house as fast as she could, never again to be seen in that city.

Before the year was out the old man's son became a father. The family was overjoyed, particularly the grandfather, who lived long enough to see his grandson enter into the yoke of the *mitzvot*. And the name of that child was Judah ben Bathyra, and he himself became one of the sages and studied under Rabbi Joshua, who gladly taught him everything he knew.

Babylon: c. Fifth Century

The Sword of Moses

In the last words spoken by Moses, before he took leave of the Children of Israel and made his final ascent of Mount Nebo, he spoke of a sword which could protect and shield his people. In the Talmud it is said that this sword was given to Moses when he received the Torah. In days of trial for the Jewish people in every generation, the thought of this sword often stirs them with longing, for they are sorely in need of a shield against their troubles. But where is the sword of Moses to be found? No one knows, but there is a tradition among the Jews of Iraq that the sword can be found in the mountains of Kurdistan.

Now there were three young Jews who longed to find the sword of Moses so that they could end the oppression of their people. They set out on a quest to the mountains of the north to see if the legend about the sword was true. It took them many months just to cross a vast desert and reach those high mountains. But they believed they were on a divine mission, and would not stop until they had succeeded in finding the sword.

Now what was it they expected from that sword? Sometimes the three friends talked about this. The eldest among them, who was the leader, said that he believed the sword would permit them to conquer armies. The second lad said he believed the sword would only serve to protect, and not to conquer. And the third of the friends thought that finding the sword might somehow bring with it the coming of the Messiah and the redemption that will come at the End of Days. They often debated these matters among themselves, but the one thing they all agreed on was that the sword had to be found, for the people were sorely in need of its protection.

Once they had reached the mountains, the three friends sought information about the sword, but no one seemed to know anything about it. Word of their quest reached the head of a nearby village, a blind old man, embittered by his affliction, who still held on tightly to the reins of power. Now this old man had heard the legend of the enchanted sword of Moses buried in those mountains, although he did not believe it. But he did believe that the Jews must intend to conquer their neighbors if they were searching for such a sword, and he decided to teach the three young men a lesson.

So this old man called in one of his servants and ordered him to go secretly to the camp of the three Jews and to bury an old, rusty sword nearby. After that, the servant should lead them to it, and when they dug it out, he was to have them arrested, for the place it was to be buried was part of that village's land.

This servant, himself a conniving and evil man, buried the rusty sword exactly as he was ordered, quite close to the camp of the three friends. Then he disguised himself as a woodgatherer and passed the camp with a load of wood slung over his back. The three friends saw him and invited him to join them in their meal. This he did, and while they were eating the three friends asked the man if he had ever heard of the sword of Moses. He acted surprised and told them that he had indeed heard of it, and that it was supposed to be buried nearby. He pointed in the direction of the place where he had hidden the rusty sword. The three friends became very excited, and decided to start searching there first thing in the morning. The evil servant took his leave and reported all that had happened to the head of the village. Then he took several men with him, and waited behind the rocks for the three young men. When the three friends succeeded in finding the rusty sword, the men jumped out and arrested them.

When the evil servant laughed at their capture, the three friends realized they had been tricked. They became very downcast, for they knew that the sword they had found must not be the sword of Moses after all. And they wondered how they could ever continue on their quest if they were prisoners of these villagers.

Not long afterward, the three friends were brought before the blind head of the village. He accused them of plotting to overthrow their neighbors, but the young men said that all they had found was a rusty sword that could hurt no one. Then the old man asked them directly, "And are you not searching for the sword of Moses?" The eldest of the three, who was also the cleverest, did not deny that this was true, since they had asked the evil servant about finding it. But he added, "You are not mistaken about the object of our search, but you are wrong about our purpose. It is not true that we want to use the sword for rebellion. No, we are searching for it because it will make us rich. And if you set us free to search for it, we will divide the money with you when we have found it."

Now this was the best thing that could have been said to that greedy old man, for although he doubted they would succeed in finding the sword, he liked the idea of sharing in the riches if they did. So he agreed to let them go free, in exchange for a vow that they would give him half the price they received for the sword. The young men gladly made this vow, since they knew well that if they did find the sword they would never sell it for all the riches in the world.

Thus the three young men were able to continue their quest, with the desire to find the sword of Moses still burning within them. But which way were they to turn? It would be foolish to start digging anywhere in the mountains, for they could spend the rest of their lives there and not find anything. No, they needed a clue; but they had none, except for the words of Moses in the Torah, which they carried in their hearts. So they called upon those words yet one more time, and raked through them as if through coals, hoping to find a clue that would direct them. Moses had said:

> *Happy art thou, O Israel, who is like unto thee?*
> *O people saved by the Lord,*
> *the shield of thy help,*
> *and the sword of thy excellence.*
> *Thine enemies shall dwindle away before thee;*
> *and thou shalt tread up their high places.*

The three each meditated on these words, as they had so many times before. Then the first of them spoke and said, "It seems as if the words of Moses are a prophecy. For is it not true that our enemies have dwindled away, and that we have escaped their clutches? And are we not now treading upon their high places?" The others realized that what he said was true—and their hope was renewed that they could succeed in fulfilling the other part of the prophecy as well, the one concerning the sword of Moses.

Then the second lad, who had also been meditating on the words of Moses, said, "Perhaps there are still other clues to be found in the words of Moses. It occurs to me that perhaps we should be seeking not only the sword of Moses, but the shield of which he also spoke when he said *the shield of thy help*. For surely that shield will be found in the same place as the sword, and a shield is much larger than a sword and should be easier to find."

His companions considered his words with great seriousness, and realized how wise they were, and they wondered why they had not thought more of the shield of Moses. But still they did not know where to start looking. Then the third lad spoke and said, "Surely we must begin by ascending one of these mountains. True, we do not know which one, but I suggest that we ascend the very tallest, which lies at the center of them. For Moses towered above all other men, and it seems to me that his sword would be hidden on the highest mountain." The other two friends marveled at the wise words of their companion, and they began the ascent.

Now by the end of the first day of climbing, the three friends had reached a small ledge on that high mountain, and to their surprise they found there the entrance to a cave. They were amazed to see a cave up that high, and they agreed that the cave must be searched. But first they made a fire and rested and ate a warm meal. Afterward they put their fire out, lit a torch, and then entered the cave.

Now the cave was quite narrow. They were able to proceed only one at a time, and even then they had to squeeze their way between the walls of the cave. And so they continued for what seemed a great distance, as the cave descended inside the mountain. In fact, they travelled so far downward that they wondered if they had descended as far as they had ascended in the first place, or perhaps even further. And as they descended in that cave, a sound began to reach their ears, like the sound of running water.

At last those narrow passages opened into a large cavern. No sooner had they entered than they saw the glittering waters of the stream that flowed from there. The three lads hurried to that stream, and when they stood above the waters they saw something glittering in its currents. "Why, it is a fish!" cried one of the lads. The others saw that not only was it a fish, but a golden fish, with golden scales, swimming in the currents of the stream. Then the eldest realized that such a golden fish must be a very important sign, and he cried out to the others, "Hurry, let us follow that fish!"

So they ran along the side of that stream, and followed the golden fish as it glided slowly through the waters. But soon they reached a place where the passage was so narrow they could not follow. And when the eldest realized that they were about to lose the fish, he suddenly reached out and grabbed it—so quickly that even he was surprised.

His companions hurried over to examine the fish in the light of the torch, and when they did they saw an amazing thing: there on one side of the golden fish was inscribed the shape of a sword! And on the blade of that sword were four Hebrew letters! How could such a thing be possible? The three friends were stunned, and they realized at once that it was a sign sent to them to guide them further on their quest.

Now of course those young men knew Hebrew, for they had

"His companions hurried over to examine the fish in the light
of the torch, and when they did they saw an amazing thing . . ."

studied the holy tongue from the time they had learned to read. And so they each read that word, but they did not know what it meant, for it was a word they had never seen before. It was the eldest of the young men who realized that the golden fish had served its purpose by bringing them this word. He said to the others, "Now let us set the fish free, for surely it was a messenger of God, and has brought us this word, which must be a great clue in our quest." The others agreed, so he set the fish free in the waters, and it quickly swam out of their sight. For a moment they wondered if they had done the right thing, but then they remembered the word, and began to wonder what secret it held for them.

So far, none of them had tried to pronounce the word. Now one of them spoke it as he imagined it must be said, for there seemed to be many ways it could be pronounced. In fact, the second lad had imagined it should be said another way, which he too spoke aloud. But the third, the eldest, had thought of still another way, and as soon as he pronounced it, the three friends suddenly found themselves standing outside again, at the foot of the mountain, at the very spot where they had begun their climb! The startled young men could not understand how they had come to be there, for just a moment earlier they had been in the cave, deep inside the mountain. They wondered if it was because of the word, but they could not imagine how that could be. All three friends agreed, however, not to pronounce the word again, since they did not understand its power, and did not know what would happen if they did. And they decided that until they learned more about that word, they must continue their search for the sword of Moses.

Now the three friends did not know it, but from the time they had left the village, they had been followed by the servant of the blind man and several of his henchmen. For the blind man was not satisfied with only half the sword of Moses; he wanted the whole thing. So he had the three young Jews followed, intending to steal the sword from them when they found it, and then take their lives.

Now when the three lads had ascended the mountain, the henchmen waited at the base of the mountain, not far from where the friends had made camp. So when they saw the three of them suddenly appear at the base of the mountain, without having seen them descend, the henchmen could not believe their eyes. The evil servant did not know what to do, so he sent a messenger back to the village. When the blind man heard what had happened, he guessed that the three had found the sword, and somehow used its magic to descend from the mountain. His lust to have such power in his own hands grew very great, and he ordered the servant to have the three killed at once, and to bring all their possessions back to him, without opening them. For the blind man secretly feared that the evil servant would try to take the power of the magical sword for himself. And he was right, the servant was planning to do exactly that: to steal the sword for himself.

So it was that the three friends were surrounded by enemies on all sides, and knew nothing about it. They were absorbed in trying to decipher the message of the golden fish and to continue their quest for the magic sword. Then all at once, they heard the cries of their pursuers, and ran for their lives. They ascended that tall mountain again as fast as they could, but the villagers had climbed mountains all their lives and drew closer with every step. The three lads climbed faster and faster, until they finally reached the peak of the mountain, and there was no place left for them to go.

What were they to do? As they stood upon that high peak and looked down, they saw that the other side of the mountain was too steep to climb down. There was nowhere for them to go, and when they heard the villagers getting ever closer the eldest lad decided to pronounce the word as he had pronounced it in the cave. And he spoke the holy Name out loud—for that is what it was—and in an instant the peak of the nearest mountain, although several miles away, moved from its place, so that it was but a single step away for them. The three companions took that step, until they stood together on the second peak. And just before the evil villagers reached the top of the other mountain, the lad pronounced the Name again, and the second mountain returned to where it had been before.

And there, on that high peak, they watched the spears and

arrows of the amazed villagers fall harmlessly into the valley below. The three companions then realized they were just beginning to understand how great was the power of that holy Name, for such power could only come from the most powerful of the seventy-two Names of God, since the Holy One is the source of all power and being. And little by little they began to understand that the sword of which Moses had spoken might not have been an actual sword at all, but that magical word itself, which served as both a sword and shield for the Jewish people. At that moment, high on that mountain peak, they realized that they had indeed succeeded in their quest. For the word that they had read in that cave deep in the mountain, from the side of the golden fish, was itself the very sword of Moses for which they had searched.

Up so high, they felt much closer to the heavens than they had ever felt before. And they knew that they would use that "sword" in their generation as Moses had used it in his—to liberate their people, the Children of Israel, so that they might end their long exile and return to the Holy Land of their forefathers. For Moses had said: *Thou shalt come in unto the land which the Lord thy God giveth thee for an inheritance, and possess it and dwell therein.* And they were certain that just as the words of Moses about the sword had been fulfilled, so too would the prophecy about the return to the Holy Land come true and that of the coming of the Messiah at the End of Days as well.

Iraqi Kurdistan: Oral Tradition

". . . when the pheasant arrived the next day with food for the
maiden, it discovered the young man inside . . ."

The Maiden in the Tree

During her stay in Jerusalem, the Queen of Sheba was the guest of King Solomon, who spent many hours speaking with her about the wonders of the Holy One, blessed be He. The Queen of Sheba listened to these tales with amazement, for they were truly miraculous. So too did Solomon tell her of how the Holy One was a matchmaker, even though each match was as difficult to make as it had been to part the waters of the Red Sea. Now when the Queen of Sheba heard this, she could not restrain herself and said, "I have believed everything you have told me of your God except for this—that the Holy One makes matches. Let me, I beg you, put this matter to a test. Let us walk together through the streets of Jerusalem. I shall select an unmarried maiden, and you will see to it that she is sent away to a distant and remote place, far from any man who might be her destined match. There let her be imprisoned in a large tree, with no way to escape. Then we shall have a fair test of whether or not your God shall provide her match!" King Solomon agreed at once to this test, and within the hour they left together and walked through the streets of Jerusalem.

Along the way King Solomon and the Queen of Sheba saw many unmarried maidens, some walking by the way, some shopping in the marketplace, some selling jewels, some selling nuts and dates, some selling all kinds of beautiful cloth. The Queen of Sheba observed all these, but passed them by. Then they came to a well, where the Queen saw a beautiful maiden pouring water from a bucket into a jug. The Queen turned to King Solomon and said, "That is the one! Let us see what will happen if she is taken to a distant and forgotten place for five years, to make her home in a tree. Then, I wonder, how your God will complete her match!"

King Solomon approached the maiden and asked her to take him to her home. The maiden was overwhelmed to find herself in the presence of the king, and she led Solomon and the Queen of Sheba to the home of her parents. There the king declared that he wished to employ the maiden for a period of five years. The sum he offered was very great, and the maiden's parents gladly accepted it. Only when the maiden had returned with him to the palace did King Solomon reveal to her that she was to live alone on an island for five years. The maiden was heartbroken, and could not imagine why she deserved such a terrible fate. Still, she did not protest, for she knew that she was powerless before the great king.

So it was that the maiden was brought to a deserted island, far from the company of men. In a forest on the island a great tree had been prepared to serve as her home. The tree was over five hundred years old, and it was wide enough to contain a small chamber. It had one door, but it was locked from without. A window was carved into its trunk, large enough to pass to the maiden all that she might need, but too small for her to escape. The room contained some furniture from the palace of the king, along with some musical instruments for the maiden to play, and even a loom on which she might weave. And that, in fact, is what the maiden did most of the time, for she was a remarkably fine weaver. As she weaved she sang all the songs that she had ever learned and many others that she made up as well. And so she passed her lonely existence in that tree, her only companion a magic pheasant that King Solomon had sent to guard over her and to bring her all that she might need. For he knew well the languages of all the birds, and he had long entrusted that pheasant with special tasks.

In this way, several years passed, and still the maiden remained alone inside that hollow tree. Many were the days and nights when she pined for her family so far away, and wondered how she had come to know such a strange fate. And yet she did not despair, for she knew that eventually she would be freed from there. Meanwhile she tried to fill her days with weaving and singing, so that the time would pass more quickly and she would not feel so all alone.

Now one day it came to pass that a ship was sailing over the sea and the son of the captain asked his father if he might steer the ship himself. The captain let him take the wheel, and just then a sudden tempest arose, which tossed the ship to and fro. The storm became stronger and stronger until some of the passengers were tossed over the sides of the ship, into the wild currents, where they drowned. And among those who fell in the water and were thought to be lost was, alas, the captain's son.

When the storm finally subsided, the captain spent many days searching the sea for survivors, especially his son. But not a single person was sighted, and it began to appear that all had been lost. At last, when there was no hope left that any of them might be found, the captain returned to his homeland. There he continued to mourn over the loss of his son, and all the time he blamed himself. He believed that if he, and not his son, had been at the wheel when the storm had struck, he might have guided the ship to safety, and his son might still be among the living.

But the truth is that his son had not drowned. Alone among all the passengers, he had clung to a plank that had floated nearby, and it had been carried over the waters until at last he had reached a distant island. Night had already fallen so he lay himself down under a tree to sleep. The next morning he was very hungry when he awoke, and he began to look for something to eat. In his pocket he found that he had carried with him only three things, a little mirror, a knife and a pair of scissors. When he found fruit on a tree he climbed up, cut off the fruit and ate it. And so he was able to sustain himself.

The island was not very large, and in his search for fruit the young man came at last to a great hollow tree. When he had just sighted it, he saw a pheasant flying toward it with a basket held in its beak. The pheasant perched on a branch next to a small opening, which looked like a kind of window. From the basket, the pheasant took out food, which it passed through the little window with its beak. Inside the tree something seemed to take the food, but the young man could not see what it was. He thought it might be some kind of animal, and he wondered greatly about all that he had seen.

So it was that the young man continued to hide himself near the tree, and finally he caught a glimpse of the maiden's dark hair as she passed in front of that small window. Now the maiden had not cut her hair in all those years, and it had grown very, very long and trailed behind her. To the young man it seemed that the long hair belonged to an animal, although he could not imagine what sort it was. At last he crept closer and peered into the window, and there he saw the beautiful maiden.

The young man knocked on the trunk of the tree three times, and the maiden inside was greatly surprised. Suddenly she was filled with both fear and longing—for she did not know who had found her in that remote place. She called out, "Who is there?" And the young man replied, "I was cast alone upon this island when my ship sank. But who are you?" Then the maiden told him how she had come to be there by a whim of the Queen of Sheba and King Solomon. The way she told him about it, he could tell at once that she was very angry at them both. He was truly amazed at the tale, for his ship had been heading for that very kingdom when it had sunk. Yet at the same time he was deeply grateful that there was such a beautiful maiden with him on that island. He talked to her through the little window for a long time, long after the sun had set. And when it rose the next day they were still talking. By this time they both knew that they loved each other.

Then the young man took out his scissors and cut away the vines around the window and took his knife and carved away the frame of the window until it was large enough for him to climb inside. And thus he and the maiden came to live inside the very same chamber in that hollow tree.

So it was that when the pheasant arrived the next day with food for the maiden, it discovered the young man inside. The pheasant flew quickly to King Solomon's palace and told him everything. Solomon was delighted at this news, but he kept it secret from the Queen of Sheba. Instead he ordered the pheasant to take enough food for them both, including the finest delicacies from the king's table.

Now the captain's son grew to greatly love the maiden who dwelt with him in the tree. One day he showed her the mirror which he had carried with him when he had fallen from the ship. She looked in the mirror and was amazed at what she saw, for she had grown very beautiful indeed during all those years, and resembled a princess. The young man, too, recognized her great beauty, and before long he asked her to be his wife. She loved him as much as he did her, and so they agreed to marry, and invited to the wedding all the birds and beasts of the forest. The birds sang, the animals danced, and it was a beautiful wedding.

A year passed and the pheasant continued to bring food for them both, as well as clothing and shoes. So too did the pheasant teach them both the language of the birds. In another year the maiden had a child, a lovely girl, whom they named Sheba, for they were no longer angry at either the king or queen. They believed that if the maiden had not been sent to that island, they might not ever have met. The pheasant reported this happy news to King Solomon, and the king told him to be sure to bring enough for them all. So too did he begin to think that perhaps the time had come to let the Queen of Sheba know their fate.

Now it happened that shortly thereafter there was the wedding of King Solomon's son. All the emperors and queens were invited to attend, and among the guests was the Queen of Sheba. King Solomon had also directed the pheasant to invite a pair of every kind of bird and beast. So the pheasant flew to every corner of the earth and proclaimed that such pairs of every kind should come to the great king's celebration. The birds flew on their own, but for the animals Solomon sent a gigantic boat, steered by the pheasant. It was the very ark of Noah that had once saved all those kinds of animals from the Flood. And the young couple emerged from the tree with their child and joined them, for they too had been invited to be guests at the wedding.

When the boat reached land, everyone jumped off and began to follow the pheasant. As they travelled, the young man noticed that next to every well they passed there was the portrait of a young man, and it was always the same picture. He thought that perhaps it was the god that the natives of the land worshipped, and he asked the pheasant what kind of picture it was. The pheasant replied, "The portrait you see is not that of an idol, for this is the land of Israel, and the people here fear God alone. It is the portrait of the son of a ship's captain who was lost at sea. His father wept greatly and lamented over his son, but people comforted him and told him not to weep, for God would have mercy on his son and would save him. So the captain had the portrait of his son put next to every well, in the hope that someone would see his son and recognize him, and know where to bring him back."

Now when the young man heard this tale, he began to cry. He told the pheasant that he was the captain's son who had once fallen into the sea. And he was still weeping when he reached King Solomon's palace. When Solomon saw his tears he asked why and the young man told him the whole story. So Solomon had messengers sent to bring the captain, and when he and his son were reunited it was a great day indeed.

So too did King Solomon see to it that the father and mother of the maiden who had lived in the tree were also present, and they were overjoyed to see her again at last. As for the Queen of Sheba, she saw with her own eyes how the Holy one had blessed that maiden and joined her with her destined one, despite everything. Then the queen's doubts were all gone, and she knew well that the Holy One, blessed be He, does indeed make matches.

/54/

And she saw as well that God is as merciful with mankind as is a father with his sons and daughters. And never again did she doubt the word of King Solomon.

Eastern Europe: Nineteenth Century

The Three Tasks of Elijah

Now it has often been told how the prophet Elijah, wearing a disguise, would bring salvation to a Jew in distress. There was one time, however, when Elijah did not disguise himself, but presented himself to a poor man whose family was starving and said, "I know about the suffering of your family, and I wish to assist you in some way. Since I have no money to give you, all I can offer is myself. Therefore I want you to take me to town and sell me to the highest bidder."

The poor man was greatly startled at these words, for he could not imagine that anyone, not even Elijah, would be willing to make such a sacrifice. He blessed Elijah for his kindness, but refused to accept his offer, for no Jew should have to serve as a slave. But Elijah insisted, and reminded the man about the pangs of hunger his children were feeling that very moment. At last the man agreed to sell Elijah, if that was what he wished. They went to market place, and the man announced that an auction was to be held for this slave.

Now among those at that auction was a servant of the king, who observed the knowing look on Elijah's face, and purchased him for the king for a sum of seventy dinars. And the poor man bought food with that money, and after that his family never went hungry again, for his business flourished and his fortune grew. And when he grew rich, he gave charity to every poor man he met, for he never forgot the sacrifice of Elijah, who had permitted himself to be sold.

As for Elijah, he was brought before the king, who at first was astonished that his servant had purchased such an old slave. "And what is it that you think this slave can do?" asked the king. "Can he carry bricks? If not, I do not need him, for the construction of my palace is shortly to take place." Then the king turned toward Elijah and said, "Tell me, old man, can you at least read?" And Elijah said, "Yes, that I can certainly do." "Well, then," said the king, "perhaps we will find something useful for you to do."

As Elijah was being led away, he heard the king say to his servant, "Go into the city and locate the finest architect and bring him to me, for I must have someone draw up the plans for my palace." When Elijah heard this, he spoke up and said, "May it please your majesty, but I too am an architect, and I do not doubt that I could design exactly the palace that you dream of." The king was pleased to hear this, for he had very particular plans of his own for his new palace and had feared an architect would have his own ideas. So he agreed to let Elijah be the first to draw up the plans.

In the days that followed, the king related his dream of a palace to Elijah, who listened intently. And when the king had finished describing it down to the last detail, Elijah set about to drawing it. The king was astonished when Elijah presented the plans to the king the very next day, and when the king looked at them, he saw that the slave had found a place for every single thing which the king had wanted. Then the king grew excited and said, "It is true, old man, that you have succeeded in puting my every wish into your plans. I doubt if any other architect could have done as well. But it is one thing to draw up plans, and another to bring them into being. Are you prepared to oversee the building of the palace as well?"

Elijah replied at once: "This too, my lord king, I can do. But if I am to serve as your builder, how can I remain a slave? For what free men will want to take orders from a slave?" The king agreed, but now that he had discovered the great skills of this slave, he was reluctant to set him free. So he said, "Freedom is the most precious thing in the world; its value cannot be calculated. If you want your freedom, building a palace will not suffice to attain it. Let us count it as one of three things you will do at my command. And if you fulfill all three commands in full, then I will give you your freedom."

Now the truth is that Elijah had the powers to free himself at any time, simply by disappearing. But he did not, because he had been sold as a slave, and as a slave he would serve until he was set free. So Elijah agreed to perform three things for the king, as he commanded—so long as they did not involve anything evil. And the king issued a proclamation, that if the slave Elijah completed the building of the palace and two other tasks as well, that he was to be set free. But he did not write down what those two other tasks were, nor did he tell Elijah at the time.

That night Elijah offered a prayer to the Holy One, blessed be He, that the palace might be built at once, for the sooner Elijah was freed from slavery, the sooner he could return to the task of assisting Jews in need. And the next morning the king and all the people of that city were astounded to see that the palace had been built, complete in every respect, exactly as the king had described it. The king was overwhelmed with joy at the splendor of his palace, and at the same time he began to realize that his slave Elijah had wonderful powers, greater than he had imagined. He was loathe to let him go, for the slave was too precious to him. So he had Elijah called in and said to him, "What you have done is a miracle, without a doubt. I am very grateful to you, and I will think of you always as I wander the halls of my new palace. But now it is time for you to complete your second task." Elijah nodded his head in agreement, for he was ready to undertake the second task at once.

Then the king said, "I have heard it said the Jews believe that when the Messiah comes, there will be precious stones that will take the place of the sun. For your second task, I would like to see these stones with my own eyes."

The king had thought long and hard about this task, for he felt sure that it was impossible to fulfill. And it was very difficult, even for Elijah—but for a reason unknown to the king. For it was written in the Book of Life that when Elijah entered the cave where the precious gems were hidden, the era of the Messiah was to begin. Yet the destined time had not arrived, and Elijah did not dare hasten the End of Days. Therefore he was silent for a long time, but at last he replied and said, "I will see to it, my lord king, that this desire of yours is fulfilled. But only if you will first agree to three conditions. The first is that you must agree to follow whoever comes to lead you to these stones; the second is that you must permit yourself to be blindfolded when you are taken there and when you return, for the location is a great secret; and the third is that you will not take any of those precious stones with you when you leave." The king was still doubtful that such precious stones even existed, so he readily agreed to these conditions. Then Elijah told the king that he would hear from whoever would serve as his guide within three days, and he bowed low and took his leave.

Now at the same time, far out at sea, there was a ship that was foundering in a terrible storm, about to sink. Among all the passengers, there was but a single Jewish boy. Suddenly Elijah appeared before this lad, although he was invisible to everyone else. Elijah told the lad that if he would agree to approach the king of the land toward which they had been sailing, he would save the ship. The boy was to lead the king to a cave, which Elijah would reveal. The boy protested that a king would not heed one so young as he, but still he agreed to do as Elijah said, for the ship had started to sink. And as soon as the boy agreed, the storm subsided and the passengers were saved. Elijah then told the boy how to find his way to the secret cave, and when he was certain that the boy understood, he vanished.

As soon as the ship arrived in port, the boy went to the palace of the king, and announced that he had come to lead the king to the precious stones. The boy was soon taken to the king, who had left orders that anyone making such a claim was to be given an audience at once. Now the king was astonished to see that his guide was a boy, but he had agreed to go with whomever Elijah sent to lead him. So too was he reluctant to be blindfolded, but because he had given his word he permitted it. But both to protect himself and to discover the secret of the location, should it prove to exist, the king ordered that the head of the palace guards should secretly follow behind them.

Now Elijah had foreseen that the king might send someone to follow them, and he saw to it that the head of the palace guards was deceived by an illusion, in which it appeared to him that the boy led the king in one direction, while in fact he was being led in another. By following Elijah's instructions, the boy led the blindfolded king to a cave some three miles from the palace. When they were inside the cave, the boy told the king to take off the blindfold, and when he did, the king was almost blinded by the bright light that shone from the precious stones gathered there. He could not believe his eyes at first, but when his eyes grew more accustomed to the great light, he realized that any one of those precious stones would be worth more than any diamond in the world. The king was so seized with the desire to possess those diamonds that he reached out to seize one of them, but at the instant he touched it all of the precious stones vanished, and the cave was pitch black. Then the king realized that such sacred stones could not be possessed, and in the face of such power he was glad he had not lost his life in seeking to make one of them his own. Then he meekly put on his blindfold and followed the boy back to the palace and bade him goodbye. He was certain that his guard would have learned the way to that sacred cave. But when he returned, the king discovered that his trusted guard had been following them when they had suddenly disappeared from his sight, and at last he had given up searching for them and returned to the palace. Then, more than ever, the king did not want to lose the great powers possessed by his slave. But in order to prevent him from becoming free, he had to think of a third task simply impossible to perform. The king gave this matter a great deal of thought, and at the end of three days he called for Elijah and told him that now that the second task had been fulfilled, he was ready to assign the third one. Elijah told him that he was ready.

Then the king smiled and took out a silken scarf and handed it to Elijah and said, "Here, my good man, is a gift. This scarf is now yours. But tell me how much would it be worth if you purchased it in the market?" Elijah looked at the scarf, which had a rainbow of colors, and said: "Since it has come from far away, and is beautiful as well, it might be worth as much as one golden coin. And considering, as well, that it belonged to the king, its value might be increased to two gold coins." The king nodded at this assessment and said: "As always, you are a very shrewd man. For I perceive that the scarf's value is exactly as you put it. Yet, as you know, it is the task of the merchant to sell something for more than he paid for it. This, then, is your last and final task, if you can fulfill it: you are to take this scarf to the market and offer it for sale. And if you are able to sell it for ten thousand gold coins, then you will have completed the final task and you will be a free man. But if you sell it for even a dinar less than ten thousand, you will have failed to fulfill the final task, and you will remain my slave for the rest of your life." The king broke out in cruel laughter, for he believed that he had finally outwitted the wise Elijah. The king knew well that he was the only one in that kingdom who possessed such great wealth. Yet Elijah showed no sign of worry. He bowed courteously, and told the king that the sale would take place in three days, and then took his leave.

Now where was it that Elijah went? Directly to the Garden of Eden, with the scarf in his hand. There he went to the base of the Tree of Life, and gathered up one hundred leaves that had fallen there, and wrapped them in that scarf. Then he returned to the city where he was a slave, and each time he met a poor Jew on the street he gave him one of the leaves and told him that by boiling the leaf in water and drinking the potion, he could cure any illness. So it was that some of the Jews were able to cure those in their families who had been afflicted all their lives with illness, and others were able to sell their leaves for a great sum, enough to sustain them for the rest of their lives.

By the time Elijah had reached the palace, he had given away every one of the leaves. But the scarf in which he had carried them had absorbed forever the fragrance of Paradise, and all who caught a scent of it knew for a moment a peace unknown in this world. When Elijah returned he went directly to the marketplace and called a crowd together in order to sell the scarf, just as the king had commanded. Now the king had come to the market that day in disguise, for he wanted to see for himself if Elijah would succeed in selling the scarf for ten thousand gold coins. At last a crowd had gathered, and one by one Elijah called them up to examine the scarf, which he spread on a table. As they did, each of them caught a scent of that otherwordly fragrance unknown outside of Paradise. And as soon as they did, each and every one of them knew that the scarf was priceless. Every man, woman and child in that crowd bid for that scarf, but none of them could offer ten thousand gold coins, for not one of them was that rich.

As for the king, he too had smelled the fragrance of Paradise and became possessed by a great longing to possess that scarf, which he had foolishly given to Elijah without realizing its value. So the king too joined in the bidding, but Elijah rejected every bid until the king shouted "Ten thousand gold coins! I must have that scarf!" "Sold!" said Elijah, and everyone turned and wondered who could be so wealthy as to buy a scarf for ten thousand gold coins.

The kijg then took Elijah aside and revealed his true identity. Yet Elijah did not seem surprised. When the king asked him why, Elijah said, "I knew that there was no one else in this land who was so wealthy, therefore the bidder had to be you. Yet you need not feel that the price is too high, for know that this scarf you have purchased will give you a priceless blessing. All you need do is to spread it out on your bed and sleep upon it, and when you fall asleep you will be transported to Paradise and permitted to share in its glory all the night. Therefore peace shall be with you for the rest of your life, and what more precious gift is there than peace?"

When the king heard this, he finally came to realize how wise Elijah was, and how great his power. He felt humble in the face of such a blessing, and such a man for as he held the scarf in his hand, he already began to feel its blessing of peace. Then the king had it announced and set down in writing and sealed with his seal that Elijah was no longer a slave, but a free man. He also gave Elijah those ten thousand gold coins, even though it was almost half his treasure. And he sent Elijah on his way in peace.

Elijah, was happy to be a free man again, free to bestow blessings on his people. It is said that he gave one of those ten thousand gold coins to each and every Jew he met, in that city and throughout the land, until every gold coin had been given out. In this way he brought on a blessed year for his people, which they never forgot as long as they lived.

Tunisia: c. Eleventh Century

The Staff of Elijah

Long ago there was an old man who had once been very wealthy and had given charity willingly, but in his old age found himself impoverished. His neighbors remembered how generous he had been when he had been rich, so they often invited him to their homes and saw to it that his needs were met. It was this old man's custom to say twice the portion of the blessing over food which mentions Elijah: "May the Holy One send us Elijah the Prophet of blessed memory to bring us good tidings of redemption and salvation."

Once, when the Sabbath was over, the old man returned home, lit a candle, and was startled to find a Jew sitting on his bed. The old man was taken aback and said, "Who are you and where do you come from?" The stranger did not answer directly, but instead asked a question of his own, "Tell me, may I remain in your home for a few days?" And the old man replied, "Certainly you may stay, but what shall you eat, for I myself am dependent on the kindness of others?" The stranger said, "No matter," and remained as the guest of the old man. The two shared the old man's food, meager as it was, and the stranger accompanied the old man to synagogue.

After three days the stranger prepared to depart, but before he set out, he said to the old man, "Take my staff; it will help you. But someday you will have to return it to its place." Now these were strange words, which the old man did not understand. "Where is its place?" he asked. The stranger replied, "On Mount Carmel." This confused the old man even more, for Mount Carmel is in the Holy Land, far away from where the old man made his home. "Who are you?" he asked. And the stranger revealed that he was none other than Elijah the Prophet. Then the old man was afraid, overcome and happy all at once. He accepted the staff from Elijah with many thanks, and accompanied him to the door and saw him off. But when Elijah had taken but a few steps, he disappeared from the old man's sight, and the old man realized that this had truly been the prophet of old.

The next day the old man took the staff with him when he went to the market. While he was walking, the staff suddenly became stuck in a crack between the stones. The old man bent down to pull it out, and when he did he found several silver pieces in the shadow of the staff. What a blessing, he thought, for now he would be able to support himself again, and even have enough to give charity.

The old man soon discovered other powers of the staff. Once, when he had walked a long distance and was feeling faint, he sat down at the edge of the road and placed his staff so that only his feet touched it. At once he felt his strength renewed, as though he had become much younger. He was able to stand up easily and returned home full of life. After that he used the staff to revive himself whenever he began to feel the burden of his age, and his spirits always lifted at the very instant his feet touched the wondrous staff.

One night the old man was awakened by the sound of screams and cries. He ran outside with the staff in his hand to see what was happening, and discovered that the Jewish quarter had been invaded by a mob who were trying to set it afire. Suddenly the old man felt filled with a great strength, and he ran directly into the mob, swinging the staff. The other Jews marveled at the old man's courage and took heart, and they too joined the fight.

In this way the rioters were quickly defeated, and never again did they dare to attack the Jewish quarter.

After this, the old man became a hero among the Jews of the town, and they decided to collect enough money for him to fulfill his lifelong wish of going to the Holy Land. So it was that he was able to make the journey after all, despite his age. After many months his ship arrived in Jaffa and the old man disembarked. His wish was to travel to the Wailing Wall in Jerusalem, but for some reason he could not fathom, he ended up in a wagon bound for Safed.

When the wagon was crossing Mount Carmel, one of its wheels broke off. There was nothing that could be done until the wheel was repaired, which would take some time. To pass the time the old man took a walk on the mountain, and along the way he spotted a tree from which a branch had been cut off. He came closer, and marveled that the wood of the tree was so similar to that of his staff. He raised up the staff against that place in the tree to compare it, and at the instant it touched the tree it fused to it and turned into one of its branches. While the old man watched in complete amazement, the branch began to bud and bear leaves, so that it soon resembled every other branch of that tree.

It was then that the old man recalled the words of Elijah, and understood that his mission was complete: the staff of Elijah had been returned to its place of origin. With a wonderful feeling the old man returned to the wagon just as the wheel was ready for travel, and he continued on his journey. After visiting the holy city of Safed, he traveled to Jerusalem, as he had first intended, and before long reached the Wailing Wall. As he stood and prayed before the Wall, a wind gusted and carried a leaf to his feet. And when the old man bent down and picked it up, he somehow knew for certain it was a leaf from the tree from which his staff had been taken. The old man kept that leaf, and it remained green all the years of his life. And he lived many more years in the Holy Land, the happiest he had ever known.

Moldavia: Oral Tradition

Romana

Once upon a time, in a distant kingdom, there lived a king and queen who were childless. One day the king said to the queen, "We have been married for seven years, and still we have no children." This worried the queen, and caused her to weep, because she was afraid that the king might marry another in order to have an heir. She walked up and down the paths of the palace garden, and then one day an old woman appeared who said, "Why are you weeping?" The queen poured out her heart, and told her of her longing for a child and of the king's growing impatience. After listening patiently, the old woman said, "Don't cry. I will see to it that you have a child." The queen looked up and asked through her tears, "How is that possible?" The old woman replied, "Here is a pomegranate which was grown in an enchanted orchard. If you eat one half of this fruit, and your husband, the king, the other half, you will give birth to a girl before the end of the year. And then you must name her Romana." The queen promised the old woman to give the child that name, took the pomegranate, ate half of it, and gave the other half to her husband, the king. And for the first time in many years, there was hope in her heart.

Now the prophecy of the old woman came true, and at the end of nine months the queen gave birth to a girl who was exceptionally beautiful, and who grew up to be gracious and charming. Her skin was very white, her lips very red, and her eyes black as night. And her name was Romana, which means pomegranate in Arabic.

After some years the queen died, and the king sought another wife. Naturally the king had his choice of every young lady in the kingdom, many of whom were quite beautiful, but he did not feel love for any of them because he still grieved for the first queen.

Now there was a scheming woman who wanted to be queen at any cost. She went to an evil wizard and asked if there was any spell she could cast to make the king marry her. The wizard told her that when she got home, she should stand in the tub. There she should cover herself with dough, and afterward bake a cake from the dough. She should then deliver this cake to the king and be certain that she was in his presence when he ate it, for he would fall in love with the first woman he saw after that.

This scheming woman did everything the wizard had said, and when she brought the cake to the king, she asked him to taste it in her presence so that she could have the pleasure of seeing if he liked it. The king did this, and as soon as he took the first bite he was suddenly filled with a need to love so great that he fell in love with the first woman he saw, who was, of course, the woman who had brought him the cake. They were wed shortly thereafter, and that is how this woman became the new queen, exactly as she had planned.

Now the new queen understood that in order to remain the only queen she had to bear the king a child. So she went back to the wizard and asked for a potion. Nine months later she gave birth to a girl of her own, whom she named Laymuna, which means lemon in Arabic. But Laymuna was neither beautiful nor charming, and so she was naturally overshadowed by Romana. This made the new queen very jealous. So much so that she went again to the wizard and asked him to tell her which princess was most beautiful. The wizard replied, "Laymuna is pretty, and you are prettier, but Romana is the most beautiful of all." Now when the evil queen heard this, she was filled with hatred for Romana, and she asked the wizard, "What shall I do to get rid of her?" The wizard gave her a ball of red yarn and said, "Take this ball of yarn, which has been dipped in blood, and tell Romana to knit a scarf from it. It carries a powerful curse. When Romana wraps the scarf around her neck, it will strangle her."

So the evil queen took the yarn and brought it back to the palace. There she hurried to tell her daughter of the wizard's plan to get rid of Romana, but, as it happened, Romana overheard all that she said, for Laymuna's room was next to her own. The next day the queen came to Romana and demanded that she knit a scarf from the yarn. She sent her outside to the palace garden to work, and told her not to return until the scarf was finished. Romana sat outside and wept, for she did not know what to do. And while she was weeping an old woman came up to her, the very same old woman who had given her mother the pomegranate so many years before. "Why are you weeping, my child?" the old woman asked. And when Romana saw her kindly face, she unburdened her heart to her, and told her all that had taken place. Then the old woman said, "Don't worry, the wizard's curse will not harm you. First, finish knitting the scarf, and then come with me."

This Romana did, and after she had finished knitting, the old woman led her out of the garden and into the fields surrounding the palace. When they were alone, the old woman said, "Not far from here there is an enchanted stream. Sometimes its waters are red, sometimes they are black, and sometimes they turn pure white. I will take you there, but you must remain on your own and wait for the waters to become white, and then dip the scarf in those waters, and also wash your hands and face in them. But take care to be patient, and do not dip the scarf into either the red waters or the black, for that would only make matters worse."

Then the old woman led Romana to the enchanted stream, and when they reached it the old woman took her leave. Romana sat on the bank and waited, for the water was then red. It remained that way for most of the morning, until just past noon, when the waters suddenly turned black. But Romana continued to wait. And when it was almost sunset the waters suddenly turned as white as the whitest sands. Then Romana did not wait; she dipped the scarf in the waters, and after that washed her hands and face in them.

Afterwards she hurried back to the palace and managed to reach the garden gate just as the sun disappeared over the horizon. So it was that she was back in time for dinner and arrived with the scarf around her neck. And when the queen and Laymuna saw her still alive, they choked on their food and became sick. For when Romana had dipped her hands and face into the pure waters, she had become even more beautiful than before and cast an aura wherever she went. The queen asked Romana how she had spent the day, and Romana told her of the walk she had taken, and of the stream she had washed in, after waiting for the waters to become white. And when she heard this, the queen told Laymuna to go to the same stream to wash. The next day Laymuna went to the stream, but she was impatient and washed her hands in the red waters, and they appeared as if they were covered with blood. Furious that this had happened, Laymuna tried to wash away the ugly stain, but not until the waters turned black did her hands appear clean again. Then she washed her face as well, hoping to become more beautiful than Romana. When she arrived back at the palace the first thing she did was to run to a mirror, where she discovered, to her dismay, that the black waters had made her even homelier than before. So angry was she, that she took her shoe off and smashed the mirror into a million pieces, and she vowed never to go back to that horrible stream again. Then she ran to the queen and told her all that had happened and they became even angrier with Romana than they had ever been before, and began at once to plot their revenge.

Not long after that, the king went off to war, and the queen decided it was the perfect time to rid herself of Romana. So the queen went back to the wizard and asked him for something that would make Romana's death seem like an accident. This time the wizard gave her a silver bracelet on which was affixed a silver scorpion. "Tell Romana that this bracelet is a gift from her father," the wizard said, "and that he had asked her to wear it day and night. Now during the day the scorpion of the bracelet is merely silver, but at night it comes to life, and its sting is fatal."

So it was that when the evil queen returned to the palace, she told Laymuna of her plan, and the two of them laughed together with glee at the thought that they would be rid of Romana at last. Then the queen wrapped the bracelet and made it appear to be a present from the king. After that she took the package to Romana and told her that a messenger from the king had delivered it that day, and that the king had sent with it the following message: "Tell Romana to wear this gift both day and night, for it is a lucky charm, and as long as she is wearing it, my armies will be safe from defeat." Now when Romana heard this, she did not hesitate, but put the bracelet on her arm, for she longed for her father to be victorious so that he could return home. So pleased was she with the gift that she walked outside into the palace garden and strolled up and down its paths, singing to herself.

But just before sunset, when Romana was about to go back inside, she saw the old woman who had helped her once before. Romana greeted her warmly, and proudly showed her the bracelet she had received from her father. And then, just as the sun was setting, the old woman pulled the bracelet off Romana's arm and threw it to the ground, as Romana watched, bewildered. At that very instant, the silver scorpion came to life, and began to crawl toward Romana. She was petrified with terror, but the old woman quickly stamped on the scorpion until it was dead. Romana almost fainted, and the old woman had to support her until she could sit down. When Romana began to recover, the old woman said, "That bracelet, Romana, was not a gift from your father, but a trick of the evil queen, who hates you and seeks your death. As long as your father, the king, is away, you will never be safe in the palace, so you must flee to save your life. Go home for tonight, but as soon as the sun comes up, you must run away." Romana realized that what the old woman said was true, but she was only a child and she wondered where it was that she could go. Then the old woman said, "Just follow whatever path you find, for it will surely lead you where you are supposed to go." After that, the old woman departed, and Romana returned to her room with a heavy heart. At the crack of dawn she left the palace behind her and made her way into the fields beyond. The first path she found was one made by the cows as they passed through the high grasses, so Romana followed it. At midday she saw a house in the distance and hurried there.

Now in that house there lived forty thieves, although they were not home at the time. When Romana came to the door she found that it was not locked, so she went inside. There on the table she saw a variety of vegetables, and because she was hungry she washed them and cooked them and ate them. Just as she finished eating she heard the thieves coming, so she hid herself in the high grasses behind the house. Now it did not take the thieves long to notice that someone had been in the house and had cooked and eaten some of their vegetables, and they wondered who it might be. So the next day, when it was time to leave, one of them hid in the house, to see if anyone came there while they were gone. Soon Romana came back into the house, for she was hungry, and the thief quickly caught her. He asked her who she was, and she told him she was a girl who was all alone in the world. This touched the heart of the thief, for he too was an orphan, and he told her that she could be their sister, and could be of help to them by cooking and keeping the house clean. So it was that Romana was accepted by all of the forty thieves as if she were their sister, and she kept the house neat and clean and cooked tasty dishes for them, and they, in return, brought her presents almost every day.

Meanwhile, when Romana was found to be missing from the palace, the evil queen assumed the scorpion had killed her, although she wondered what had happened to her body. Just to be certain, she returned to the wizard and asked to know which princess was the most beautiful. And the wizard replied: "Laymuna is very pretty, and you are even prettier, but Romana is the most beautiful of all." When she heard this, the queen flew into a fury and shrieked, "But Romana is dead and gone, for I myself saw her put the silver bracelet on her wrist!" But the wizard said, "No, Romana has somehow escaped the spell once more, and now she lives in the wilderness with forty thieves." When she heard this, the eyes of the evil queen grew narrow, and she said, "What can I do to get rid of her for good this time?" Then the wizard took out a gold ring and gave it to the queen and said: "See to it that Romana gets this ring, for when she puts it on she will fall into an endless sleep, from which none will be able to wake her." Then the queen asked, "And how shall I find her?" And the wizard replied, "Just follow the cow path behind the palace garden, and eventually you will arrive at the house in which she is staying."

Then the queen took the ring and went back to the palace. There she disguised herself as a jewelry merchant, and followed the cow path as the wizard had told her to, until she arrived at the house in which lived Romana and the forty thieves. She knocked at the door, and when Romana opened it, the evil queen saw to her delight that she was alone there. She pretended to be friendly and showed Romana her wares. Romana did not recognize her, for the queen had disguised herself very well. She showed Romana various trinkets, and last of all she showed her the gold ring. Now Romana found it to be very beautiful, but she explained that she did not have any money. The disguised queen insisted that she keep it anyway, and that she would come back later when she had money, and she could pay her then. But first, she said, Romana should try it on, to be certain that it fit. And as soon as Romana put it on her finger, she fell to the floor. The evil queen cackled to see her lying there, asleep, and left certain that this time she had gotten rid of her for good.

Now when the forty thieves came home and found Romana lying in that death-like sleep, they all cried over her because they had come to love her very much. And because they could not bear never to see her again, they put her in a glass coffin so that they could still look upon her lovely face.

Now one day the prince of a neighboring kingdom was out hunting in the high grass. He saw a white deer there and raised his bow, but when he saw how beautiful it was, he could not let the arrow fly. Instead he pursued the deer on his horse, hoping to capture it alive. But the deer was very fleet, and after the prince had chased it for seven days and nights he still had not caught up with it. In this way the prince came to the kingdom of the sleeping princess, and there he came upon a hut, and because he was thirsty he tied his horse to a tree and went to the door and knocked. When the door opened, he was greeted by an old woman, the very same old woman who had given the queen the pomegranate and had shown the princess the stream. And to the prince's complete astonishment, he also saw in the darkness of the hut the eyes of an animal reflecting the fire—it was the white deer he had chased all that time. The old woman said, "I see that my pet deer has led you here, as I told it to do." Now the prince could hardly believe his ears, and he realized that this old woman must have great powers indeed. Then he said, "Why did you want me to come here?" And the old woman replied, "Forty days before a person is born, a voice goes forth in heaven and announces whom they are destined to marry. Now there are not many who can hear that voice beside the angels, but there are a few and I am one of them. And so I heard the voice that announced who it is that you are destined to wed."

When the prince heard this, he did not doubt that what the old woman said was true, for he had already seen her power. So he said, "Tell me, then, who is my destined one . . . if you are permitted to reveal this." "Yes, I shall reveal it to you," said the old woman, "for that is why I brought you here in the first place. Know, then, that you are destined to wed the princess of this kingdom, whose name is Romana. But for a long time she has been cursed with an endless sleep. That is because the gold ring she is wearing has cast a spell on her. If only that ring were removed, the princess would be freed from the spell and would wake up." "Gladly would I free her from this spell," said the prince, "but how can I find her?" "That is easy," said the old woman, "just follow the white deer." And in a flash the white deer bounded out of the hut into the fields, and the prince quickly mounted his horse and rode after it.

The prince soon arrived at the house of the forty thieves, and as he approached it he heard one of them humming a dirge-like tune. He came up to him and asked, "Tell me, why is it that you are singing such a sad song?" And the man replied, "Because our sister, Romana, has fallen into a sleep so deep that no one in the world can wake her." "And what would be the reward of the one who succeeded in waking her?" asked the prince. "O, if such a thing were possible," said the man, "the one who woke her would truly deserve to marry her." "Perhaps I can succeed in doing this," said the prince, "for I am acquainted with many of the mysteries of healing." "Please try your best," said the man, "for my brothers and I all long to see her awaken."

Then the man, one of the forty thieves, took the prince inside the house, where he saw the glass coffin in which Romana lay with her eyes closed, as beautiful as ever. The prince's heart leapt when he saw her, and he knew that he loved her, that he could never love any other, and that what the old woman had told him of Romana being his destined one was surely true. Then, with all forty thieves watching, the prince sat down beside the glass coffin, and took Romana's hand in his own. And while it appeared to the others that he but stroked her hand, he slipped off the ring. At that very instant the princess opened her eyes. When the forty thieves saw this, they let out cries of glee, and hugged each other. And when Romana opened her eyes and saw the prince sitting there, she recognized him at once—for she had seen his face before. She had met him and grown to love him in the dream which had lasted the entire time she was asleep. And so it was that being awake was like continuing the same wonderful dream, a dream which had suddenly come true. And Romana and the prince embraced, in the knowledge that they had found each other at last.

Then the forty thieves prepared a great feast for Romana and the prince, and each of them gave a precious gift to the happy couple. Afterwards, Romana and the prince returned to her kingdom. When the king saw Romana he was overjoyed, for he had mourned her as if she were dead. The king soon realized how much Romana and the prince loved each other, and he agreed that they would be married, and ordered plans for the wedding to be made. But the evil queen was furious when she saw that Romana had been revived, and she wasted no time in seeking out the evil wizard again.

This time the wizard gave the queen a golden pin, and he said, "Have Laymuna give this pin to Romana as a wedding present when she is alone in her room. Tell her to pin it in Romana's hair herself, and when she does Romana will be transformed into a dove and fly away. Then you will be rid of her at last." The queen wasted no time. She took the pin and returned to the palace, and gave these instructions to Laymuna, who went directly to Romana's room, where she found her alone. Laymuna acted very friendly and showed her the golden wedding gift. Romana was so deliriously in love with the prince of her dreams that she was not on her guard, and forgot all the hatred that her step-sister held toward her. She hoped that Laymuna had changed her ways, and she graciously accepted the wedding gift. Then Laymuna smiled and said, "Oh, let me pin it in your hair." And when she did, Romana was immediately transformed into a white dove, which flew out the window of the room.

Before long it was realized that the princess was missing again. Although the king and the servants searched everywhere, she was not to be found. The prince who was about to become her groom was filled with despair, for he did not know what had happened to her, and he knew he could not love any other, since she alone had been destined to be his bride. As for the princess who had become a dove, she remained near the palace, sitting in an orange tree. The dove that was Romana sang of all that had happened to her, and cried for help, but since no one knew the language of the birds, no one understood.

Now each time the palace gardener tried to prune that orange tree, the dove would chase him away, and eventually this strange behavior came to the attention of the prince. One day he saw the dove chasing after the gardener, and he came to the man's assistance, taking a net and capturing the bird. The prince kept the dove in his room and cared for it, and he found that the presence of the dove consoled him in his grief over the missing princess.

Now that the evil queen had finally gotten rid of Romana for good, she went back to the wizard and again asked him, "Which princess is the most beautiful?" And the wizard replied, "Laymuna is very pretty, and you are even prettier, but Romana is the most beautiful of all." "How is that possible," screamed the queen, "for Romana has become a dove!" "That is true enough," said the wizard, "but the prince has caught the dove and is taking care of her. Who knows, perhaps he will find the secret of turning the dove back into a princess." "Is that all?" said the queen. "Well, in that case there is nothing to worry about, for I am certain he will never figure out how to do that!"

But one morning when the prince awoke and looked out his window, he saw to his amazement that the white deer of the old woman was standing in the garden, beneath the very orange tree in which he had captured the dove. The prince wondered greatly at this, and decided that the old woman must have sent the deer as a sign that he should seek out her advice at once. So he said he was going out to hunt, but instead he went to the hut of the old woman, and told her all that had happened. Then he asked her if there was any way he could find Romana, for he was willing to go the ends of the earth to save her. Imagine his surprise when the old woman said, "You have already saved her, and you are taking very good care of her as well." "What do you mean?" asked the prince, who was quite confused. "The dove you have made your pet is none other than the princess Romana, who has been put under a spell." "Ah," said the prince, "that must be why I have grown to love that bird so much! But tell me, how can she be freed from this spell?"

"I will tell you what to do," said the old woman. "First, take the dove with you into the presence of the king and queen. When you get there, offer the dove as a gift to the king. He knows how much you love it, and he will be touched by this gesture." Then the old woman gave the prince a blue ribbon to which was attached a small golden bell, and she said, "Once the king has taken the dove in his hand, give him this ribbon and tell him it is for the dove to wear so that he will always be able to find her. When the king puts the ribbon around the dove's neck, the princess will be restored to her human shape." The prince was delighted with this plan, and he thanked the old woman and hurried back to the palace.

So it was that the prince did as the old woman had told him to do, and brought the dove to the king and offered it as a gift. The king gladly accepted it, and the queen was also pleased with it, but for another reason—for now that it was out of the prince's possession, she planned to poison the bird, and so be rid of Romana forever. Then the prince took out the ribbon and golden bell and gave it to the king as well, and when the king slipped the ribbon over the neck of the dove, Romana was at once restored to her human form. She stood before them all, much to the amazement of everyone, especially the queen and Laymuna. They tried to run away as soon as they saw Romana, because the they knew their role in casting the spell was about to be revealed. When Romana told the truth to her father, the king had the evil wizard put to death and banished the evil queen and her daughter to a faraway island at the end of the world.

At last the wedding of the prince and princess could take place, and it was the most joyous celebration that anyone in the kingdom had ever attended. So it was that the prince and princess lived together in love and harmony all the days of their lives, and the old woman was made godmother of all of their children, for it was she who had brought them together and had made it possible for their destiny to be fulfilled.

Egypt: Oral Tradition

The Princess Who Became
the Morning Star

Long, long ago, in the days before Noah and the great Flood, there lived a king who ruled a vast kingdom. This king had two daughters, Istahar and Naamah, and they were the flowers of the realm, beloved by everyone. Now in those days it happened that two angels, Shemhazai and Azazel, descended from heaven and came to walk upon the earth. How had this happened? These angels had come before the Lord and had complained about the evil ways of men. The Holy One had told them that if they lived on earth, they too would be swayed by the Evil Inclination and would also be led astray. The two angels insisted this would not happen to them, and they begged the Lord to let them show Him how well they would sanctify His name.

The Holy One agreed to permit the angels to descend to earth in the form of men, but He warned them that they must not reveal the secrets of heaven, nor could they marry the daughters of men. The two angels vowed to obey these commands, and so they became flesh and blood, and descended Jacob's ladder until they reached the earth.

Now since Shemhazai and Azazel were angels, they were

possessed of great powers and knew a multitude of secrets. And although they respected their vows and did not reveal the secrets of heaven, they did make use of their powers to perform feats that amazed everyone. They cast spells and performed exorcisms, divined from the stars and cut roots and herbs with which they healed the sick. Before long their fame had spread to the furthest corners of the earth. Thus the king was intrigued to hear that these famed sorcerers had arrived in his kingdom and that they sought an audience with him. The king agreed to receive them, and when they arrived the two princesses were also present, for they too had heard of these great men.

The two angels were a splendid sight when they entered the palace, for they were taller than most men, and far more handsome. So it was that the two princesses, Istahar and Naamah, lost their hearts to them at the very moment they saw them. And when the angels beheld these beautiful princesses, they were filled with passion for them as well—Shemhazai for Istahar, and Azazel for Naamah.

The king welcomed the sorcerers, and asked them to demonstrate their powers. Then, with his gaze fixed on Istahar, Shemhazai pronounced a spell and, to the amazement of all, transformed himself into an eagle that flew out the palace window and returned a moment later with a flower in its beak, coming to rest on the arm of the chair in which Princess Istahar sat. When he restored himself to his human form, Shemhazai gave the flower to Istahar and bowed low before the king as the court applauded.

After this it was Azazel's turn. He too pronounced a spell, and all at once the walls of the palace disappeared. The king and the royal court found themselves surrounded by the sea on all sides, although there was no sea anywhere in that kingdom. At that moment chaos broke out—maidens screamed and strong men wept. Everyone was terrified as they saw the huge waves rising and falling around them, and the king soon cried out for the spell to be broken. Then Azazel pronounced another spell, and they found themselves safe within the palace, the waters gone. It was then that the king and all his court realized that Azazel had created a mirage, and they were amazed at his powers.

Now the more the king thought about the two sorcerers, the more he longed to have them at his beck and call. For with such powers he could rule the world. And the king had noticed that the sorcerers seemed to be attracted to his daughters, as well they might, since Istahar and Naamah were known to be the most beautiful young women in the world. Thus a plan took form in the king's mind, in which he decided to ask his daughters to entice the two sorcerers, that they might wed them, and then their powers would be at the king's command.

The king spoke with Istahar and Naamah, and was pleased to discover that they approved heartily of such a match. When the king learned this, he decided to raise the matter with the sorcerers, for he felt that their power was almost in his grasp.

Now the two angels were themselves filled with longing for the two princesses. As soon as they had filled their eyes with their beauty they had forgotten the holy vow they had made never to marry the daughters of men. So when the king proposed to them that they might marry the princesses, the two angels quickly agreed to make the king's daughters their brides.

Soon after this Princess Istahar had a dream in which an old man named Enoch, told her that the two sorcerers to whom she and Naamah were engaged were not sons of men, but angels who were sons of God. It had been decreed in heaven, the old man continued, that if any of the sons of God should marry the daughters of men, the product of their union would be cruel giants who would poison the world with evil, forcing the Holy One, blessed be He, to destroy all life on earth. The old man told Istahar not to marry the angels at all cost. In the dream Istahar asked the old man how she could resist Shemhazai's charms, and he told her to pry the secret Name of God from Shemhazai, for with that in her possession she would be able to escape his embrace.

When Istahar woke from that dream it was still the middle of the night. She was deeply frightened, for she saw that the fate of the whole human race depended on her and her sister. Then Istahar hurried and woke Naamah and told her the dream. But Naamah refused to take the dream seriously, and insisted she did not believe that the sorcerers were angels—and nothing Istahar said could make her change her mind.

With grief in her heart, Istahar went back to sleep, and once again she dreamed that she met the old man. He told her that it had been decreed in heaven that if both she and her sister married the angels, God would have no choice but to destroy all life on earth. But if only one of the sisters married, the evil unleashed on earth would be lessened: rather than destroy all life, the Holy One would protect one man and his family, and a pair of each kind of bird and beast. And if by a miracle both sisters resisted the angels, then the curse brought on by the Fall of Adam and Eve would be lifted, and the age of the Messiah would begin.

When Istahar awoke from this second dream she felt much better, for she had decided that she would do everything in her power to prevent her union with the angel from taking place. And if she could not control the decisions of her sister, at least she would know that all life on earth would not be destroyed.

So it was that the next time Istahar was alone with Shemhazai she told him that she knew he was an angel. Shemhazai was quite startled to hear this, and he pressed Istahar to tell him how she had found out, but she refused. Then he asked her if she was going to reveal it to her father. He begged her not to, for he was afraid that there would then be no wedding. Now the truth is that Istahar understood that if her father, the king, knew the sorcerers were angels, he would be even more eager to have them marry his daughters. But she pretended to be certain that the king would break the engagement if he knew the truth. And when Shemhazai offered her anything to remain silent, Istahar asked him to reveal to her the secret Name of God.

Now Shemhazai was astounded when Istahar asked this, for this Name is the most prized mystery of all of heaven, and among the angels there were only a handful who shared the knowledge of the Name. In fact, this mystery had been revealed to Shemhazai and Azazel only when they descended to earth, for it was by pronouncing the Name that they were able to exist in this world in the form of human beings.

". . . at that instant, she was transported from this world to the world above, where she was reborn as the morning star."

Thus Shemhazai was very reluctant to reveal the great powers of the Name to Istahar, who was only a mortal. But when he saw that she was determined to reveal the truth to her father, Shemhazai at last relented and revealed the secret to her. The moment she knew it, Istahar pronounced the Name out loud, and at that instant she was transported from this world to the world above, where she was reborn as the morning star, the brightest in the sky. The Holy One was filled with admiration for the chaste maiden Istahar, who cared more for the future of the human race than for her own pleasures. He made her immortal, and gave her abundant blessings to dispense to every generation. And Shemhazai, who witnessed the great sacrifice of Istahar, realized the extent of his sin and repented. In his grief he suspended himself from heaven, head down, and thus he hangs even to this day. But Azazel never repented, and thus he was punished by the Holy One, blessed be He, by being hung upside down by iron chains, and fastened to a canyon beyond the Mountains of Darkness, where he still remains for having broken his sacred vow.

As for Naamah, Istahar's sister, she did marry the angel Azazel, and the product of their union were the terrible giants known as the Nephillim, who filled the earth with evil, so that the day came when the Holy One had no choice but to bring on the great Flood. But because the righteous maiden Istahar put her trust in God and in His messenger, Enoch, one family was saved from that Flood, the family of Noah, and they served as the bridge by which the human race managed to survive. And that is why men in every generation have turned with admiration to the beautiful morning star. For were it not for Istahar, we would not be here to gaze at its beauty.

Germany: c. Thirteenth Century

The Secrets of Azazel

After the pious maiden Istahar resisted the fallen angel Shemhazai and was transformed into the morning star, the angel realized the extent of his sins, and repented. In his grief at having failed to honor the vow he had made to the Holy One, Shemhazai did penance, suspending himself between heaven and earth. But Azazel, the other angel who had descended with Shemhazai, did not repent. Instead he married Naamah, the sister of Istahar, fathered her children, and put his great powers at the command of the king. And because the king was evil, he commanded the fallen angel to perform many evil acts. A great deal of blood was spilled which cried out from the earth.

When the cries of the victims reached the circles on high, the holy One decided that the evil angel Azazel must be punished. It was the angel Raphael who was sent to carry out the punishment. First Raphael put Azazel in chains, for Raphael carried the power of the Name, against which all of the fallen angel's evil came to naught. Then Raphael cast Azazel into a canyon of sharp and pointed stones in the desert Dudael, hung him upside-down, and covered him with darkness. There he was condemned to remain until the End of Days.

Yet even in that dark and forsaken place, Azazel did not repent. Instead he thought up evil plots that he would carry out if only he were set free, although he knew very well that since the Holy One had passed judgment on him, nothing in existence could change his fate. Then Azazel decided that if he could not perform evil by himself, perhaps he could still inflict it on the world. He used his magic powers to seek out the most evil soul in the world, and when he found this soul, he sent him a dream in which he revealed his existence to him. The fallen angel told this evil man, who was already a magician, how to reach that forsaken place in the desert Dudael, the dwelling place of demons, beyond the Mountains of Darkness. When the evil magician awoke and recalled the dream, he decided to set out at once to reach the den of Azazel, for he lusted after the unlimited powers the fallen angel could give him.

But the evil magician was not the only one who heard the siren call of the fallen angel. All kinds of evil beings in that desert sensed his presence, and were drawn to him there. And so it was not long before a great many demons, spirits and fiery serpents had placed themselves under the domination of that unrepentent angel.

Now the magician was already familiar with many of the darker secrets, and using these, he completed the journey through the barren desert and across the Mountains of Darkness in a fraction of the time it would have taken a common traveller. There in the dark mountains he was met by two demons who called out to him at once, for Azazel had forewarned them that he was coming. Then two big and fiery serpents surrounded him, and led him directly to the place where Azazel, the Prince of Darkness, had been imprisoned.

When the magician reached the canyon in which Azazel had been chained, the presence of evil was so strong it hung in the air like a sword. The magician, who had always revelled in evil, knew that he would gladly serve the wishes of the fallen angel. So too did Azazel quickly recognize that the magician was in his sway, like the demons and spirits that swarmed around in that dark place. So he taught him a great many of his secrets there in the darkness, and even though the magician never saw the evil angel face to face, he listened carefully to all that he said and forgot nothing.

For fifty days and nights the evil magician remained in that cavern, soaking up the dark secrets that Azazel revealed, secrets of magic and witchcraft that had never before been revealed to one of the living. When it was time to leave that cavern, the magician fell to his knees and worshipped Azazel and burned incense before him. Then he was led out of the dark cavern by the fiery serpents. When he emerged, the magician was the most dangerous man in the world. He could work his will on almost anything. And he intended to stop at nothing short of ruling the world in the name of the evil angel.

Now it did not take long for the evil reputation of that magician to become widely known, for everywhere he went he used his terrible powers to bring everyone under his rule. When word of his awesome powers reached King Solomon, the king knew that he had a terrible adversary in the magician. For King Solomon was not only the wisest man of his time, he was also the most powerful of all sorcerers, because he drew his power from the Holy One, blessed be He, while other magicians drew upon the forces of evil. But from what he heard of the reports about this evil magician, he would have to harness all of his knowledge and power in order to defeat him. The evil magician was also well aware that only Solomon stood in his way. So he was already plotting to overcome King Solomon, before Solomon could have a chance to challenge him.

Now the evil magician knew that King Solomon's greatest power came from his signet ring, for its four precious stones had been presented to him by four angels and each stone had engraved on it one of the four letters of God's Name. The magician knew that if he could rob Solomon of that ring, he might be able to defeat him. But how could this be done? Solomon wore the magic ring day and night; he never took it off. And it was impossible to remove it while it was still on Solomon's finger. The magician meditated on this problem for many days, and at last he came up with a plan.

The evil magician knew that King Solomon could not resist a woman who was both beautiful and wise. Such was the Queen of Sheba. The magician pronounced a spell and conjured up a female demon who was most astonishingly beautiful. So too was she wise, for the magician endowed her with his own knowledge. This demon's name was Lilith, the same Lilith who had once been married to Adam, but she had left him and flown out of the Garden of Eden by pronouncing God's Name. She lived in a cave beside the sea, and she took all the demons who lived there for lovers. When God had sent three angels to order her to return to Adam, she refused. After that she became a night demon who preyed on unsuspecting men, as well as a witch who delighted in strangling little children.

It was this terrible demon that the evil magician brought forth using a spell he had learned from Azazel. The magician was confident that if anyone could free King Solomon of his magic ring, it would be Lilith. Not only would this make Solomon helpless, but it would give the magician boundless power as long as the ring was in his possession. And this was exactly what Azazel wanted, for the fallen angel still hoped that some power might succeed in freeing him from those chains. So it was that both Azazel and the evil magician lusted after the ring of Solomon, for it held the most powerful magic in the world.

Lilith flew like a shadow to King Solomon's palace, and entered by an open window. She found her way to Solomon's bedroom, and although the door was locked, she still managed to enter, by making herself as slim as a shadow and slipping beneath his door. At that moment Solomon was reading the Torah, when he noticed something very strange—the letters on the scroll began to quiver, as if they were alive, and suddenly they took flight, so that a few seconds later the parchment of the scroll was blank! Solomon could scarcely believe his eyes, yet at the same time he realized that this must be a sign of grave danger, for it must be a very great evil from which the letters of the Torah would take flight.

Just then Lilith reached out her hand and touched Solomon, and greatly startled him. And when he saw that most alluring maiden standing in front of him, he found himself falling under her power. In order to cast her spell over Solomon, all that she needed to do was to make him speak one word to her. Solomon, of course, did not know this, but just as he was falling into that deep well, from which he might never be able to climb out, King Solomon came to his senses and realized that this must be no ordinary woman, but an evil being whose presence had caused the sacred letters to depart.

Then, when Lilith reached out to embrace Solomon, he took her by the hand and without saying a word beckoned her to come with him. She assumed that he meant to join her in an embrace, and willingly followed. But Solomon had another plan in mind, and in a moment he brought that dangerous beauty to the golden framed mirror that hung on the wall of his chamber. And before she realized what had happened, Lilith found herself face to face with that mirror, except that her reflection did not appear in it. And when that happened she realized that Solomon had seen her for what she was, and thus she had lost all her seductive power.

Defeated, Lilith vanished from before Solomon's eyes, cast out of this world until another evil wish would call her back. But it was not only Lilith that King Solomon had defeated, but the evil magician as well. For when Lilith took flight from this world, so too did the evil soul of the magician. It found itself drifting through the Other World in futile circles, and there it remains to this day, cut off from all that is sacred.

And not only was the evil magician defeated, but Azazel, the Prince of Darkness, lost the evil tool he had chosen to work his evil ways. Now that the magician's soul had been exiled from this world, it would be many centuries until one of such evil would reappear in the world of men. And all that time Azazel brooded in the darkness at the defeat that came so easily at the hands of King Solomon.

As for Solomon, he learned from this that the letters of the

Torah were the only guide that he needed. And he was greatly relieved when he turned back to the scroll of the Torah and found that the letters that had flown from it had returned, for he knew that the danger had passed.

Holland: c. Seventeenth Century

The Wise Old Woman
of the Forest

There once were two brothers, one rich and one poor. The wealthy brother was a miser, who hated to part with a penny, but every year he at least gave his poor brother enough wheat to bake matzot for Passover. One year, however, the rich brother decided to give no charity of any sort. And when the poor brother arrived to receive the wheat, the rich brother kept putting him off, telling him to come back the next day. With no other choice, the poor brother continued to return day after day only to be put off again and again. For the rich brother assumed the poor one would eventually give up and go away, but he did not. At last the rich one lost his temper and shouted at his brother, "Go to Azazel!" meaning, "Go to the Devil." But the poor brother, not knowing very much about devils or angels thought that his rich brother was sending him to someone else for wheat. So he innocently set out to find Azazel, whoever and wherever he was.

Now all the poor brother took with him on his journey, beside a little bread and water, was his *tallis* and *tefillin*. He walked for a day or two, wondering where he might seek out this Azazel.

Finally he came to a stream and decided to rest. He ate some dry bread and drank some water, and as he sat there he saw a house in the distance. Perhaps, he thought to himself, this was the house of Azazel. So he got up and went to that house, and there he found three sisters who were busy spinning. One of them was spinning gold thread, one woolen thread, and the third silken thread. The three girls welcomed him warmly, for it had been a long time since any visitor had come there. They offered him a fine meal and were very kind to him, but the poor man could not help but notice that all three seemed very sad.

At last the man asked the sisters why they were sad, and they told him that they had been spinning gold, wool and silk for years, all the while looking out the window to see if any young men were arriving who would marry them. But the young men had never come, so they had grown very sad. Their plight touched the heart of the poor man, and he told them that when he reached Azazel he would try to find a way to help them, and they were very grateful about this.

In the morning the poor man set out on his journey once again, and after walking for a day or two he came to a giant tree and decided he would rest in its shade. That tree was filled with delicious looking fruit, and the poor man picked one and tasted it, but it was very bitter. This amazed him, and he said out loud, "Why would such a fine tree have such bitter fruit?" Then, to his amazement, a voice came forth from the tree, and said, "It is true that my fruit is bitter, but I do not know why. If only I knew the reason, perhaps something could be done about it." When the poor man heard this, he felt sorry for the tree and said, "When I reach Azazel I will ask why·this is, and if I find out, I will return and let you know." And the tree replied, "I would be very grateful for that."

So the poor man continued to seek out Azazel. In a day or two he reached a very wide river. Now the poor man wondered how he could ever cross that river, when he happened to notice a ferry boat near the shore, with a ferryman in it. This made the poor man very happy. He came to the ferryman and asked if he could take him across. This the ferryman agreed to do, but as he rowed the poor man noticed that tears were streaming from his eyes. "Why do you weep?" he asked him, and the ferryman replied, "Over the years I have rowed many people back and forth across this river, but I myself cannot leave the ferry." The poor man took pity on his plight, and he promised the ferryman that when he reached Azazel he would try to find out if there were some way he could be relieved of this endless duty. The ferryman was very grateful for this, and wished him luck on his journey. Then the poor man set off on the far shore of that river to continue his quest.

Now the poor man found himself in a dense forest where there were no paths to follow. Another man might have turned back, but he knew that Passover was soon to come and that every family must have wheat for matzoh, no matter how poor they were. So he made his way through that forest as best he could, and at last he came upon a small hut. Evening was about to fall, so he decided to knock on the door and seek lodging there. He found that an old woman with long white hair lived there. She invited him to come inside and was very kind to him, for visitors rarely came her way. While they ate, the poor man told her of his quest to find Azazel and also of the sad sisters, the tree with the bitter fruit, and the ferryman who could not leave his post. The old woman listened carefully, and when he had told her everything she said, "You may not know it, but you have come to the right place, for I think that I can help you and those that you met." For the lucky poor man had found his way to the wise old women of the forest, who knew the answer to everything.

So it was that she told him that if the three sisters would stop spinning long enough to sew bridal dresses from the cloth they had made, the young men they were awaiting would show up by the time the dresses were ready. As for the tree with the bitter fruit, this was because a great treasure was buried in the roots of that tree. Remove the treasure, and the fruit of the tree would soon become sweet. And with that treasure in his possession, the poor man would no longer be poor. As for the ferryman, he would be able to leave his post as long as there was another to take his place.

The poor man was filled with happiness when he heard this.

He thanked the wise old woman of the forest with all his heart and hurried off to help those he had promised to help. The first one he reached was the ferryman, who was overjoyed to learn that it might be possible, after all, for him to escape from that endless task. But who, he wondered, could he get to take his place? Not long afterward the poor man reached the tree with the bitter fruit. He began to dig beneath it and soon struck a chest buried there. It was filled with gold and silver and precious stones of every kind, as well as a gold menorah that was the most beautiful he had ever seen. No sooner did he remove the chest, than he plucked one of the fruits of the tree and bit into it, and found that it was the most delicious he had ever tasted. Then the voice of the tree thanked him again and again for his help and wished him well, and the man set out on his way home, no longer a poor man.

A day or two later he reached the house of the three sisters. He told them what the wise old woman had said. They began to sew their bridal gowns at once, and by the time the man awoke the next day he found that all three sisters had completed their gowns, one more beautiful than the next. They accompanied him outside as he took his leave, and while they were standing outside their house, wearing those beautiful gowns, three handsome young men happened to ride by. When the young riders saw the three sisters, they lost their hearts. And so it was that the three sisters found the loves they had been waiting for.

Now when the man returned home with all his new found wealth, the first thing he did was to purchase a large store of wheat so that his family would have enough matzoh for Passover. So too did he buy many fine foods to enjoy at the Seder, and he invited his brother and his family to join them. Now his rich brother greatly wondered at his brother's new found wealth, and asked about it. Then the once poor brother told him that all his good luck had come about because he had gone to find Azazel, just as his brother had suggested.

So it was that the rich brother set out the very next day on the very same path in hope of finding as great a treasure as had his brother. When he had walked for several days, he reached the river where the ferryman still remained at his post. He told the ferryman to take him to the other side so that he could find his way to Azazel, and this the other did, but no sooner did they reach the far shore than the ferryman leaped out of the boat onto the shore, and the rich man had to remain behind as the new ferryman for all time.

So it was that instead of the poor brother going to Azazel, this was the richly deserved fate of the selfish brother.

Morocco: Oral Tradition

The Palace of Tears

Long ago, in the days of King Shacarial, there was a poor Jewish fisherman who lived near the shore. Every day the fisherman went out to sea and cast his net four times, catching as many fish as he could. But one morning he didn't catch any fish the first three times he cast his net, and the fourth time, although the load was very heavy, all he brought back was sand and stones and a small iron chest. In his disappointment the fisherman consoled himself with the box, thinking that he would sell it to a jeweler and at least make some money from it. Just then he heard a noise from inside the chest, and he took his knife and pried it open. And as he lifted the lid very heavy smoke poured forth, that turned little by little into a terrible and frightening demon. As the fisherman moved toward the back of his boat, the demon said, "Prepare to die, fisherman!"

The fisherman pleaded with the demon and said, "What harm did I do to you? I did you a great favor by setting you free from this chest!" The demon replied, "Listen to what I tell you, and you will understand why I intend to kill you."

And this is the tale that the demon told: "Long ago I was a minister of King Solomon. He called me forth during the building of the Temple in Jerusalem, and I served him faithfully for many years. But once I disobeyed him, and he commanded that I be imprisoned in this chest, and the chest was cast into the sea. During the first thousand years I swore that I would reward the one who released me by making him a great ruler. In the second thousand I swore that whosoever released me would become the ruler of the world. But when no one set me free in all that time I grew bitter, and vowed that I would kill whoever released me without feeling any pity for them. Now it is you who have saved me, and so I am going to kill you."

The fisherman saw that he was truly in grave danger. So he said to the demon: "Before you kill me, please answer one question, and swear in the name of God that you will answer truthfully." The demon agreed, and swore as the man asked. Then the fisherman said, "Swear to me that you were truly inside this little chest, for your size is far greater than it." The demon swore that he had indeed been inside it, but the fisherman insisted that he was not satisfied, and would not believe him until the demon proved it to him by making himself small and getting back in. So the demon made himself small and squeezed himself into the chest, and at that moment the fisherman slammed the lid shut so that the demon was trapped inside it once again.

Then the demon begged him from inside the chest to release him, and swore that he would not harm him. And the fisherman said, "I'll only release you if you'll swear as well that you will make me rich." The demon swore, and at last the fisherman opened the chest again. This time, as soon as the demon was free he picked up the chest and cast it into the sea, where it soon sank. Then he turned to the fisherman and said, "Take your nets and follow me." The fisherman did this, and the demon led him until they arrived at a very small lake, in a place surrounded by four hills. And on the other side of the lake there was a black palace. When they reached the lake the demon said, "In this lake there are four kinds of fish, red, green, yellow and blue. If you fish in it and bring the fish to the Sultan, he will reward you well. But remember, you must not cast your net more than once a day. Nor must you attempt to enter that palace."

When the demon finished saying this, he vanished in a puff of smoke. Then the fisherman cast his net as the demon had said, and he caught four large and beautiful fish, one of each kind. He was tempted to cast his net again, but he remembered the demon's warning, and decided not to. Then he brought the four fish to the palace of the Sultan, and when the Sultan saw how beautiful they were, he paid the fisherman four hundred silver coins, and told him that he wanted him to bring four such fish to him every day. After that the fisherman went home very happy, and he told the whole story to his wife and children, and they too celebrated their father's good luck.

Now in the palace of the Sultan a servant cleaned the fish and put them in a pan to cook over the fire. At that moment the wall suddenly opened and the servant saw a woman emerge wearing a scarf, and she looked at the fish and said: "Fish, fish, are you ready?" The fish lifted their eyes and said, "If you are ready, we are ready. If you are going, we are going." Then, all at once, the woman disappeared, and the fish in the pan turned into coals. Then the frightened servant ran to the vizier and told him what had happened, and the vizier told the Sultan that the servant had burned the fish by accident and had been properly punished. And though the Sultan was disappointed, he accepted this explanation.

The next day the fisherman brought four more of the fish and was paid for them as before. This time the Sultan let it be known that the fish had better not be burned, so the vizier joined the servant and watched as she cleaned the fish and put them in the pan to fry. So it was that this time both the vizier and the servant saw the vision in which the wall opened and a woman wearing a scarf stood there and spoke to the fish. So too did the vizier hear the fish reply to her and then turn to coals in the frying pan. And the vizier knew that he must inform the Sultan of this strange event, and that is what he did. The Sultan was so amazed by this tale that he ordered the fisherman be brought to him that very day, and when he arrived the Sultan ordered him to bring him four more of the fish at once. But the fisherman explained that he could not bring the fish until the next day, for he was forbidden to cast his net in that place more than once a day. He told the Sultan the tale of how he had found the chest with the demon inside it, and how the demon had brought him to that lake. And the Sultan and the vizier were much amazed by this tale, and began to suspect that the fish of that lake might be enchanted. So they told the fisherman to bring them four more fish the next day.

This the fisherman did, and as soon as he brought the fish the Sultan and vizier went to the kitchen themselves and did everything the servant told them to do. And lo and behold, they saw the same vision of the woman wearing a scarf, and saw how the fish replied to her and then vanished. After that the Sultan demanded that the fisherman take them along with him to the lake, and although the fisherman was reluctant to reveal exactly where he had caught the fish, he was wise enough not to refuse the Sultan.

So it was that the fisherman served as their guide, and led the Sultan to the lake. When they reached it they were very surprised indeed, for it was quite close to the Sultan's palace, and they could not understand how it could be so near without anyone knowing of its existence. And they were even more amazed when they saw the black palace on the other side of the lake, which was also unknown to any one of them. The Sultan especially was very curious to know more about this palace, so near to his own. But he did not want the others to accompany him, for he did not know what he would find. So he ordered the fisherman to cast his net, and they watched as he did so and saw how he soon brought back the four fish, one of each kind. And they returned with the fish to the palace, where the same miraculous events occurred when they tried to cook them.

The Sultan was truly astonished by all that had occurred, and he decided to explore the area around that lake for himself. So he had the vizier tell the ministers that he would be gone for a few days. Then he dressed in ordinary clothes, took his sword, and went on his way. This time he went directly to the black palace on the far side of the lake, and when he reached it he found that it was surrounded by a wall of black stone. The Sultan went up to the gate and picked up a rock and knocked on it. But when no one came to the gate, he opened it himself and entered. The courtyard was empty, and the Sultan found that the door of the palace was open, so he went inside. He went from one room to another, astonished at the beauty of the palace and filled with curiosity to know who lived there. From time to time he called out, hoping to find someone, but there was no reply.

At last the Sultan reached a bedroom at the other end of the palace, and there he sat down, marveling at all that he had seen. While he was sitting there he heard a voice sobbing nearby and he jumped up and tried to find where it was coming from. He went down one of the halls, entered a room, and heard the voice coming from behind a curtain. When he moved the curtain he saw a handsome young man wearing the clothes of royalty and seated on a chair, his face very sad. The Sultan approached him and greeted him and the young man returned his greeting by nodding and then said, "Forgive me. I would rise and come toward you to welcome you, but I cannot, and I hope that you are not insulted." Then, all of a sudden, the young man opened his robe, and the Sultan saw that he was half man, half marble. This both frightened and amazed the Sultan, who said, "Now I well understand why you cannot stand up. But how is it that you have become half marble? Tell me, and I will do all in my power to help you."

The young man then told the Sultan his story: "I am the son of the king of Persia. Shortly after I ascended the throne I married a beautiful maiden from another kingdom. For five years my life was peaceful. Then, one afternoon when the queen was not present and my eyes were closed as if I was asleep, I overheard two servants as they spoke. One servant said, 'The poor king. If he only knew that the queen does not love him.' 'Yes,' said the other, 'every night she puts some kind of potion in his tea, that she prepares herself, and then he falls asleep and she goes out into the forest to meet her lover.'"

"Just then," the king continued, "I opened my eyes and

/100/

yawned as if I had awakened from a very deep sleep, and at the same time the queen entered and we sat down to dinner. When we finished, she gave me the tea that I used to drink every night. While her back was turned I poured it out the window and then I told her that it was as good as always. Then, when we went to bed and she thought I was asleep, I heard her say 'Sleep, sleep. I hope you will sleep forever.' Then she got up and left.

"As soon as she was gone I got up, dressed, and followed her. She went into the darkest part of the forest until she reached a place where there was a gate. She spoke words of magic and the gate opened by itself. That was the first time I realized that she was a witch. Soon after she was met by a man, her lover. A terrible fury took hold of me and I took my sword and struck him. Then I escaped unseen. I knew that I had killed him, but the queen was able to save his life with her magic powers. However, the wound was so severe that even her powers were only able to preserve signs of life in his eyes. Otherwise he was unable to speak or eat.

"Back at the palace I pretended that I was asleep. After some time, she returned. The next morning, when I woke up, I found her wearing black and saw that she had cut her hair. She told me that she had received three messages of disaster: about the death of her brother in a battle, and the deaths of her father and mother out of grief over him. For one year she continued to mourn. Then she asked me permission to build a palace in the name of her parents, to be known as the Palace of Tears. That is this black palace in which you have found me. Once it was built she brought her lover here and visited him every day. But despite all her efforts and magic, she was unable to heal him, and he continued to barely cling to life.

"One day I went to visit the Palace of Tears and I heard her talking to her love. She said, 'My beloved, my moon, will you be dumb forever? Please speak, speak, only one word, just a single word. Then everything will come to life. If you want me to move this palace behind the mountains, or if you want me to turn the entire kingdom into ruins, where only foxes will roam, just say so and I will do it.' Hearing this I became so furious that I ran into the room, cursing them both. Then the queen looked at me with a terrible look, and she said, 'Don't think that I don't know that you are the source of my trouble.' Then she pronounced a few magic words, and said, 'From now on you are going to be half man and half marble!' And no sooner did she speak then it came to pass—and that is how I came to be in this terrible state, completely frozen in place. With scorn she rolled me into this room and left me here. After that she came every day, bringing me a few crumbs to eat and dregs to drink, berating and hitting me, while I was helpless to defend myself. Then she went to visit her lover, continuing to try to heal him, but to no avail.

"Soon after she turned me into a man half marble, the witch put a spell over the entire capital city and turned it into a lake, and all the people in it were transformed into fish. And she used her magic to move the palace of tears beside the lake. And that is the end of my sad tale."

Now of course the Sultan was amazed to hear this tale, which explained how the palace and lake had suddenly appeared in that place. And he did not doubt anything that the young king had said, for he merely had to look at him, half man and half marble, to know that he was telling the truth. The story greatly moved the Sultan, who wanted to help the poor king seek his revenge. Then the Sultan said, "Tell me where the room is in which the queen's lover is to be found. I shall go there and seek your revenge." Then the king told him, and the Sultan went to that room in the dark of the night, cast the lover from his bed and took his place.

When the queen arrived in the morning, she first went to the room of the king, left his pathetic meal and struck him several times. After that she came to the room of her lover, while the king lay in the bed, his head turned toward the wall. When she saw him she began to speak, and said, "My beloved, my life, will you be dumb forever? Speak but a few words to me and my barren life will blossom again." Then the Sultan pretended as if he had woken up from a very deep sleep, and he said: "Where am I? What place is this?" And the queen became delirious with happiness and in a flood of words she told him of all that had happened, and how she had avenged herself on the king and the rest of the capital.

/102/

Then the disguised Sultan said, "Perhaps your revenge is the cause of my long illness. Go, release the king and the rest of the kingdom from the spell, and perhaps my strength will return in full and we can be lovers again." Hearing these words the queen did not hesitate, but agreed at once that she would do as he asked, for her happiness at his having spoken at last knew no bounds.

So the queen went and released the spell that had turned the king into a man who was half marble, and as soon as he was free he ran away from the Palace of Tears as fast as his legs could carry him, for he was terrified of what the queen would do if she discovered the Sultan's hoax. After that the queen went to the lake and pronounced a spell, and suddenly all the fish turned back into people and the lake turned back into the capital, and the people found themselves back in a bustling city.

After this the queen returned to her 'lover,' and she told him that she had obeyed his wishes. Then the Sultan said, "Good. Now let us see if the spell under which I have suffered for so long has been lifted. Let me try to sit up. Please, close your eyes, and only open them when I tell you." Then, trembling with hope, the queen closed her eyes, and the Sultan sat up, took out his sword, and cut off her head. And the moment he did, both the head and the body of the witch vanished in a puff of smoke and were gone. And at that moment the sun, which had been hidden behind dark clouds all the while, shone on the city for the first time, and the young king knew that the spell of the witch had finally been broken.

Then the young king came back to the Palace of Tears and met the Sultan, and they embraced. The Sultan told him how he had defeated the witch, and the king saw to it that he received great rewards: gold, jewels, and thousands of horses and donkeys. Then the king called all of the people together and revealed to them the sad history of all the years that they had been enchanted, and told them of how the Sultan had set them free. And they declared a great holiday that day, which was celebrated among them forever after.

As for the fisherman who had led the Sultan to that lake in the first place, the young king gave the Palace of Tears to him as a reward. And there the fisherman and his family were so happy that in time it became known as the Palace of Peace, for they lived there in joy and peace for the rest of their lives.

Morocco: Oral Tradition

The Disguised Princess

There once was a king whose only daughter was always pale and distracted. Many doctors were summoned, but none could find the cure. The king was very concerned about his daughter, and asked his wisest ministers for advice. One of them suggested that the king send the princess and her friends to a beautiful garden far from home, away from the cares and responsibilities of the palace. By the end of a year, surely, her spirits would greatly improve.

The king considered this advice, and it seemed good to him, so he took the princess and the daughters of the ministers, who were her closest friends, to a delightful garden in a corner of that kingdom. There the maidens were indeed very happy, and spent their days playing games, dancing and singing, and enjoying the finest foods. Thus a year passed, and the good spirits of the princess returned at last.

At the end of the year the king journeyed to the garden to visit his daughter, and saw how beautiful she appeared, and how satisfied, and he was very pleased. He asked her if she wanted to return home, but she replied that she preferred to stay in that garden for another year. So the king agreed to let her remain there with the daughters of the ministers for a second year, and promised to return at the end of that time to bring them all back to the palace. Then he wished his daughter well, kissed her goodbye, and took his leave.

So it was that the life of peace and relaxation continued for the princess and her companions. Every day, after they had sung, danced and talked, they took an afternoon nap, each beneath a different tree, each out of sight of the others.

Now it happened that a prince from a nearby kingdom was out on a hunt when he spied a white gazelle running through the fields. The beauty of that animal made him want to catch it, but each time he caught sight of it anew, it vanished. The prince was a determined man, and he chased the gazelle for many days, until he saw it leap over the wall of a garden.

The prince tied up his horse and climbed over the wall, intent on tracking down the beautiful gazelle. But as soon as he climbed down into the garden, he was amazed to see how lovely it was, and recognized at once that it must belong to royalty. From where he stood, the prince saw a young maiden asleep beneath a nearby tree. He drew closer to her and saw that she was the most stunning and beautiful maiden he had ever seen in his life. From the first, he knew that he could not love any other. So the prince took off the golden amulet he wore around his neck, and placed it in the hand of the sleeping princess.

Just then the prince saw the gazelle leap back over the wall, and he left the garden to continue the chase, even though his heart now belonged to she who was asleep there.

When the princess awoke and found the golden amulet in her hand, she was astonished, for it was very beautiful, and she had no idea whence it had come. She asked the other maidens about it, but all of them had been asleep except one, who had awakened just as the prince had climbed back over the wall in pursuit of the gazelle. This maiden described the prince to the princess, and when she learned how handsome he was, she fell in love at once, even though she had not yet looked into the prince's eyes.

In the days that followed, the princess could not sleep, so

filled with longing was she to find the one who had given her that golden amulet. At last she decided she must leave the garden and search for him herself. She told the maidens of her decision, but they were very frightened, for should the king discover that the princess was not with them, they would surely lose their lives. Now the king was not expected for nearly a year, so the princess promised that she would return before the arrival of her father, and that she would come in the company of the one who had left the golden amulet in her hand.

Even though the maidens shed many tears and begged her not to go, the princess set out on her journey. She walked for a long time, and when evening was about to fall, she reached the gates of the capital of a nearby kingdom. An old woman was standing there, so the princess went up to her and said, "Please, let me come home with you, for I have no place to sleep and I am very weary." The old woman took pity on her and brought her to her house, where the princess slept on straw.

Now since there had been nothing in that garden for the princess to buy, she did not have any money. All that she possessed was a ring and the golden amulet, and of course she would never part with the amulet. So she gave the old woman the ring and told her to take it into the city to sell for the highest price, and with the money she would be able to buy food for them to last for some time. The old woman did this, and she received more money for that ring than she had ever seen in her life.

The princess rested there for many days while she considered her plan. At last she said to the old woman, "Today I want you to take me to the market and sell me as a slave to some rich gentleman." The old woman did not want to do this, but the princess insisted. And so it was that the princess, disguised as a poor slave, was sold to one of the king's ministers as a companion for his ailing daughter.

The minister took the disguised princess to his home, and told her that he wanted her to watch over his daughter and to keep her company. But that night, when the princess was with the minister's daughter, an amazing thing happened. The girl, who had been in bed as if ill, stood up and turned first into a horse, then into a cow, and finally into a camel. The camel ran from place to place, and terrified the princess, who dropped the candle she had been holding, causing its flame to go out. With no way to light the flame, she became even more frightened, and not wanting to be alone in that dark room with a camel, she jumped out the window, landing on the ground below. There she saw a dim light in the distance and hurried to see if it was someone who could help her. But when she approached, she heard whispering and soon realized she had come upon a group of witches who were casting spells on the poor daughter of the minister, turning her into one animal after the other.

So the disguised princess returned to the house of the minister, and told him all that had happened. When he learned that his daughter's plight had been caused by witches, he asked the king's sorcerer for help. The sorcerer came to the house the next night, and cast yet another spell which caused the spells the witches cast to be cast back upon themselves. So the witch who turned the girl into a cow, herself became a cow, and the witch who turned her into a horse became a horse, and the witch who made her into a camel became a camel. The minister then sold the cow, the horse and the camel, and he gave the money to the disguised princess, and gave her her freedom as well.

After that the princess returned to the old woman, who was very happy to see her. The princess remained with her for some weeks, but then she asked the old woman to take her into the market to sell her again. The old woman refused with all her might, but again the princess insisted, and this time she was sold as a slave to a wealthy man.

Now this man had a daughter who had not spoken a word in years, which caused her parents great distress. He told the disguised princess that he wanted her to be the girl's servant and companion. That evening, when they were alone together, the mute girl offered the princess coffee into which a sleeping potion had been poured. The princess drank the coffee and soon fell into a deep sleep. The mute girl pinched her to make sure she was really sleeping, then took out a key and opened a secret doorway, which led to a small cupboard. She slipped bread and water under the cupboard door and then she called out: "Will you marry me now, or would you rather stay in there forever?" And a voice firmly replied: "Never will I marry you! I will only marry she to whom I gave my golden amulet!"

The next day the princess awoke feeling exhausted—and sore, as if someone had been pinching her. She realized at once that the coffee the mute girl had given her had a sleeping potion in it. So she did not drink the coffee the girl offered her that night, and only pretended to be asleep, even when she was being pinched. And when the girl opened the secret door and called out to the prisoner in the cupboard, the princess heard him say what he said the night before. Then she realized at once just who that prisoner was—the very prince for whom she was searching! She also realized that the mute girl was not mute at all, but that she could speak as well as anyone else.

That night the princess switched coffee cups and made the girl fall asleep. Then she took the key from a chain around the girl's neck, opened the secret door and knocked on the wall of the locked cupboard. The prince, thinking it was his tormentor, said, "Go away, I have already sworn I will never marry you!" But the princess whispered, "I am not the one who has imprisoned you, but the one who would set you free." "Oh, I would be so grateful," said the prince. "And tell me," said the princess, "would you marry me if I set you free." "No, that I cannot do," said the prince, "for I have vowed to marry only the maiden to whom I gave my golden amulet." "I see that you are a man of your word," said the princess, "but tell me, how did you come to be imprisoned here?" Then the poor prince told her how he had been chasing a gazelle through a field when his horse stumbled and he fell off and struck his head against a stone. "And when I awoke," he said "I found myself locked in this cupboard, the prisoner of this evil girl." "Oh, you poor man," said the princess, "I will do everything I can to help you. Tell me, where can your parents be found?" The prince told her that they were the king and queen of that very kingdom, and that the girl who had imprisoned him would rather see him die than let him marry anyone else. The princess told him not to lose hope, for she would save him very soon.

The next day the disguised princess told the girl that she had seen and heard everything, and would reveal the presence of the prisoner if the girl did not stop pretending that she was mute. With no other choice, the girl began to speak to her parents again. They were so delighted that they set the slave girl free at once.

Then the princess returned to the old woman, who was certain that this time she would remain with her. But no, before very long the maiden insisted that the old woman sell her as a slave to the king and queen of that kingdom. And when the old woman saw how determined she was, she accompanied the girl to the palace and easily sold her as a slave—for even though she was disguised as a slave, the princess was still very beautiful.

There the princess found herself in the presence of the king and queen, and she noticed at once that they were in mourning. She asked another slave why this was, and she was told that their son, the prince, had disappeared. Then the disguised princess went to the king and queen and told them that she knew where their son could be found. They were amazed to hear such a thing from a slave, but when they heard her entire story, they accompanied her at once to the house where the prince was imprisoned. The king's guards burst into the house, and the poor prince was soon found, almost at death's door. When the girl who had imprisoned him saw that, she ran away and was never seen again.

The prince was quickly brought back to the palace where he soon recovered. When he was healthy enough to sit up, he asked how it was that he had been saved. Then they told him about the slave girl who had known where he was imprisoned. He asked her to be brought forth, and when he saw the princess he recognized her at once as the sleeping girl to whom he had given his amulet in the garden. When the princess saw him, she took out the golden amulet and showed it to the prince. Then they embraced, for they had been reunited at last, and the king told his parents about how they had met, and the princess revealed her true identity.

So it was that just before the year ended, the princess returned to the garden as she had promised, in the company of the prince. And when her father arrived the princess introduced them to each other, and the prince asked the king for his daughter's hand. The amazed king was overjoyed that his daughter wished to marry so wealthy and handsome a prince, and gladly gave his permission. So it was that a great wedding was celebrated, which both kings and queens attended. And that was the most joyous event in the history of both kingdoms, for the prince and princess who had been destined for each other had been brought together at last.

Tunisia: Oral Tradition

The Boy in the Cave

King Nimrod was once the most powerful ruler in the world; it was he who built the Tower of Babel. He had vast armies at his command, and his treasury was so filled with jewels and gold that the silver had to be stored elsewhere. None of his enemies dared attack him, and his fortresses seemed impenetrable. But one night there was a strange sign in the heavens: an enormous comet suddenly appeared and coursed its way across the sky. On its circuit, it swallowed up the brightest star in the sky, the one that shone directly above King Nimrod's kingdom. Naturally, everyone who had witnessed that astonishing sight wondered what it meant. King Nimrod also wondered, and he ordered his soothsayers to seek out the meaning of this omen.

The soothsayers studied the stars, and they did not like what they learned. For the sign could only mean that a child was about to be born who would overthrow the most powerful king in the world, which they all understood could be none other than King Nimrod. At first the soothsayers were afraid to report this interpretation, out of fear of Nimrod's wrath. But then they decided that if he learned about it later, his wrath would be even greater, so they told him about the meaning of the sign.

Now King Nimrod grew pale when he learned the prophecy of the stars, for he had never known the stars to be wrong. Still, he had no intention of simply losing his kingdom, so he decreed at once that all pregnant women must go to a special place to give birth. So too did he tell those he appointed to oversee the births to be certain that none of the infants boys be allowed to live, while the mothers of infant girls were to be awarded many gifts.

Naturally this decree threw terror into the hearts of every family in that kingdom in which a child was about to be born. And among those there was the woman Emtelai and her husband, Terah. They could not bear the thought of having their child delivered to death if it were a boy, for reports of the slaughter of the infant boys had already reached their ears. Therefore Terah led Emetlai to a cave in a remote area outside of the city, where he helped her deliver the child. But neither father nor mother could remain there with the infant boy, whom they named Abraham. Fearing for their own lives, they left the infant in that cave and commanded his soul to fate.

Now the Lord on high saw all that took place down below and sent the angel Gabriel directly to the infant Abraham to sustain him. Gabriel cared for the infant and gave him milk, which flowed from the finger of his right hand. So too did the angel hang a glowing stone around the infant's neck. This stone cast a wonderful light in that cave at all times, so that the infant was never in the dark. Abraham wore that jewel around his neck for all of his life, and whoever looked into it was healed of any sickness. So too did he discover that the stone could also serve as an astrolabe, with which he could observe the stars.

Now the truth is that the milk the infant Abraham received from the angel Gabriel was the milk of Paradise, and the light that shone from that stone was of the light God had created on the first day, known as the primordial light. Sustained with that milk and that light, a remarkable transformation took place; the infant Abraham grew at a miraculous rate, until after a period of two weeks he resembled a ten-year-old child. So too was he well versed in Hebrew, the holy tongue, for that is what the angel had taught him to speak, since that is the language of the angels. And the angel Gabriel also revealed to him the secrets of heaven, that one Lord God had created heaven and earth and ruled over all the world.

It was then that Abraham's sorrowing mother returned to the cave to learn the fate of her child. For she had not been able to sleep since she had left the infant there, and she naturally assumed the worst. So it was that when she entered the cave and did not find the infant there, she broke down and wept bitter tears, believing that the child had been devoured by wild beasts. But when she walked outside the cave she saw a young boy standing on the bank of the river that ran nearby, and hoping that he might know something of her baby's fate, she hurried to him and asked if he had seen an infant near here.

At first Abraham pretended he did not know of whom his mother spoke, and he asked her to explain how she had come to abandon a newborn infant in such a barren place. But when he saw how much she grieved over her loss, he finally revealed that he was her son. Although at first she found this impossible to believe, after Abraham explained the miracle that had taken place, and showed her the glowing stone he wore around his neck, Emtelai understood that he was indeed her newborn son. She asked him what god was responsible for such a miracle, and Abraham told her that it was the Lord who ruled over the world. So too did Abraham tell his mother that he would devote his life to God and follow in His ways, for he had had ample proof of his mercy and power.

So it was that Emtelai was the first after Abraham to recognize the true Lord, and she too became a devout and pious believer for the rest of her life. For she saw how God had saved her infant, and how he had grown in such a short time into a child possessed of great wisdom.

Not long after Abraham and his mother returned to the city, King Nimrod began to receive reports of a wonder-working child who was said to possess a healing stone of miraculous power. It was said that this child spoke of a God not only greater than the idols the people worshipped, but even greater than Nimrod himself. For at that time the people believed their kings to be gods, and Nimrod was thought to be the most powerful god of all. These reports infuriated the evil king, who sought counsel among his ministers. Then Satan came in the guise of one of the advisors and convinced the king to send his army against this young man. He told the king that although the youth appeared to be an ordinary boy, he was, in fact, possessed of immense power, and must be stopped before it grew even greater.

The king took this advice and sent his army marching against Abraham. But the Lord saw their evil intentions and sent down a cloud of darkness so dense that all of them thought they had gone blind. Only when the soldiers turned back did the dark cloud lift.

Now when Nimrod learned how his troops had been turned back, he grew afraid for the first time. All at once he looked up and saw the boy Abraham standing before him in the royal chamber. The king could not believe his eyes. He asked Abraham how he had entered there, and the boy explained that he had arrived at the palace even before the retreating troops, since the jewel he wore around his neck could illumine the deepest darkness. Then the king commanded that his guards take that jewel from Abraham, but when a guard touched the jewel it burned his hand. And this happened to all those who tried to take it from him, although the jewel rested cooly against Abraham's chest. When Nimrod saw this, his blood began to boil, and he shouted for the guards to seize the boy. And Abraham did not resist, but allowed himself to be led to prison to await Nimrod's sentence.

Now Nimrod was quite certain he would sentence the boy to death, but he wanted the sentence to be carried out in a way that no one would ever forget, so that no one would challenge the king for a very long time. Again Satan came forth in disguise and told the king that a great catapult should be built that would cast Abraham into a blazing furnace where he would meet his end. The king liked this idea, and had the catapult and furnace built on a vast plain, where all of the inhabitants of that city could gather to observe the execution.

"... he was stunned to see there a garden as beautiful as the Garden
of Eden itself."

Meanwhile Abraham waited serenly in his cell, confident that the Holy One, blessed be He, would protect him against all danger. Then, on the day of the execution, when everyone had assembled, Nimrod stood before Abraham and loudly proclaimed that if Abraham would bow down and worship him as the greatest king, his life would be spared. Abraham's mother, seeing that her son's life was in such danger, begged him to save himself, but Abraham replied that he did not fear the fire, for the fire of man can be quenched with water, while the fire of God burns eternal.

So it was that Abraham did not resist when he was placed inside the catapult and shot from a great distance directly into the blazing flames of the furnace. But at the instant he landed there, the flames died down, and suddenly all of the logs and branches, which had just been burning, began to bud, and then to blossom, and then bore fruit. And when Nimrod himself opened the door of the furnace to see what had happened, he was stunned to see there a garden as beautiful as the Garden of Eden itself. When he saw this, Nimrod realized that Abraham and his God were far more powerful than he, and he took to his heels along with all of his advisors. Abraham knew that since they had been disgraced in the eyes of their subjects, Nimrod and his evil ministers would never again have power over the people.

Then Abraham turned to the great crowd gathered there and in a booming voice proclaimed that the Lord God is one. And all who saw and heard him knew that what he said was true, for they had witnessed the miracle themselves. And so it was that Abraham brought the light of the Lord to a great multitude that day. They entrusted their fate to him, in the knowledge that he himself was guided by the true Lord of Hosts, may he reign forever and ever!

Italy: c. Thirteenth Century

Alexander Descends
into the Sea

When Alexander the Great had explored and conquered the world, he said to his wisest men, "Although I have seen what is to be seen in this world, I am still not satisfied. Therefore I would like to descend into the sea and learn what is under the ocean. Make me, then, a hollow bell of glass, in which I will descend into the deep." His men did not fail him, and seven days later Alexander climbed inside the glass bell, taking with him provisions, a living fowl, and a stone that gave off light, which he had come to possess in one of his conquests, and which he now wore around his neck. The men lowered the glass bell into the water, until they ran out of rope. Then they tied the other end to a tree and secured the knot. Now Alexander had told them to wait up to a year before pulling the rope back in, unless he sent them a sign to pull it up before then. So they left a watchman there at all times to wait for Alexander to send them a sign that it was time to pull the rope back in. But before seven days had passed a giant eagle swooped down from the sky and cut the rope, and the bell slowly sank toward the bottom of the sea.

Now Alexander did not realize that the rope had been cut.

Instead he imagined that his men had woven more rope and had decided to lower him even deeper into the sea. He was greatly pleased at this, for the further he descended the more fascinating were the sights he saw. In this way Alexander came to see what no other man had ever seen—the wonders of the ocean, filled with fish of every kind, coral and anemones, and shells a thousand years old. So too were there creatures unlike any ever seen upon the land, with all kinds of strange shapes. Alexander marveled at what he saw, and never closed his eyes to sleep, so fascinated was he.

Now Alexander had no way of knowing for certain how much time had passed, since the stone illumined the deep both day and night. Nevertheless, time flew by, and when he thought it had been about a year, Alexander strangled the fowl, causing its blood to rise to the surface, where Alexander hoped his men would recognze it as a sign. Little did he know that he had drifted many miles from shore, and that he had arrived in a sea of great purity. This sea was so pure it did not retain blood, and waves arose to wash the intruding blood from its pure waters. And these waves eventually carried Alexander to shore, casting him among a strange people whose language he did not understand.

The natives of that land had broad faces and only one eye. Alexander was the first man they had ever seen with two eyes, and they assumed he must be some kind of god and bowed low before him. They appointed him as king, and Alexander studied their ways and for nine months ruled over them, for he was a natural ruler. Then he bid them farewell and told them that he had to return to the land of the other gods, who, like himself, had two eyes. The natives did not try to stop him, for they saw him as destiny itself, and so Alexander soon found himself alone in the wilderness, with no sense of how to find his way back to his Kingdom.

When it seemed like Alexander had been wandering for months, he came upon a lion. At first he was terrified, and climbed a tree. But the lion approached him peacefully and lay down like a lamb at the foot of the tree. Alexander saw that the lion did not seem intent on evil, but still he did not dare descend from the tree until it departed. So it was that he spent the night there, and in the morning he found that the lion had gathered fruits and berries for him, and had placed them at the foot of the tree. Then Alexander realized that this was no ordinary lion, and he descended from the branches. When he had eaten the lion's offering, Alexander mounted the lion, as he understood he was supposed to, and it departed, bearing him on its back.

The lion carried him for seven days, and at last it reached a cave, where it let Alexander dismount and then took its leave. Alexander entered the cave and passed through it, every passage lit by the stone he still wore around his neck. At the end of seven days he reached the end of the cave, and there he found an old man, sitting before a fire. The old man looked up when he approached and said, "Art thou Alexander?" Alexander was very surprised and he asked the old man how he knew his name. The old man replied that he could see many things in the dark of the cave, peering into the past as well as into the future. Thus he had seen Alexander being brought to the cave by the lion. "What lion is that?" asked Alexander. And the old man replied, "That lion is known as the lion of Ilai, for it makes its home in the forest Ilai, which is the forest you have entered."

Then Alexander told the old man that he had been lost when he had met the lion. But the old man already knew that, and knew as well everything that he had seen in his descent beneath the sea. His knowledge of every detail amazed Alexander, who greatly wondered who he was. But when he asked the old man his name, he refused to tell him. His name was known only among the Jews, he told him, for it was a secret that could not be revealed. Then the old man told Alexander that if he vowed never to harm the Jews and to protect them in every way, he would lead him back to his kingdom. Otherwise he would be forced to wander in that cave for the rest of his life.

Of course Alexander made the vow, and then the old man led him to one of the cave's many passages. Alexander bid him farewell and traveled down that long passage for seven days. And when he emerged from the cave he found himself on the shore of the sea, with his army facing him on the far shore. He quickly gathered logs, bound them with vines, and sailed across to return to them on a raft. His men, who saw him floating on the sea, thought that he had finally risen up from the bell, for it was exactly one year since he had first descended. For if the truth be known, after the line had broken they had given up hope. But they had returned that day, because it was the anniversary of his descent. When they saw him floating calmly toward them, he seemed more like one of the immortals than a living man.

When Alexander was reunited with his army he told them all that had happened to him, and they were much amazed. From that time forward Alexander always saw to it that the Jews were protected and lived in peace in all the lands that he ruled.

Italy: Eleventh Century

The Waters of Eternal Life

The birth of Alexander the Great was preceded by many signs, read by many astrologers. For two stars were seen together in the sky at night, a pair of twin suns burning brightly. All the diviners recognized this as a sign of greatness, but they also saw in it the prophecy of an early death. So it was that Alexander always knew of the destiny foretold for him, and he fulfilled the first part to the hilt, conquering the world. But once he had succeeded in this enormous quest, Alexander began to worry about the second part of the prophecy, that his life would be brief. So it was that he undertook his second great quest—to locate the Waters of Eternal Life.

The legend of such miraculous waters is found in every land, and Alexander heard of it wherever he went. Since he had managed to conquer the world, he undertook the quest to locate those waters without fear or hesitation for above all he longed to conquer death.

Alexander set out with a dozen of his finest soldiers, well aware that many obstacles might lie before him. From an old soothsayer—one of those who had foreseen his birth—Alexander learned that the Waters of Eternal Life were to be found beyond the Mountains of Darkness. But none who had tried to go there had ever returned. This did not discourage Alexander; he set out at once, confident that nothing was insurmountable.

Thus the king and his men travelled for many weeks, and at last they reached the towering mountains. Alexander saw that it would take his men several more weeks to cross them, and he was loathe to take that much time. Then he noticed several giant eagles flying overhead, and an astonishing idea occurred to him—to leash some of those eagles together, to carry him to the other side of those mountains. Alexander decided to try such a crossing for himself, while his men would cross on foot. If he succeeded, he would meet them on the other side of the mountains in a few weeks.

So it was that Alexander ordered his warriors to bring him four of those giant eagles. Before long four of the largest were captured in a net. The king then ordered their food to be withheld for three days. Meanwhile Alexander ordered his men to weave a basket that was large enough to carry him, with a lid that could be closed to protect him from falling out during flight.

Next Alexander ordered that four long iron spikes be affixed to a board, with four pieces of meat affixed to the spikes. After that Alexander told the men to take the four eagles and bind their legs to the four corners of the board. And he had ropes hung from the board, from which the basket was suspended, with Alexander inside it. The eagles, seeing the meat above them, flapped their wings attempting to reach it. Thus the basket was carried high into the clouds. And from a narrow slot in the basket, which had been left so that he could view the land below, Alexander looked with amazement upon the mountains beneath him. And as he was carried higher, he began to see the entire continent, which seemed to him like a cup floating on the waters of the ocean.

When the heat of the sun began to weary him, Alexander pulled a rope, which turned the spikes downward, so that the eagles followed them in that direction until they finally landed on the earth. When Alexander emerged from the basket he released the eagles and then looked about. He found that he had indeed been carried across those Mountains of Darkness and had landed beside a mighty river. The land on which he stood was barren, but across the river he saw a great many trees, filled with fruit. He wished that the eagles had landed on the far side, of the river but since they had not, he had to find a way to reach it, for there he could sustain himself. Alexander decided to build himself a raft.

He bound logs together and then strapped the basket to the raft and climbed inside. Now the currents of that river were quite swift, with many dangerous rapids. Before the raft had crossed the river half way, it split apart and the basket with Alexander in it was cast into the currents, where it floated on the waters like a barrel. Inside it, Alexander was turned over and over, tumbling ceaselessly. At last the basket was cast out of the waters and onto the shore. When the weary Alexander climbed out, he found that he had indeed reached the far side of the river where the rich fruit grew.

Now Alexander was famished after all he had gone through to fly over those mountains and cross that river, and the fruit of these trees beckoned him as no other food had in all his days. Alexander reached out and plucked one of those ripe, alluring fruits, but the moment he did he heard shouting from all sides, and in an instant he found himself surrounded by strange and frightening looking beings. Although their form was human, they had wings and cast no shadows. Even so, Alexander was not afraid, but before he could do anything, four of the beings took hold of him, and in an instant Alexander found himself wrapped in chains. His captors then set out through the forest with Alexander as their prisoner.

So it was that Alexander found himself taken to a magnificent palace, far greater than that of any king he had known. He could barely believe his eyes as he stared at the mighty size of that palace. He asked the guards who walked at his side whose palace it was, and they told him it was the palace of Asmodeus, king of demons. Alexander was deeply shaken, for now he realized who had captured him, and while he had no fears among men, he knew nothing of the ways of demons.

So it was that Alexander the Great, conquerer of the world of men, was brought in chains before Asmodeus, king of demons. Asmodeus had a very stern and frightening bearing, and Alexander began to fear that he might have reached the end of his days. Asmodeus spoke loudly, and said, "You, sir, are accused of very serious crimes. First of all, none born of woman are permitted to set foot in this land, the kingdom of the demons. The penalty for this crime is death! Second, you have been accused of picking one of the fruits of the trees in my royal orchard. The penalty for this crime is also death! Therefore you have twice been condemned to death. Is there anything you wish to say in your defense before the sentence is carried out?"

Alexander was well aware that only his wits could save him. He replied, "My lord monarch, I have come to your realm on a quest, for I am seeking the fabled Waters of Eternal Life. Instead it appears that I have found an early death."

Asmodeus was much impressed both by the directness of Alexander's reply and by the nature of the quest. And he wished to know more of his captive. So he said, "Tell me, before the sentence is carried out, who you are, so that your fate will not be lost to the world."

Alexander then revealed his name, and when Asmodeus discovered the identity of his famous prisoner, he was greatly surprised. The king of demons rose from his throne and embraced Alexander, much to Alexander's amazement. "Welcome, oh great king, Asmodeus said, for the conquests of Alexander are known not only in the world of men, but in our world as well. Had I only known who you were, you would never have been subjected to such trials. For a king such as yourself is always a welcome guest."

Alexander could scarcely believe his ears, for the very stern judge of a moment earlier was now embracing him as an equal. Alexander gratefully acknowledged the kind gestures of the king of demons, and then said, "Some men believe that I care for nothing except conquering. But this is not true. Above all, I am an explorer, drawn to the far corners of the earth. And now that my days of conquest are behind me, I have chosen to devote myself to searching for these secret waters. If you can help me in this quest in any way, I would be eternally grateful and I would seek to repay you in any way that I could."

Now Asmodeus could be the most deadly enemy, but he could also be the most trusted friend. And he had long admired the exploits of Alexander, who at such a young age had conquered the world of men. Thus Asmodeus replied, "Would that I could lead you there myself, my lord Alexander. But this is not possible, for it has been decreed in Heaven that neither angels nor demons may reveal the locations of those miraculous waters to mortal men. But since you have overcome all obstacles to reach this distant land, I will assist you as much as I can. And if I may not reveal the location myself, I can at least tell you how this secret can be learned. For the only one permitted to reveal this secret is the Speaking Tree."

Alexander was astonished to hear that there actually was a tree that spoke. "Where, then, can this Speaking Tree be found," Alexander asked, "for I am prepared to set out even today to seek it out." Asmodeus was pleased that Alexander was truly devoted to his quest. "Stay with me tonight and be a guest at my table," he said, "and in the morning I will tell you how to reach this tree and send you on your way." This Alexander readily agreed to, and so his hunger and thirst were quenched that night at the table of the king of demons.

So it was that Alexander was the first of men ever to taste the far more exquisite food of demons. Alexander asked Asmodeus why this was, and the king explained that the wonderful taste of those foods derived from the fruits that grew only in that royal orchard in which Alexander had been discovered. For they were enchanted fruits, which Asmodeus himself had brought into being by a spell.

That night Alexander slept in a bed fit for a king, and in the morning he breakfasted with Asmodeus, who revealed the only way possible to reach the Speaking Tree. First, he must travel to a certain forest, in the midst of which were sweet waters. There Alexander must go upstream until he reached a cave from which the waters flowed forth. Then he must wade through that cave to their source in a spring, beyond which he would see at once a large red tree—that was the Speaking Tree. It spoke on the third hour of the day and would reply to whatever was asked of it, except to reveal the day destined for a man's own death.

Alexander was deeply grateful to learn this, and he asked Asmodeus if he could show his gratitude by bringing him some of the Waters of Eternal Life when he had found them. But Asmodeus explained that he and all other demons were immortal, and therefore had no need for these waters. However, Asmodeus added that there was one thing Alexander could do for him, which he would greatly appreciate. Alexander vowed to do whatever the king asked of him, and Asmodeus said, "The Speaking Tree replies to three questions; three and no more. For one of these questions I would like you to ask where a glowing pearl can be found. For I have every kind of jewel in my crown except for the glowing pearl, and if you should bring me the reply to this question, I would be very grateful. And if you should somehow happen to bring back one of these pearls, I would give you a great reward."

Alexander assured Asmodeus that he would make this one of his three questions to the tree, and, if fate permitted, he would seek out the glowing pearl as well. Then he set out on the quest. He found the way to the forest exactly as Asmodeus had described it, in the midst of which sweet waters were flowing. The king then followed the path alongside those waters until he reached the entrance to a cave. Alexander was certain that this must be the cave beyond which lay the Speaking Tree.

Alexander waded through the waters of the cave for twenty-nine days. And though the waters were up to his neck-and sometimes even a bit higher—he often found himself wondering what the third question to the Speaking Tree should be. Alexander knew that he could not ask the tree how long he would live, since this question alone was forbidden, so he decided to ask how he would be remembered in the future. For the impression a man leaves behind is even more important than the perception of him during his lifetime.

At the end of twenty-nine days Alexander at last reached the source of the stream and stepped out of that cave into the light. The first thing he saw there was a towering red tree, and he knew at once that this must be the Speaking Tree. Alexander looked at the sun and decided that it was almost the third hour of the day, the hour when the tree could speak. So Alexander approached it and asked his first question: "Tell me, oh Speaking Tree, where can the Waters of Eternal Life be found? I have come here from very far to hear your reply."

Alexander had to wait only a moment, for exactly when the third hour arrived, the Speaking Tree replied: "You have taken the right path. Continue on and you will reach those waters. For it is destined that you will find them." Alexander was filled with joy when he heard this, for he was certain that if he reached those waters he would achieve his ultimate aim—eternal life.

Then Alexander asked the second question: "Where can one of the glowing pearls be found?" And the Speaking Tree replied: "Whoever descends into the Well of Living Waters will find it on the very bottom."

This reply threw Alexander into a dilemma. The tree would reply to only one more question, and he wanted to ask about his future reputation. But he did not know where the Well of Living Waters could be found, nor might he ever find out if he did not ask the Speaking Tree. So Alexander had to ask, "How can the Well of Living Waters be reached?" The Speaking Tree replied, "The first light of the full moon shall reveal the well."

Now this reply mystified Alexander, for the tree had not told him where to go. He decided to meditate upon the words of the oracle, and since night was about to fall, Alexander sat down beneath the Speaking Tree. Before long he saw a feather of light on the horizon and soon realized it was the first light of the rising moon. As Alexander watched, this feather seemed to gain wings, which shone on a single spot in the forest. Alexander suddenly recalled the words of the Speaking Tree, and rushed to the place illumined by the light, which was inside a circle of trees. But when he got there, he was disappointed; he had hoped to be led to the Well of Living Waters, but there was nothing there but a clearing in the forest. He sat down and soon fell into a deep sleep.

As he slept, Alexander dreamed he was floating on the waters of a river, drifting as if weightless. It was a very pleasing dream and it lasted all night. When Alexander awoke at dawn he recalled the dream and wondered at its meaning, especially since he had been searching for a well.

As he thought about this, Alexander noticed the outline of a circle around him. He felt with his hand and discovered it was a circle of stones, with only a small portion of each stone protruding from beneath the earth. Suddenly it occured to Alexander that this might be the well he was seeking, and that it was covered with a layer of dirt. Alexander began to dig there at once, and although he only had sharp stones to dig with, he managed to clear away several feet, so that he was soon digging from the bottom of a pit. Then, all at once, the crust of earth on which he stood broke, and Alexander fell a great distance, finally plunging into ice-cold water with a great splash. Any other man would have been terrified, but Alexander was delighted, feeling certain that this must be the Well of Living Waters.

Yet even if this were so, what good could it do him if he remained trapped in that well? As Alexander treaded water there, wondering how he might find his way out, he suddenly noticed a light glowing from the very bottom of the well. Alexander was quite curious to know what this might be, so he took a deep breath and dived below. He descended a great distance, and began to run out of breath just as he reached the bottom. He picked up the glowing object in his hand and shot to the surface as fast as he could, gasping for air as he emerged. When he reached the surface of the water, he saw at once that things had changed, for when he had dived below the waters were pitch black, and now a light shone on every stone—the glowing pearl! He had found it. And when Alexander realized this, he regained his confidence and felt certain that he would not only find a way out of that well, but also complete his quest to find the Waters of Eternal Life.

With the light cast by the glowing pearl, Alexander examined the sides of the well. He spotted a stone ladder that had been built into the round wall. Alexander swam over to the wall and just as he was about to grip the first stone rung, he remembered that this was, in fact, the Well of Living Waters. He wondered what was special about those waters, so before he climbed out he decided to taste them. He put the pearl in his pocket, and filled his cupped hands with water. No sooner had he tasted that wonderful water, than he felt refreshed and filled with strength. Alexander understood that these were indeed living waters that brought new life to whoever tasted them.

With his newfound strength Alexander was able to ascend the ladder inside the well, the glowing pearl held in his teeth to light the way. It took him several hours, but at last he climbed out of that deep well. By then he was exhausted, and he decided that he must have some more of those refreshing waters, but there was no bucket to be found. So Alexander plucked a gourd which grew in that place, hollowed it out, and made a long rope out of vines. And when this rope and bucket were ready, he lowered them into the well until they reached the waters far below, and when he had filled the gourd, he pulled it back up. When he tasted those waters this time, they seemed even more delicious, since he had made such great efforts to obtain them.

Invigorated once more, Alexander turned his thoughts back to the quest that had brought him there in the first place—the Waters of Eternal Life. For although the waters of this well were surely wonderful, he was seeking the even more wonderful waters that provided not only vigor, but also eternal life. He recalled the oracle of the Speaking Tree, which had guided him to continue on the same path. Yet what path was it, since he had travelled on so many? While Alexander was considering this matter he happened to notice that the light cast from the glowing pearl in his hand seemed to form a path before him. It was a miracle, Alexander decided, and holding the pearl in front of him, he followed that path wherever it led.

In this way Alexander was led a great distance through the forest, and after he had travelled for many days and nights, sustained by the fruit that grew wild on those trees, Alexander came to a great gate. Before that gate shone a mighty light, like a small sun. Alexander was very curious to know what garden that was, and what was the source of that light. He hurried toward the gate, shielding his eyes from the light, and when he reached it and stood off to one side, he was able to see that the light was given off by a flaming sword being spun at amazing speed by a mighty angel stationed at the gate. And when Alexander saw such a gatekeeper, he knew that this must be the Garden of Eden, of which he had often heard. Inscribed on the gate of the Garden, which arched above the angel, letters were engraved, which read:

> Lift up your head, O ye gates, and be elevated, ye gates of the world.
> For this is the gate of the Lord, through which the righteous shall enter.

Alexander gazed in amazement at the angel with the spinning sword of fire, and he wondered if it had been placed there to guard the way to the Waters of Eternal Life. Alexander decided that he must find a way to enter that Garden, although it appeared to be impossible. Then Alexander explored the wall of the Garden, which rose up to such a great height that he could not see the top of it. It seemed to be circular, and great trees grew around it, with their tops reaching into heaven.

Alexander studied that wall and decided that the only way to climb it would be by climbing one of those immense trees. Therefore he sought out a branch within his reach and pulled himself up, for he had climbed many trees when he was a boy, though none were of such a great height. At the end of the first day of climbing, Alexander still had not climbed the first third of the tree. He had to climb another full day to reach the second third. And only after the third day of climbing did he reach the top of that tree and look down from that dizzying height at the world below.

But now, for the first time, he could see the top of that high wall, which was within his reach. So it was that Alexander very carefully climbed from the top of that mighty tree onto the high wall. And when he looked down, he saw the most splendid sight of his life—a Garden that looked like a paradise, perfect in its abundance, with four rivers branching from a spring that flowed forth from a mighty tree in the center of the garden, its top branches reaching into the palaces of heaven. Alexander then knew for certain that he had reached the fabled Garden of Eden, and he sensed at once that the Waters of Eternal Life could not be found anywhere else; perhaps they were the very waters flowing from the roots of that wondrous tree.

Alexander then decided to climb down into the garden, and by holding on to the thick vines that grew against the inside of the wall, Alexander was able to descend to the world below. Climbing down went much faster than climbing up, and before long Alexander found himself on the ground once again. Then he hurried over to one of the rivers that flowed nearby. He was filled with curiosity to know if these were indeed the waters he had sought so long. But how was he to find out? Suddenly an idea occurred to him. He opened up his pack, in which he carried his provisions, and he took out a salted fish. He quickly tossed that fish into those waters, and instantly it came to life and swam away, its tail swishing back and forth. Alexander rejoiced to know that he had finally reached the precious waters. Now he would be able to obtain eternal life.

Alexander leaned over and filled his cupped hands with water and was just about to drink when a solemn voice said, "Wait! Before you drink of those waters, do you not want to know the consequences?" Then Alexander looked up and saw a radiant being standing before him, like the one at the gate of the Garden, and he knew it must be an angel. Alexander was filled with awe. The eyes of that angel cast an aura, and when Alexander felt that light upon himself, he felt the presence of the angel all around him, and knew its sacred purpose. Alexander said simply, "Yes, please tell me." Then the angel Raziel—for that is who it was—said to Alexander, "Know, then, that whoever drinks these waters will know eternal life, but he will never be able to leave this garden."

These words greatly startled Alexander, for had the angel not stopped him, he would already have tasted of those waters and become a prisoner in that paradise. For a life of peace and meditation in that garden was not what Alexander wanted. Instead, he longed to explore every hidden corner of the world and to found a great city that would bear his name. Alexandria. At that moment Alexander understood that he could not drink those waters, for he preferred to live in the world of men, even if it meant giving up eternal life. All at once he found himself standing outside the Garden walls once again, not far from the angel that guarded the gates its flaming sword still spinning.

Then Alexander turned around, and much to his amazement, he saw the palace of Asmodeus before him. He could not understand how that was possible, and when he turned back to the Garden gate, he found that it was no longer there. Somehow he had returned to the palace of the king of demons, far away from the Garden in which he had stood just moments before. Alexander was very confused.

When Alexander stood before the king of demons once more, he asked how it was possible for the king's palace to be so near the Garden, he had travelled such a great distance from one to the other. Asmodeus replied, "In this kingdom, Alexander, distances are not what they seem. They are different for each man, according to his fate. When you set out on your quest, you had many trials and obstacles to overcome. But after your decision to give up the Waters of Eternal Life, even when they were in your grasp, your fate was changed, and the distance reduced itself to almost nothing. But I see that you have brought the glowing pearl with you. Know that at the very moment you picked it up from the bottom of the Well of Living Water, another such pearl appeared in my crown, glowing for all the world to see." And it was true—a pearl just like Alexander's glowed from the king of demons' crown Asmodeus continued, "The pearl in your possession, Alexander, is therefore your own. Let it lead you for the rest of your days and you will not go astray."

So it was that Alexander realized that his quest had not been in vain after all, for that glowing pearl was invaluable, since it would guide a man wherever it was that he had to go. Then Alexander thanked Asmodeus for helping him, and set out on his own with the light of the pearl leading the way. For it was time to return to the Mountains of Darkness, to meet his men, who were about to descend the final peak. And when they did, they found Alexander waiting there, though they had no idea of how far he had travelled since they had parted.

When they were reunited, Alexander told his men of his adventures, and showed them the glowing pearl. Now the men were astonished at this tale, but the thought of turning back when they had just crossed those mountains distressed them greatly. Then Alexander asked the glowing pearl to show them the shortest way across, and all at once it shone upon the entrance to a cave, which none of them had noticed before. They entered that cave, which the pearl illumined for them better than any torch, and before a day had passed they reached the other side of the Mountains of Darkness, simply crossing beneath them. After that they let the glowing pearl lead them wherever they needed to go, for it always led them to the right place. And so it was that although the life of Alexander was not long, as had been prophesied at his birth, his days were filled far more than those of most men, and his life was a rich one.

Italy: c. Eleventh Century

The Princess Who Became a Garland of Flowers

There once was a king who had an only daughter. When his daughter was quite young, his wife died and he remarried, for a king must not be without a wife. At first his new wife pretended to be kind to the king's daughter. But in time, when she had a daughter of her own, she started to behave in a hateful manner towards the princess. She made life hard for her in every way, until the girl could not bear it any longer. But the king knew nothing of any of this, for he was very busy with the matters of his kingdom.

At last the princess ran away from home. She left the city and walked and walked until, toward evening, she arrived at a pool of water surrounded by trees. Now the princess did not know it, but this was an enchanted pool. All kinds of miracles and strange occurances were said to have happened there: a sparrow that had dived into the pool was said to have emerged as an eagle; a donkey was said to have emerged as a stallion; and a frog from a nearby pond was said to have emerged as a horned owl. This was widely known in the town nearest that pool, but of course the princess knew nothing of it. She felt that she could not go any further, so she climbed up one of the trees there and slept in the branches.

The next morning the prince who lived in that city went riding on his white stallion, as he did every morning. He brought the horse to that pool to drink, but when he led the horse to the water, it caught a glimpse of the reflection of the princess, who was just waking up in the tree. This so frightened the horse that it reared backward. Every time the prince tried to persuade it to drink, the horse recoiled. So the prince got off his horse and pulled the reins, trying to bring the horse to the pool. It was then that he glimpsed the reflection of the princess in the tree. He was greatly astonished, stepped closer, and saw that the girl in the pool was very beautiful indeed. And just from looking at her reflection there, he fell in love with her at first sight.

The prince turned around with his heart in his mouth, afraid for a moment that the reflection might exist only in the water—for he had heard tales of beautiful demons who were said to make their home there. But when he saw that she was a real person, even more beautiful than her reflection, the prince stared in speechless amazement. At last he found his tongue and asked the beautiful girl if he might help her down, and she gladly took his hand and climbed down. When at last they stood face to face, the prince asked who she was and why she as sleeping there, but the truth is that it did not matter to him, so smitten with love was he. The princess told him of all that had happened to her ever since her father, the king had remarried. When the prince heard all the hateful things the stepmother had done, he agreed that the princess had had no choice but to flee. And he vowed that he would not only protect her from all harm, but that if she so wished, he would wed her as well. And the princess, who had fallen in love with the prince as much as he had with her, gladly agreed that she would become his bride.

The prince was filled with a soaring joy, for at last he had found the love of his life. He told the princess that his father and mother would gladly accept her and welcome her into their home. He took off a beautiful golden charm that he was wearing and placed it around her neck. And he told her that he would depart and come back soon with his family, so that they could greet her with proper honor. Then he galloped off back to the city, and the princess sat down on a rock overlooking the water.

Soon after the prince had left, a maid from the nearby town reached the pond, where she had been sent to fetch some water. Now the water of the pool was not often used for drinking, because of all the tales told about it. But since the nearby well had become muddy there had been no other choice but to make use of the pool.

It was a much further walk to reach the pool, and when the maid got there she was in a terrible mood. For this maid had a horrible disposition in the first place, and she was also very ugly— her cheeks were pock-marked, her eyes squinted, her hair was thin and her legs were crooked. Had this maid known how ugly she was, she would have been even nastier. But she did not know since there were no mirrors in the land. The maid came to the pool and leaned over to fill the urn, and when she caught sight of the princess's reflection, she thought it was her own. She said out loud: "If I am so beautiful, why must I serve others?" And she threw the urn down, so that it broke into many pieces, and she returned empty-handed.

When she was asked why she had not brought the water, the maid told them that the urn had broken. So they gave her an empty wine-skin and told her to fetch the water in it at once. She went back to the pool, but when she saw the reflection of the princess again, she tore the wine-skin to pieces, threw it away, and returned home. They asked her why she was empty-handed, and she said that a dog had attacked her and torn the wine-skin to pieces.

This time they gave the maid a brass pitcher and warned her not to return without it. But when she came to the pool and saw the reflection of the princess once more, she smashed the brass pitcher on a rock. The princess, who had observed all that had taken place, could not keep still any longer and called out, "Why do you break all the vessels? That's not your reflection you see in the water—it's mine." The maid was greatly startled when she heard this, and she turned around and saw the princess sitting on the rock overlooking the pool. Then she looked again into the water and saw, for the first time, her own reflection. And when she saw how ugly she was, she was filled with hatred for the beautiful maiden sitting on the rock nearby. And deep in her heart she vowed to destroy her.

Then the maid got up and sat down next to the princess. She stared at her beautiful gown, as well as at the diamonds and golden jewels she wore. Never before had she been in the presence of a princess, and she pretended to be friendly, even though she was gripped by a jealous rage. She asked the princess why she was sitting there, and the princess told her that she was waiting for the prince, who would shortly return. When she heard this, the heart of the maid was filled with even more hatred, and she vowed that it would be she, and not the princess, whom the prince would marry.

The maid told the princess that she had never seen such a beautiful dress before, and she asked to try it on, just to see what it was like. The princess, who was very generous, agreed to let her wear it for a moment, and took off the dress.

After the maid had put it on, she asked to borrow the precious pearl necklace of the princess, and the princess let her put it on as well.

After that the maid asked to try on the rings of the princess, who gave them to her.

After that she asked to try on her diamond earrings, and the princess took them off.

Finally when the maid was wearing everything that had belonged to the princess, she shoved her a little, and said: "Move over." The princess moved over on the rock. Then the maid shoved her a little more, and then a little more until finally she pushed the princess off the rock and into the enchanted pool. And no sooner did she touch the water, then she became a garland of the most beautiful flowers, which floated on the surface near the shore.

Just then the prince rode up, and when he approached the princess, he was staggered. For she was wearing the same gown, the same necklace and earrings, and ring, but she did not seem to be the same person at all. The prince stuttered, still in shock, and asked her, "What has become of your long, silken hair?" And she replied, "While I was waiting for you, crows pecked at my head and plucked out my hair." Then the prince asked, "Why are you squinting?" And she replied, "Because I stared into the sun searching for you to return." Then the prince asked, "Why is your skin so rough?" And she answered, "The branches scratched my face." Finally the prince asked, "Why are your legs crooked?" And she replied: "Because I ran after you but I couldn't catch you."

The poor prince found it hard to believe that this was the same girl whom he had promised to wed, but he was a man of his word, and he felt he had no choice but to take her with him. As he lifted her up on the horse, he looked down in the pool and saw the beautiful garland of flowers floating on the surface. Its beauty was the only reminder of the enchanting princess he had met in that place, and he reached down and picked it up and took it with him. He kept that garland in his room and cared for it himself, and he felt much happier in its presence than with the maid who pretended to be the princess.

The maid also saw how the prince loved that garland of flowers, and she was filled with jealousy and hatred. So one day, when the prince was not there, she crushed all the flowers. But the moment she did, the flowers turned into a piece of parchment. The maid was furious, for the parchment was too strong for her to crush or tear. So she took the skin and threw it into the fire. All the while it burned she laughed, nor did she stop until the fire had burned itself out.

When the prince returned, he went over to the fire to light it again, and in the ashes he found the parchment. Miraculously, it had not been damaged by the fire at all. Instead, the flames had inscribed a portrait on one side of the skin—the very portrait of the princess, exactly as the prince remembered her. And when the prince saw that wonderful portrait he suddenly realized that the true princess must have been enchanted and that the ugly one must be an imposter.

The prince turned with fury on the maid and accused her of casting a spell on the true princess. And when the maid saw the portrait, she was so terrified that she confessed in terror, and the prince had her cast into the dungeon and threw away the key. He then placed that portrait of his beloved in his room in a place of honor, and stared at it day after day, shedding many tears, and wishing he had taken her with him in the first place, and not left her behind.

About that time a strange thing happened. One of the servants of the prince came into his room to clean it, and found that it was already perfectly in order. The servant asked the prince about this, and the prince wondered who could have been in his room and cleaned it. This happened again the next day, and the next—and each time the servant reported this strange occurance to the prince. Finally the prince's curiousity was so great that one day he only pretended to leave, and hid outside the door of the room. He waited until he heard the sounds of someone moving about inside, and then he flung the door open. Lo and behold, there was the beautiful princess, a broom in her hand. For when the prince was not present, she was able to emerge from the portrait and enter his room. Knowing something about the way spells work, the prince dashed inside and snatched up the piece of empty parchment, rolled it up, and threw it into the fire. This time the parchment burned like a dry leaf, and was consumed in an instant. At the same time the spell was broken and the princess was freed from that portrait and restored to her own form for good, radiant and beautiful as ever. The prince and princess were overwhelmed with joy, and they embraced. Then the prince took her with him through the palace to tell the good news to his parents, the king and queen. Not long afterward they were wed, and the day of their wedding was the greatest celebration the people of that kingdom had ever known, and it is still observed as a joyful time to this very day.

Afghanistan: Oral Tradition

The Tale of the Magic Horse

In one of the cities of Afghanistan there was a poor rabbi who served as a *moyel* for the Jews of several nearby cities, where not many Jews were to be found. One day, as he traveled from one city to another, he reached a crossroad, just as it grew dark, and sat and rested under a tree. At the same time, two other men arrived at that crossroad from two different directions, who also decided to sleep there and continue in the morning. One of these was a carpenter and the other a shoemaker. The three of them gathered some wood, made a fire and cooked a modest meal, and afterward they went to sleep.

Now the rabbi and the shoemaker fell asleep right away, but the carpenter remained awake. So to pass the time he took a large piece of wood and began to carve a horse from it. He worked on the horse for hours until it was finished, and then he fell into a deep sleep. Soon afterward the shoemaker awoke, and when he saw the horse standing next to him he was frightened, but he soon discovered it was made of wood. The shoemaker was so charmed by the carpenter's creation that he took some leather and made some reins for the horse, and when he finished he went back to sleep.

So it was that at dawn, when the rabbi awoke to say his morning prayers, he discovered the wooden horse, complete with leather reins. It was so finely crafted that he thought it deserved to be alive, and so he wrote out an amulet containing holy names and put it inside the left ear of the horse. And lo and behold, at the very moment he did this the horse came to life, and started to move. Just then the others awoke and saw with amazement that the horse had come to life. Then the carpenter said, "The horse is mine because I carved it." And the shoemaker said, "The horse is mine because I made its reins." And the rabbi said to them, "You each contributed to its body, but it was I who caused the spirit to enter it and bring it to life. Therefore it is mine." Since they all recognized how precious that magic horse was, each argued that it was his. At last they agreed to go to the king of that city and to let him decide to whom the horse belonged.

Now when they reached the palace of the king, they brought the magic horse with them, and they were quickly given an audience with the king. They told the king their story, and the king was very surprised to see such a miraculous horse, constructed of wood and yet fully alive. The king's son, the prince, also listened to their tale with amazement and stared in awe at that enchanted horse, wondering if it were possible to ride on it. He asked this of the three men, and the rabbi told him that if the left ear of the horse were turned, the horse would move. Then the curious prince mounted the horse and turned the left ear, and all at once the magic horse rose up into the air, taking the prince along with him. Before anyone could stop it, the horse flew out of the window of the palace and disappeared on the horizon. When the king saw this, he called on his guards to try to bring him down. In the confusion that followed, the three creators of the magic horse realized their lives were in danger, so they ran away from there as fast as they could.

Meanwhile the poor prince found himself carried through the air at a great height, as the magic horse flew across the heavens. At first he only held on for his life, but after they had flown for a full day and crossed a great distance, he began to recover his wits, and wondered if there might be some way to make the horse descend. Then it occured to him that since he had turned the left ear to make the horse ascend, that perhaps turning the right would cause it to land. So he turned the right ear, and lo and behold the horse immediately flew down to earth.

Now it was night when the prince finally stood on land again, and from what little he could see it appeared that he had come to a very isolated place. Then he noticed a dim light in the distance. Leading the magic horse by its reins, he went in the direction of the light and soon found himself standing before a small wooden hut. The prince knocked on the door and an old woman opened it. He told her that he was a wanderer seeking shelter for the night. She welcomed him, saying, "Please come in, for a guest is a gift from God." Then he asked her if he might be permitted to bring in the horse as well, as it was his only possession. The old woman, who herself had very few possessions, understood his fear of losing it and agreed that he might keep it inside the house. Then she brought him a bowl of soup and pita bread and after he had eaten he thanked her for her hospitality and went to sleep.

In the morning the prince decided it would be best for him to stay there until he found out where he was and could figure out how to return to his own kingdom. He took a gold coin out of his pocket and gave it to the old woman and told her that it was hers to keep if she would permit him to remain there for a few days. This the woman gladly agreed to do, for she had never held a gold coin in her life. She soon left to go into town and buy food enough for them both.

That evening, as they sat down to have dinner, the old woman lit a candle. The prince said to her, "Now that you have enough money, why don't you buy a decent lamp, so that we won't have to sit in the darkness like this?" The old woman replied that the king had passed a decree that no one was allowed to have a lamp, since he had built a tall tower that cast a strong light which was supposed to illuminate the whole city. The prince wondered at such a strange decree, and said, "Where is this tower?" "Wait a little while," said the old woman, "for in a short time the light in the tower will be lit."

Before long, a strong light could be seen in the distance, and the old woman told the prince that this was the tower of which she had spoken. The prince was taken with a great curiosity to know more about it, so he mounted his magic horse, turned its left ear and flew directly to the tower, landing on its roof. There he left the horse, and climbing down from the roof he found himself outside of a window. And when he looked within he saw in the brilliantly lit room a beautiful girl who was sound asleep.

The prince quickly opened the window and climbed inside. When he saw the precious objects that filled that room—golden candlesticks, magnificent portraits and priceless antiques—he knew that this girl could be none other than a princess. Under her bed he noticed a pair of golden slippers, and on the table next to the bed there was a fine meal waiting. So the prince sat down on the edge of the bed, and without waking the princess, ate the meal. When he had finished, he took the candlesticks that were near her head and put them on the floor, and he took her golden slippers and put them near her head. So too did he change the order of the pictures and move other things around. At last he went to the girl and kissed her, and then climbed out of the window back onto the roof, where he mounted his magic horse and flew back to the home of the old woman.

When the princess awoke she reached for the candlesticks at the head of her bed. But instead she found her golden slippers. And when she looked where the slippers were supposed to be, she found the candlesticks. Confused, the princess sat up and looked around her room, and at first she thought she must still be dreaming. For everything had been moved around—and instead of rice and roast chicken, all she found was an empty plate. Who could have been there? Surely no servant would so jest with the king's daughter; he would soon enough lose his head! And how, she wondered, could anyone have gotten into the room in the first place? For her father had hidden her in that tower, away from everyone, for reasons she could not understand. The princess did not know what to do, but she decided to wait until morning before telling anyone what had happened, and so she went back to sleep.

In the morning, when the princess awoke, she remembered all that she had discovered that night, and saw that indeed there had been a visitor to her room in the tower. When she looked into the mirror, she saw the mark of the prince's lips on her cheek, for her skin was so delicate even the lightest touch would leave a mark. All day long she wondered who had been there. And since she detected whimsy, not malice, in the changes in her room, she decided to refrain from telling anyone about what had happened. Instead, she would stay awake all night to see if this visitor returned.

The prince did return to the tower that night, riding his magic horse. He left the horse on the roof as before. When the princess heard the sound on the roof she pretended to be asleep, but she secretly observed the prince as he repeated his jest, eating her food and moving the objects around in her room. She even kept her eyes closed when the prince tenderly kissed her goodbye, but by then she knew that she loved this man, whoever he was, and that her life would never be the same.

On the third night, the prince again visited the room, and the princess again pretended to be asleep. But this time the prince left a letter in which he revealed his identity and confessed his love. He asked her to remain awake the next evening. The princess read the letter over and over and held it to her heart.

In the evening the prince arrived and saw that the princess was awake, anxiously waiting for him. The moment he saw her sitting there, he knew a sense of happiness greater than he had ever known. That night the prince and the princess spent the whole night talking, telling each other of their lives. Thus the prince revealed the strange manner of his arrival, on the flying wooden horse, and the princess told him of her father's strange decision to lock her up in that tower, away from all the world. Before he left that night the prince and princess exchanged a long and tender kiss, and the prince promised to return the next night.

So it was that the prince continued to spend his days sleeping in the old woman's hut and visiting the princess every night. In the course of time the princess discovered that she was with child. She concealed this for as long as possible, but as it became more evident, she became afraid that her father, the king, would find out about the nightly visits of the prince and that his life—and even her own—could be in danger. She told the prince of these fears and they decided that they would escape together that night rather than risk losing their lives.

So the prince had the princess mount behind him on the magic horse, and they flew off together, crossing a vast desert. But while they were in flight the princess felt the first pangs of birth, and told the prince to descend at once. This he did, and before very long the princess gave birth to a beautiful son, whom the prince delivered. The child resembled him as do two drops of water.

Now the prince knew that he could not move the princess and the child so soon after she had given birth, and that he must get food and water for them. So he left them in the shade beneath a tree, mounted the magic horse and set off to find the nearest town. When he reached it in but a few hours time, because of the swift flight of the magic horse, he purchased everything that he needed. He also took along a torch, so that he might make a campfire in the desert for the princess and their child.

Now as fate would have it, as the prince stop the wooden horse flew across the sky, a spark of the flames of the torch was carried by the wind to the amulet in the left ear of the magic horse. The amulet caught fire and began to burn. As it was burning, the horse began to descend in the desert, far away from where the princess and their child awaited him. And by the time the horse reached the ground all its magic was gone and the poor prince found himself stranded in the middle of the desert. There was little else to do but begin wandering in the hope that he might someday find the love of his life and his newborn child.

Meanwhile, the princess waited in the desert alone with her child for the whole day, and still the prince did not come back. She could not understand this, but she was not too worried because the prince had left her with what little food they had, and she was able to feed the baby with her own milk. But when he did not come back on the second day, nor on the third, she began to fear that something terrible had happened, and that she might be stranded there and in grave danger.

Then it happened on the seventh day, when the supplies of the princess were about to be used up, that a caravan passed near her, and when they saw her they came her way. The princess threw herself at the feet of the leader of the caravan and begged to go with them wherever they were going. Now the leader of that caravan was a pious and generous man, and when he saw the plight of the princess and her child he told her that he would take her in like his own daughter, and the baby like his grandson. So it was that the days of the princess passed in the shelter of his kindness, although she could never forget the prince she had loved so much.

Now the pious man not only cared for the princess, he also taught the child to read and write and saw to it that he was well educated in every way. By the time the boy had reached the age of fifteen he was handsome and kind. One day, though, this boy was teased by the other children, who said that he had no father. Now he had always assumed that the man who took care of them was his father, and he asked his mother about this. She told him that the kind man was his grandfather, and then, for the first time, she told her son the full story of his birth, and how she had met and lost his father, the prince.

The young man heard this tale with awe, and was filled with a great longing to know his true father. But his mother explained that she had not heard from the prince in all the years since the boy had been born, and had no idea where he was to be found, or even if he was still alive. Then the boy asked her if there were any signs by which he could be known, and the princess told him yes, there were two: there was a dark spot on his left ear and a scar on his right shoulder.

Now the more the young man thought over the story of how his mother and father had been separated, the more he wondered if the prince might not have become a wanderer in the desert. So he made it known that any wanderer who arrived in town would be welcome in their home. He saw to it that their servants gave these wanderers a bath, and told them to look for the two marks of his father, the prince.

Now many wanderers passed through that charitable house, and they all were grateful for the kind treatment. One day a man arrived whose clothes were decayed and torn, his hair uncut and his nails long. He came to the house of the young man because he had heard he would receive a little bread there. But when the servants bathed him, they discovered the two marks and quickly told the young man about them. Then the boy arrived and invited the man to join him and his mother for the evening meal. But when he offered the man roast chicken and rice (the meal his mother had so often eaten in her high tower) the man refused it, saying that he would prefer to eat bread. The boy asked him why this was, and the man started to cry. But then he stopped himself and said, "There is no point in my telling you, because it just throws salt on my wounds." The boy begged him to tell his story, and finally he did. And so it was that the boy heard from his father's lips the miraculous tale he had already heard from his mother, who listened with amazement, and sought to recognize the prince in the grim man who told this sad tale.

Then, when the prince had revealed his broken heart, the boy revealed who they were, and that his long quest had at last been completed. At first the prince refused to believe them, but when the princess added details of the story he had not mentioned—how the magic horse had ascended when its left ear was turned, and descended when its right ear was turned—the prince realized that it was true and that his long wanderings had at last come to an end. Then the prince embraced his wife and son and almost fainted out of sheer joy and relief. It took many weeks before he fully recovered from his long and tortuous quest to find them, but little by little he regained his strength. And when he was well again, he decided they should journey to each of their parents' kingdoms to let them know of their fates.

Now the kind man who had sheltered the princess and her son all those years shared in the joy of the reunited family, and led the caravans that travelled to both kingdoms. There it had long been assumed that the prince and princess were dead, so of course their families were filled with joy to discover that they were alive. Their wedding was twice celebrated, and there was great rejoicing in both lands, and the prince and princess knew happiness at last. So too did their son discover what it meant to be a prince, one of the wealthiest in the world, and the heir to two kingdoms. And the day came when he ruled both with wisdom, and joined them into one mighty land.

Afghanistan: Oral Tradition

The Enchanted Well

Long ago there lived in Jerusalem a handsome young man who had studied not only the sacred texts, but also all of the sciences and other fields of learning. But there was one realm he had not been able to explore, and that was the study of sorcery and other kinds of magic. Now at that time the greatest magicians and sorcerers in the world were to be found in Egypt, so that is where this young man decided to go.

Not wishing to journey to Egypt on his own, this young man joined a caravan that was setting out for the city of Cairo. In that caravan was a merchant with whom the young man conversed. This merchant had been to every corner of the world, and he had seen and done a great many things. When they had become friends, the young man confided his desire to learn of the magical arts. The merchant then told him the name of a certain sorcerer who lived in Cairo and the quarter of the city in which he could be found.

So it was that soon after the young man reached Cairo he found a man by that name, living exactly where the merchant had told him to look. But the young man was very disappointed to find that he did not appear to be as wealthy and powerful as he had expected. Instead he lived in a modest house, where few books were to be seen. The young man suspected that the merchant had mocked his desire to explore magic by sending him to a very ordinary man. Still, he did not want to leave without finding out if the man was a sorcerer or not.

So the young man introduced himself, and told the man of the merchant's advice that he seek him out. When the man asked what it was that he wanted, the young man told him that he sought to study with a magician, a sorcerer, or a wizard, if one could be found. The man replied that the merchant of whom he spoke was one of his closest friends, and since he had sent the young man, he would be willing to accept him as an apprentice, for he was indeed a sorcerer, well versed in the magical arts.

Now even when he heard this, the young man did not believe it. He still worried that the merchant had decided to trick him, and had told the man to pretend that he was a sorcerer. The young man fumbled a bit and then said that he was actually seeking someone as young as himself to study with. The sorcerer recognized that the young man doubted his powers, so he decided to show the young man some of his magic. And he said, "Certainly, my good sir. I can understand your desire to study with one your own age. Rest here for the evening, and tomorrow I will introduce you to someone young who is already a master of the magical arts. Surely he will be more than happy to accept you as his apprentice."

The young man was quite relieved to hear this, and he hoped that the sorcerer he was to meet would be an authentic one. Meanwhile the young man sat down to eat at the sorcerer's table. The sorcerer poured wine for him from an old bottle, and told him it was of a rare and precious vintage. The young man took one drink of the wine, and found that it was truly the best he had ever tasted. Just then there was a knock at the door, and the sorcerer, who was busy preparing the meal for his guest, asked the young man if he might open it. The young man stood up and walked across the room to the door, but on the way there he suddenly saw a well in the middle of the floor. He had not noticed it there

/151/

before, but the discovery came too late. All at once he found himself tumbling down inside it. This was no ordinary well, though, for he fell for the longest time, confused and gripped by terror. It seemed like hours before he at last plunged deeply into water, sinking down, down . . . for the well seemed to have no bottom. Just as he was beginning to run out of breath, he started to float upward, and so he swam toward the surface as fast as he could.

When his head emerged from beneath the water, the young man found that he was no longer in a well, but in a quickly moving river. He swam in that direction across the current, and since he was a fine swimmer, he managed to reach land. There he found a beautiful garden, filled with a multitude of trees of every kind, including date trees and fig trees on which the fruit grew beautiful and ripe. The young man was amazed to find himself in that paradise and realized that he was very hungry. He plucked some dates and figs and ate them, and they were the most delicious he had ever tasted.

His strength restored, the young man decided to explore the garden. He found that it was vast, and that the trees had all been planted in the form of a labyrinth. He soon realized that he had walked so far into it that he did not know how to find his way back to the river. He was lost in that labyrinth for the longest time, but at last he reached a bridge at the end of the maze. Greatly relieved to have escaped, he hurried across the bridge in hope that he might meet some people who could help him find his way back to Jerusalem.

Beyond the bridge there was a road, and the young man followed it until he reached a splendid city. In the center of the city was a market crowded with merchants and customers bidding for their wares. When the young man came closer, he saw that this was a market for jewels and precious gems and wonderful paintings and vases and other precious objects. From these riches, he surmised that he had reached a wealthy kingdom, whose inhabitants had cultivated the finest arts.

In that marketplace there were also the public scribes, who wrote out letters and documents for the people. Now all of the scribes were busy at work except for one, so the young man went over and greeted him. The scribe asked how he could be of assistance, and the young man told him that he wished to send a letter to his family far away. The scribe asked him what city the letter was to be sent to, and the young man told him Jerusalem. At this the scribe seemed quite confused. He turned to a nearby scribe and said, "Look, here is a traveller from a distant land. He says that he is from the city of Jerusalem. Have you ever heard of such a city?" The other scribe shook his head that he had not, and went on with his work. The young man was amazed at this, for who in the world had not heard of the glories of Jerusalem? And he wondered what land he had come to, that was so far from the Holy Land that its inhabitants did not even know it existed.

The scribe asked the young man if he still wanted him to write the letter, and the young man confessed that he knew how to write, but was actually seeking to know about the land that he had reached, and how he might find his way back home. The scribe wished to see his writing, so the young man wrote down a few words, and the scribe marveled at the young man's beautiful script. He showed it to the other scribes, each of whom expressed admiration. And all the scribes agreed that one with such a fine script should serve in the royal court.

So it was that the young man was brought before the king. The scribes spoke of him most highly, and the king too was greatly impressed with the young man's script. Without hesitation he offered to let him serve as chief of the palace scribes. The young man had not expected this, but he realized that he could not reject the king's offer, so he agreed to serve as his scribe.

As time passed, the young man came to realize that he had been very fortunate in receiving such a high position immediately upon entering that foreign land. So too did his relationship with the king deepen, until he became one of the king's confidents, and in time he was also appointed chief of the king's counselors. Yet the young man was never happy with his good fortune, for he was determined to return home, though no one there could tell him which way to go.

At last the young man found an opportunity to reveal his

intentions to the king, but the king was very sorry to hear that the young man desired to depart, for he had become very attached to him. He begged him to put off his departure for a year, and the young man agreed to do this.

A year passed and again the young man asked the king about leaving. Now the king had hoped that the young man would abandon this notion, but when he saw that he had not, he offered to let the young man marry his only daughter, so that one day he would inherit the throne. The young man was startled and overwhelmed by this unexpected offer, but he soon realized that it was a truly wonderful turn of events. Besides, the king would not like being turned down, since he had offered him his beloved daughter. So the young man agreed to the betrothal, and in a short time the joyous wedding took place, to which all of the inhabitants of that kingdom were invited.

After the wedding, the young man soon discovered that he loved the beautiful princess, and for the first time he was grateful for the strange twists of fate that had brought him to that land. In a few short years the young man became the father of a son whom he adored. Thus the young man's life in that kingdom prospered, and he was prepared for the role of succeeding the king.

Then one day a terrible thing happened. As the young man was playing in the palace garden with his son, the boy ran to the side of the well in the garden, leaned over, and fell in. His cries caused the young man to come running, and without thinking he jumped in after his son, determined to save him at any cost. But instead of falling into the water, the young man continued to fall through that well as if it were bottomless. Nor was there any sign of his son. He could not understand what was happening, and he was filled with fear and confusion. After a long time he struck the surface of the water and sank below, and when he managed to return to the surface for air, he found himself in the home of the sorcerer in Cairo. He climbed out of the well and looked about bewildered. The sorcerer, who seemed to be expecting him, said, "Well, have you learned anything of the magical arts?"

At that moment, all the young man knew was that his son had fallen into the well, and he began to weep and lament over his loss. Then the sorcerer said, "Do you not understand anything at all? Your son and everything else you experienced in that kingdom was but an illusion." The young man protested that he had been the chief counselor of the realm, he had married the king's daughter and was in line to succeed to the throne. He related everything that had happened to him since he had arrived in that land. But the sorcerer insisted that it all had occurred in only an instant, brought about by the potion that the sorcerer had given him to drink. The young man still found it hard to believe it had only been a mirage, and he looked for the well in the floor, but there was none. Then the young man finally realized that what the sorcerer had said was true, and that he was a powerful conjurer indeed.

After he had recovered from that ordeal, the young man asked the sorcerer if he might study with him after all, and the sorcerer agreed to teach him the secrets and mysteries of the magical arts. So it was that the young man became his apprentice, and delved into these mysteries for many years, until he himself became a renowned sorcerer whose mastery was recognized throughout the world.

Spain: Thirteenth Century

The Golden Amulet

Joseph, our righteous ancestor, was his father's favorite, as his brothers well knew. But when Jacob gave Joseph the splendid coat-of-many-colors, the envy of his brothers waxed hot, until they were ready to slay him. But Reuben, the oldest brother, told the others not to slay him, but instead to take him out into the wilderness and cast him into a pit. This the brothers did, abandoning him there, certain that he would never escape.

There, in that pit, the world went dark for Joseph, as dark as the darkness into which he had been cast. That was Joseph's bleakest moment, and out of grief and anger at his betrayal, he suddenly began to dig like a madman into the bottom of that pit, as if in that way he might somehow escape it. And after Joseph had dug in this fashion for some time, he suddenly struck something hard, something that was buried there. His curiosity was awakened, and he dug even faster to discover what it was.

All at once bright rays of light shot out of the bottom of the pit, startling Joseph and filling the world around him with light. And when his eyes had grown accustomed to the sudden light, Joseph saw that he had uncovered a glowing stone in the bottom of that pit, and what is more, he saw that there were words inscribed on it. Then with a curiosity greater than any he had ever known, Joseph pushed away the dirt on all sides, until he had fully revealed the writing on that glowing stone. At first the words were blurred in the light, but when he focused on them word by word, he was able to make them out.

Joseph rejoiced when he saw that the words were written in Hebrew. But the first words he read there warned him not to lift up that stone, nor to try to take it from that place. Then Joseph grew afraid, and recognized that he was in some kind of sacred place. For he soon learned that the stone was none other than the Foundation Stone, which held back the waters of the Abyss. So too was it the stone that Jacob had slept on as a pillow when he had dreamed the dream about the ladder reaching to heaven, with angels upon it. And after Jacob had departed from that place, which he named Beth El, the stone had sunk deep into the earth, in the place where Joseph had found it. And among the secrets that were revealed to him, Joseph learned that someday that stone would serve as the cornerstone of the Temple in Jerusalem. And he read as well that anyone who discovered that stone might read in it his true destiny, that which is hidden from all others. And Joseph, still deeply grieved by his brothers' betrayal, was suddenly filled with great hope as he read all that was written there for him. For there he read his fate in the Book of Life, which the Foundation Stone reflected as if it were a mirror.

Thus did Joseph discover his true destiny, with all its abundance—except the name of the woman he was destined to wed. So too did he read there the secret of how to escape from that pit. For it was Joseph alone who freed himself from that place, without the help of any others—that is why Reuben could not find him when he came to take him from the pit. But the secret of how Joseph escaped has long been lost. And by so escaping the dark pit, Joseph came into the possession of his new powers, which had not been revealed to him until that time. These included the ability to interpret dreams, and to rule with wisdom. And in this way Joseph was able to follow the path of his fate without straying from it, and thus he was one of the few who ever fulfilled his true destiny. For the Holy Spirit rested upon Joseph and led him in all matters of wisdom like a shepherd leads his flock.

Later, when Joseph was cast into the dungeon in Egypt, he never lost faith for a moment, for he knew that he had but to follow the path of his destiny and he would reach his true destination. Likewise, when he reached the pinacle of power in Egypt, second only to Pharoah, he never forgot what it had been like in the dungeon and the pit. Thus he never abused his power, and he became beloved of all.

Now Dinah, the daughter of Jacob and the sister of Joseph, was with child. In this way did it come to pass: Dinah was one to stay in her tent, out of modesty, and was rarely seen outside it. Still, the reports of her beauty were legendary, and Shechem, the son of Hamor the Hitite, longed to see her for himself. So he brought dancing girls who played on pipes to pass near her tent. Dinah heard the music and went out of the tent to watch the dancers, and when Shechem saw her astonishing beauty, he was overcome with a desire to take her for his own. He seized her, and violated her innocence—and thus had she conceived. Now this was a great tragedy in the family of Jacob. The tribes of Israel were up in arms because of this unborn child. They wanted to cast the child into a pit and abandon it, and Jacob worried greatly over the child's safety. After all, it was still the child of his daughter, and he wanted no harm to befall it.

When Jacob saw that his attempts to protect the child might prove futile, he made a golden amulet for her. He hammered it out himself and inscribed on it the Name of God, followed by these words: "Let all who read these words know that the bearer of this amulet is the child of Dinah, daughter of Jacob, also known as Israel. Know too that this child bears the blessing and protection of the House of Jacob and of the Lord God as well. Whosoever joins himself to this child joins himself unto the seed of Jacob."

Jacob then gave the amulet to Dinah, and when the day approached on which Dinah was to give birth, she went out into the wilderness with Jacob's maidservant, Serah, who had served as midwife at the birth of all his offspring. Before they departed, Jacob bid Serah to guard Dinah, and see to it that she was cared for when she gave birth. And he told Serah to take the child to a place of safety, so that no vengeance might be taken upon it for the sin of its father.

One night soon after, alone in the wilderness, with only the light of the moon to guide her, Serah delivered Dinah's child, a girl. They were much amazed when the infant's face gave forth a strange, ghostly light, like an aura. And both Dinah and the midwife knew at once that the child bore a great blessing. Then Dinah did not hesitate, but placed the gold amulet her father had given her around the infant's neck.

They remained there for seven days, and Dinah nursed the child with love and affection. On the seventh day, however, an eagle of great size suddenly swooped down where the child lay in a basket, and carried both child and basket aloft. Now the eagle's nest was in Egypt, where it received sustenance from the sacrifices given to the Egyptian god On. The eagle flew with the child in the basket to the altar, where its food was placed by the priest Potiphar every day. And when Potiphar came to offer sacrifices the next day, he found the infant there, in the basket next to the altar, protected by the outspread wings of the eagle. Much amazed, Potiphar assumed that the child had been sent by the god On, whose altar it was, and soon the news spread of this miracle. Potiphar and his wife adopted the child and secured a nurse for her, and both rejoiced exceedingly, for they were childless. They named her Asenath, and treated her like a princess, although this meant keeping her apart from everyone else.

When Asenath grew older she did not resemble the daughters of the Egyptians, but she was like the daughters of the Hebrews in all respects. She was tall like Sarah, charming like Rebecca, and beautiful like Rachel. Many suitors sought her hand, but Potiphar never permitted them to even meet her. Instead he had a magnificent palace built for her, where she remained alone in a chamber in the tower, attended by seven maidens, who dwelt in the other chambers of that lofty place. And among the people of Egypt as well as the Pharoah's court she was regarded with awe, as if she were indeed the daughter of a god. But Asenath herself was very lonely, for she could not bear her extreme seclusion.

From that lonely tower Asenath observed the world. So it was that she noticed Joseph's chariot passing through the streets, and the women of Egypt, including the daughters of princes, climbing to the top of the walls and the towers to watch him. And as he would ride by they would throw necklaces, rings and bracelets in his direction, hoping he would raise his eyes and look at them, if only for an instant. Joseph, however, spurned their gifts, ever mindful of the commands of his father. And from her tower window Asenath watched for Joseph to pass, for he had also stirred the longing in her heart as had no other.

During that time Joseph had a long and vivid dream. In the dream he found himself alone in a tent with his father, Jacob. Jacob motioned for Joseph to follow him, and let him out of the tent into the surrounding wilderness. At last he led him to a cave, hidden behind a bush. Lighting a torch, Jacob led Joseph into that cave and through its narrow passages. At last they reached a hidden passage, and there Jacob reached into a crevice and took out an object—a small wooden box with four candles on it, one in each corner. In the dream Jacob handed the box to Joseph, making it clear to him that it was precious.

Joseph held the box close to him as they departed from the cave, and when they stood once more in the sun, he opened it. And as soon as he did, a bright light shone from within, and Joseph saw that there was a golden object inside. He picked it up and saw that it was a key—a golden key. Then he looked closer, and saw that something had been inscribed on the key. He tried to read the words, but he could not. Just then Joseph looked up in the dream, and saw that Jacob was no longer there—he was alone. In confusion Joseph looked down again at the key, and found that it now was the shape of a golden branch, as if it had grown on a golden tree. So too were words inscribed there, and this time when Joseph looked closely at them, he saw to his delight that they were written in Hebrew.

Once more Joseph looked up, to see if his father had returned, but he had not. Then Joseph looked back at the branch to read it, and he saw to his amazement that it had changed its appearance once more, this time resembling an amulet, hammered out of the purest gold. Joseph contained his amazement and read the words written there, and learned that forty days before he had been born a voice had gone forth which had announced the name of his beloved. But when Joseph tried to read the name that was written there, he could not, for it was blurred. Just then Joseph woke up, with the dream still vivid in his memory. And he wondered greatly about it.

Meanwhile, one day, Asenath, whose love for Joseph had grown so great that it possessed her, impulsively took off her golden amulet and threw it from the window of the tower, so that it landed at Joseph's feet. Now that was the amulet she had been wearing when she had been discovered on the alter of On. No one knew what was written there, for it was inscribed in Hebrew; yet even so, it was her most precious possession. And now it lay at Joseph's feet.

When Joseph first saw the glittering object, he thought it to be another necklace or braclet. But when he saw that it was an amulet, he suddenly recalled his dream, and his heart began to beat rapidly. He looked up, to see if the amulet had fallen from heaven, and caught a glimpse of Asenath, peering out of her window, as she pretended to turn her gaze away. And even before he read the amulet, Joseph knew with an inner certainty that it must have been she whose name had been sung out in heaven along with his own. And when he picked up the amulet, and discovered that its owner was none other than the daughter of his sister, Dinah, he gave thanks to the Lord for blessing him in this way.

By making inquiries, Joseph soon discovered that the girl in the tower was none other than Asenath, adopted daughter of Potiphar; and so too did he learn of the miraculous manner in which she had reached them. Now Joseph had already been a slave in Egypt when Dinah had given birth, and since he had been separated from his brothers for so long, he did not even know that the child had been born. Nor did he know the sorry history of her birth. All he knew was that this was the first contact he had had with any member of his family in eighteen years, even if Asenath did not know who he really was.

And Joseph told Potiphar that he wished to have an audience with his daughter, and had her brought down from the tower. And when they stood face to face, Joseph took out the amulet and held it out to her. But Asenath said that it belonged to him, and Joseph then asked her if she knew what it said. He was most amazed when she said no, and he understood that she knew nothing at all of her true family. It was then that Joseph revealed himself as her kinsman.

Then Joseph asked for the hand of Asenath, and Potiphar gladly gave his approval. Before the year was out their marriage was celebrated, and Joseph was united with one of his kinsman, as had been Abraham to Sarah, Isaac to Rebecca, and his father Jacob to his mother Rachel. And in this way Asenath was re-united with the seed of Jacob from which fate had torn her. For when Jacob came down to Egypt with his family, Dinah came as well, and when Joseph finally told her of the manner in which the infant Asenath had come to the house of Potiphar, and showed her the swaddling-clothes in which she had been found, Dinah realized that Asenath was her long-lost daughter, and mother and daughter were reunited at last. Nor did they suffer the pain of separation again for the rest of their lives.

Palestine: c. Eighth Century

David's Harp

Now King David had a wondrous, magic harp, which he hung by the window of his bedroom chamber. And at midnight the North wind came and blew across its strings, and made wonderful music. That music gently woke King David and called him to take up his pen, and he wrote the psalms in a trance. The words rose up from within him effortlessly, and the Holy Spirit spoke through him as if he himself were a kind of harp. That is how the Psalms came to be written.

Nor was this the only blessing brought by this magic harp. For the notes plucked by the fingers of the wind also carried King David into the future, even beyond the time of his death, so that he had a vision of the Temple in Jerusalem that his son Solomon would build in the days to come. But so too did he have a vision of the future days in which the Temple would be destroyed, and the people of Israel would be driven into exile to Babylon. That is when David wrote the words of this psalm:

> By the rivers of Babylon,
> there we sat down, yea, we wept,
> when we remembered Zion.

We hung our harps upon the willows in the midst thereof.
For they that carried us away captive
required of us a song,
and they that wasted us
required of us mirth, saying
sing us one of the songs of Zion.

How shall we sing the Lord's song
in a strange land?

Thus the day arrived when the bleak exile of David's vision took place: the walls of the Temple were torn down and the people were driven into exile. It was a bitter time indeed. Yet the day also came when the Jews returned to the Holy Land and set about rebuilding Jerusalem. In those days there lived in Jerusalem an old man whose name was Shabbatai. And this old man had thought long and hard about the wonders of David's harp, for he himself was a maker of lutes and harps. Every time he carved and strung another harp, Shabbatai thought of the harp of David and wondered what had been its fate. For he knew well the tales of its wondrous ways, and the legend that its strings were made from the sinews of the ram which Abraham sacrificed instead of Isaac at Mount Moriah. The thought possessed him that if that harp could be found, perhaps the Holy Spirit could once again emerge and bless Jerusalem as it had in the days of King David.

But where could David's harp be found? It had disappeared at the time of the Babylonian exile. And the more the old man thought about this, the more certain he became that King David's harp had surely been among those hung in the willow trees in Babylon. For the people had no doubt recognized that David's prophecy in the psalm had come true, and to honor the prophecy they surely must have hung David's harp among their own.

In this way, the notion of searching for David's harp in the willow trees by the rivers of Babylon took root in the old man's mind. He shared this thought with everyone he knew, but they all thought he had taken leave of his senses. Eventually the longing to search for the wondrous harp overwhelmed Shabbatai, and he decided to undertake the journey to Babylon no matter what the obstacles, and he made preparations for the journey.

His wife and children tried to convince him to abandon the mad notion that Kind David's harp could still be found. Besides, he was an old man, how could he complete such a journey? But every night, Shabbatai dreamed he glimpsed David's golden harp hung in the branches of a willow, just beyond his reach. So one day he simply set out with no more than a waterbag, a pouch filled with dates and figs, and a staff which he had carved himself.

Now it was a terrible wilderness the old man had to cross, and his journey was as difficult as that of the Children of Israel in their desert wanderings. Yet Shabbatai felt as if he were guided by the distant strains of David's harp, calling to him as it had to King David at midnight. In this way he was inspired to overcome every obstacle, and managed to cross mountains and valleys, rivers and streams, and the desert wilderness that seemed to stretch before him endlessly.

This great effort took its toll on the old man, and left him worn and frail by the time he finally reached Babylon. There he searched along the shores of every river for the willow trees in which the harps might be hung. He looked among the branches of many a willow tree, but not one of them contained even a single harp. Yet, only when he was certain that he had searched beside every river in Babylon did Shabbatai become discouraged, and begin to fear that he had failed in his quest.

With no one to turn to for help, the old man sought out the burial place of the righteous sages who had died in that land of exile, and he called upon the dead to come to him and reveal where the harp could be found. For a long time Shabbatai prayed before the tombs, but all he heard was the whispering of the wind.

Then, all at once, Shabbatai saw a shadow cast from behind him, and when he turned around he saw an old man standing there who did not have the appearance of one of the living, but of one who had come from the Other World to greet him. The ghost-like figure spoke and said, "What is it that you wish to know?" Shabbatai poured out his heart and pleaded to be guided to the willow tree in which King David's harp could be found.

When the ancient sage heard this, he said, "You are right to search for David's harp, but you are looking in the wrong place. For the psalm does not say that the harps were hung in Babylon, but in the willows of Zion, for the people hung them there before they departed, knowing from the first they could never sing the songs of the Lord in a strange land. It is in Zion that the harp can be found. Not in the land of our exile." Then this the ghostly figure began to fade from view until he vanished from before Shabbatai's eyes. And although he had not dared to ask, Shabbatai was certain that the sage could have been none other than King David himself, who had come there to guide him. So that day he started back to the Holy Land. He was not discouraged that he had come all that distance in vain, because at the end of that journey he had learned a valuable secret. And the hope of finding David's harp still inspired him and served as his guide.

So it was that the long journey back to the Holy Land seemed but a moment to the old man, who once again heard the distant calling of David's harp. And as he approached the boundaries of the Land of Israel, it seemed to Shabbatai that he could see a divine presence hovering above the trees and flowers, and he realized that the Holy Land had lost none of its holiness since the time of King David, but that it had been hidden from his sight and that of the other inhabitants. Now it had been revealed to Shabbatai's eyes at last.

The old man's family was so overjoyed to see him again that they did not even ask about his mission, they just assumed he had failed. Nor did Shabbatai reveal all that had happened to him, for he had decided to say nothing about it until he had succeeded in finding the harp.

But where was Shabbatai to seek the harp in the Holy Land? He could not look to the rivers of Babylon to lead him to the willows; in the Holy Land willow trees grew everywhere. Where was his search to begin? Shabbatai considered this question for the longest time, and one day the answer dawned on him as a great revelation. He took leave of his astonished family and set out once again, this time for Mount Zion. For although all of the Holy

Land is called Zion, there is one specific mountain that bears that name.

When he reached Mount Zion, old Shabbatai found that he was able to climb it as if he were a young man, so inspired was he there. He searched the mountain until he was familiar with every willow tree, but he did not find a single harp. This was more than the old man could bear. He had been so certain this time. He sat down in despair and put his head in his hands, and in that moment his heart almost broke. But just then distant strains of a music more beautiful than anything he had ever heard reached his ears. And all at once a sense of peace came over the old man.

Then he arose like one in a trance and followed the music. When he turned in the right direction, the music seemed to grow louder, and when he turned the wrong way it grew dim. In this way Shabbatai was led to a cave, whose entrance was hidden behind a willow tree. He entered the cave, and found it filled with a glowing light, and he passed through it, still led by the hypnotic strains of the wondrous music. At last he reached the other end of the cave and came out into a garden that seemed to be surrounded by an aura. He knew he had reached a very sacred place. When he looked up Shabbatai's breath was taken away—for there, in every tree, he saw a harp, its strings plucked by the wind. This was the unearthly music which had led him there. But most wonderful of all was a gleaming, golden object that Shabbatai saw in the upper branches of the finest willow tree of all, one which towered above all of the others. It was at that moment that the old man completed his quest, for he had found the harp of David he had sought for so long. He seated himself at the foot of that lofty willow, and listened to the very strains that had wakened King David himself on so many nights and inspired him to write the immortal psalms. And there, beneath that tree, the old man remained, and some say that he can be found there still, listening as the music of the Holy Spirit drifts across the Holy Land, far more beautiful than anyone can imagine.

Palestine: Nineteenth Century

The Eagle's Treasure

In one of the villages of India lived two brothers who were farmers. One of them succeeded in everything he did. His rice fields gave good harvests and his wheat barns were always full. But the second brother seemed to have no luck at all. The little rice that he and his family picked in the fields was not enough to sustain them, and sometimes there weren't even enough seeds left to plant for the season to come. To make matters worse, it was a year of drought and the harvest in the villages was very small.

The planting season arrived—all the farmers of the village started to prepare their land for the new seeding. So too did the poor brother prepare his land, in the hope that his neighbors would let him borrow seeds, which he would return after the harvest. But when he went to his nearest neighbor, he refused to lend him anything. He said he did not have enough seeds for himself.

So he went to a second neighbor, and that one also refused him. This neighbor said, "Why don't you go to your rich brother?

Why do you come to a poor man like me?" Sad and disappointed, the brother returned home and told his wife that the neighbors had refused him.

"They are right," said his wife. "Why don't you ask your brother? It's not that he couldn't help you if he wanted to. Isn't he the flesh of your flesh?" "But," mumbled the poor man, "he doesn't want to hear from me." "There is no other choice," said his wife. "You must go to your brother and tell him about our unbearable situation."

The man knew his wife was right, there really was no other choice. So the man went to his brother, who lived in a beautiful palace. When he arrived there, he found the gate locked. He stood and knocked on it, but no one came out to open it. At last one of the windows opened and the wife of his brother cried out, "Why are you knocking?" "I want to ask my brother to have pity on me and give me some rice seeds for planting," said the man. "For if I delay the time of the planting, there will be nothing to harvest this year, and we will not be able to live."

She said, "We know that you fail at everything you touch. You couldn't even save a little rice for planting, and now you come to bother us."

The poor brother wanted to speak but the words choked in his throat, and he remained silent.

Then the wife of his brother said, "Wait by the gate, you worthless beggar, and I will bring you some rice to plant." She closed the window, went to the kitchen and took some rice from the pot on the stove. She put it in a bag, and gave the cooked rice to her brother-in-law, knowing full well that it could not serve for planting.

The poor man did not check the seeds until he returned home, and when he discovered that the rice in the bag was soft and cooked, he was so downcast he felt his life had come to an end. But then he remembered his wife and children, who depended on him. He was ashamed to tell his wife how his sister-in-law had humiliated him, so he decided to go to the fields, and to plant the cooked rice as if it really would grow. He put his faith and hope in God to save them. But the rice that he planted did not grow, and the man was very disappointed. With nothing else to hope for, he had hoped for a miracle.

One day when he came to the field as usual, however, the poor brother noticed a very odd plant growing from the earth. He did not know what kind of plant it was, but his heart told him that this plant would somehow be his salvation. So he guarded that plant, the only one to grow, and did not tell anyone else about it. When the harvest time came, he took the scythe and went to the field. His wife looked forward to a big harvest that year, for it had been a fertile season for all the other farmers. The poor brother took the scythe and cut down the plant with one blow. At the same instant, a huge eagle descended from the sky and snatched the plant and flew away. The man managed to grab the other end of the plant and held on to it with both hands so that the eagle pulled the man with him and carried him far up into the sky.

After flying for a long time, with the poor man holding on for his life, the eagle began to fly lower, until it reached a small mountain, where it landed. Scattered on the top of that mountain were jewels and golden objects of the most precious kind. The man stood in awe before the magnificent treasure and did not know what to do. Then, all at once, the eagle spoke and said, "Take all the jewels and gold you want; fill your pockets with them! But remember that in an hour we must depart from here, or otherwise we'll be lost. For then a huge fire will rise up from the mountain and consume everything."

The man replied, "I am already willing to depart." When the eagle asked him if he had filled his pockets with jewels, the man said, "I took one gold object and one jewel. That is enough for me. I do not need any more." The eagle was surprised and said, "If such a small amount is enough, then a great future awaits you. Now let us take our leave."

This time the man climbed upon the back of the bird. With one hand he held on to the eagle, and with the other clung to the precious plant. In this way the eagle soon returned him to his field. When the man came down from atop the eagle, he offered it the plant. The eagle took it, and said, "It is proper that we make this exchange; the precious objects for you and the plant for me."

Then the man said, "But what is the secret of this plant?" And the eagle replied, "This plant was grown from a tear of the Lord, shed over the plight of the poor in the world, and it is the food of the Messiah." When the brother heard this, he knew he was in the presence of a holy being, and knew as well that the Lord had heard his prayer.

When the eagle had taken its leave and departed, the man took the golden object to town and sold it for a great amount of money, enough to buy much food and clothing for himself and his family. The golden object sustained him for a very long time, so that their lives were much better than before.

The man also bought more land bordering on his own. He planted all of these lands and became the richest man not only in his village, but in the whole province.

When his sister-in-law saw this remarkable turn of events, she was very surprised and couldn't understand how it had happened. After all, not long ago her brother-in-law had come begging for a little rice to plant, and now he was even wealthier than they were. So she asked her husband to invite his brother to visit them, in the hope that they might find out his secret.

At first, the man hesitated to accept the invitation, but in the end he decided to go. This time his brother treated him with respect. He offered him wine, and said, "Tell me, how did you become so wealthy?" "I'll tell you," said the man, "even though you treated me so badly and wouldn't even meet me face to face, even though you sent your vicious wife, who gave me cooked rice to plant. I planted that cooked rice rather than reveal my brother's treatment of his family. And, amazingly, a large plant grew up from that rice. I took good care of it and guarded it well, and at the harvest time, as I cut it down, a great eagle swooped down, lifted me up as I clung to the plant and carried me across the sky. We flew a long time, until finally the eagle landed on the top of a mountain on which was scattered a great treasure of jewels and gold. Then the eagle told me to take as much as I wanted, and I filled my pockets."

"Splendid," said the brother, but in his heart he made plans to obtain an even greater treasure for himself.

So the next season the rich brother planted one field of his land with cooked rice and tended it day by day, always hoping to find the miraculous plant growing there. And one day he did see such a plant starting to grow, and he guarded it well. At harvest time he went to the field with a scythe in his hand and cut down the plant. Once again the eagle swooped down and tried to take it away. But the rich brother was ready for the eagle and held on to the plant with both hands.

The eagle asked him as it flew, "Why are you holding on to my plant?" The man replied, "I want you to take me to the place where the treasure can be found." "Are you a poor man?" asked the eagle. "Yes," lied the rich brother. "In that case I will take you there," said the eagle.

When they reached the mountain top where the jewels were scattered, the eagle warned the rich brother about the fire that would appear in an hour and consume everything except for the jewels and gold. "Therefore fill your pockets, take everything that comes into your hands, and try not to take too much." "I will do as you say," said the rich brother. But in his heart he thought differently.

He searched for the largest and most valuable jewels, for he imagined that he was an expert at selecting the best ones. He did not notice that the hour was about to pass. The eagle warned him again and again, but the rich brother always answered, "Another minute, another minute; I want to fill my hat as well." The eagle waited until the very last moment, and then flew off without him.

Suddenly the rich brother felt heat rising up from the earth and realized that the danger was close. He ran to look for the eagle, but it was gone. As the fires rose, a great cry rang out from the mountain, and the rich brother perished with his pockets full.

India: Oral Tradition

The Prince of Coucy

Long ago there were two brothers who lived in the city of Coucy in France. The name of the elder was Samson, and the name of the younger was Hayim. Now while Samson was a rabbi, rich in the knowledge of the Torah, he was quite poor in material possessions. But his brother Hayim, whose ships went to the ends of the earth in order to recover the rarest spices, was numbered among the richest men in the land. Since Hayim loved and admired his brother, and recognized that Samson best served God as a scholar, he saw to it that his brother's family did not go in need. So too did Hayim respect the opinion of his brother, and always consulted with him on every matter, large and small, for Samson's wisdom had proven to be invaluable to him. Thus they each assisted the other and lived together in love and peace.

Once Hayim came to the House of Study where Rabbi Samson spent his days, and said: "My beloved brother, I would be grateful if you would accompany me to the harbor, where we can consult aboard one of my ships, for I have a secret that I must tell you in a place where no one else can hear us."

When Samson heard this, he became worried, and agreed to

come with his brother at once. But first the rabbi gathered up a pen and paper and ink, as he always did when he left the House of Study, in order to write down any new thoughts about the Torah that might cross his mind.

Thus Rabbi Samson went with his brother to the ship. When they boarded it, Hayim ordered the captain and the sailors to depart for the shore, so that they might be alone. Then Hayim revealed to his brother what was on his mind. "I have had a dream that deeply disturbs me," said Hayim. "And since the Talmud says that a dream left uninterpreted is like a letter unread, I felt that I must ask you what it means." Now it is true that Rabbi Samson had the greatest respect for the truth revealed in dreams, and he wondered what kind of dream would cause his brother to be so secretive. He listened carefully as Hayim continued: "My brother, the dream concerns you as well as me, and I am very afraid of what its meaning might be. In the dream, I found myself alone with you in a foreign land, a cold and pitiless place. In the end I left you there and returned alone. Many other things transpired in the dream, but that is all I could remember when I awoke. Yet this was enough to horrify me, for my love for you holds no bounds and I could never imagine leaving you behind. Yet I fear this dream may reveal some secret hatred of which I have never been aware, and I was greatly ashamed of myself. Therefore I have asked you to join me here so that we might discuss this dream where no one would overhear us."

Now Rabbi Samson was astonished, for since a dream, the sages teach, is a sixtieth part prophecy, the dream might portend a time to come when the two brothers would become enemies, though he could not believe such a thing could happen. But before he had time to meditate on the dream and consider its meaning, the ship was suddenly shaken by a great blast of wind, so powerful it tore the ship free from its moorings and carried it far from shore. This happened so quickly that the brothers did not realize what had happened until they tried to go up to the deck. There they were driven back by the great wind as a great storm battered the ship from all sides. Then both brothers prayed with a fervor as never before, imploring the Holy One to spare them from that terrible storm.

The tempest lasted all night, but at dawn it began to subside, and soon afterward the skies became clear. When the two brothers were at last able to reach the deck, they found themselves surrounded by the sea on all sides—but there were no blue waves and no sound of water lopping against the boat; only cold grey water, smooth, hard and silent. Suddenly they realized their ship was frozen in a Sea of Ice. Their hearts sank and they feared that their time had come at last. For they had heard the legends sailors tell of that fateful place, and how any ship trapped there is doomed to remain until the End of Days.

They looked around them and saw many other ships, also frozen there. When they saw this, they lost almost all hope. Still, Rabbi Samson prayed to God, and vowed to devote himself to the study of the Torah even more if only he were freed from that terrible plight. Hayim also cried bitterly and poured out his heart to the Creator of the Universe, pleading that his soul be saved from that Sea of Ice. Even though his chances of escape appeared to be very slight, Hayim believed that he would be saved because of his righteous brother.

After a time, Rabbi Samson said to his brother, "Let us use our mast to reach one of the nearest ships, and we'll see what is in it. So they took down the mast and used it to form a bridge, putting one end on their own ship, and the other end onto the hull of the closest one. Then they walked across. But when they stepped on that other ship's deck they became very frightened, for they saw sailors lying everywhere, all of them dead, their bodies frozen. Samson lifted his eyes, and saw that on the walls of the ship were written the names of the crew and their cities. He thought to himself, "This is probably the custom of those lost at sea, so that if another storm someday moves the ship from this frozen place, their families may learn of their fates, and their wives would be free to remarry.

So Samson took out the paper and pen and the ink he had brought with him. He wrote down every name on the walls of that ship, and vowed that if he were ever freed from there, he would do everything in his power to tell the families about the fates of these sailors.

Hayim also explored the ship, and discovered a vast treasure of precious jewels—diamonds, sapphires, and pearls. He was very surprised to see all that treasure and decided to take some of those riches with him. He vowed to use them for charity if he were ever saved from that terrible fate.

After this the two brothers used the mast to reach another ship, which was frozen beside a high wall so high they could not even see its top from where they stood. The wall was very smooth, with no place for their hands to grip, nor any crevices to support their feet. When he saw this, Rabbi Samson prayed to God and said, "Dear Lord, pilot of Israel, give me the strength to climb up this terrible wall. Perhaps there I will find a way to be rescued." He took a knife and made a hole in the bottom of the wall, large enough for his foot. Then he made a hole above that, in which he put his hands. And in this way, little by little, he climbed up that great wall, eventually, and with the help of God, reaching the top. When Hayim saw this, he tried to follow in his brother's footsteps. But tied around his waist was the bag of treasures he had taken from the ship, so when he climbed on the wall it weighed him down. Before very long he lost his grip and fell backward. He called up to his brother, and Samson also called down to him. But neither could hear the voice of the other.

After several hours, when Samson did not return, Hayim began to lose hope. He feared that he might freeze there when night fell, and he decided that if he were to die in that forsaken place, it would be better to be in his own ship. So, with great difficulty, he managed to cross back over the frozen sea, to his ship. When he reached his ship he cried bitterly, for not only had he lost his last chance of being saved, but he had been separated from his beloved brother as well. So he sat alone and barely ate anything out of sorrow, although he had plenty of provisions. After many days Hayim found a book of Psalms in the ship, and he sat the whole day, pouring out his heart before God.

Meanwhile, Rabbi Samson had climbed over that wall. There

he saw a vast orchard filled with beautiful fruit trees and fine fruit the likes of which he had never seen before. He wandered there the whole day amazed at what he saw, and when he felt hungry he ate that delicious fruit. As night fell, Rabbi Samson climbed one of the high trees, and slept in its branches.

In this way Rabbi Samson lived there for thirty days, wandering by day and sleeping in the branches at night, until one day he reached the end of the orchard. He saw before him a huge valley, wide and beautiful, with fragrant grass and beautiful flowers. He slowly walked into that valley and was enjoying its beauty, when off in the distance he saw a tall palace. He thought to himself that perhaps he would find a place to rest there. But when he approached the palace, he became afraid. His heart started beating very quickly, but he strengthened himself and approached the palace door. When he reached it, a young man dressed in white came toward him. The young man said, "Shalom, my teacher and my rabbi."

Rabbi Samson was very surprised to find someone there who knew his name. He asked him who he was, and the young man replied, "I was once your student, but I died at a young age and came to this pleasant world." Rabbi Samson then said, "Do you know a way for me to return to my home?" The young man said, "Sit here, and I will go ask the righteous ones who rule in this palace."

While Rabbi Samson was waiting there, he saw the entrance to a small cave nearby. It was covered by a curtain on which were inscribed many symbols which he did not recognize. He was curious to know what was in that cave, so he lifted a corner of the curtain, and when he did, a great blast of wind escaped and blew him off his feet. The wind tossed boulders into the air as if they were apples, and tore down huge trees in the forest that had been planted there on the sixth day of creation. For Samson had unwittingly opened the cave of the storm winds. Had he lifted the entire curtain, the storm would have returned the whole world to chaos and void, but this wind was only strong enough to tear the ships free of the frozen sea, including the ship on which Hayim had been trapped. Then the wind carried the ships to where the waters of the sea were no longer frozen. And when the storm passed, Rabbi Hayim replaced the mast and raised the sail, and eventually reached a familiar port from which he finally found his way home.

When Hayim returned to Coucy, the whole city celebrated, because everyone there had assumed that both he and his brother had been lost at sea. But when Rabbi Samson's wife and sons learned that Hayim had returned alone, they cried bitterly over their loss. Hayim told them everything that had happened along the way, and he comforted them, saying: "I too am worried about my dear brother. But I pray to God, who saved my life, to save the life of Samson as well. For it was destiny that carried us to that distant sea, and it was destiny that brought me back. And I feel confident that destiny will return Samson to us when he has accomplished all that he is fated to do." Thus Rabbi Samson's family did not abandon hope.

Now when Rabbi Samson lifted up the curtain of the cave, the storm that was set free lifted him high in the air and then dropped him back to the ground, where he fainted. When the young man returned he looked for Rabbi Samson everywhere. When he finally found him, he managed to restore him by holding an apple beneath his nose. Then the rabbi told him what had happened, and the student said, "I want you to know that the righteous ones decided to give you the honor of entering the Garden of Eden while you were still alive. But because you released the winds stored in that cave, which had not been set free since the time God created the whole world, you can no longer enter there. All I can do for you now is to show you how to leave this place. Will my teacher and rabbi accompany me?" Rabbi Samson grieved at his error, but there was nothing he could do, so he followed his student until he finally stopped and said, "I am not permitted to go beyond here. But if you continue along this path, my master, you will eventually reach a city." Then the student handed Rabbi Samson an apple, and said, "I could not take you to the Garden of Eden, but I can give you this apple from the Tree of Life. It was with this apple that I restored you. Use it well and it will someday bring you back home." Then the student disappeared.

Rabbi Samson stood there for a while, lonely and distraught, but he realized that there was no turning back, and he continued along that path until he became very tired. Then he sat down and took out that precious apple and examined it. And when he smelled its wonderful scent, his spirits were revived.

With no other choice Rabbi Samson continued on his way, and in the distance he saw a very large city. When he came closer, he saw that it was surrounded by walls and that its gates were closed. So he slept outside the gates that night, and in the morning, when they were opened, he entered the city. While walking through the streets, he noticed that everyone seemed very downcast. Some of the Jews even wept openly.

At last Rabbi Samson went to an inn, and asked the owner to tell him why everyone was so sad. The owner said, "The princess, so precious to our old king and queen, suddenly became ill, and now lies near death. The king brought doctors from the four corners of the earth, but all of them have said there is no hope left for her. When the king heard this, he sent for the Jews and told them, 'I know that your God can cure ills and revive the dead. Therefore I command you to pray to your God for my daughter. And if your God cures her, your lives in my kingdom will flourish. But if not, you will all be expelled without any possessions at all, without even the clothes on your back.' That is why all the Jews of this land cry out to God, and hope and pray that He will hear us and cure the princess."

When Rabbi Samson heard this, he remembered the apple from the Tree of Life and its remarkable powers, and he told the man, "Stop crying and hurry to the king, and tell him that a poor Jew has arrived who has promised to cure the princess before it is too late." The innkeeper looked at him with suspicion and laughed. "In the house of the king sit the most famous doctors in the world. If they are unable to find a cure for his daughter, how can you?" And Rabbi Samson said, "Don't ask questions, but do as I say, and you will be better off." The innkeeper saw how certain Rabbi Samson was, and decided to do as he asked.

So the innkeeper went to the palace of the king. And when he stood before the throne, the innkeeper fell to his knees. The

king asked, "Why are you here?" And he answered, "Your majesty, may you live forever, I have come to deliver a message to you. A poor Jew came to me today, a stranger to our kingdom, who told me he could cure the princess. Therefore I came here to tell you, but I cannot be responsible for what he promises, for I do not know if it is true or not." Now this was at least a ray of hope, so the desperate king ordered the Jew to be brought before him at once.

When Rabbi Samson came before the king, he bowed low, and the king said to him, "Are you willing to risk your life in order to cure my daughter?" And Rabbi Samson said: "God will cure your daughter if she still has a living soul within her body." The king took him to his sick daughter, and when the rabbi approached her, he saw that her pulse was very weak, her breathing was very light, and her eyes were growing dim. So he turned to the king and the queen and said, "Now I must be left alone to prepare and administer medicine to the princess. Return in two hours." The king and the queen left the room and closed the door, and

Rabbi Samson sat in front of the sick girl with the apple from the Tree of Life in his hands.

When the princess caught the remarkable fragrance of the apple, her soul revived and began to grow stronger. After two hours, the king and queen rushed back to the bed of their daughter and they saw that she was breathing more strongly than before. Then Rabbi Samson said to the king, "Now I will leave, and in two hours you can send for me again." So they sent him in the king's chariot to the inn, and they ordered that he be washed and dressed in the finest garments like those worn by the doctors of the king. They also commanded that he be given whatever he desired to eat and drink.

Two hours later, the king sent his chariot to bring Rabbi Samson back to the palace. As he walked past the king's doctors, they mocked and laughed at him, and said among themselves, "Look at this foolish Jew, who is pretending that he can cure the princess!" But Rabbi Samson paid no attention to them and went directly to the chamber of the princess. This time he put the apple beneath her nose, and as she breathed in the delectable scent, her eyes opened. When the king and queen returned and saw this, they were so happy they wept.

Once again the rabbi departed, only to return four hours later. The king and queen could not wait to see what would happen next. As soon as the rabbi was alone with the princess, he again held the apple beneath her nose, and soon she began to speak, calling out for her father and mother. Then he said to her, "Do you see me standing here?" And she said, "Yes." He then asked her what was in his hand, and she replied that it was an apple. And he told her, "I want you to know this apple revived you, and you owe your life to its wonderful powers. But you must hide this secret from everyone, even from your father and mother." The princess vowed never to reveal the secret, and Rabbi Samson gave her the apple to keep until she had fully recovered. When she held it in her own hands and breathed in more of that heavenly fragrance, she revived enough to sit up on the bed. When Rabbi Samson opened the door for the king and queen and they saw their daughter sitting up and heard her speaking to them, they were overwhelmed with happiness and embraced and kissed her. Then Rabbi Samson told them to bring all the doctors in the palace there to see that only God can help. And when the doctors saw the miraculous recovery, they were astounded, and stood in awe at the rabbi's powers.

A few days later, the princess left the bed and began to walk again, and after a month had passed she was completely recovered. Then she returned the wondrous apple to the rabbi, vowing once again never to reveal the secret. And when it became clear that the princess had fully recovered, the king brought Rabbi Samson—whom everyone now called "Our Master, the Doctor"—to the royal treasury. When Rabbi Samson entered, he was astonished at the beauty of the precious gems that sparkled like stars, and the gold that shone like the sun. The king told him, "My Master, the Doctor, whatever you wish to take from here is yours." And Rabbi Samson said, "My lord, may your kingdom grow and flourish for many, many years. The generosity of your heart is all the reward that I wish. Besides, wealth only binds its owner in chains." The king was truly amazed to hear this, for he had never before met a man who did not covet gold and precious gems.

Then the king asked his advisors how he might reward the doctor for bringing his daughter back from the brink of death. One of the advisors said, "If it please your majesty, there is no greater reward for which a man can ask than to be made a ruler of one of your cities." The king thought this to be a fine idea, for he recognized at once that Rabbi Samson would make an ideal ruler, since his wisdom was very great and he could not be bribed. So the king called together his entire court, including all of his lords and advisors. He had Rabbi Samson sit at his right hand, and said to him, "My Master the Doctor, I wish to make you ruler of one of my great cities." Rabbi Samson said, "A ruler must devote himself entirely to the needs of his people. And to rule a great city a man must be willing to think of nothing else day and night. But I am above all a scholar of the Torah. All I ask is that you make ready a ship and take me back to my family in Coucy." Naturally the king agreed to this request, but he decided to appoint Rabbi Samson ruler of Coucy as well, for that city was part of his empire. He declared that thereafter Rabbi Samson was to be known as the Prince of Coucy. So too did the king decide to accompany Rabbi Samson on his voyage home, along with the queen and the princess, who was now strong enough for an ocean voyage. Thus a fleet of ships was readied, filled with the nobles of the kingdom, all of whom came to proclaim Rabbi Samson the Prince of Coucy.

During that voyage the king spent many hours alone with Rabbi Samson, since he greatly admired his wisdom. One day he finally asked him something he had wondered about for so long: how had he cured the princess? For she had strangely refused to reveal the slightest detail of her cure. Now the rabbi was very reluctant to reveal the secret, because if that apple were possessed by a king, he could use it to revive the dead and make himself into a god. Still, Rabbi Samson did not want to lie to the king, so he told him everything that had taken place, right from the day he had left the House of Study with his brother. He let the king hold the apple, and when the king smelled its fragrance, all his aches and pains disappeared, and he felt as if he were young again.

Suddenly, a great wave arose and rocked the ship, wrenching the apple out of the hands of the king, so that it fell into the sea. The king cried out when he saw this, for if the truth be known, he had vowed from the first instant he had held the apple that he would make it his own. But heaven had decreed otherwise, and Rabbi Samson, although saddened, was relieved that the apple had been lost to the sea and had not become the tool of a king. Rabbi Samson consoled the king by telling him that the apple had come into his hands only to cure his daughter, the princess, for the fate of our lives and whether we live or die must remain in the hands of God.

When the fleet reached Coucy, the people were astounded to see the royal flag, since the king had never visited their city before. They watched in awe as the chariots, with their glorious white horses, rode off from the port, bearing the splendor of the king and his entourage. The people honored the king by bringing him to the house of the richest man, who was none other than Hayim, Rabbi Samson's brother. But the people of the city did not recognize that it was Rabbi Samson who stood at the king's side, for he was dressed in the garments of a royal minister and appeared to be a member of the court.

That evening, at Hayim's mansion, the king introduced Rabbi Samson as the Prince of Coucy, who would henceforth govern the city. Then Rabbi Samson greeted the city elders, among them, of course, his brother Hayim. But he did not reveal himself, even to his brother. Instead he asked Hayim about life in the city and about his own family. And Hayim spoke to the new prince, but did not recognize him at all. When Hayim began to grow comfortable in his presence, he said, "My prince, I once had a very precious and dear brother. He was a great scholar of the Torah, whose wisdom was without equal. Everyone loved him, and if he were with us today, he would have shared his wisdom with you." Then the Prince of Coucy said, "If he is not here, where is he?" And Hayim told him what had happened to him and his brother with a few words as possible, for his pain was still very great.

Rabbi Samson decided that the time had come to reveal his true identity, so he placed his arm around the shoulders of Hayim, and he said, "Know, my beloved Hayim, that I am your long lost brother Samson. Although I may look like a stranger to you, but if I tell you the name of your brother's wife and children and the name of your uncles and aunts, and the names of all the men in this room and their wives, will you then believe me?" And Hayim stared at the Prince in complete amazement, and suddenly realized that it was truly Samson who stood there before him, and his heart leaped for joy. He hugged and embraced his brother, and then gave thanks to God for saving them both and for bringing them out of darkness into light.

Then Rabbi Samson told Hayim all that had happened to him since they had become separated, and everyone gathered there was amazed at the miracles that God had performed until he had safely returned. That reunion was a wonder to behold, as was that of Rabbi Samson and his wife and children.

That very day Rabbi Samson took off his royal garb and wore the clothes of his fellow Jews once again. The first thing he did was to send word to each and every widow of the sailors who had perished on the frozen sea. Then he returned to the House of Study, and sat in his usual place, and governed the city from there as he studied Torah. And from that day on Rabbi Samson was deemed the Righteous One of his generation, bringing justice and peace into the lives of everyone whom he governed in the city of Coucy.

France: Fourteenth Century

The Eagle Prince

Once upon a time there lived a king and queen who longed to have children. Many years passed, and many remedies were tried, but nothing succeeded in bringing them the blessing of a child. Then the king learned from one of his viziers that there was a witch in that land who had an enchanted pomegranate tree behind her house. If a man and woman both ate half of one of the pomegranates that grew on this tree, they would be certain to have a child of their own.

The king was heartened to hear this, and he told the vizier to send a servant to pay the witch whatever she wanted for one of those precious pomegranates. The vizier told the king that the matter was not so simple, for this evil witch would never sell even one of her pomegranates, no matter how much was offered. The king asked the vizier why this was so, and the vizier told him that it was because the witch was not the rightful owner of the enchanted tree. It had once been tended by a holy sage, but the witch had come into possession of it, and she drew her pleasure from withholding its fruit from the world. For nothing pleased her more than that others should be unhappy. So she guarded the fruit of that tree like a hawk, and great was her magic that it was impossible to overpower her.

The king was greatly saddened when he heard of the evil ways of this witch. For it was a most personal matter for him—that witch stood in the way of his heir, without whom all his conquests would mean nothing. The king asked his vizier if there were anything he could do. The vizier replied, "I am afraid that in this case, all his majesty's powers are of no use. For the fruit will only serve he who has picked it. Perhaps, my lord, you might go to the tree yourself and try to pick a pomergranate without being seen."

The king told his wife, the queen, what the vizier had said, and when she realized that their only hope lay in those magic fruits, she begged her husband to attempt to steal it. The king told his wife that he would at least try, for his desire for a child was as strong as hers.

So it was that the king mounted his horse and set out for the house of the witch. When he was almost there, he tied up the horse nearby so that he could escape on it once he had obtained the fruit, and then walked the rest of the way to the witch's house. Soon, beneath the full moon, he saw the beautiful pomegranate tree and the ripe fruit it bore.

The king looked for a sign of the witch, but there was none. He stood there for some time, listening to every sound, trying to hear if the witch were home, or if fate had led him there on a day when she was not. At last, when the king was certain there was no one around, he ran up to the tree and picked one of the largest and reddest fruits. But the instant he plucked it from the branch, a terrible thing happened: the king became frozen like a statue, unable to move a single muscle, his upraised arm clutching a pomegranate.

The king remained there, frozen in place, for what seemed an eternity, even though only a short time had passed. At last he heard terrible laughter coming from nearby, and he realized that the witch had returned. She came up to the king, who stood there helpless with a pomegranate in his hand, and she said, "Well, now, what have I caught in my web this time?" She shrieked with laughter and said, "Did you think that I left nothing to guard my precious tree? Hardly! I cast a spell so that anyone who touched it would be frozen in place, but the spell must be growing weak. Somehow you managed to pluck the fruit before the spell took effect. I will have to attend to that. As for you, the fruit is yours to keep—it belongs to whoever picks it. But listen carefully while I tell you about the other spell I have cast on this tree, and then decide if you still want to eat the fruit."

The king, still frozen in place, heard all that the evil witch said. When he learned that the fruit was to be his after all, he was filled with hope, but then the witch shrieked again with evil laughter. She began to speak of the other spell, and his heart sank. "Before I set you free, my lord, keep this in mind: Because you stole that fruit on the night of the full moon, the child that will be yours will belong to me every full moon, and I will take it whether or not you agree. On that one night each month your child will become an eagle—and will fly here and do my will. Know too, great and powerful king, that if anyone in the world, other than you and your wife, finds out that your heir becomes an eagle, the next time he is transformed into one, he will remain that way for the rest of his life! And know that there is only one thing in the world that can break the spell, the witch cackled with laughter, "but I have no intention of telling you what that is!" And with that she went inside her house. And as soon as she closed the door, the king found that he could move again. And once he realized that he had been freed from that terrible spell, he ran from there as fast as he could, the pomegranate tightly in his grasp. He raced to his horse and set out for his palace as fast as he could ride, both out of fear of the witch behind him and desire to share that magic pomegranate with his wife. For he did not believe such a strange curse could come true—how after all, could a child become an eagle? The king rode all night, and by dawn he at last reached the palace.

He hurried inside and told the queen all that had happened. When he told her about the witch's curse on their child, his wife agreed that such a curse should not be taken seriously, and certainly should not stop them from having their own child at last. So they cut the pomegranate open, and the king and queen slowly and carefully ate each and every ruby seed, and marveled at its wonderful taste. Sure enough, a short time later the queen found that she was with child, and at the end of nine months she gave birth to a beautiful son, who was the pride and joy of all the kingdom.

Now to the great relief of the king and queen, the first full moon came and went, and nothing changed in the slightest—their baby remained as he was and did not change into an eagle. The same was true for every other night of the full moon until the prince was ten years old. By then the king and queen had almost forgotten the witch's curse. But on the night of the first full moon following the prince's tenth birthday, the terrible transformation suddenly took place right before the eyes of the king and queen, and the eagle their son had become flew at once out the open window.

No one can imagine how much the king and queen despaired when they saw that the curse had come true nor how they both wept that night over the loss of their child. But at dawn, when the eagle flew back into that room and again became a boy, the king and queen wept tears of joy to see him. And after that they saw to it that they alone remained with their son on every night of the full moon, so that no one else would see him change into an eagle. For they had not forgotten that if this came to pass they would lose their son for good, and he would be cursed to spend the rest of his life as an eagle.

Now what was it that happened to the poor prince when he suddenly found himself transformed into an eagle? He found that he was compelled to fly directly to the witch's house. There she gave him orders to fly halfway around the world, to a cave in which there was an old woman who spun golden thread. The old woman would place in his beak a very long thread that stretched behind him for many cubits. And the eagle had to fly with it back to the witch's house, where she took it from him and gathered it into a golden spool. Then the eagle was free to return to the palace, where he arrived just before the dawn.

This same strange ceremony took place every month, each time the enchanted prince flying in the form of an eagle to that cave and bringing back one of those long, golden threads. What the prince did not know was that the witch was very slowly making a garment out of those golden threads. In fact, it took ten years for the witch to complete a golden blouse—for that is what she had woven.

Naturally, the golden blouse was enchanted. For the witch had cost a spell that would make the prince fly directly to that golden blouse, no matter where it was in the world, and when he arrived, fall hopelessly in love with whoever was wearing it. Now the witch's plan was to see to it that the blouse was worn by an ugly old hag, so that the prince would pine away over a woman old enough to be his grandmother. The witch shrieked her terrible laughter every time she thought of the wonderful plan. For she was not satisfied ruling the life of the prince one day a month. No, she wanted to ruin his entire life, and what better way to do it?

One day, a toothless old beggar woman happened to make her way to the witch's house, hoping for a crust of bread. As soon as the witch set eyes on her, she decided that she was the perfect choice to be the prince's beloved. She took the old woman in and gave her a good meal. Then she took out the golden blouse, and when the old woman saw it, she put her hands over her eyes, so brightly did it reflect the light. The old woman could not understand why the witch was giving her a blouse fit for a queen, but of course she did not argue. She took the precious blouse and carried it off. But the one thing that she did not do was to put it on, for it seemed much too beautiful for a hag such as herself. Instead she put it in her bag, and took it out to admire from time to time.

Now in another kingdom there was a king who had three daughters blessed with all the virtues, and whom the king loved very much. Once, the king had to travel over the seas to a far-away land. On the day before departing he said to his daughters, "What gifts do you want me to bring you? For whatever you desire, be it ever so rare, I will grant your request."

The eldest daughter arose and said, "My father, I wish for a bracelet made of precious gems." The second daughter said, "And I would like a comb made out of pure gold, set with diamonds." But the third daughter did not know what to ask for. Her father told her not to worry, for she could tell him the next day, before he departed.

Now that night the youngest princess had a dream in which she was wearing a magnificent blouse woven out of gold. In the dream she saw herself wearing it in a far-away place, which she had never seen before, and she was with a very handsome man, whom she loved at first sight. So it was that when the princess awoke she was very sad that it had only been a dream. But even if she could not make it come true, at least she could ask her father for a blouse woven out of gold, and that is what she did. So before he departed, the king kissed his daughters and told them that he would not return until he had found the gifts they had each requested.

When he reached the distant land, the king went to a master goldsmith and asked if he had a bracelet made of precious gems he could purchase. The goldsmith told him he did not have one in his shop, but that he could fashion such a bracelet for a thousand gold dinars. The king agreed to this price and said he would return in three days, when the bracelet was to be completed. Three days later the king went to the goldsmith and received the bracelet, and it was a fine one indeed.

In the same manner did the king purchase a comb of pure gold set with diamonds for his second daughter. But try as he might, he could not find the blouse woven with gold thread for the youngest daughter, and this made him very sad. Then it happened that a rumor reached the king that a poor beggarwoman was said to possess such a blouse. The king could not understand how something so precious could be in the hands of a beggar, but he decided to see if it was true. When the king finally found the old beggar woman, he approached her most gently, gave her some gold coins, and only when she trusted him did he mention that he was a king who was searching for a blouse woven out of golden thread, and would be happy to pay a great deal for it, if only he could find it somewhere.

Now when the old woman heard that he was a king, she was delighted, for here was someone worthy of that precious blouse. The old woman asked, "And for whom are you seeking such a treasure?" And the king said, "I wish to give it as a gift to my youngest daughter." "Is she beautiful?" the old woman asked, and the king replied, "She is the most beautiful girl in all the land." When she heard this, the old beggarwoman lit up. She took the magnificent golden blouse out and showed it to the king, who was astonished by its beauty as well as its great worth. The king could not believe his ears when the beggarwoman said, "Here, it is yours! Give it to your daughter, the princess, and let her wear it in good health!" A stonish and grateful, the king thanked the old woman with all his heart. So too did he refuse to let the old woman go unpaid, and gave her a bag filled with gold coins. This was more than enough to keep her in great comfort for the rest of her life, so the old woman left, happy with all that had happened, and the king joyously returned to his kingdom, laden with gifts for his beloved daughters.

It was on the night of the full moon when the king returned. He gave the gifts to the princesses, who were amazed by their beauty. But above all they were astonished at the rare beauty of the golden blouse. Then the youngest princess left to try the blouse on, but it happened that at the very instant she put on the golden blouse, an eagle suddenly appeared. It caught her in its beak, lifted her onto his wings, and flew off with her. The king and queen saw the princess as she was being carried off, but with all their wealth and power there was nothing they could do to bring her back.

The eagle flew with the princess on its back all night, and just before dawn they reached another palace in a far-away kingdom and flew in a chamber window. The eagle left the princess there and flew back out the window. The frightened and confused princess looked around the room and found it was as beautiful as her own chamber in the palace of her father, the king. Suddenly there was a knock at the door, and a young man entered the room. Although it was the first time the princess had met that man, she recognized him at once. For that was the prince she had seen in her dream—when she had tried on the golden blouse! As for the prince, he took one look at the beautiful princess, in that golden blouse, and he lost his heart to her forever, for that was the nature of the spell. But the princess was both beautiful and worthy of his love, and in this way the plan of the evil witch was foiled. And so the princess came to be grateful to the mysterious eagle that had snatched her away from her home for she had found the prince of her dreams.

The parents of the prince were also delighted that their son had fallen in love at last, and with such a fine princess as well. Shortly a wedding took place, attended by the happy parents of the princess and celebrated with great joy in both kingdoms.

Now the marriage of the prince and princess was ideal except for one thing—the curse of the full moon. For on those nights the prince became an eagle once again, as had been his fate for so long. The one thing that terrified the young prince was that his bride would discover this secret, and then he would become an eagle forever. So the prince told his wife, as each full moon approached, that he had to go on a journey, and he pretended to leave the palace, but actually remained in a hidden room, where he became the eagle and flew off to serve the witch.

Now after the eagle prince had brought enough golden thread to weave the blouse, the witch gave him a new command, and again he was compelled to obey. She ordered him to fly to the boiling waters of Gehenna and dip in those terrible waters. And only after he had been scalded and sapped by the waters of Hell was he permitted to dip into the waters of Paradise, which always restored him. But each time, the eagle prince suffered greatly in the waters of Gehenna, and the prince wanted nothing more than to have this torture ended, and to become like all other men.

Then it happened one day that when the eagle prince returned just before dawn, a single feather fell to the floor when the eagle changed back into a man. When the princess found that feather, she wondered where it came from. The more she studied it, the more it seemed familiar to her. At last she recognized it—it was exactly like the feathers of the eagle that had carried her away from her kingdom. When she showed it to the prince, he seemed greatly shocked to see it, and fell silent. The princess began to wonder what the meaning was of his strange response, and she decided to follow him on the next full moon.

So it was that the princess came to discover her husband's terrible secret, and she realized that she was married to the same eagle that had carried her to that land! And when he returned the day after the full moon, she told him that she had recognized the feather, and she made him confess that he was the eagle who had abducted her in the first place. The prince was crushed, for he knew what it meant if his secret became known. Filled with grief, he told his wife of the witch's spell, and how her knowledge of his secret would doom him, after the next full moon, to remain an eagle for the rest of his life. The princess was filled with horror, for she had in this way brought an end to their life together, which had been her greatest happiness.

Then the princess grew very angry. "We must fight back!" she said. "The witch said there was one way to break the spell. I must go to her before the next full moon, and discover her secret."

"What are you saying?" said the prince. "Have you forgotten how dangerous the witch is?"

"No," said the princess, "but how else can we break the spell? She would recognize you if you tried, but she does not know me, for she thinks you married that old hag. I will disguise myself as a witch and try to trick her."

Now this was a very dangerous plan, but the prince could not bear the thought of being an eagle for the rest of his life, separated from his beloved wife. So the prince agreed to let the princess go.

Now the princess made herself look exactly like a witch, and went to the real witch's house and knocked on the door. While she was standing there she saw the pomegranate tree, just as the prince had described it, still filled with beautiful ripe fruit. Suddenly the door opened and there stood the wicked witch, a foul look on her face. But when she saw it was another witch, she brightened up, happy to have some company.

"Come in, come in," said the witch. "That is, if you are a sister in evil." "Of course, I am," said the princess. "Why I have just turned a farmer and his family into stones, and I tossed them into the sea." "Ho, ho," said the witch. "Let us trade tales of evil." And the princess went inside.

Once they were seated, the real witch told her how she had

caught so many fathers trying to pick the fruit of the enchanted pomegranate tree, and how she had frozen them with her spell, and thrown them off the cliff behind her house. "Did none of them ever pick a single fruit?" asked the princess. "Only one foolish king," the witch replied, "but I got even with him." And then she proceeded to tell the disguised princess the tale of the eagle prince. And when she came to the part about the old hag bride, she rolled on the floor with laughter.

Then the disguised princess laughed too and said: "I'll bet you fixed it so that he will never figure out how to set himself free from the spell." "Oh, that I did!" chortled the witch. "He would never think to burn his wife's most precious possession—her golden blouse. It is not woven of regular gold, but enchanted gold, and if it is cast in a fire it will simply go up in smoke, and the spell along with it. But who would burn such a priceless possession?"

The princess could hardly wait to return to the palace and give the prince the good news. But she had to get out of there safely, so she continued to giggle until it was getting dark, then said she must leave, for she had some evil tricks to do that very night. She left the witch's house and hurried back to the palace and told the prince what had happened.

So it was that the prince embraced his wonderful wife for wrenching that secret out of the evil witch. They built a fire at once and cast the golden blouse directly into the flames. Instantly it went up in a puff of smoke and disappeared. At that very moment the evil witch also vanished in a puff of smoke, and that was the last anyone ever heard of her, for she had bargained with her very soul to cast that powerful spell. So it was that the prince never again turned into an eagle during the night of the full moon. The spell that prevented the fruit of the pomegranate tree from being plucked was broken, and its delicious fruit served once more to provide the blessing of a child to those who had been barren. No longer did the prince fear the coming of the full moon. Instead he and the princess celebrated every full moon, and lived together in love and peace all the days of their lives.

Persian Kurdistan: Oral Tradition

The Stork Princess

There once was a poor family that barely had enough food to eat. One day a stranger came to the house and offered to give work and good wages to the youngest son, Aaron, if his parents would permit the boy to accompany him on a journey as his helper. And although his parents were reluctant to let Aaron go, their dire condition left them no choice, for in his absence there would at least be one less mouth to feed.

The next day Aaron left in the company of the stranger, each riding a camel. They rode through the desert for three days until they reached the base of a very high mountain. When they had made camp there, the man told the boy that there was a vast treasure in the cave at the top of the mountain. He told Aaron to ride his camel there, tie it to a tree, and search in the cave until he had located the treasure. Then he was to carry all the treasure out of the cave, load it on the camel, and send the camel down the mountainside. After the man had unloaded the camel, he would send it back up to bring Aaron down.

Now when Aaron looked up at that high mountain, its top reaching into the clouds he was very frightened at the thought of

/196/

having to go up there by himself. But he knew that his parents desperately needed the money he would earn from his work, and so he did as the man said. He rode the sure-footed camel up the treacherous slope, and slowly but surely made his way to the top of the mountain. When he got there he tied up the camel, just as the man had told him to. Then he lit a torch and went inside the cave. Before he had gone very far inside, he was suddenly startled by a glittering reflection, and when he looked to see what it was, he could hardly believe his eyes—for there was a vast treasure, consisting of every kind of precious jewel and many golden objects. In fact, there was enough treasure for four or five camel loads, not just one.

Then, with his heart beating quickly, Aaron began to carry out some of the treasure. When he had made enough trips to load the camel, he sent it down the mountain. And when the camel reached the bottom, the boy heard the man shout for joy as he examined the treasure. Then Aaron waited for him to send the camel back up, but instead the man, who believed that the boy had loaded all of the treasure at one time, shouted up to him, "Did you really think I would send the camel back up for you? How would I carry the treasure back? Enjoy yourself, foolish boy, because you will stay there for the rest of your life!" And with that the evil man took his leave, abandoning poor Aaron at the top of that steep mountain.

When the boy realized how he had been tricked, he shed bitter tears not only for himself, but for his parents as well, who would be so distraught when their beloved son did not return. After a while, however, Aaron became hungry, and decided to look around from that high place to see if there was any way he could descend safely. The mountain was far too steep for him to climb down, and on the other side of the mountain was the sea. He was trapped.

At last, when hunger began to make him desperate, Aaron decided that he had to get down from that mountain one way or another. Since he could see that his chances of going down the steep slope were slim, and that even if he succeeded he would still be alone in the desert without supplies, he decided that way was closed to him. Since he was a very fine swimmer, he decided to descend the other side of the mountain as far as he could, and then dive into the sea, in the hope that he could somehow reach safety that way.

This Aaron did, climbing very cautiously down the other side of the mountain until he could descend no further. Then he prayed to God for protection and, taking a deep breath, dived off the side of the mountain into the sea. He started to swim, and swam for three days and nights, until he was completely exhausted. Just as he was about to give up hope, he sighted land and made his way to a beach.

When he was safely on the beach, Aaron collapsed in exhaustion. He slept all that day and night, and awoke early the next morning. By that time he was truly famished and decided to search for something to eat. Before long he came to a large house, and he knocked on the door. To his joy a sweet young girl opened the door, and when she saw his ragged and gaunt appearance, she invited him in at once, and gave him some hot and tasty soup. After Aaron had eaten and rested, the girl asked him how he had gotten there, and Aaron told her the terrible tale of the stranger who had abandoned him on the top of the mountain. When the girl heard where he had come from, so far away, she told him that he might stay and live with them, for she and her six sisters had always longed to have a brother. Aaron agreed that he would stay if the other sisters agreed, and he asked the girl how it was that she and her sisters had come to live there. Then she told him that the house had been the house of their parents. When they died, the sisters decided to remain together and live there.

Before long the other sisters returned, and they all happily accepted Aaron as their new brother, so that he felt as if he were truly a part of their family. They lived together in peace for many months, until one day the sisters received a message from their uncle inviting them to a wedding. The sisters did not think it would be a good idea to take Aaron with them, so they gave him forty keys and left him in charge of the house. They told him that they would be gone for forty days, and during that time he should open one room a day. But there was one room he was forbidden to enter.

Now he was very lonely while his 'sisters' were gone, so Aaron opened two rooms a day in order to pass the time. Before very long he had opened all the rooms except for that one he was not permitted to enter, and his curiosity grew very great. At last he could not stand it any longer and opened that forbidden door, for he told himself that no one would ever know what he had done. When the door was open he found himself facing a beach on the shore of a great sea. There on the beach were three storks, each standing on one foot. There was really nothing that seemed forbidden or dangerous, and Aaron wondered why his 'sisters' had told him to keep that door locked.

Then, all at once, the three storks dropped their feathers and were transformed into three beautiful girls, each prettier than the other. With just one look, Aaron fell in love with the prettiest of them, who appeared to be the youngest as well. But as soon as the girls caught sight of him, they were frightened and became storks again and flew away. After they were gone, Aaron found that he was lovesick and could not get the beautiful girl out of his mind.

Then the boy went to the forbidden door every day and peered out of it, hoping to find that the storks had returned. But they did not, and the days passed very slowly for him, until at last his seven 'sisters' returned.

Now when his 'sisters' saw how downcast Aaron seemed, they guessed at once that he had opened the forbidden door. They begged him to tell them the truth, and at last he confessed that it was true, and then he told them what he had seen. They said, "We warned you not to open that door for just this very reason. For we knew that once a month the three stork princesses come to wash in the sea, and then fly back to their palace. And any young man who glimpses them when they are not storks is sure to lose his heart, just as you have lost yours. For they are the three most beautiful girls in the world, and the one that you love, the youngest, is the most beautiful of all."

Now when Aaron heard this, he was very afraid, for the love

that drove him was the most powerful emotion he had ever known. He said to his sisters, "But might not she love me as much as I love her?" And his sisters replied, "There is no way to be certain of that, but there is a way for you to find out." And when Aaron heard this the flames of love rose up again in his heart. "Wait until next month," the sisters continued, "when the storks return. While they are washing themselves, steal the feathers of the youngest, so that she cannot turn back into a stork. Then she won't have any choice but to follow you. And once you have led her through the door of this house, she will have lost the power to become a stork and will remain a girl for all time."

Aaron could hardly wait for the day to arrive when the storks would return. When it did, he hid behind the forbidden door and opened it just a crack, until he saw the storks alight on the beach. Then, when the storks had shed their feathers on the beach, became girls again, and were washing in the sea, Aaron crept outside and carried off the feathers of the youngest princess. When the princess found that her feathers were gone, she was distraught, and started to search for them. Then Aaron opened the door and held them out to her and told her that if she wanted them back she would have to follow him. In this way Aaron coaxed the princess to come inside, and when that had happened she lost the enchantment that enabled her to become a stork, and thus had no way to return with her sisters to their kingdom.

So it was that the princess came to live in that spacious house. At first she wept because she could not fly home, but as she got to know Aaron she grew to love him. And when he asked her to marry him, she agreed at once. His 'sisters' prepared the wedding, and held it at their home, and it was a day of joy for them all.

After the wedding Aaron began to feel homesick for his father and mother, and longed for them to meet his wife. So too did the princess miss the king and queen and her sisters. So they decided to take their leave of the seven sisters and to make a journey together to both their homes. It was a long journey, but because Aaron and the princess loved each other so much, the weeks passed like minutes, and before long Aaron found that they were approaching the very same mountain from which he had dived into the sea. He had not forgotten the wonderful treasure hidden at the top of that mountain, and he told the princess about it. Just then they saw a caravan passing in the desert, and the princess suggested that they barter some of their wedding gifts for two of the camels of the caravan. This they did, and with the two camels Aaron was able to ascend the high mountain once again. He loaded a vast amount of treasure on the back of one camel, and rode the other back down the mountain, where the princess waited for him.

Thus they continued through the desert with a treasure fit for a king. Along the way, they came upon a great pit, and when they peered down into it, they saw at the bottom the body of the evil stranger who had abandoned Aaron at the top of the mountain, and scattered all around him were the jewels the boy had gathered for him. Then Aaron understood that the greedy man must have tried to make his way in the dark, rather than wait for the light, so that he might enjoy his wealth sooner. He had fallen into that pit, never to know the pleasure of his wealth. Aaron climbed down into the pit, tossed up the jewels and gold, and loaded them onto the second camel, so that their wealth was double what it had been. They continued until they reached the house of Aaron's parents, who could not believe their eyes when they saw him, for they had thought him dead. And when they saw the vast treasure he carried, and the beauty of his wife, the princess, they were so stunned they were speechless.

Aaron and the princess remained there a fortnight, and before they left Aaron gave his family a portion of the treasure, so they would never be poor again, and he took the rest of it with him. When the princess reached her palace and introduced Aaron to her parents, the king and queen, and to her two sisters, they were all overwhelmed with joy to see her again, and to meet her handsome and wealthy husband. So it was that Aaron became a member of the royal family, and lived in joy and love with his beautiful wife and was one day himself declared the king.

Persian Kurdistan: Oral Tradition

The Donkey Girl

In one town there was a rabbi who was loved and respected by all. Now the wife of this rabbi had given birth every year to another son, and there were already six fine boys. But while his wife was with child for the seventh time, the rabbi travelled from that city to visit a sick man, and on the road he met an old woman who was leading a donkey. Now this old woman was in truth an evil witch, and the donkey she was leading was the very old man that the rabbi was going to visit. For the witch had come into his house when he was too weak to resist her, and had cast a spell on him that had turned him into a donkey. But because he had been sick at the time, he became a lame donkey which struggled along the road while the old woman beat it mercilessly.

When the good rabbi saw how this old woman was mistreating the donkey, his heart went out to the poor animal. He approached her and said, "Why are you so harsh with this donkey. Surely you can see that it is lame and that it is moving as quickly as it can." "Why don't you mind your own business!" hissed the witch, beating the donkey even harder. The rabbi could not bear to see this, so he said, "Perhaps you would be willing to sell this donkey to me?" "Oh, I would sell it to you," said the witch, "but the price would be too high." "And what is it that you are asking?" said the rabbi. "That you give me your next child for this donkey!" screamed the witch. The rabbi was shocked when he heard this, and he said, "I would never give away a child of mine, even if it had the head of a donkey!" "And that is exactly what your child *will* have!" shrieked the witch, and she led away the poor donkey, beating it all the time. The rabbi looked back at them, and his heart was filled with sadness for the plight of the donkey, but he did not think for a moment that the curse of the witch might come true. But when he came to the house of the sick man and saw that he was not there, he wondered what could have become of him. He noticed donkey tracks leading away from the house, and he became afraid. He decided that he had better hurry back to his home, for his wife might be giving birth at any time.

Not long after the rabbi returned home, the rabbi's wife gave birth. But she did not give birth to a normal child. She gave birth to a very strange creature, whose body was that of a girl, but whose head was that of a donkey. When the midwife saw this strange being she was very frightened. She called for the rabbi and said to him, "Rabbi, your wife has not borne you a son this time, but instead a very strange creature." "What kind of creature?" asked the frightened father. "I have never seen one like it," said the midwife, "but you who are wise and well-versed in the Torah, perhaps will have heard of a being such as this."

The rabbi's astonishment and terror grew as the midwife described the baby to him. He then understood that the old woman he had met must have been a witch, and that she had cursed him with a terrible curse which he and his wife would have to bear for all of their days. These thoughts made the rabbi reel in confusion, for he did not know what to do. At last the midwife suggested to the rabbi that he kill the newborn child, but the rabbi rejected this at once and said, "The Torah forbids the slaying of a soul. And every living being has a soul!"

Finally the rabbi decided to conceal this tragedy from his wife, and he commanded the midwife to take the girl from her mother, and to say that the baby was sick and must be cared for. He also told the midwife to put the baby in a special room, and to give her food and drink in isolation.

The midwife did as the rabbi ordered, but the mother never ceased asking about how the baby was doing, and wanted to go to her. At last the rabbi revealed to his wife the truth about the strange creature that had been born to them. The mother broke into heart-rending sobs, and the rabbi hurried to comfort her. But the truth is that his heart too was broken.

The girl grew and developed and was healthy and strong, only her head and ears were like those of a donkey. Each day her parents brought food to her special room, and when she began to speak, her father began to teach her Torah. It turned out that the girl was really quite clever and she absorbed all that she was taught with astonishing swiftness. And because her father was a brilliant scholar, the girl attained great knowledge of the sacred texts.

Now this rabbi was also a generous host to those needing shelter. One day a youth came to him from a great distance, whose one desire was to study Torah. The rabbi received him into his house and began teaching him. One evening the student asked a question, and because it was summer and the heat was great, the rabbi replied, "I will answer your question another time." Meanwhile the rabbi's daughter, who was listening to her father's teachings from her room, heard his response and answered the student's question herself. The student heard the answer and asked, "Who is that wise young woman who knew the answer to my question?" The rabbi replied, "She is my daughter." "I wish to take her as my wife," declared the young man. The rabbi took his student to a corner of the room and tried to persuade him to give up his plan. "My daughter is ill and is not right for you," said the rabbi. But no pleadings or explanations on the part of the rabbi had any effect. It was clear that although he had never seen the young woman's face, the young man was lovesick and was not about to change his mind.

So it was that the engagement was arranged, all fitting and proper, and the time of the wedding was fixed. In those days it was forbidden for the groom to see his bride until their wedding night, so during the ceremony under the canopy, the rabbi's daughter was heavily veiled. After the feast, to which hundreds of guests were invited, the groom entered the bride's room, and what did he see? The face of a donkey peering out at him from the bed. Horror-struck by what he saw, the groom sat down in a corner of the room and began to weep.

"Why are you crying" his bride asked. "No tragedy has occurred. Everything can be repaired in this world."

"I am ashamed before your father," replied the young man. "How often I asked him to give you to me, and I repelled all his attempts to prevent the marriage. What will I tell him now? How will I explain to him my desire to leave you?"

"I will not stop you from going," said the bride. "Just stay here until morning."

He remained with her until day break, and then he left, saying, "I am leaving you, but I want to give you three gifts as a rememberance." First he gave her his ring. "Every time I see this ring I will remember you," she said. Then her husband gave her a book which his father had given him in order to guard him on his journeys—a book that was very precious to him. "Thank you," she said as she accepted the book. "Every time I open this book I will think of you." Then the young man handed her his beautiful prayer shawl on which was woven his name and the name of his father. She thanked him for this gift as well and said, "Every time I touch this prayer shawl I will be reminded of you." Than they said goodbye, and he left.

When the bride's parents came to see what had happened, she told them everything. Her mother was so grief-stricken that soon afterward she died. Now after a month's time the bride began to feel that she was with child, and after nine months she gave birth to a son, who was as like his father as are two drops of water. She was greatly relieved that her son did not have a donkey's head, but she mourned that her mother had not lived to see the birth of the child. The girl raised the baby with great love and said in her heart, "At least there will be someone to say kaddish after me."

The rabbi, grandfather of the child, helped his daughter raise the boy and taught him Torah, so that he succeeded mightily in his studies. One day, when he was already on his way to becoming a young man one of the men in the synagogue began to test him in Torah and the youth answered every question with ease. All present, especially the fathers who had sons his age, were jealous of him and one of them said to him, "Do not be proud. It would be good for you to go and find your father!" "What do you mean?" asked the astonished youth. "Behold, the rabbi is my father." "No," said the troublemaker, "the rabbi is not your father, but your grandfather. You had best seek out your father."

The youth returned home very upset and asked his mother, "Where is my father?" "You live and study Torah with him," answered his mother. "No, mother," said the boy "that is my grandfather, not my father." Then his mother saw that he had discovered this secret and, through tears, she told him the truth.

Then the boy asked her if she had anything that belonged to his father, and she showed him the ring, the book and the prayer shawl. The boy took them and said, "I am going off to search for my father." "No, no, do not be hasty," pleaded his mother. "How will you know where he lives? I have no one else in the world but you; what will I do without you?" But her pleading and beseeching did not change his mind. The boy had decided to go out to seek his father no matter what. He took provisions for the road and the three gifts his father had left, and went on his way.

One evening, tired from his wanderings and with his food almost gone, he sat under a tree to rest. So tired was he that he fell asleep, and he began to dream. In his dream an old man approached him; it was none other than Elijah the Prophet. Elijah greeted him and asked, "Where do you come from, young man, and where are you going?" The boy replied, "I am coming from my mother, and I am seeking my father." "You are not far from your father," said the old man. Two more cities lie before you and in the third city you will meet him. Now know that the leaves of the tree you are sleeping beneath can cure your mother of the terrible spell that has afflicted her. Boil leaves from this tree in water and have her drink it, and she will be cured." When the boy awoke, he remembered the dream clearly. And he arose and plucked many leaves from that tree, put them in his pack and continued on his way.

Now in every city the boy had come to he would enter the synagogue, go up to the pulpit, and ask if anyone in that city knew his father. This is what he did when he arrived at the third city. An old man sitting near the pulpit reached up and took the book from his hand and opened it. When he did, a look of great surprise crossed his face, and he said, "This book is mine, and I gave it to my son. How do you come to have it?" "It belongs to my father," said the boy. Then the old man embraced the boy, kissed him and cried, "I am your grandfather and my son is your father!" The boy asked that his grandfather not reveal this to his father. "Where can my father be found?" he asked. "He comes to this synagogue every day," said the grandfather. "He should arrive shortly." "Good," said the boy, "I will wait for him."

But for some reason, on that day the father did not come to the synagogue. After the services, the grandfather and grandson walked together to the grandfather's dwelling and the old man said to his son, who also lived there, "There is a young man here who wants to ask you something." Of course the father did not recognize his son, and the son had also never seen his father. But when the boy took out the *tallis* and asked, "Do you know a man by this name?" the father was thunderstruck, and was not able to speak a word. At last he said, "Where did you get this?" "From my mother," answered the boy. Then he embraced his son and kissed him, and the boy immediately asked his father to return to his mother. "I cannot return!" said the father. "But, said the boy, "you are my father and my mother's husband. I have received a remedy from Elijah the Prophet himself, and when my mother drinks the water in which I have boiled the leaves of a certain tree, she will become as beautiful as any woman." And so he persuaded his father, who returned home with him.

Now when they reached his home, the young man entered the house first and said to his mother, "I have brought you a potion, mother. You must boil these leaves in water and then drink it. I received this remedy from Elijah the Prophet himself, and he promised that after you drink it, you will become like all other women." His mother boiled the leaves and drank the water and behold, her face began to be transformed. Her donkey ears disappeared, and before long she had become a woman as beautiful as any other, and in fact far more beautiful than most. When her husband came in and saw his beautiful wife, he could not believe his eyes, and he gladly came back to her. So it was that after this, father and mother and son lived together in comfort and happiness, and they never forgot the blessing of Elijah the Prophet, who saved them from the terrible curse.

As for the witch, one day she made the mistake of pronouncing a spell while she was standing next to a mirror, and she immediately became a donkey. And when the poor man she had turned into a donkey saw this, he gave her a powerful kick, and at the same instant he was transformed back into a man. Then he got on the donkey that was the witch and began to beat her, and did not stop until he had returned to his house, where she had cast the spell on him in the first place. He tied her up outside the house and forced her to serve him from then on for as long as she lived.

Iraq: Oral Tradition

The Healing Waters

According to legend, King Solomon built a wonderful Mikvah, a ritual bath, whose waters healed all those who purified themselves therein. This bath, with its miraculous powers, continued to help all who sought healing even after the death of King Solomon. But it was destroyed along with the Temple in Jerusalem, and the secret of those healing waters was never discovered.

Now the miracles and wonders of King Solomon were known not only among his people, the Jews, but they were spoken of throughout the entire world. Tales of Solomon were carried to every corner of the earth. So too were the tales of Solomon told among the Arabs of Turkey, so that the legend of the healing waters was well known.

Now it happened in the days when Sultan Abdul Aziz ruled Istanbul, that an evil minister of the Sultan, who also served as the court artist, decided to use this legend to bring harm to the Jews of that kingdom, and to one Jew in particular whom he hated, David ben Abraham. For he was the most influential advisor in the court, and the evil minister resented him greatly.

Therefore the evil minister approached the Sultan one day and said, "Surely the Sultan is familiar with the reports of the wonderful bath built by King Solomon and its healing waters." The Sultan acknowledged that he knew the legend, and the evil minister said, "In the time of King Solomon, Jerusalem was the capital of the world, but in our time Istanbul is the greatest city on the earth, and you, its ruler, are the most powerful king since the time of King Solomon. Would it not be appropriate for one such as yourself, Oh great Sultan, to have a wonderful bath, such as that of King Solomon?"

Now the Sultan was flattered by the comparison of himself to King Solomon, although in truth he was not nearly as wise nor as great a ruler. But the devious words of the evil minister convinced him that if he could only possess such a miraculous bath with healing waters, all the world would kneel at his feet. Yet he did not know if the secret of that bath had been preserved, so he asked the minister, who replied, "The secret has been kept among the Jews, your majesty. In fact, it is known to your trusted advisor, David ben Abraham. But I do not think he will be willing to reveal it to you."

The Sultan was shocked at this suggestion, and said, "I trust David ben Abraham before all others, and he has shown many times that he would hold back nothing from me!" This was exactly what the evil minister was hoping the Sultan would say, and he replied, "Surely the Sultan is correct. Still, this secret has been kept among the Jews for many centuries. But if the Jew were to hesitate to reveal it, the Sultan has many powers of persuasion at his command." And the Sultan said, "I will call in David ben Abraham at once, and you will witness all that takes place." Then a messenger was sent to bring David ben Abraham to the Sultan at once.

With his Jewish advisor standing before him, the sultan said, "It is true, is it not, that you are well-acquainted with the traditions of your people?" David ben Abraham said, "Yes, and if I have any wisdom at all with which to serve your majesty, it derives entirely from these sacred studies, to which I have devoted myself all the days of my life." The king nodded and said, "In that case, are you familiar with the legend of the wondrous bath of King Solomon?" David acknowledged that he knew of this tale, and then the king said, "That is good, for I now command you to construct such a bath within one year, exactly like that of King Solomon. Furthermore, the waters of this bath must be miraculous, like those in the bath of Solomon. They must be able to heal all who set foot inside them! And if you succeed in building this bath, I will appoint you governor of all of Istanbul for the rest of your life. But if you fail, you and all your fellow Jews in this land will forfeit your lives!"

David ben Abraham heard these words with disbelief, for the Sultan had never spoken to him in this manner before, and the order was so impossible as to be perverse. For he knew that the plans of the bath of Solomon had been lost since the days of the destruction of the Temple, nor was the secret of where or how Solomon had obtained those healing waters known. David, who was indeed a wise man, recognized at once that the king did not think of this diabolical plan himself. He understood that the evil minister must have put him up to it. And he was overwhelmed with fear that such an evil decree had fallen upon him and his people.

David returned home, filled with bitterness and deep in mourning, and wondered what he must do to prevent this evil decree from coming to pass. At last he decided he would visit the man whom he knew to be the wisest in all the land. This was Moses ben Maimon, the great Maimonides, or, as he was known to his people, the Rambam. For at one time the Rambam made his home in Istanbul, far from Alexandria, where he now lived.

When the Rambam heard of the evil decree he was deeply shocked, and recognized that a great curse hung over the heads of the Turkish Jews. He immersed himself in his studies and sought to discover all that he could about the miraculous bath of Solomon. Because he could not only understand the meaning of all that was written down, but could read between the lines as well and derive the hidden meanings, the Rambam at last succeeded in deciphering the dimensions of the royal bath, which had served as the holy Mikvah in the Temple. So too did he discover the spell cast by

King Solomon that made the waters heal all who purified themselves therein.

Now in order to pronounce that spell, it was required that the secret Name of God be spoken, but the true pronunciation of the Name had been lost at the time of the destruction of the Temple. And even though the Rambam knew every word of the spell, he could not complete it, since he did not know how to pronounce the Name. The Rambam prayed with great intensity to the Holy One, blessed be He, to reveal this secret to him only long enough that he might cast the spell on the waters of that bath.

The Rambam opened the pages of the Torah in order to delve further into this mystery, when his eyes fell upon the line *And it shall be as a Covenant between us.* He then understood that God had decided to answer his prayer. That night, in a dream, the angel Raziel delivered the secret of the Divine Name to the Rambam, so that it was on his lips when he awoke. And when he awoke the Rambam went at once to David ben Abraham and told him that he could now go to the Sultan and declare that he was ready to built the royal bath.

So it was that by using the dimensions discovered by the Rambam, David ben Abraham was able to build a royal bath that had not seen its equal since the time of Solomon. After that a spring was dug that supplied the bath with fresh water, and on the night the bath was completed, the Rambam came there with David ben Abraham. The Rambam asked him to remain outside, to see that no one entered. Then he immersed himself in the waters of the bath, and spoke the secret Name he had learned in his dream. All at once he felt the weight of the years fall away, and a great peace and sense of calm came over him.

Then, when the Rambam stepped outside of the bath, he found that a scar he had on his arm had vanished, and that all of his wrinkles had disappeared. But so too did he find that he no longer knew the secret of how to pronounce the Name. Thus he understood that the Holy One had seen fit to protect his people in that time of danger, and that the waters of the bath were indeed as miraculous as those in the bath of King Solomon.

Now when the Sultan saw that majestic bath, he was astonished at its beauty. And when he immersed himself in those healing waters and discovered how wonderful they were, he was overwhelmed with gratitude to David ben Abraham. For now he felt certain he would be hailed as the greatest ruler since King Solomon. But when the evil minister found that instead of destroying the influence of the Jew, he had greatly enhanced it, he grew sick at heart. To make matters worse, the king called upon the minister, as court artist, to paint the walls of the bath in a manner worthy of their splendor. But the minister soon found that the paint peeled off the bath almost as quickly as he applied it, and he realized that in this way he was being punished for his evil plan.

When the time drew near for the painting of the walls of the bath to be completed, the evil minister became frantic for he greatly feared the Sultan's wrath. At last, in desperation, he threw himself on the mercy of David ben Abraham. Even though David knew full well that the evil minister had been behind the king's order to build the bath with the healing waters, still he had compassion on him and revealed the secret of how to paint on those walls. For any paint with lead in it failed to cling to those pure walls; only pure oil paints could be used.

In this way the minister was finally able to paint the walls, completing his work just in time by never stopping to eat or sleep. The Sultan was greatly pleased with his work, but the evil minister was too exhausted to feel anything except relief. And in his perverse way, he blamed David ben Abraham for his suffering, rather than feeling gratitude for his assistance. And the evil minister vowed to himself that he would one day have his revenge upon the Jew.

Meanwhile the Sultan looked upon David ben Abraham with great favor, and appointed him Governor of Istanbul. He consulted with him daily, in long walks by the shore of the sea. Then one day it happened that as they were walking near the waters, the king's ring, on which the royal seal was affixed, slipped from his finger and was carried off by the tide. The king was devastated, because that ring and its seal had been in his family for many generations, and it was the symbol of his rule. The king feared that this might be an evil omen, and in his confusion he blamed David ben Abraham, with whom he had been walking, and said, "The loss of this ring is a terrible sign, I fear. And since it occured in your presence, you are somehow responsible for it. Does it portend that the Jews are going to revolt, perhaps, with you as their leader?" David ben Abraham could not believe these words, yet he also recognized that the Sultan was deeply upset over losing his ring. Still, he looked into the Sultan's eyes and said, "No such revolt is portended, nor is it planned. I thought the king had recognized that my loyalty and that of my people is assured."

But the Sultan did not feel in the least reasonable, so he said, "If your loyalty is all that you profess, then recover my ring within thirty days. If you do, I will eliminate all taxes on the Jews, and give them my full protection. But if you do not, you and your people will surely suffer!" Then the king turned around and walked off alone, still distressed by the loss of his royal ring.

David ben Abraham realized that another disaster had befallen the Jews, and he hurried once again to consult with the wise Rambam. At first even the Rambam was at a loss as to how the Sultan's ring could be recovered. But the Rambam studied the sacred texts and read between the lines and discovered a spell by which it would be possible for David ben Abraham to descend into the sea, to the palace at the bottom where Leviathan rules the underwater world.

At that very time, however, the evil minister, who had learned with great delight of the king's new ultimatum to the Jews, had come up with a plan to ruin David ben Abraham once and for all. To be certain that David could not recover the Sultan's ring, the evil minister had spies report all that he did. One day he learned that David had ordered a new pair of shoes to be made. So the evil minister went to the shoemaker, and offered him a royal sum to sew into those shoes papers in which the Muslim religion was questioned and the Sultan himself was attacked.

The shoemaker did as he was paid to do and the shoes were delivered. Then the evil minister informed the king of a plot against him, to be led by David ben Abraham. The king ordered David to be arrested at once, and his shoes to be examined to see if anything was sown into the soles. And when the incriminating papers were discovered, the king grew very pale and ordered that he be executed at once, by being cast into the sea.

Now when a great crowd passed near the home of the Rambam, he wondered what had taken place, and he was told of the purpose of the procession to the sea—to send David ben Abraham to his death. The Rambam hurried until he reached the shore, and just as he did, he saw them cast David ben Abraham into the depths of the sea. At that instant he pronounced the spell he had learned, causing David to be protected as if surrounded by a shell of air, so that he could breathe as he plunged into the waters. So too was he carried directly to the bottom, to the kingdom ruled by Leviathan.

There, far beneath the surface, David was greeted as if he were the greatest ruler, for the beauty of the bath he had built was known even in the kingdom at the bottom of the sea. There Leviathan told him that he could have any wish, and David wished that the king's ring might be returned to him. Leviathan gave the order, and before long the fish that had swallowed the ring was found, and the ring brought to David. He gave thanks and asked to be returned to the world above. Leviathan agreed to do so at once but asked David to request on his return that the evil minister be sent to the underwater kingdom as well.

So it was that while the great mob of people stood on the shore, waiting for the body of David ben Abraham to rise to the surface, he suddenly appeared, very much alive, even though more than thirty minutes had passed since he had been cast into the deep! The people were astounded to see him step out of the waters, and even the king was terrified, thinking that he was seeing a ghost. Imagine his surprise when David approached him and without saying a word handed him his lost ring! Then David described all that had taken place, and everyone was astounded.

Now among those gathered to see the Jew executed was the evil minister. He stared with disbelief as David emerged alive from what had seemed a certain death. And as he looked on, David said to the Sultan, "Even in the world below they speak of your wonderful bath, your majesty, and they are considering building one of their own. Therefore Leviathan, the ruler of the deep, discussed the matter with me, and now he would like you to send below the court painter as well, so that he may consult with him on painting the bath." The Sultan, staggered by this tale, did not hesitate, but ordered that the honored painter be cast into the waters at once. And the painter, who was the evil minister, was vain enough to believe that Leviathan had really called upon his help. So he did not protest when he was cast into the sea. And no sooner did he plunge beneath the surface than a great fish swallowed him and carried him straight to Gehenna, where he is still being punished to this day, painting a bath very much like that of King Solomon, but no sooner is his painting complete than the flames of Gehenna consume it, and he is forced to paint the walls all over again.

As for David ben Abraham, he lived for many years honored by all, and the Sultan never doubted his loyalty again. And of course he continued to consult the Rambam and to learn Torah from him, for the Rambam was the finest teacher the world has ever seen. And that was a fertile period as well in the lives of the Jews of that land, who flourished in the shelter of the Holy One, blessed be He.

Turkey: Oral Tradition

The Reincarnation of a Tzaddik

In a faraway land lived a baker and his wife and daughter. This baker had been quite old when he had married, and so even though he was a father, he was old enough to be a grandfather. The baker's daughter, who was fifteen years old, always helped her father with the baking. One day, while she was baking loaves of bread, she opened the door of the oven and something small, round, and black rolled out and fell into her hand. When the girl held it up to see what it was, the ball jumped straight into her mouth, and before she knew it, she had swallowed it. She did not know what it had been, but she guessed it was a bit of dough that had fallen off and become burned, and she thought no more about it.

Then it happened that a few months later the girl's belly became swollen, as if she were with child. This greatly disturbed her parents, who had always found her to be exceptionally pure. When the girl swore that she was innocent, her parents believed her, for they knew she would not bring them to shame. At last she remembered the strange incident with the black ball and told her parents of it. The story astonished them, but they did not doubt that it was true. Nine months after she had swallowed the ball, the girl gave birth to a boy.

The girl's mother raised the child as if it were her own, which is what they told the world. Then it happened that when the child was only a few days old he opened his mouth and spoke in the voice of a child but with the words of a grown man. He asked for the same food they ate, and not the food of an infant. This completely astounded everyone in the baker's family, and they realized that the child was as strange as was his origin.

When the child was a year old he asked to be dressed so that he could accompany the baker to the synagogue to pray. The boy also insisted that clothes be made for him so that he would be dressed properly in the House of Prayer. The girl and her mother both worked on these clothes, and when they were ready, the boy walked with his grandfather to the synagogue, taking the path that ran alongside the sea. As they set out, the boy asked his grandfather to promise that no matter what he did until they returned home from the syunagogue, he was not to question it. Since the child was not an ordinary one in any respect, the grandfather agreed to this strange request.

On the way the boy told his grandfather that he was tired, since he was not used to walking such a distance, and he asked to stop at the house they were passing. The grandfather agreed to this, and knocked on the door. When the people opened the door, he asked if they could rest for a while, and they welcomed them in and offered them food and drink. So it was that they rested there and the people were exceptionally kind to them. Then, just as they were about to leave, the boy picked up the beautiful silver candelabra that was the couple's only valuable possession, and threw it out the open window into the sea. The boy's grandfather was shocked by this seemingly evil deed, and the people were heartbroken, although they did not hold the old man responsible since the deed had been committed by an infant. The grandfather wondered greatly at why the boy had done this and wanted to ask him about it, but he remembered his vow and remained silent.

As they were walking together along the path they came to a

house that was being built. Many builders were working there, and they all seemed exceptionally cruel. They often struck one another, cursed and fought. When the boy approached them and asked if he might rest there, they shouted at him and chased both him and the baker away. Then the boy raised his arms, and the building was suddenly completed. The boy and the old man hurried off, before the builders realized that it had been the boy who had performed that miracle. But such a reward for such evil people completely confused the baker, and he wondered greatly why the boy had so used his great powers. But he did not ask, since he had vowed to remain silent, and they continued on the way together, until they reached the synagogue. There the infant boy amazed all those present by praying as well as any man, and all who heard him had no doubt that he would grow up to become a great Tzaddik.

By the time they left the synagogue, night had fallen, and the boy said that he was again in need of rest. There was an old woman who was coming toward them on the path, and the boy asked his grandfather to ask her if they might come to her house. This the old man did, and the woman gladly welcomed them to be her guests. She told them that she lived alone with her only son, since her husband had died, and although they were very poor, they would gladly share their food with the old man and the boy.

The widow treated them with every kindness and gave them a tasty meal, and when she offered them a room where they could spend the night, the old man gratefully accepted, since it is dangerous to walk in the dark. But after everyone else had gone to sleep, the infant boy got up, took a sharp knife from the kitchen, and killed the cow that was the widow's only possession in the world.

In the morning, when this deed was discovered, the boy pretended to be as shocked as everyone else, but the old man knew that he was responsible for this foul deed. Then he grew greatly angered, and when they were alone he accused the boy of having slaughtered the cow. The boy confessed that he had done so, but reminded his grandfather of his promise not to question his deeds until they had returned home. But the old man was so outraged by the boy's deeds that he demanded to know the reason for them, even though the boy warned him he would later regret having asked.

Then the boy revealed that a wicked neighbor of the couple whose candelabra he had thrown into the sea had falsely accused them of having stolen it, and the king's guards were on their way at that very time and would have arrested them for theft had the boy not thrown the candelabra out the window. As for the wicked builders, they had the souls of those who built the Tower of Babel, and their souls would never know any peace. Now there was a great treasure buried in the place where they were erecting that building, and the boy had magically completed the building so that they would not discover the treasure they obviously did not deserve.

As for the widow's cow, the boy had heard a heavenly voice announce that her only son was shortly to die, and the boy had killed the cow as a sacrifice in place of her son, who would now be permitted to live a long life.

After this the boy revealed that he was the reincarnation of the soul of a Tzaddik who had not finished all of his destined deeds in this world when he had died, and so came back to complete them. But now that the deeds had been performed and his identity revealed, it was necessary for him to depart from this world. When the old man heard this, he burst into tears, for he had broken his vow to remain silent. And when he raised his head to bless his grandson, he found that the boy had disappeared.

Then the grandfather returned home and told his wife and daughter all that had happened, and although they missed the boy very much, still they were very proud that they had been chosen to help bring a Tzaddik into the world.

Egypt: Oral Tradition

King Solomon's Ring

There was once in the city of Cairo a king of the House of Israel, wise and pious, who poured over books of learning day and night. This king had a son, whose name was Bulukiya. When the king grew old and was near death, he informed the Council of the Elders that his son Bulukiya was to be his successor. Then he heaved a last sigh and took his leave of this world. And after the funeral of the king his son Bulukiya was made king in his stead. He proved to be a just ruler and the people had peace in his time.

Now one day Bulukiya entered his father's treasuries, and discovered a hidden door to an inner chamber he had never seen before. He opened it and entered, and there he found a tiny room, not much bigger than a closet. In it was a marble column, on top of which was an ebony casket. He opened this and in it he found a casket of gold, containing a book. He read the book and found a secret account of the Messiah, and how he would arrive in future days. And the book revealed how the prophecies of the coming of the Messiah had been concealed in the Torah and the Books of Abraham.

Bulukiya was startled at this discovery. He wondered why his father had never revealed it to him. Perhaps he had not thought him ready to receive this secret information, and assumed that he would one day discover that door for himself, as he indeed had done. In any case, that book changed Bulukiya's life. He resolved to wander over the earth, in search of this Redeemer, or else to die of longing for him. He informed the Council of the Elders, who then told him that his father had in fact planned for such a day. As he had suspected, the book had been intended for him, when the time was right. And his father had commended the council to permit him to set out on that journey, for to do so was his destiny, which the soothsayers had read in the stars at the time of his birth.

Bulukiya was very gratified to hear this, for all men love to think that they follow the path assigned to them by fate. He changed his royal garment for one of goat's hair, and put on coarse sandals and set out on his solitary quest. He traveled toward Syria, and when he reached the sea he found a ship and signed on as one of the crew. They sailed for many weeks until they reached an island. The ship stopped there, so that the crew could replenish its store of water, for that island was known to have a fresh-water pool. Bulukiya went to shore with the rest of the crew, and set out to explore the island, which was overgrown with foilage and fruit trees of every kind. He ate his fill of fruit, then he sat down to rest at the foot of a tree. Now one of those fruits caused him to grow drowsy, and before long he fell asleep. When he awoke several hours later, he discovered that the ship had set sail without him. At first Bulukiya was very distressed, and clutched his hair in anguish. But at last he accepted his fate, and thanked God that at least the island was abundant in food and water, so he set out to explore the rest of the island.

As Bulukiya traveled toward the island's far side, he thought he heard faint strains of something that sounded like a chant. At first he was certain that the island must be inhabited, and he was greatly relieved. So too did he assume the inhabitants to be peaceful, for their prayers proclaimed the greatness of the Holy

One, blessed be He. But then, when he reached a place where he was close enough to see who it was, he discovered, to his great astonishment, that it was a large group of snakes who were praying, snakes far larger than any he had ever seen. All at once Bulukiya found himself surrounded by snakes, and he trembled with terror, but the snakes did not attack him. Instead they ordered him to follow them, and brought him to their queen. And when the Queen of the Serpents saw that there was a man on the island, she was astonished, and she demanded to know where he was from, and how he had come to be there.

Bulukiya, who was himself amazed to speak to a serpent, told the queen that he was a ruler among the Children of Israel, and that he had set out on a sacred quest. So too did he ask to know where he was, and who were the snakes that inhabited that island. The Queen of the Serpents said, "Know, king among men, that I am the Queen of the Serpents. We are dwellers of Gehenna, and we were created to punish those souls sent to Gehenna to be purged of their evil aspects. Twice a year, in the summer and the winter, Gehenna boils over and casts us forth, onto this island. Before long Gehenna will inhale and draw us back down again."

Bulukiya laughed when he learned this, for he had been seeking the holy Reedemer, and instead he had arrived at the very gates of Hell! The Queen asked him why he had laughed, and when he told her she said, "Know, Bulukiya, that there is nothing I long for more than that the time of Redemption should arrive. For when the time of the Messiah is nigh, the punishments of Gehenna will come to an end, and we will be free to live in peace. Thus if you will vow to inform me of any knowledge you acquire in your quest, I will reveal a great secret to you, which will prove invaluable." Naturally Bulukiya made this vow to the queen, and she, for her part, led him to a place on that island where a small, circular patch of a very rare and exotic herb grew which was not to be found anywhere else in the world. And the Queen of the Serpents said, "This herb, Bulukiya, is more precious than all the gold in the world. When pounded and squeezed it will form a juice, and when this is rubbed upon the soles of your shoes it will confer on them the power of walking upon the sea itself, as if it were dry land. Furthermore, all that is required is that you state where it is that you wish to go, and your feet will be guided there. Surely this will greatly aid you in your quest."

Bulukiya could barely imagine that such a wonderful herb could exist, but then he realized that if there could be a kingdom of serpents who spoke and prayed, then such a magic herb might also be possible. And he thanked the Queen of the Serpents with all his heart for revealing this great secret, and picked a handful of those herbs. As the queen watched him, he squeezed them between two rocks, until its juice began to run out, and caught this juice in a large leaf and poured it into his leather pouch. Then he rubbed that which remained on the leaf onto the soles of his shoes, and, very cautiously, he stepped into the water and found, to his immense wonder, that he could indeed walk on the waters, that they supported him as fully as if they were land. So too could he make great strides, much longer than those he made when walking on the earth. Bulukiya was so enthralled by this amazing ability that he soon found himself in the middle of the sea, and when he tried to find the island, he could not. For a moment he was frightened, but then he remembered that the Queen of the Serpents had told him to simply announce where he wanted to go. So he spoke his wish to return to the island of the serpents, and in a flash he found himself spirited across the waters and at the shore of the island, at the very place where the Queen of the Serpents still waited for him. That is when Bulukiya began to realize the wonders he might accomplish with such a magic herb, and he gave grateful thanks to the Queen of the Serpents, and promised to return once he had completed his quest. Then he took his leave of her and as he stepped upon the sea he stated his wish to travel to the Holy Land. And an instant later he found himself sailing across the waters, much faster than any ship.

In this way Bulukiya soon managed to cross the sea and reach the Holy Land in a single day. From there he walked until he came to the holy city of Jerusalem. For all of the prophecies of the Messiah said that he would come there, to the site of the Temple, which the Messiah would restore with a single motion of his hand. Bulukiya made his way to that place, and prayed with great fervor at the Western Wall, which was all that remained of the Temple. Praying beside him was a man who was also absorbed in his devotions, but when he finished praying he noticed Bulukiya and observed by the clothes he wore that he was a stranger. And when Bulukiya turned to go, this man approached him and hailed him as a true believer, and asked him what his name was, and from where he had come. Bulukiya told him that he was a stranger from the city of Cairo, who had made a pilgrimage to the Holy Land. Then the man, who said his name was Affan, invited Bulukiya to come with him to his lodging and to remain as his guest. And this, of course, Bulukiya was more than glad to do.

Before long Bulukiya and Affan became close friends, and when Bulukiya decided that he could trust him, he told him the true purpose of his quest, and of his good fortune at the hands of the Queen of the Serpents. Affan could barely believe that anyone could cross the sea by foot, and he begged Bulukiya to demonstrate the power of the magic herb for him. So they set out together for the sea, and when they reached the water Bulukiya spread some of the juice of the magic herb on the soles of their shoes and, lo and behold, both found themselves nearly flying over the face of the waters.

When they returned to shore, Affan was wildly excited, and it was then that he confided to Bulukiya a quest of his own that he had desired to undertake for many years. For once, when he had been a very young man, Affan had met an old prophet who had confided to him the secret of the resting place of King Solomon, and the fate of the enchanted ring that he had worn, which enabled him to perform his many feats of magic and wonder. The prophet had said that a genie, obeying Solomon's dying wish, had borne his body to a palace carved out of rocks upon an emerald island at the end of the Seven Seas. The genie had set his body upon a throne there, with the ring still on his finger, and there Solomon's body was still said to be found, perfectly preserved. The prophet had taught him seven conjurations to repeat should he ever reach that enchanted island, to protect him from the forces that guarded Solomon.

Ever since, Affan had been possessed by a great desire to seek out that island and obtain that magic ring for himself. But, of course, he could not, since he had no idea where the island could be found. But now that he knew of the magic herb, which could take them wherever they wished, they surely could find that island, and once they did the ring would be theirs! Bulukiya now saw the hand of fate in his meeting with Affan, for should they succeed in obtaining King Solomon's ring they could use its magic in order to hasten the coming of the Redeemer for whom Bulukiya so longed, making possible the restoration of the Temple in Jerusalem and the abundant blessings that the secret book had promised were to begin in the End of Days.

So it was that Bulukiya and Affan made a sacred vow to set out together to seek the magic ring of King Solomon. And they vowed as well that should they succeed in obtaining it, they would use its magic to bring about the coming of the Messiah and not for any selfish purposes of their own. Now this is indeed what they vowed, but the truth is that Affan's desires were not the same as those of Bulukiya. He secretly thought to himself that once he had the magic ring in his possession he would not use it to bring about the End of Days, but rather to establish himself as a great ruler, as great as King Solomon himself. And then, when he did not need Bulukiya's help any longer, thought Affan, he would simply wish him out of existence.

Soon afterward, when they had gathered supplies to sustain them in their journey, Bulukiya and Affan came back to the shore of the sea, rubbed the juice of the magic herb on the soles of their shoes, and announced that they wished to travel to the island where King Solomon's body had been brought. Then, in an instant, they found themselves traveling over the face of the waters at a great speed, and in every hour they covered a distance greater than a speedy ship can travel in a month. For seven days and nights they sailed over those waters, crossing, in that way, each and every one of the Seven Seas, and on the eighth day they came in sight of a mountain, soaring high in the air, which shone with a green glow, as if it consisted solely of emerald. Soon they came to the shore of the island on which that mountain rose, and there they rejoiced and embraced each other, for they were certain that the precious ring was within their grasp.

They entered the passes of the mountain and walked on, until they saw from afar a cavern surmounted by a great dome, shining with light. They continued until they reached that cavern, and as soon as they entered it they beheld a throne of gold covered with every kind of jewel, and lying at full length upon the throne they saw, as they had hoped, the body of King Solomon, perfectly preserved. He was clad in robes of green silk woven with gold and embroidered with precious jewels, and his right hand lay upon his breast, and on his middle finger they saw the seal ring, whose luster outshone that of all other gems in the world.

Now Bulukiya started to go toward that throne, but Affan stopped him and told him that it might be very dangerous for Bulukiya to try to obtain the ring, and that it would be better if he, Affan, made the attempt. He asked Bulukiya to repeat the conjurations that he had taught him, in order to protect them from the powers that guarded the body of King Solomon. This Bulukiya agreed to do, and he repeated the spells as Affan went forward to obtain the ring. At that moment Affan was overcome by a lust and greed far greater than any he had ever known, and he could barely wait for the moment when he would hold the ring in his hands. So possessed was he that he forgot to repeat the spells himself, as the prophet had told him to do. Instead he could only think of what he would do once he had made the ring his own. Long ago he had decided that his first wish, to test the powers of the ring, would be to cast Bulukiya into oblivion, so that he might have sole possession of the ring. Then, with the power of the ring combined with the powers the magic herb gave him, he would be invincible, and would soon become the most powerful ruler in the world.

Now as Affan drew near the throne a mighty serpent slid from beneath it, and cried out at him with a cry so terrible that the floor began to tremble. Sparks flew from its mouth, and it said, "Begone, fool, or you are a dead man!" But Affan was so filled with lust to possess the magic ring that he did not turn back, but continued to approach the throne. Then the serpent blew a fiery blast at him, so that the cavern was almost set on fire, and cried out, "Woe to you! Unless you turn back I will consume you!" Hearing these words Bulukiya began to tremble and left the cave, for he sorely feared for his life. But Affan, as if in a trance, went forward until he reached the throne of King Solomon. Then he put out his hand and touched the ring and tried to draw it off of Solomon's finger. But at that moment the serpent blew a great blast of flame at him once more, and he became a heap of ashes. And when Bulukiya saw this from the entrance to the cavern, he fell down in a faint.

Now, unknown to Bulukiya, the spirit of his deceased father had been watching over him all along and followed him wherever he went. And when his father's spirit saw the great danger he was in, should the fiery serpent turn upon him, he hurried to the angel Gabriel and begged and pleaded that the angel descend to earth without delay to rouse him and protect him from that great danger. And because of the high regard for the pious soul of Bulukiya's father in Paradise, the angel did indeed descend, and roused him from his faint. Now Bulukiya almost fainted again when he found himself face to face with the angel, but when the angel mentioned the name of his pious father, Bulukiya felt himself strengthened. Then the angel asked him what he was doing there, and Bulukiya told the angel of his great longing to call forth the Messiah, so that he might bring the End of Days.

Then the angel Gabriel spoke and said, "Know, Bulukiya, that the time of the coming of the Messiah is set in heaven, and it is not possible to hasten that time, even with the power of King Solomon's ring." Bulukiya was downcast at these words, for he felt that all of his efforts had been futile. And when the angel saw this, he said, "Despair not, Bulukiya. For your quest has been a good one in many ways. For now you have earned the kind of wisdom necessary to rule your kingdom with the wise justice for which

King Solomon was so justly famous." And Bulukiya understood that this was true, and that the time had come for him to return to the kingdom that he had abandoned so long ago.

Then the angel Gabriel took his leave and ascended into Paradise, and Bulukiya left the cavern of King Solomon and crossed the mountain and returned to the sea. Once more he rubbed some of the juice of the magic herb upon the soles of his shoes, and then he stated his wish to return to the island of the Queen of the Serpents, so that he might inform her of his discovery that the time of the Messiah could not be hastened.

So it was that Bulukiya did indeed fulfill his vow to the Queen of the Serpents, and after that he traveled through each and every one of the Seven Seas and had many other adventures and learned many things, until he had become one of the wisest men since the days of Solomon himself. And when he returned to his kingdom the Council of the Elders recognized that he had gained great wisdom in his long journey, and gladly restored his throne to him. And in the years that followed Bulukiya ruled with an even hand and was famous for the justice of his decisions throughout the world. So too did he continue to immerse himself in the sacred texts of the Torah and the Books of Abraham, until all recognized as well that he was a pious man of the stature of his own father, worthy of the admiration of all.

Egypt: c. Eighth Century

The Magic Lamp
of Rabbi Adam

Over the years, Rabbi Adam protected his people, the Jews, from every kind of danger, and tales about his marvels were told everywhere. These tales reached the ears of the ruler of the kingdom in which Rabbi Adam made his home. The king had little use for the Jews in the first place, and his hatred was fueled by his vizier, a truly evil man. The vizier often spoke of the dangers Rabbi Adam posed to the kingdom, should he ever lead the Jews in revolt. At last the king decided that they had better do something about him.

The vizier wanted to have Rabbi Adam killed, but the king feared that this might drive the Jews to revolt, the very thing he was trying to prevent. So instead he had Rabbi Adam sent into exile into the wilderness far from the habitats of man. An armed troop of guards led Rabbi Adam there—it took them a year to reach their destination and a year to return, so isolated was that place.

Now Rabbi Adam might have resisted those guards; he might simply have pronounced a spell to become invisible, for he was a great sorcerer. But he put his faith and trust completely in God, for he knew that if he was being sent to a distant place, it was for a purpose, even if he did not know what it was. So he did not resist. When he was alone in that wilderness, Rabbi Adam wondered what mission awaited him in that desolate place. For two days and nights he wandered, eating the wild berries and fruits he found growing there, sleeping in the branches of a tree. But on the third night, as it grew dark, Rabbi Adam saw a light in the distance, and he walked toward it.

Eventually he reached a small house in the woods, a wooden hut. He knocked on the door, and an old woman answered. Now Rabbi Adam needed to take no more than one look at that woman to know that she was a witch, for he could see the presence of evil in her eyes. But he revealed nothing of this to her, and told her he was a lost traveler in search of food and water and a place to spend the night. The old woman laughed and invited him to come inside.

Once inside, the old woman told Rabbi Adam that if he wanted to stay there, he would have to promise to work the next day. Rabbi Adam readily agreed, and the woman served him food and drink. Now Rabbi Adam knew better than to eat the food of a witch, but he created the illusion that he had done so, not wanting to alert her. And when he slept that night he slept with one eye open, for she might try to harm him. For Rabbi Adam knew the ways of witches, and how to protect himself as well.

But the witch did not harm him that night. She had already decided that he might be useful to her—to recover the lamp in the well. For in the well was a magic lamp, containing a genie. This genie could be used for good or evil, depending on the nature of whoever possessed the lamp. It had been placed in the well by its last owner, who feared its great power. Before he had commanded the genie to sink to the bottom of the well and to remain there in the lamp, he had the genie pronounce a spell making it impossible for anyone to recover the lamp unless he was a pure soul. The way was blocked to anyone evil, and that is why the witch, who coveted that lamp more than anything in the world, could not retrieve it.

Now just as Rabbi Adam had recognized the evil in the old

woman's eyes, so too had she recognized the pure aura that surrounded him. And just as he was wary in her presence, so was she wary in his, but like him she kept the secret of her knowledge to herself. So she did not at once reveal the true purpose for which she intended to use him.

Now the witch's plan was to frighten Rabbi Adam until he was in her power. And thus she had put a magic potion into his food, which would cause him to lose his will. She believed that he had eaten the food, and thus was under the power of the potion. So the next morning she told him that his life was as good as lost, for the soul of anyone who tasted her food was in her power for the rest of their life, unless he was able to accomplish three tasks that she assigned. The old woman cackled as she explained this, and asked Rabbi Adam if he preferred to give up his soul at once, or if he wanted to try to undertake the tasks. Rabbi Adam was very solemn, and told her that he would surely choose the tasks, for his soul was his most precious possession.

Then the witch led him outside into the forest, which stretched around them as far as the eye could see. There the witch gave him the first task: to pick up all the firewood in that forest and pile it up behind her hut all in one day. She led Rabbi Adam into the forest and told him not to come back until his work was done. When she left him, she was laughing, for a thousand men could not finish that task in one day.

Rabbi Adam waited until the witch had returned to her hut, then he took out the magic whistle he carried with him at all times, with which he could call upon the birds and beasts. He blew the whistle one time and in a flash, one of every kind of beast from that forest gathered around him. Rabbi Adam, who spoke the language of them all, told them of the task, and asked for their help in completing it. All through the night, the animals gathered firewood and flung it onto a great pile, until the forest had been stripped of all its dry wood. By morning, a mountain of firewood loomed behind the witch's hut.

When the witch awoke the next morning, it was still dark. She could not understand why, but when she looked outside the window she saw the great mountain behind the hut, and she could not believe her eyes. From the window she could not see the top of it! She ran outside, and there she saw it reached almost to the sky, like some kind of tottering Tower of Babel. The witch shrieked when she saw it, for she knew that somehow Rabbi Adam had completed the task, but how? Then she realized that he was no ordinary wayfarer, but himself a great sorcerer. And she knew that she was in for the fight of her life.

Still, the witch did not reveal her fears, acting as if it had been a simple matter to build up a mere mountain of firewood. She coldly went on to the second task. He must turn that mountain of wood into a blazing fire, she ordered, but if so much as a spark of that fire touched her hut right beside it, his soul was as good as lost. Now the witch did not care what happened to the hut, since once she had the lamp in her possession she would no longer live there, but rule the world from some great palace.

At first Rabbi Adam wondered how such a thing could be done, how one could contain such a mighty blaze. And he worried too that if the fire got out of control it could burn down the forest and destroy all the animals that made their home there. Then Rabbi took out the whistle and blew on it twice, and soon one of every kind of bird that lived in that forest came to him. He told them of the task, and then instructed the birds to fan a great wind with their wings, which would keep the fire from burning down the hut or anything else.

Then Rabbi Adam took a torch and lit the mountain of firewood. The witch, who watched him do this from her window, quickly left the hut and hid in the forest, a good distance away. She watched as that fire grew and grew, and then she watched in amazement as great flocks of birds hovered in the air and beat their wings above the flames. They remained there all that day and all night, until the fire completely consumed the mountain of wood. The next morning the witch was amazed to see that her hut was still standing, untouched by the flames; with Rabbi Adam standing next to it, smiling.

The witch had to struggle to restrain her fury, for she wanted more than anything to defeat Rabbi Adam once and for all. Then she told him, in a voice filled with rage, the third task: He was to descend into the well and bring her the lamp that was down there. Once again Rabbi Adam accepted the task, and followed the witch to the well. He lit a torch and climbed into the bucket and the witch lowered him into the well. It was so deep that by the time he reached the bottom, Rabbi Adam could not even see the witch at the top of the well, but could only hear her voice. There, in a crevice just above the level of the water, Rabbi Adam saw the glimmer of the golden lamp reflecting the fire of his torch. Rabbi Adam took the lamp in his hand and marveled at its beauty.

Just then he heard the voice of the witch, terrible and commanding, asking to know if he had found the lamp. Rabbi Adam called back that he had. The witch screamed for him to put it in the bucket and she would raise it, but he said that he would bring it up himself, when she pulled him up. The witch told him that although it was not difficult to lower him into the well, it would be too much for her to pull him up. She told him to send up the lamp and she would call upon the genie of the lamp to raise him up. But Rabbi Adam refused to let go of the lamp. He told her that if she told him how to call upon the genie, he would do it himself, just to be certain that he was not left behind in the well. And although the witch bitterly hated to reveal the secret to him, she saw that it was her only hope of getting the lamp, for Rabbi Adam would not give it up as she had hoped.

So the witch told him that the lamp had to be rubbed three times, in a special way in order to invoke the genie. Rabbi Adam did this, and the genie appeared right there in the well, so large that he reached from the bottom of the well to the top. When the witch saw the genie she screamed at him to give her the lamp. But the genie looked at her with disdain and said, "It is not you, but he who called upon me; so too is it he who possesess the lamp. I am at his command, not yours." When Rabbi Adam heard this, he said, "Let this be the first command, then: See to it that I am removed far from this well, along with the lamp, while the old witch remains at the bottom of the well in the form of a heavy stone!" The witch shrieked when she heard this command, but it was too late. An instant later Rabbi Adam found himself outside the witch's hut, where he could hear the great splash of a heavy rock as it sank to bottom of the well.

Now that Rabbi Adam had defeated the witch, he knew that he must return to the kingdom from which he had been exiled. It was then that he thought of a way to convince the king to repent, and to change his evil treatment of the Jews. Rabbi Adam rubbed the lamp in his hand three times, in the special way the witch had told him to, and again the genie appeared. And Rabbi Adam told him to snatch the princess after she had gone to sleep, and to bring her there.

That night the genie returned with the sleeping princess in his arms. Rabbi Adam gently woke her, and the princess was amazed to find herself in a strange place. She begged Rabbi Adam to help her return to the palace, but Rabbi Adam told her that she could not go back until she cleaned up the hut. She swept and cleaned it all night long, then he called upon the genie to take her back.

Now the next day, when the princess came to her father, the king, and told him that she had been kidnapped and taken into the forest and made to work all night, he thought that she must have had a vivid dream, or that she had only imagined it to take place. But when the princess slept all day long, and came back with the same story the next day, the king began to wonder, and on the third night he stationed a guard in her room.

The genie, however, merely put the guard to sleep, and for the third night she performed tasks for Rabbi Adam. He told her to inform her father that it was he who held her in his power, and that she would never have another night's sleep for the rest of her life unless the king revoked his decree sending him into exile—and revoked as well all of the evil decrees against the Jews. When the king heard this threat, and saw how exhausted and miserable his daughter had become, unfit for any suitor, he quickly agreed to revoke all the decrees as Rabbi Adam had demanded. So it was that Rabbi Adam was able to return to the kingdom, a hero to his people, whose days of persecution had come to an end.

Now the king had learned his lesson, and had no longer any

desire to challenge Rabbi Adam. But the evil vizier could not bear to see Rabbi Adam and the Jews victorious. He was certain that Rabbi Adam drew his powers from some magical object; and he was determined to find out what it was and to steal it for himself.

So it was that the vizier spoke to the princess every time he was alone with her about her ordeal with Rabbi Adam. He asked her to repeat every detail she could remember of what had happened, and in this way he learned of the magic lamp and of the genie that inhabited it. The vizier was certain that this was the source of all of Rabbi Adam's power, and he wasted no time hiring thieves to steal the lamp and bring it to him.

Thus it happened that Rabbi Adam returned to his home one day and found that his magic lamp was gone. He was greatly disturbed, not only for his loss, but because of the danger of that lamp falling into the wrong hands. Rabbi Adam went to his magic mirror, which permitted him to see anything he wanted. He learned that the lamp had come into the possession of the evil vizier, who spent all his time trying to make the genie come out of it, but so far without success. Rabbi Adam knew that he must get the lamp back before the vizier discovered the secret.

Therefore Rabbi Adam came up with a plan. He used his great powers to make the palace of the king vanish, and in its place he created a palace of illusion, identical to the first. Then he used his powers to disguise himself as the king, so that no one, no matter how close to the king, would have been able to tell the two of them apart. After this he sent for the evil vizier, commanding him to come at once. Of course the vizier obeyed the command of the king and soon stood before the disguised Rabbi Adam.

Rabbi Adam told the vizier that he urgently needed his advice on an important matter. He said, "Listen carefully, for I depend greatly on your wisdom. In this kingdom there is one who possesses a great treasure—a golden dove which lives and breathes although it is hammered out of gold. Such a treasure is fit, of course, only for a king, and knowing this, the man has kept the golden dove a secret. What do you think should be done to such an unfaithful subject?" The vizier answered at once: "It is well known, my Lord, that the king possesses all that lies within the boundaries of his kingdom, and all that his subjects possess they do so only at his behest. Therefore the matter is simple. Command this disloyal subject to return to you that which belongs to you by divine right!" "This, then, I shall do, exactly as you have said," Rabbi Adam, disguised as the king, responded. "And therefore I am commanding you, my subject, to bring me the golden lamp in your possession. And if you have not placed it in my hands within a single hour, your life is lost!"

Then the vizier grew terrified. He understood very well that the subject of whom the king had spoken was himself, and he ran as fast as he could and brought the lamp from his home and placed it in the hands of Rabbi Adam. No sooner did he do so than the palace and everything in it vanished, and the vizier found himself stranded in a wilderness. No matter where he went he was lost. At last he lay down to sleep, and in the morning he again found himself before the palace, where the king's guards woke him and asked to know what he was doing asleep there. The astounded vizier could only reply that the king surely understood, since it was he who had taken possession of the golden lamp. But since the king had no idea what lamp this was, he concluded that the vizier had lost his mind and ordered him to be locked up as a madman. Before long the vizier had indeed gone mad, and raved of nothing else but a genie who would serve the will of whoever possessed a certain magic lamp, which everyone knew, of course, could not exist.

Now Rabbi Adam made good use of that magic lamp all of his days, but only for purposes of good and for the protection of his people. He kept it in a well-hidden place, so that it should never be used for evil again. And the lives of the Jews of the land flourished as never before, for the king was no longer their enemy, and the evil vizier no longer held any power over them.

Egypt: Oral Tradition

Rabbi Adam and the
Star-Gazing King

Once there was a king who knew how to read the stars. He had been taught in his youth by a great soothsayer, and by listening carefully, the king had learned how to discern the secrets of the past and how to forecast the future. Every night he stood on his balcony and searched the stars with a wonderful telescope that had been a present of his father.

Now since the king understood so well the truths hidden in the stars, and recognized the importance of the stars in forming a man's character, he became very curious to know who had been born on the same day and at the same time as he. This question burned in his heart, and he spent every night searching for this secret in the stars.

At last the king discovered the name and city of someone who had been born under his constellation. This turned out to be a rabbi, none other than Rabbi Adam. Now Rabbi Adam was himself a great soothsayer and sorcerer, whose knowledge of the Other World was very deep. And he was possessed of great powers, including the knowledge of how to read the stars.

So it was that Rabbi Adam, in a faraway city, saw that the king was searching for him in the stars. But because Rabbi Adam was even more adept at reading the stars than the king himself, he saw that there was a secret purpose in the king's search, which even the king did not recognize. And so he awaited the arrival of the king, in the certainty that he would come.

The king announced to his vizier that he had decided to journey into his kingdom, to learn for himself the true needs of the people. He had decided to disguise himself as a merchant, so that no one would know his true identity, and he would leave his trusted vizier to rule in his absence until he returned. Then the king exchanged his royal robes for the clothes of a merchant, and set out on a horse for the city in which Rabbi Adam made his home.

Once the king arrived, he asked for the way to Rabbi Adam's house, and was told that he lived in the forest outside the city. This surprised the king, for he had expected that the one who shared his constellation would possess the finest mansion in the city. And his curiosity about Rabbi Adam grew even greater.

There in the forest the king found the hut of Rabbi Adam, and was astonished to see that it was built entirely of wood, like those of the poorest of men. He knocked on the door, but there was no answer. At last the king entered and found that although a fire was burning in the fireplace, the hut was empty. But he had not come all that way to give up, so he decided to wait there until Rabbi Adam returned.

The king looked about and saw that Rabbi Adam's only possessions were books. Then he noticed a small, silver mirror hanging on the wall, the only possession of any worth at all. The king stood up and went over to the mirror and peered into it. But he did not see his own image reflected in the mirror. Instead he saw his wife together with his vizier, in the chamber of the king. The king was somehow able to overhear them, and he heard the vizier and his wife plotting to take over his kingdom. They intended to have him arrested when he returned and to have him executed before he was able to reveal himself as the king. They would then announce that the king had died, and the king's wife would marry the vizier and they would rule together. The king was staggered to see and hear such terrible things. Not only was it unexpected, but the betrayal of his wife and the vizier shook him to the roots.

Deeply shaken the king sat down on a chair, and just then Rabbi Adam returned. He greeted the king as if it were the most natural thing in the world to meet him there. "Welcome, my lord king," Rabbi Adam said, "I have known for some time that you would be coming. So too have I been aware of the true reason for your visit here—to see the vision which has just taken form in front of your eyes in my mirror. For this mirror once hung in the Garden of Eden, and our father Adam looked in it to see the future generations that would arise after him. So too was it possessed by many other sages, including our father Abraham, and King David, and his son, Solomon, of whom I am certain you are familiar. And now that the truth about your wife and the vizier has been revealed to you, what do you wish to do about it?"

The king understood at once that he had sought out Rabbi

Adam in order to learn this painful truth. "My good rabbi," he said, "I put myself in your hands, for I see that your knowledge and wisdom is far greater than my own. Tell me, what is there that I can do to free myself of this terrible danger?"

Then Rabbi Adam took out an unlit candle and handed it to the king and said, "Light this candle in the fire and then take it into the mirror. Wait until the evil vizier is facing you in the mirror so that you can see his eyes, and then, while the head of your wife is turned, blow out the candle."

The king did as Rabbi Adam had said, and soon stood with the lighted candle in front of the mirror. At once he saw the vizier plotting with his wife, and when he was able to see the vizier's eyes but not those of his wife, the king blew out the flame of the candle, and at that instant the vizier fell to the floor, dead. Now the queen had no idea of what to do and was very frightened, for they had been alone in the chamber of the king. The queen became frantic and ran to the window, and there in the palace garden she saw the court priest walking. She called for him to join her, and when he did she showed him the body of the vizier. He examined the body, but could not understand why the vizier had died. He asked the queen to tell him the truth why had they been there and what had they been discussing—and she confessed all that had taken place.

After the queen had revealed their plot to the priest, he said to her, "Tell me, in all truth, for I swear never to reveal it to anyone else: did you yourself kill the vizier?" The queen swore that she had no hand in the matter, and the priest decided that she was telling the truth. "Rest assured that I believe you." he said, "Now if you will do everything I tell you to, we will get rid of the vizier's body and no one will know this has happened. But you must agree to testify that the leader of the Jews had the vizier kidnapped, and that the Jews murdered him and hid his body."

The frantic queen was willing to agree to anything in order to get the body out of the king's chamber before anyone else found it there. So she agreed to the priest's evil plan and promised to testify as he had instructed. Then the physician took the body down to the palace wine-cellar, where he dug a grave and buried it.

Now the king had witnessed all that had taken place in the mirror of Rabbi Adam, and when he saw what his wife had done he trembled with rage. Then he turned to Rabbi Adam and related all that he had seen, and told the rabbi that he must return to his palace at once. Rabbi Adam gave him his blessings, and told him to act with wisdom and moderation and to keep the Jews of the land safe from their persecutors. The king swore he would do this, and then took his leave.

After a journey of several days the king arrived in the capital and found it seething with disorder. For the priest had spread the lie that he and the queen had seen with their own eyes how the Jews had kidnapped and murdered the vizier, and had taken the body away. In this way the priest had incited the people to attack the Jews and avenge this evil deed. On his return to the palace, the queen and the priest again testified to the lie, and insisted that the king order that all the Jews of the city be killed to avenge the vizier's death.

The king listened in silence to all that they said. Then he said, "Tomorrow I will assemble the king's counsel to discuss this matter and reach a decision concerning it."

The next day the counsel members met and each of them arose and argued that the Jews of that city must be punished for their foul deed. The king was the last to speak, and when he rose he said, "Honored members of the counsel, I have heard what you have said, and I am prepared to order the destruction of the Jews. But I fear that if we do this other nations will rise up against us. Therefore I suggest that we invite representatives of all the nations and tell them about the terrible things the Jews did. We will permit them to be judges, and this way they will concur in our decision and understand that our revenge is just."

The ministers were pleased with this suggestion and directed that a great reception be held for the representatives of all the nations. The king saw to it that Rabbi Adam was invited as well. On the day the matter was to be judged, all the representatives met in the court of the king. When they had all been seated, their glasses were filled with wine, and just as all began to drink, Rabbi

Adam arose and said, "My apologies, your majesty, but this wine is tasteless." And as soon as Rabbi Adam said this, all of the guests noticed that the wine was suddenly tasteless, and they wondered why they had not noticed it sooner. Then the king directed an angry glance at the priest, who was in charge of the wine-cellar, and the priest sent servants to go at once and bring fresh bottles of wine for all the guests. But as soon as they tasted the new wine, all of the guests agreed that it was even worse than before.

His hands trembling, the priest went down to the winecellar himself and brought up the finest bottles he could find. But when these had been tasted, all the guests agreed that they were the worst of all. Then Rabbi Adam asked the king if he himself might be permitted to select the bottles from the wine-cellar, and would the king and his guests accompany him there, so that they might see the king's splendid wine-cellar.

Now when the king, the rabbi, the priest and all the ministers of state reached the wine cellar, Rabbi Adam asked them if they were not aware of a foul odor. None of them had noticed it, but now it suddenly became apparent to all, and they were very embarrassed for the king. Then Rabbi Adam walked around in the wine-cellar, and suddenly he pointed to a specific place on the floor and said, "This is where the foul odor is coming from!"

The king's servants were immediately called, and they dug where the rabbi had pointed while the priest watched in terror. Before long they reached the body of the vizier, and when it had been uncovered, everyone was deeply shocked. Enraged, the king turned to the priest and said, "So, you buried the vizier here! Why then did you testify that the Jews kidnapped and killed him?"

The priest, filled with terror and having lost his tongue, fell into a deep faint. He was carried back into the court of the king, and when all had assembled there again, the king turned to the queen and asked her why she had given false testimony. The frightened queen confessed all that had happened, and then the priest who by then had recovered and saw that his scheme had been found out, also confessed. Then the king asked the ministers to serve as his judges. They all condemned him to death, and he was hung that very day. As for the queen, the king sent her into exile, where she spent the rest of her days. Then the king had it proclaimed throughout the land that the Jews had been found innocent. And he thanked Rabbi Adam for having saved him, and told him that he was proud that they had been born on the same day.

Greece: Oral Tradition

The Enchanted Palace

Now there once was a holy sage whose name was Rabbi Adam. He possessed the powers of the mightiest sorcerer, although he did not depend on magic as did other sorcerers, but solely upon the power of God. For he was familiar with the true pronunciation of God's most secret Name, revealed to only one Tzaddik in each generation. And whoever possessed that true pronunciation had unlimited powers, so long as they were used for good. For God's sacred Name may only be used only to create, never to destroy.

In time rumors about Rabbi Adam reached the king of the land in which he lived. This king decided to have an audience with the rabbi and to ask for proof of his powers. The king was encouraged in this by the king's minister, who was a very evil man. This minister did not believe in the tales of Rabbi Adam's exploits, but he hoped that the Jew would make a fool of himself in front of the king, thus humiliating his people and his faith. For this minister had a deep hatred of the Jews, and sought to turn the king against them every chance he got.

Rabbi Adam was not surprised when he received the king's

invitation to attend a royal banquet, for he knew how to read the future in the stars and saw that it was coming. Now since Rabbi Adam did not use his powers for his own benefit, he was poor and lived in a small hut in the forest outside the city. But he knew that when he went to the court of the king he must not dress like a peasant. For even without using the sacred Name, it was in his power to create any illusion he chose. Thus he created the illusion of wealth, so that when he arrived at the palace he appeared to be dressed as well as the richest of the nobles who had assembled there.

When the evil minister saw Rabbi Adam's noble appearance, he could not believe his eyes, for he knew him to be one of the poorest of men. He assumed that the Jews of his city had collected coins in order to purchase garments for him to wear. These elegant clothes only increased the minister's hatred, and he was even more determined to find some way to humiliate Rabbi Adam and to cast a dark shadow on the lives of the Jews. These thoughts so filled the mind of the evil minister throughout the long banquet, that he did not enjoy a single morsel of the finest delicacies, which were served with the most delicious wines. Just as the final serving of the banquet was being taken away, the minister whispered into the ear of the king, who was sitting beside him, "Now that the famous Rabbi Adam is in our presence, why don't you introduce him to all the nobles and ask him for a demonstration of his powers, of which so much is rumored."

The king agreed it would be a fitting occasion and he rose and introduced Rabbi Adam, as the minister had suggested. Then he called upon the rabbi to show the assembled nobles a glimpse of the remarkable powers he was said to possess. Rabbi Adam said he would be happy to grant the king's wish, and he asked the king to think of an object, anything at all, that he would like to find in the pocket of his royal robe. Then the king should whisper to one of the nobles what object he had thought of. The king did this, and the noble to whom he whispered nodded that he had heard. Then Rabbi Adam told the king to reach into his pocket. He did this, and all at once he took out an enormous diamond, perfectly cut and far larger than any diamond the king had ever seen. The king was stunned to see this, and the noble acknowledged that a great diamond was in fact what the king had wished for. Then the king thanked Rabbi Adam, and told him he had certainly provided them with a fine demonstration. And the nobles applauded the rabbi, who once again took his place at the table.

Now the evil minister almost choked when he saw the size of the diamond the king drew out of his pocket. For he realized that his plan to humiliate Rabbi Adam had backfired. His evil mind searched for another way to bring wrath down upon the rabbi and his people. So he turned to the king once again before the banquet had ended, and whispered that it would only be appropriate for Rabbi Adam to invite the king to dine at his table, as the king had seen fit to invite the good rabbi to his. The king spoke of this to Rabbi Adam as he was about to take his leave, saying that he hoped to dine with the rabbi on some future occasion. Rabbi Adam did not blink, but invited the king and all of his court to join him in thirty days time. The evil minister was delighted when he heard this, for he thought that the Jew was certain to bring shame upon himself, since the poor hut in which he lived was certainly not worthy of the king. And he looked forward to that evening with great pleasure.

In the days that followed the royal banquet, the evil minister was very curious to know what kind of preparations Rabbi Adam was making for the king. He sent servants to spy on the rabbi, but they always reported that he could be seen through his window, pouring over the sacred books of the Jews. No effort had been made to rebuild his tiny little hut, which barely had room for the rabbi and the king, much less the rest of the court. The rabbi had not even begun to purchase foods and wines for the occasion. The evil minister felt reassured with each of these reports that the king would be offended by the poor table Rabbi Adam would offer, and he hoped that the king might take his revenge on all the Jews. Thus the minister bided his time, waiting for Rabbi Adam to fall into his trap.

On the day of Rabbi Adam's banquet, the king and his court set out for the rabbi's home. That evening, shortly before the king and his court were to arrive, Rabbi Adam spoke that most secret and powerful Name. When the king's party reached the small path in the forest that led there, the minister was astounded to see a royal highway, exactly wide enough to permit the king's court to pass through in comfort. And that fine road soon led to the most astounding palace anyone in that court had ever seen. It was made of marble, and decorated with gold and silver objects whose value alone was more than all the gold in the king's treasury. The king could not understand how he had never known about that magnificent palace, and he felt awe in the presence of Rabbi Adam, whom he now regarded as a lord whose wealth was almost equal to his own.

As for the evil minister, he was in a state of shock. Where had that magnificent palace come from? What had happened to the tiny hut of Rabbi Adam that his servants had spied on so often? The head of the minister was spinning, so that he did not even notice the taste of the wonderful delicacies that Rabbi Adam's servants served—for, yes, there were dozens of servants in that palace, all of whom catered to every desire of the royal guests.

The evening passed for the king and his court as if they were in a dream, for they had never experienced such wealth and elegance in their lives, but the mood of the evil minister was black. Since he had failed in every way to belittle Rabbi Adam in the king's eyes, he decided to profit at least another way—by stealing one of the golden goblets in which the wine had been served. For he imagined it was worth a small fortune, and could support him for the rest of his life. So when he thought no one was looking he hid the goblet inside his vest. But Rabbi Adam saw him, for nothing escaped his vision. And the rabbi smiled to himself.

At last it was time to go. The king and all of his guests rose to depart, but the evil minister remained in his seat. The king was annoyed when he saw this. He motioned for the minister to rise, but the minister remained sitting. Then the king grew angry, and ordered him to stand in his presence, but the minister did not rise. He pleaded that he was somehow unable to stand up, even though he had been trying to all along. The king turned to Rabbi Adam to apologize, but Rabbi Adam told the king it was no fault of his own, but had been brought about by the minister himself. The king wondered at this and asked Rabbi Adam what he meant. Rabbi Adam said, "The only reason that anyone would be unable to arise from this table would be if he had taken something that did not belong to him." The face of the evil minister grew red when he heard this, and the king stared into his eyes and asked him if he had, in fact, taken anything. The minister assured the king that he had not, but the king ordered him to be searched, and the goblet was found beneath his vest. When it was taken from him, the minister was finally able to stand up. Then the king ordered that the minister be arrested at once, and vowed to judge him without mercy for the humiliation he had brought on the court. So too did the king offer his apologies once more, which Rabbi Adam graciously accepted, and the king and his court took their leave, in awe at the wealth and power of Rabbi Adam.

Now in the days that followed a strange report reached that kingdom. It seems that in another land, far away, the marble palace of the emperor had disappeared on the day a great feast was to be given, only to reappear the next day. This mysterious occurrence was spoken of everywhere with great awe, for who could imagine how such a thing could ever happen?

Eastern Europe: c. Seventeenth Century

The King Descended
from Haman

There were two powerful kings who had waged war for ten years for possession of a land which lay between them. Despite all those years of conflict, nothing had been decided, and the war continued to bleed their treasuries dry. Finally the two kings grew weary of their war, and secretly met. They agreed between themselves that since both believed the land to be theirs by inheritance, they would each search into their own genealogy, and whoever turned out to be the nobler of the two would get the land for his own.

So both kings called in their scribes to determine their ancestry. The one king found out that he had descended from a line of ten kings, while the other king discovered, to his amazement, that he was descended from nine kings, and from Haman, the evil vizier to King Ahashverosh who had tried to destroy the Jews. And since Haman was only a vizier, and not a king, the other king won their wager, and it was he who took over the lands.

Now the king descended from Haman was truly bitter at this end to the long and bitter struggle, the war that had been fought for so many years. He was angry about his loss and angry as well about his ancestry, which had been surpassed by his rival. And since he could not seek revenge by means of war, for peace had been declared, the king decided to seek satisfaction as did his ancestor, Haman, by bringing misery to the Jews of his kingdom.

Now it happened that the most honored man among the Jews of that land was named Mordecai, just as had been the case in Haman's time. The king had this Mordecai taken prisoner, and proclaimed that if a tribute of ten thousand silver shekels were not paid to the king in a very short time, Mordecai would be put to death.

Naturally this evil decree greatly distressed the Jews of the kingdom. For even if all of the Jews of that land emptied all of their savings, they could not amass such a sum. Clearly, the king did not expect to receive such a ransom, and was planning to put his prisoner to death. And who knows what disasters would occur after that? So the leaders of the Jews gathered together, and discussed what should be done. They agreed that since it was hopeless to try to raise such a ransom, they must have some other plan. But no one knew what steps should be taken other than to call for fasting and prayer until the danger had passed.

The leaders sat silent for a long time, lost in thoughts of how to escape that deadly situation, when at last the oldest among them spoke and said, "When I was a child, a similar danger came upon us, and we were saved by a wonder-working Tzaddik, whose name was Rabbi Adam." The others all agreed that such a holy sage might save them, but none could imagine that Rabbi Adam might still be alive. Still, when they realized there was nothing else to do, they decided to send one of them to seek out this Rabbi Adam, if he were anywhere to be found. At least he might find his grave and pray there on their behalf.

The one who was chosen to search for Rabbi Adam was Rabbi Simeon, the youngest rabbi among them. He set out at once, for he understood the urgency of his mission although he was also aware of its likely failure. He travelled from city to city—as time was running out—but found no clue about the wonder-working Tzaddik. One day, however, when he entered a city and asked if anyone there knew of Rabbi Adam, he was told to seek out the old beggar who sat before the walls of the city.

Rabbi Simeon found this old beggar without any difficulty, for he had been seated at those gates for many years. Even though his clothes were ragged, Rabbi Simeon saw that the beggar had the look of wisdom on his ancient face. He asked the beggar if he knew where he could find Rabbi Adam, or even if he knew if he was still alive. The beggar said, "He is alive." And when he heard these words, a shiver ran down Rabbi Simeon's spine. His words rushed together as he asked, "Tell me where can he be found?" And the old man said, "Tell me first why you are seeking him." Then Rabbi Simeon poured out his heart to the beggar, and he saw that his words moved the man deeply. When he had finished speaking, the beggar said, "You need not fear, for Rabbi Adam will prevent this tragedy from coming to pass. I myself will tell him of it. You may now set out for home, and by the time you arrive, the danger will have passed."

Now Rabbi Simeon could scarcely believe his ears, so joyous was the prophecy. But at the same time he did not want to return unless he had some proof that the words of the beggar would come true. So he said, "With all my heart I pray that all that you say shall come to pass. But what sign that the danger will be averted can you show me?" Then the old beggar looked into the eyes of the young rabbi, and he said, "Know, then, that I am Rabbi Adam. And I have sat at this gate all these years in the guise of a beggar in order to watch over the Jews of this city, and see that no harm comes to them. For I can take one look at the face of every man who passes through this gate and recognize his fate. And if I see danger hovering above a fellow Jew, I come to his aid. Because my protection is such a blessing, the Holy One, blessed be He, has allowed me to live this long." "And how long is that?" asked Rabbi Simeon with wonder. "I am now one hundred and sixty years old," said Rabbi Adam. And Rabbi Simeon realized that all that he said was true, and that he was in the presence of one of the holiest sages who ever lived. Then Rabbi Simeon embraced Rabbi Adam and took his leave, with faith that Rabbi Adam would indeed save Mordecai and the Jews of his kingdom from a terrible fate.

Shortly afterward, a strange thing happened to the evil king who was descended from Haman. He was an early riser, and one day when he awoke at dawn he saw someone standing in his room—a ragged beggar who appeared to be a Jew. The king was stunned, since his chamber was surrounded by armed guards on all sides, and he could not imagine how the beggar had entered. At first he was afraid that he was an assassin, but as light filled the room he saw that it was a very old man, whose age he could not even guess. The king grew furious at the thought that the Jews feared his sentries so little that they had sent an old man to kill him. Before the old man could say anything, the king grabbed a spear and threw it at the intruder. But the spear never reached Rabbi Adam—for that is who it was—but just disappeared into thin air. Rabbi Adam then raised his hand, and the king found himself lifted up by invisible arms, and carried out the window across the countryside over uncounted miles. All at once the king was set down in a cemetery, with a wall that seemed to reach to the very heavens, and where not a single living soul was to be seen.

At first the king could not understand what had happened, and for several days he wandered about the cemetery in a daze. Each day, before the sun set, the old beggar that the king had seen in his room appeared to him and gave him a little bread and water, so that he might be sustained. But the beggar never spoke a word to the king, because the king had never permitted him to speak.

Now on the third night that the king spent in that cemetery, a remarkable thing happened. The king, lying downcast at the foot of a tree, saw how, just after sunset, the cemetery was suddenly filled with spirits, which he understood must be the spirits of those buried there. When he realized how he was surrounded by spirits on all sides, the king feared for his life, and wondered if he himself had become a spirit like those he saw around him. And that day, when Rabbi Adam arrived, the king begged him to help him escape from that place, for he was terrified of the spirits that roamed there at night.

Then Rabbi Adam said to the king, "All of those buried in

this cemetery were victims of you or your ancestors." When the king heard this, a cold chill passed through him, and he was more frightened than ever that these spirits might take revenge on him for all that he and his dynasty had done. And he threw himself at Rabbi Adam's feet and offered to do anything if he would only help him escape from that hellish place. Then Rabbi Adam took out a scroll, on which was written an edict revoking any decree against the Jews, and making the Jews equal with all other peoples in that kingdom for as long as the dynasty of that king would last. And the king gladly signed it, for in that moment of great danger, it was not too high a price to him. And after he had signed it, the king affixed his seal. No sooner had the seal touched the parchment, than the king found himself back in his bed, and the sun newly risen in the sky.

When he realized that he was back in his royal chamber, the king could not believe his eyes, for he could not imagine how he had gotten there. He wondered how many days had passed since he had been carried off to that terrible cemetery. He called in his guards, and they were surprised at the question, and told the king that only a single night had passed, for they had accompanied the king to his chamber the very night before. The king was astounded to learn this, and once more was beset with confusion.

Just then a messenger arrived with a message for the king. The king accepted the scroll of the message, and when he opened it he saw the decree that he had signed freeing the Jews from all accusations. And the hands of the king shook as he held it. He did not withdraw it, but announced it at once and saw that it was enforced. For nothing in the world frightened him more than the thought of that cemetery in which he had been imprisoned. And because he still thought about it every day, he would dream about it every night. So it was that this evil king descended from Haman was punished for the hatred in his heart. And the Jews of that kingdom celebrated as never before, and gave thanks that the Holy One, blessed be He, had seen fit to give the world a sage as great as Rabbi Adam, who had somehow brought about their salvation.

Eastern Europe: c. Seventeenth Century

The Demon's Tail

There once was a poor man whose sole desire was to gain great wealth. He was willing to do anything to accomplish this, even to delve into magic. He heard that there was a wizard who lived alone in the forest, and one day he went to see him. The wizard lived in a little hut, but when the man stepped inside, he found himself in a great palace. "Oh," he thought to himself, "if only I had wealth like this, I would be a happy man." The man told the wizard of his desire to be rich, and asked if there was some way to call forth a spirit from the underworld who would satisfy his every wish.

The wizard said, "Yes, such things can be done. But they are very dangerous. Take my advice and go home and put this idea out of your head." But the man wanted to be rich no matter what, and he begged the wizard to help him. The wizard said, "The only way to make one of these spirits your slave is to capture the demon who commands it." The poor man had not expected this, but he was willing to try anything. He asked how the demon could be caught, and the wizard said, "Not far from here, in the forest, there is a clearing in which the demons come to dance when there is a full moon. This clearing is in the shape of a circle, and there is a tall tree in the center of it. Go there during the day and hide yourself in the tree in the center of the circle. Wait there until the demons come to dance, and remain hidden all night—and be quiet, for if the demons find you, your life is as good as lost. Know that the demons will also depart before dawn, because they are forbidden to be in this world during the day. Watch as they depart, and when there is only one left, climb down from the tree and grab him by the tail. That is the only way you can keep demons from harming you, for whoever holds their tail holds them in their power. So don't let go for any reason. The demon will beg to be set free, but tell him that you won't let him go unless he vows to send you a spirit from the underworld to serve as your slave. He may be reluctant to give up his slave, but if you can hold on until dawn, the demon will give in, for he fears nothing more than being caught in this world once the sun has come up, for then he is powerless."

The man listened to the wizard's words with complete concentration, and he assured him that he would be very careful. Then he asked the wizard how he might repay him for all that he had done. The wizard said, "If you succeed in obtaining such a slave, just keep him away from me." Now the man thought that this was a strange request, but he was not about to argue with it, and he told the wizard that he would be sure to obey. Then he hurried off to search for the clearing in the forest, for the moon would be full that very night, and the man did not want to wait another month for the chance to obtain the riches he so dreamt of having.

The man followed the wizard's directions, and before long he found the very clearing he had described. He knew it was the right one, for it was a perfect circle and there was a tall tree in the center. He climbed this tree and perched high in the branches, hidden in the leaves, and there he waited anxiously for night. Time passed very slowly, and even before the sun had set the man began to be hungry and thirsty, but he ignored this, thinking instead that he would soon be wealthy, and he would have all that he ever needed to eat and drink. At last night fell, and soon after it had grown dark the man heard the sounds of laughter and shouting, and soon he saw a whole cadre of demons enter the clearing. One of them lit a fire by touching his finger to a stone, and in a moment all of the demons began to dance wildly around the fire, singing in ghastly voices an eerie and horrible tune. High above them, in the branches, the man watched all that took place with great fear, for he suddenly realized the dangerous situation situation into which he had put himself, and for the first time he began to doubt the wisdom of having come there.

For hours the man kept completely still, barely daring to breathe, in terror that the demons might discover him. Then, during the night, the wind began to blow quite hard. It shook the tree, and the poor man was afraid that he would fall out, right into the clutches of the mob of demons. The wind also carried his human scent, which the demons soon noticed. One of them said, "I smell a human!" Another said, "Let's roast him!" Another said, "I get a leg!" Another said, "I get an arm!" Then they all said, "Let's find him!" So the demons ran into the forest surrounding the clearing, searching everywhere for their victim, while the poor man trembled in terror, certain that his life was as good as lost. But the demons never thought of looking in the branches of the tree in the center of the circle, and so they did not find the frightened man. After a while, they came back to the circle and decided that the wind had carried the scent from the edge of the forest, where there were a few huts. And they forgot all about finding a victim and went back to dancing and cavorting together.

At last, many hours later, the demons began to drift back into the forest, until finally there was but one demon left, slumped at the bottom of the tree, completely exhausted. The man in the branches knew that this was his only chance, and as quietly as he could he crawled out on a branch right above the demon and dropped on top of him. The demon was startled, of course, and in the instant before he realized what had happened the man grabbed his tail with both hands and held on as the demon roared and leaped wildly from side to side. Now the demon hoped to frighten the man into letting go of its tail, but the man knew that if he did, not only would he never become rich, he would not live to see another day. So he held on to the demon's tail with all his might, and at last the demon realized that he was in the man's power and that it would soon be dawn.

Then the demon began to beg the man to set him free, promising to give him whatever he wanted. The man then spoke for the first time, telling the demon that he wanted him to turn over his slave from the underworld, who would respond to his every command. When the demon heard this, he roared again, this time with laughter. Finally, when he stopped laughing, he said, "Believe me, the last thing you want is my slave. But if you really want him, he's yours." The man felt certain that the demon was trying to trick him out of his slave in this way, and he gladly accepted the demon's offer. But before he let him go—just seconds before the sun was about to rise—he made him vow that he would give him his slave at once, and that he would find him when he reached his home. The demon, who was becoming increasingly desperate, made this vow and disappeared the very second the man let go of his tail.

The man could barely believe his luck. Not only had he survived the night in that tree, right under the nose of all those demons, but he had even forced one of them to turn over his slave to him. He could hardly wait to get home, and ran through the forest as fast as he possibly could. Along the way he passed the hut of the wizard and was tempted to go inside and tell him what had happened, but he remembered that the wizard had asked him to keep the slave away from him, and since he was afraid that he might change his mind, he passed the hut without going in.

At last, when he was truly exhausted from running so hard, the poor man reached the turn in the bend from where he could see the river and his little hut. There he saw a great giant, as tall as the tree he had climbed, standing outside his door. This sight frightened the man at first, but then he remembered the demon's vow, and he reminded himself that the giant was his slave. Why, with such a slave he could accomplish anything! And so the man plucked up his courage and approached the giant. The giant also saw him as he approached, took a single step, and stood in front of him. The man had to lean his head all the way back in order to see his face, and when the giant spoke, his voice sounded like thunder, but the man could still make out the words: "My master, your wish is my command. Command, my master, or I will kill you!"

The man was surprised at this threat from his slave, but he ignored it and told the giant to make him a palace with every comfort and amusement. And no sooner had he finished speaking than such a palace, more dazzling than even that of the king, stood before him. The man ran to the palace door, overwhelmed with curiousity to see what it looked like inside. But the demon blocked his way, and again he thundered: "Command, my master, or I will kill you!"

The man did not like being threatened just as he was about to enjoy the fruits of his success, so he told the giant to make him a garden with every kind of fruit tree and flower, along with lakes and fountains, and with colorful singing birds and beasts. He thought this would keep the giant occupied while he discovered the pleasures of his palace, but he had barely walked inside when he heard the voice of the giant thunder again: "Command, my master, or I will kill you!" Astounded, the man looked out the

window and saw that the giant had indeed fulfilled his command —acres of garden covered the lands, with ripe fruit hanging from every tree and the sound of singing birds filling the air. But the man barely had time even to consider these, for he saw the angry eyes of the giant staring into his own, and he knew that he must give him new orders at once.

Then the man told the giant to fetch him singers of every nationality, and many servants as well. He thought that this would keep the giant busy, running around the world. But no sooner were the words out of his mouth than the man saw that he was surrounded by servants and singers, all of them waiting to serve him. But he was not able to give them a single order before he heard the roar of the giant once again, demanding to be given another task. Now the man, no longer poor, but wealthy beyond his wildest dreams, became truly afraid for the first time. For he could not think of anything else that he needed; the giant had provided everything. So he told the giant to come back tomorrow, for he had done enough wishing for one day. Then the giant roared: "If so, I must kill you!"

The man was terrified and tried to flee into the rooms of the palace, but the giant reached through a window and grabbed him. The man shook with terror as the giant carried him out of the palace and held him high in the air, prepared to smash him to the earth. In his desperation he shouted to the giant: "The river! The river! Do something about it!" "What do you want me to do?" thundered the giant. "Turn it around," said the man. "Make it run the other way. I don't like the way it runs now."

No sooner had he finished speaking these words than the giant put him down and hurried off to the river. He reached into the water and scooped it up in his great hands and spun it around, so that for a moment it looked like he had succeeded in turning the current. But a moment later the water continued to flow as before. Again the giant scooped it up and spun it, but not for long. So the giant scooped it up once more and tried again, with the same results. By the tenth time, the man realized that he had won himself a little peace. He went back to the palace and took a seat by the window, where he could see the giant. He had his servants bring him a dinner fit for a king, and while he ate he had the singers sing lovely songs to him. And all the time he looked out the window at the frustrated giant, he smiled.

Eastern Europe: Oral Tradition

The Grateful Dead

There once was a wealthy man whose only son was born in his old age. This man lived in the city of Jerusalem, and decided that his son would not be exposed to the frivolous things of the world, but only to the study of the Divine Law. So he found a master with whom his son could study, and had both master and pupil live in seclusion for ten years. As one would expect, his son came to acquire a vast amount of knowledge.

Now by this time the boy's father was himself a very old man who was well aware that his days were numbered. He realized that his son had been left ignorant of the practical ways of the world, and that he might not be able to manage his inheritance when the time came. So the old man sat with his son and began to teach him what he had learned of world affairs. He found his son to be an excellent student, for in having learned the Divine Law he had also learned how to listen and comprehend what he was being taught. And the day came shortly after the father completed his lessons to his son, that he died and took leave of this world.

Now after the period of mourning was over, his son decided to take the fortune he had inherited and travel forth to see the world. For while he was rich in learning, he still lacked worldly experience. He traveled through many countries, and finally reached Turkey, where he traveled to the capital. There, while he was walking in the street one day, he saw a strange sight: an iron coffin suspended from a chain between two pillars. The young man wondered greatly about this and asked the guard what it was, but he was merely ordered away from there. The young man did not give up, and because he had learned something of the ways of the world, he offered the guard a piece of silver to tell him the reason a coffin had been hung there.

The guard told him that the coffin contained the body of a Jew who had once been the closet adviser of the Turkish Sultan. The Sultan had trusted him, but the Jew had many enemies, jealous of his influence, who had finally convinced the Sultan that the Jew had robbed him of a great fortune. In the end the Jew had been executed and his body placed in that iron coffin, where he was subjected to public scorn even after death. The king had commanded that the coffin be left there until the Jews paid back the sum that the king had accused the advisor of stealing, but it was an impossible sum for them to collect.

The young man was very moved by this tale, and when he learned the amount required by the Sultan, he realized that it was within his power to supply it with his inheritence. So he went to the Sultan and offered to pay the ransom so that the Jew could be buried according to Jewish custom. The Sultan was happy to receive the great sum, and readily agreed not only to free the coffin for burial, but to clear the man's name, and to invite all of the inhabitants of the city to attend the funeral, including the Jews. And thus the poor Jew received the honor in death that he deserved.

Now the Sultan was very favorably impressed with the young man, and offered him a place in his court, but the young man explained that it was his intention to return to his home in Jerusalem. Soon afterward he boarded a ship bound for the Holy Land, but a great storm arose that sank the ship with all its passengers, except for this young man, who saved himself by grasping a plank. And while he was floating on that plank in the wild waters, a white eagle suddenly appeared out of the heavens and flew directly to him. The eagle hovered above the waters, and the young man understood that this must be a heavenly messenger sent to save him, and he mounted upon its back. Then, as the young man held on for his life, the bird took flight and carried him directly to Jerusalem, to the house of his father that now belonged to him. Then, just as quickly as it had appeared, the eagle disappeared, and in the darkness the young man could make out a figure in a white shroud. At first he was frightened, but then the figure spoke and told him that he was the dead man whose honor he had retrieved in Turkey with his generous deed, and that it was he who had appeared in the form of the white eagle to save him from certain death. And before the shrouded figure vanished, he told the astonished young man that his life in this world would be blessed, and that a great reward awaited him in the World to Come. And indeed all that came to pass.

Eastern Europe: Seventeenth Century

The Golem

During the reign of the Emperor Rudolf, there lived in Prague a wonder-working rabbi whose name was Rabbi Judah Lowe. He had been taught in these mysteries by Rabbi Adam, whose power had been unsurpassed since King Solomon. Nor did Rabbi Adam withhold anything from his disciple, and thus Rabbi Loew served as the Tzaddik of his generation, as Rabbi Adam had the generation before him.

One year it happened in the spring that Rabbi Loew had a long and vivid dream, in which he found himself in the Christian quarter of Prague, outside the Jewish ghetto. There he witnessed a terrible crime, in which a child was murdered and thrown in a sack, then carried to the Jewish section of the city, and left inside one of the houses there. In the dream Rabbi Loew saw the face of the murderer; it was the face of the evil sorcerer Thaddeus, a great enemy of the Jews who spent his days plotting ways to harm them. And Rabbi Loew understood that Thaddeus was in this way plotting to accuse the Jews of a Blood Libel. This terrible accusation had been made against the Jews in almost every generation. For the claim that Jews use blood in order to make matzot for

Passover was a terrible lie. Never had such a thing been done. And now Thaddeus was planning to accuse the Jews of this falsehood again.

In the dream Rabbi Loew found himself helpless to do anything when he suddenly heard the sound of beating wings and looked up and saw a flock of birds flying in formation, spelling a word that he read clearly in the heavens. It was God's most sacred Name, which holds the power at the source of all being. And in the dream Rabbi Loew wrote that Name down on a piece of paper, and slipped it into the pages of the Bible he was carrying in his hand. No sooner had he done this, than he looked down at his feet, and suddenly saw the outline of a large body in the earth. Before his eyes the features of the body began to take form, and the word *Emet*, which means Truth, appeared on its forehead. Just as the eyes of the man of clay opened, Rabbi Loew awoke, the dream still vivid in his memory.

Now the rabbi recognized from the first that he must decipher this dream. For the Name of God was the most sacred word of all, and its appearance in a dream must portend matters of grave importance. He realized that it could have no other meaning than to warn him that Thaddeus was about to accuse the Jews of Prague of the Blood Libel, which would doubtless unleash a terrible pogrom against them. Thus the dream had come as an urgent warning, but surely it also contained the method by which the plot of the evil Thaddeus could be foiled. But what way was this? Rabbi Loew was uncertain.

Rabbi Loew decided to open the pages of the Torah and consider the first line his eyes fell upon. For in this way heaven was able to guide and advise him. He opened the Torah at random, and when he did, the first thing he saw was not a passage from the Torah, but the very slip of paper on which he had written the Name of God in the dream. It had miraculously passed through the dreamworld into the world in which he was awake! Suddenly Rabbi Loew understood that his task was to bring something else into this world—that man of clay he had seen in the dream. But how was this to be done? Perhaps by inserting that slip of paper on which the Name was written into the mouth of that clay creature.

And from where would this creature come? He himself would have to help bring it into being.

Rabbi Loew realized there was no time to be lost. He decided that he must undertake that strange creation that very night. Rabbi Loew hurried and awoke his son-in-law, Isaac, and his disciple, Jacob, and told them to get dressed and to come with him at once. They wondered greatly what urgent matter had arisen, but dared not ask, knowing that the rabbi would tell them when he was ready. And in fact he said nothing at all, but led them through the darkness to the banks of the river Moldau. There Rabbi Loew told his helpers to dig out enough clay to equal the weight of the three of them. This they did, and Rabbi Loew began at once to shape that formless mass into a clay man of immense size. And once he had completed the outline, Rabbi Loew added the features, adding last of all the word *Emet* to the forehead, just as he had seen in the dream. Then Rabbi Loew took the slip of paper on which he had written the Name out of his pocket and put it inside the mouth of the man of clay. He then walked around the clay man—seven times in one direction, and seven times in the other. As he did this, the body of the clay man began to glow, and Isaac and Jacob could hardly believe their eyes. At last, when Rabbi Loew completed the seventh circle, he stood before the clay man and recited a magical formula he had learned from Rabbi Adam, but which he had never pronounced before. At that moment the clay man opened his eyes and sat up, then looked at Rabbi Loew and nodded his head.

It was then that Rabbi Loew realized that the clay man would always be mute. He turned to Isaac and Jacob and told them that the man they had created was a Golem, which had been sent to protect them from the designs of the evil sorcerer Thaddeus. They were to call him Joseph. Then Rabbi Loew went to the bag that he had brought with him, and took out huge clothes, and the largest shoes Isaac and Jacob had ever seen. They dressed the Golem with these clothes, and then they all walked back to town together. And Isaac and Jacob marveled that just three of them had set out that night, and now four of them were going back!

Rabbi Loew presented the Golem to everyone as a new

servant who would be living with them. When he was alone with him, Rabbi Loew told the Golem that he must set out at once and discover where the evil sorcerer Thaddeus had hidden the body of the child he had murdered. Rabbi Loew went with the Golem, and they walked out together early in the morning and passed before every Jewish house in the community. The Golem strode swiftly past each one, and Rabbi Loew hurried to keep up with him. At last the Golem stopped in front of a house near the gate of the ghetto, and pointed to the front door. Rabbi Loew went with him to the door and knocked. The door was opened by an old man, a pious Jew, who was very surprised to see Rabbi Loew at his door so early in the morning—and surprised, as well, at his strange companion.

Rabbi Loew hurried inside and asked the old man if there was a cellar in that house. The man said that there was, although it had not been used for many years. He showed Rabbi Loew and the Golem how to get there, and descended the steep stairway with them. There they found at the bottom of the stairs the sack Rabbi Loew had seen in his dream, in which Thaddeus had put the child's body. Just then there was a loud knocking at the door, and when the old man climbed the stairs to answer it, the police demanded to be let inside. In the cellar, Rabbi Loew heard what was happening upstairs, and realized they were in terrible danger, for Thaddeus had no doubt reported the murder to the police and told them where to go. They must know as well, the Rabbi thought, to look for the body in the cellar.

Rabbi Loew turned to the Golem in desperation. Understanding full well the danger they were in, the Golem picked up the sack with the body in it and carried it with him, while directing Rabbi Loew to follow. He led him to a secret door in the floor of that cellar, which was hidden beneath a rug. They descended the steps and closed the door behind them. This stairway led to a dark tunnel, through which they walked for a distance of several miles. At last they arrived at another stairway, similar to the first. They climbed it, and found it led to another hidden door in another cellar. Quietly they entered, and heard loud laughter coming from above them. Rabbi Loew instantly recognized the voice of Thaddeus, and heard him boast that he had fixed the Jews this time, and that their blood would begin to flow that very day. Then Rabbi Loew motioned to the Golem to leave the body there, and they returned to the dark tunnel.

By the time they had returned to the house of the pious Jew, in which Thaddeus had hidden the body, the police had already searched the whole house, including the cellar. When they found nothing, they reluctantly departed. Then Rabbi Loew went to the captain of the police and reported a rumor he had heard: a child's body could be found in the cellar of the sorcerer Thaddeus. The captain did not want to take this accusation seriously, but when he saw the Golem towering over him, he decided he had better go there and investigate. He insisted, however, that Rabbi Loew accompany him, for he intended to jail him if his accusation proved to be false.

So it was that the police arrived at the mansion of the wealthy sorcerer. Thaddeus was astounded to see Rabbi Loew and the powerful servant in the company of the police. And when the sorcerer saw the word *Emet* inscribed on the Golem's forehead, he began to tremble with fear, for he knew that Rabbi Loew had used his great powers to bring him into being. The captain informed Thaddeus of Rabbi Loew's accusation, and Thaddeus scornfully replied that they were free to search his entire house, not only the cellar. But the police said they only wanted to see the cellar, and Thaddeus took them there. Imagine his surprise when he found the body of the child he himself had murdered, there in his own home! He nearly fainted, and when he had recovered enough to stand, the police took him into custody and thanked Rabbi Loew for having uncovered this terrible crime. Thus was the evil Thaddeus punished for his sin, and the Jews of Prague were spared the terrible pogrom that would have raged had the body been found in their part of the city.

After that the Golem remained in Rabbi Loew's home for many years, and every day and night he could be seen strolling through the streets of the ghetto, looking for anyone acting in a suspicious manner who might be trying to bring harm to the Jews. And when the enemies of Jews saw what a powerful protection they had, they ceased to plot against them, for they saw that the Jews could not be defeated. And thus Rabbi Loew and the Golem brought many years of peace to the Jews of Prague, for which they were deeply grateful. But when they tried to thank him, Rabbi Loew would always remind them that all help comes from on high, and that it is the Holy One, blessed be He, who is their guard and benefactor. And the people gave thanks as well to the Holy One, for protecting them from the plots of the enemies of Israel.

Eastern Europe: Nineteenth Century

The Demon in the Jug

There once was a man who became lost in a forest. He walked until he could walk no further, and sat down beneath a tree. While he was resting there, he noticed that the trunk was hollow, and that there was a jug hidden inside it. As he was very thirsty after walking such a long distance, and thinking that the jug might contain something to drink, the man reached inside the hollow tree and pulled the jug out.

The man held the jug up to the light of the afternoon sun, but he could not see through its brown glass. Curious to know what was inside, the man tried to loosen its cork, but it had been put in very firmly. At last, however, he succeeded, and when he did, a cloud of smoke poured out. And before the startled man's eyes, that cloud took form and became some kind of spirit, a very large one indeed, that suddenly burst into laughter.

The man's knees began to tremble, and he wondered if he had done a terrible thing. On the other hand, he had heard stories of spirits who had rewarded those who set them free. And he greatly wondered what it was that was standing before him, but he was afraid to ask.

The demon, however, did not hesitate to speak. For the demon had read the man's mind—that is but one of their powers—and had decided to pretend that it was a benign spirit rather than a dangerous demon. So it spoke sweetly and said, "I am deeply grateful, my good sir, that you have freed me from this terrible prison." The kind manner of the demon reassured the man, and he found the courage to ask, "How did you come to be in there?" The demon replied, "An evil witch cast a spell and trapped me in that wretched jug, and there I have lived for a good many years. Yes, I am certainly grateful to you. And I will gladly reward you, by giving you three wishes."

The man was overjoyed, for he did not know that the demon was lying. For the truth was that the demon had been captured and imprisoned in that jug by none other than Israel ben Eliezer, the Baal Shem Tov himself, when he had been but a young boy. He had defeated a witch who had caused a drought and caused the doors of the Ark to become locked. The boy Israel had found the way to break both of these spells, and when he had defeated the witch, he had also captured her demon, who was one of the most troublesome sort. He had imprisoned the demon in the jug, and hidden it deep in that forest, thinking that no one would ever find it. And for thirty years no one did, until one day this man, also a Jew, stumbled on the jug and released the demon, naively believing everything it had said.

The man did not have to think very long before he made his first wish. He said, "I wish you would return me to my home, for I was lost in this forest when I saw the jug inside the hollow trunk." Without a word, the demon clapped his hands, and the man was whisked through the air, and set down before his house. The man was greatly relieved to be back home, and was overjoyed that the demon seemed to be a good spirit after all. He straightaway began to think about what his next wish might be.

When the demon saw that the man was about to make his second wish, he spoke first and said, "Take care now, my friend. Do not waste your wishes. There are only two left. Meanwhile I will be happy to remain here with you, for I enjoy living in a house as much as any man."

The man considered these words, and they seemed wise enough to him. So he invited the demon to remain as his guest until he had was certain about his other two wishes. And that is exactly what the demon wanted, for it had no intention of ever departing from that house. It was a very nice one, in a modest way, and the demon had decided it was an ideal home for him to possess.

The man thought about the remaining wishes all evening, and by the time he went to sleep, he still had not made up his mind. That night he slept very poorly; his bed seemed quite uncomfortable. When the man woke up in the morning, his neck was very sore, for his body was doubled up in the bed. And the reason was that the bed was half as big as usual! The man sat up startled, and felt as if he were a giant in the room of a dwarf. Everything in the room was half as big as it had been the night before: the pots and pans were half as large, although still the same shape; the mirrors had also been reduced by half—even the money in his pocket was only half as much. The man understood at once that his house had been possessed, and he was terrified that such a thing had happened. Suddenly he remembered the spirit and wondered if it might be a demon instead. It did not take him very long to realize that that must be the case. And there, sitting at the man's table, which was only half as large, was that very demon, helping himself to some of the man's food and drink. Now the truth is that demons have no need at all for food and drink, at least not the human kind. But the demon thought it fun to pretend he did, for that way he could waste a lot of the man's provisions. The demon looked up from a cup of the man's best wine (which was only half as large as the night before) and said with feigned innocence, "Have you decided on your next wish?"

In a fury the man shouted: "Yes! Make everything in my house the proper size, and never cause it to be any smaller again!" The demon smiled and said, "I happily obey your wishes." Then the demon waved his hand, and everything in the house was restored to its proper size. At first the man was greatly relieved, but then he recalled the strange words of the demon. And he said to him, "Why did you say 'wishes' instead of 'wish'?" "Why?" said

"The man sat up startled, and felt as if he were a giant in the room of a dwarf."

the demon, "because you *did* make two wishes. One was that I restore the things in your house to their old size, and the other was that I not make them smaller any more. And I assure you that I will obey these wishes. But now that you have used up all three of your wishes, know that I am taking possession of this house. For the time being, I will let you live here, although the day may come when I will drive you out"

The man understood that a great calamity had befallen him when he had set that demon free from the jug. He grieved over his error and wondered what he might do. For he could not simply abandon his house, nor was anyone likely to give him anything for it. So he went to the holiest man he knew, the Baal Shem Tov, and begged for his help.

The Baal Shem then called upon his scribe, and asked him to write amulets for this man, one to be hung in every room. He told the man to hang the amulets up the next day, after he had opened the doors and windows, and that the Baal Shem would then come to see if the evil spirit had fled. This the man did, and as soon as the last amulet was hung in the last room, a whirlwind circled through the house and whisked out the front door, which the man had left open just as the Baal Shem had told him to.

Now the Baal Shem arrived just in time to see the whirlwind rushing out of that house, and swirling around it outside, until it disappeared. Then the Baal Shem rushed into the house and told the man to quickly close his doors and windows. When this had been done, the Baal Shem took down the amulets from each room in which they hung, and gathered them all together in his right hand. Then, accompanied by the man, he walked around the house, searching for the demon's hiding place. They looked beneath the house, and in the cracks in the walls. Then the Baal Shem noticed a barrel of water, its lid slightly ajar. He told the man to lift off the cover entirely while he held out the amulets. When the man did this, the whirlwind burst out of the barrel. First it spun around them and then went over the garden wall.

Once the lid on the barrel had been replaced, the Baal Shem walked to the gate, and there he saw the angry demon swirling furiously. As the Baal Shem stood and watched, the demon (slowly took) on a terrible shape—for it had finally revealed its true nature. And the Baal Shem recognized it at once: it was the very demon he had captured and sealed in a jug so long ago. "So you've escaped from the jug I put you in!" said the Baal Shem. And suddenly the demon seemed less threatening, and it said meekly, "Who are you?" "The very boy Israel who defeated you once and will defeat you again!" shouted the Baal Shem Tov, and he made straight for the demon. As he did, a remarkable thing happened: the closer the Baal Shem came to the demon, the smaller it became. Where once it had towered above the trees, now it was no larger than a small nut. By the time the Baal Shem reached it, it simply disappeared. Now the man was mystified, but the Baal Shem smiled to himself, for he knew that the demon was back in the jug where it had been in the first place. Only this time the Baal Shem made certain the demon would never escape again.

Eastern Europe: Eighteenth Century

The Princess and
the Baal Shem Tov

It was said that King David once wrote down the psalms in a book, each in his own hand. And it was also said that whoever could find that book and return it to the Holy Land would be able to bring the Messiah to this world; the End of Days would begin, and everyone would receive his just reward. But no one was able to find that book, not in all the years that passed since the Temple in Jerusalem was destroyed.

Now there was one man who was certain that the book still existed. And that man was Israel ben Eliezer, better known as the Baal Shem Tov. He vowed that he would seek out that book and bring it to the Holy Land, for he longed for the coming of the Messiah more than anything else. But where was he to look for it? The Baal Shem suspected that no one had found that book for so long because the secret of its location had been erased from this world. But he knew that it could be learned in heaven, for all mysteries come from the celestial realm. And since he desired the coming of the Messiah so urgently, the soul of the Baal Shem departed from his body and ascended into heaven, and did not stop until it had reached the very Throne of Glory. The soul clung there and pleaded to learn where the holy book of King David was to be found. At last his soul heard a voice in those upper realms which revealed to him that the book was to be found in Istanbul, in the library of the Turkish Sultan.

After this, the joyous soul returned to the body of the Baal Shem, who decided at once that he would set out for Istanbul as soon as possible, and somehow obtain the sacred book from the Sultan. Now sailing to Istanbul was not so simple, for the voyage there was long and difficult, and it was the coldest time of the winter. But the Baal Shem simply scoffed at all these obstacles and forged ahead. He left on his journey after Rosh Hashanah, at the start of a new year, and he reached Istanbul by Passover.

Now the first thing the Baal Shem did when he disembarked in Istanbul was to pray by the grave of Rav Naftali, a Tzaddik who had attempted to sail to the Holy Land, but had died in Istanbul before completing his journey. His grave had become a stopping place for all who passed there on their journey to the Holy Land. That night Rav Naftali appeared to the Baal Shem in a dream. He told the Baal Shem that heaven had decreed that he might fulfill the task of restoring the book of King David to the Jewish people, but that his desire to carry the book to the Holy Land would be thwarted, for the time had not yet come for the Messiah to bring the End of Days.

When he awoke, the Baal Shem recalled this dream vividly and he was overjoyed to learn that his quest for King David's book had found favor in heaven—but he was also downcast to know that he would be unable to complete his quest to bring the Messiah in his own time. Still, the Baal Shem understood very well that each man must fulfill the destiny that is given him, whatever it may be.

The next day when the Baal Shem went walking in the streets of Istanbul, trying to think of a way to present himself to the king, he noticed that the people seemed very sad. At last he saw a Jew in the crowd, and asked him why everyone seemed to be in a state of mourning. The man told him that the king had just announced that his daughter, the beloved princess, was desperately ill, and that the best doctors in the land could not cure her. The Sultan had proclaimed that whoever could succeed in healing the princess would be rewarded with half of the kingdom, but whoever tried and failed would be be put to death.

Now when the Baal Shem heard this, he recognized it as a sign from above, directing him to the Sultan and the book of King David which the Sultan had in his possession. But before he presented himself to the Sultan, the Baal Shem needed some clue as to how to cure the princess, for surely he would be given one chance to do so, and one chance only. So the Baal Shem returned to the grave of Rav Naftali and prayed to have this secret revealed to him. And that night the Baal Shem again dreamed that Rav Naftali came and told him that the princess could be cured only by a particular kind of flower that grew only in the absence of light. And, Rav Naftali revealed, this flower could be found in a cave outside of the city, in the side of a mountain.

Once again, when he awoke, the Baal Shem recalled everything that Rav Naftali had told him, so he set out the next morning to find the cave of which the Tzaddik had spoken. To his delight, the Baal Shem was able to reach the cave that very day. He lit a torch and entered the cave at once, and before he had gone very far, he reached a place where he saw something remarkable—a bed of flowers flourishing in the dark. Although they were pale white, and did not have the bright colors of other flowers, they were also exquisite and beautiful. The Baal Shem regretted having to pick even one of them, but he knew how precious they were, both to the princess and to himself. So he took one of those delicate flowers with him and returned to the city.

The Baal Shem came to the palace and announced that he wished to cure the princess. The king gave him an audience and was surprised to see before him a man dressed like the poorest of peasants. But the king was desperate and willing to try anything to save his daughter. The Baal Shem asked the king to describe his daughter's illness, and the king said that she had become possessed by a dream which recurred every night, until it had driven her mad. The Baal Shem asked what the dream was about, and the king told him that she continued to dream of a particular flower, but that when she awoke and drew it, all agreed that it was not to be found. Yet she was pining away for it, even though it only existed in a dream.

Then the Baal Shem took out the pale flower he had picked in that dark cave, and showed it to the king. The king was startled when he saw it, because it resembled exactly the drawings of his daughter, of which she had made hundreds, since she could not get the shape of that flower out of her mind. The king took the Baal Shem at once to the princess, and when he handed her that flower, she burst out crying and sobbed for the longest time. But when she had calmed herself, she clutched the flower to her breast and told her father that her dream had come true at last. And after that, the princess never dreamed of that flower again and was freed from her obsession with it. And when the Sultan saw how quickly his daughter recovered, he was filled with gratitude for the man who had saved her, and he told the Baal Shem that he could have anything that he asked for, including half of his kingdom.

Imagine, then, when the Baal Shem told him that his only request was to be permitted to look through all of the Sultan's library, and to be able to select one book from there as his own. The Sultan was overwhelmed at this modest request, and told the Baal Shem that he could surely take any book that he wanted.

So the Baal Shem prepared to search through every shelf in the Sultan's vast library, the largest in all the land. Trying to find one volume in that maze of shelves would have been like trying to find a needle in a haystack, but fate led the Baal Shem directly to the precious book he had been seeking. And when the Baal Shem opened it and saw the words that King David himself had written there, words which had long been engraved on the Baal Shem's heart, he knew such joy as he had never before experienced in all his days.

So it was that the precious book was restored to the Jews after so many centuries. The Baal Shem thanked the Sultan and took the book with him. He returned to the grave of Rav Naftali and placed the book there, so that the soul of the sage could share in its blessing. And that night the Baal Shem dreamed of the great rabbi once again, and this time Rav Naftali told the Baal Shem that he had accomplished a great feat in restoring that precious book to the Jews. But until the time had arrived when the book could be carried to the Holy Land, it must remain safely hidden. So it was that the sage told the Baal Shem to take the book with him back to Poland, since he could not continue his journey to the Holy Land. And when he arrived there, he should seal the book in the side of a mountain near the city of Kamenetz. And the sage also told the Baal Shem the holy names that would make it possible for the mountain to open and close, so that the book would be hidden from all except the one who was destined to set it free, when the time had come at last for the footsteps of the Messiah to be heard throughout the land.

The Baal Shem did as the holy sage Rav Naftali instructed him in the dream, and the book is still hidden in that mountain to this day, awaiting the one whose destiny it is to set it free and carry it to the Holy Land. And when this happens, the world we know will be transformed, for the days of the Messiah will finally be at hand.

Eastern Europe: Nineteenth Century

The Demon and the
Baal Shem Tov

Now it was the greatest wish of the Baal Shem Tov to travel to the Holy Land at least once in his lifetime. But it had been decreed in heaven that the Baal Shem not set foot there, for his spirit was so pure and profound that merely his presence in the Holy Land would force the coming of the Messiah and the End of Days.

Of course the Baal Shem did not know this, and he made several attempts to get there. Once he set out for the Holy Land in the middle of the winter, but as soon as his ship departed from Istanbul a terrible storm broke out, threatening to drown all the passengers. It was only when the Baal Shem announced to the four winds that he was turning back that the storm subside.

Some time after that, the Baal Shem decided he would sail across the sea on a handkerchief, and asked Rabbi Zvi Sofer, one of his disciples, to accompany him. The Baal Shem explained to Rabbi Zvi that there were certain dangers involved, for both of them would have to concentrate at all times on a certain combination of holy letters and words. And if they became lax even for an instant, they would be doomed. Rabbi Zvi was frightened at this prospect, and he convinced the Baal Shem Tov to make the journey in a ship. So they boarded a ship but when they had been at sea for only two days, a violent storm carried them off course. When the storm subsided they found themselves near a small island. The captain decided to cast anchor there and let the passengers go ashore, so that they could recover from the fear that had gripped them during the storm.

Then it happened that at the moment the Baal Shem and his disciple set foot on that island, both of them forgot everything they knew. The Baal Shem was deeply frightened, and asked Rabbi Zvi if he could recall any of his teachings. But Rabbi Zvi replied that he could not recall anything except the alphabet. "In that case," cried the Baal Shem, "recite it at once and I will repeat after you, for while we are without our learning we are completely at the mercy of evil forces." So Rabbi Zvi began to recite the alphabet with fervor and the Baal Shem repeated it after him, and they continued to do this the whole time they remained on that island.

When, at last, the passengers returned to the ship, the two men discovered to their immense relief that their memories had returned, but they wondered greatly at the strange episode on the island. Then, all at once, one last passenger ran to the ship and boarded it, just before it set sail. He was in a panic, and when he calmed down he told the others what had happened. It seems that he had wandered off alone and somehow had come to a cave, where he had heard many voices whispering. He hid and saw a whole crew of strange creatures—surely demons—emerge from that cave. They were armed with every kind of weapon, and he heard one of them say to the other, "Now he has forgotten everything, except for the alphabet. And when he reaches the Holy Land he will be deprived of even that!" The passenger was gripped with terror, when suddenly all the demons became frozen in place, and could neither speak nor move. They remained that way the entire time the passengers were on the island, but when the ship was boarded once again the demons suddenly began to move and chased the poor man all the way to the ship.

And yes, from the ship everyone could see the demons standing on the shore, shooting arrows in their direction and throwing spears that fell short, and when the Baal Shem and his companion saw this, and considered what the passenger said, they realized that fate had decreed that the Baal Shem not attempt to reach the Holy Land after all, and when they reached the next port they reluctantly turned back.

When the Baal Shem returned home, he wrote a letter to the great kabbalist known as Or Hahayim, who lived in the Holy Land, to see if such a journey were possible for him. The kabbalist agreed to seek out the answer in the heavenly realms, and when he did he saw the figure of the Baal Shem there quite clearly, except for his feet. So it was that the Or Hahayim concluded the Baal Shem would never realize his hope of reaching the Holy Land. The kabbalist wrote a letter explaining this to the Baal Shem Tov, but the Evil One saw to it that the ship carrying the letter sank, so that it was never delivered. For Satan had hopes of tricking the Baal Shem into acting against the wishes of God, and thereby to deprive the Baal Shem of his powers, if not of his very life.

So it was that the Evil One sent a demon to tempt the Baal Shem Tov. This demon came to him in the guise of a holy sage and said, "It is well known, both on earth and in heaven, how great is your longing to reach the Holy Land. So too is it known that your attempts to reach it by ship have failed, and it is said you fear that you are not destined to fulfill your hope of setting foot in Eretz Yisrael. Yet I have come to tell you of a dream in which I was informed that the decree against your reaching the Holy Land is in effect only when you travel over water, but not if you travel over land."

Now the Baal Shem had great faith in the mysteries revealed through dreams, but he could make no sense out of this decree, for he knew of no way to reach the Holy Land without crossing the sea. The Baal Shem pointed this out to the disguised demon, who had fully expected this reply. Then the demon said, "Of course it is believed that a sea journey is the only way to reach the Holy Land. But in this same dream I saw an enchanted cave, and I was sent to reveal it to you. For by means of this underground cave you can depart from here and reach the Holy Land in only a matter of days!"

When the Baal Shem heard this, his longings for the Holy Land were kindled anew. In his rapture and hope that his dream of reaching the Holy Land might still be realized, the Baal Shem failed to look closely enough at the stranger. He regarded him simply as a messenger from on high, perhaps even Elijah himself, who had been sent there to help him fulfill his life-long wish. And the Evil One, seeing all that took place, revelled in thinking that he was at last about to defeat the Baal Shem Tov.

So it was that the disguised demon led the Baal Shem Tov to a cave with a hidden entrance, not far from his village. Had the Baal Shem been suspicious, he might have noticed that the man cast no shadow, and thus recognized that he was a demon. But for once the Baal Shem did not concentrate as he should have, so filled was he with longing to reach the Holy Land that he followed the demon as if in a dream.

The demon entered the cave first and the Baal Shem followed. They walked through that cave for many hours, until the Baal Shem became very exhausted, and from time to time the demon would announce that they had just passed through another country, and were that much closer to their goal. In this way he spurred the Baal Shem on, even though he was very worn out.

At last the Baal Shem felt that he could not take another step. He said, "Please, let us stop and rest for a while. I don't think I can go any further without resting."

But the demon was very anxious to complete his dirty work, and he also knew that the Baal Shem was much more dangerous when he was alert and rested. So the demon said, "As I recall, the dream warned that we were not to rest until we reached our goal, and that we would come to our destination after we had crossed a log that lies across some deep quicksands. And look, I believe I see those quicksands before us, so that we are almost there."

Indeed the Baal Shem recognized the quicksands ahead of them, and saw the log lying across them, and he was filled with hope that he was about to reach his goal. But he was also supicious, for he had never heard of quicksands inside of a cave before, and he had begun to have doubts about his companion, since he so often added new details about his dream. So the Baal Shem began to concentrate for the first time, and since it had grown very dark in that cave, he said, "Just a moment. Before we come to the log lying over quicksands, let us light a torch, for otherwise it will be too risky to cross."

Now this was just what the demon did not want to do, since his plan was to push the Baal Shem into those quicksands, which he himself had created with his evil magic. So to convince the Baal Shem that it was not difficult to cross the log, he stepped upon it and called out that it was quite wide and posed no problem. But the Baal Shem insisted that he would not cross unless they lit a torch, so the demon reluctantly agreed to wait while the Baal Shem did so.

Now at the very moment the flames of that torch illumined that cave, the Baal Shem saw that the man he had been following for so long did not cast a shadow, and knew he was in the gravest danger. But at the same time he was so angry to have been misled that he suddenly shouted, "Look out! Your shadow is missing!" This cry so confused the demon, that in his panic he fell into the very quicksands he had brought into being, and the moment he struck them, both demon and quicksand disappeared, and the Baal Shem suddenly found himself standing at the entrance of that cave, near his village, where he had entered so many hours before. Then he gave thanks to the Holy One, blessed be He, for saveing him at the last minute, despite his attempt to undertake a journey that was forbidden to him. And after that he never again thought of going to the Holy Land.

Eastern Europe: Nineteenth Century

"... for the fabric was like moonlight, exquisitely woven and
without any sign of stitches or seams."

A Garment for the Moon

Once upon a time, the moon came to the sun with a complaint: the sun was able to shine during the warmth of day, especially during the summer, while the moon could shine only during the cool of night. The sun saw that the moon was unhappy with her lot, particularly in the wintertime, so he told the moon he would have a garment sewn for her, to keep her warm. Then he called upon all the great tailors to make a garment for the moon. The simple tailors also wanted to help, but they weren't invited, so they said among themselves, "We're not going to go."

After discussing the matter for some time, the great tailors came to the conclusion that it was simply impossible to sew a garment that would fit, because the moon is sometimes little and sometimes big. What measurements were they to use?

But after the great tailors gave up the task, the simple tailors decided to try. When the great tailors heard about this, they said, "If we couldn't do it, how can you expect to succeed?" But the simple tailors refused to give up. They met among themselves to discuss how this garment might be made. Many suggestions were given, but none of them could solve the problem of the moon's changing size.

Just when they were about to give up, one poor tailor among them stood up and said, "I have heard of a faraway kingdom where there is a fabric which has the substance of light. This fabric stretches to whatever size is required: it becomes large if the object to be fitted is large, and shrinks as much as necessary if the object is small." The other tailors all cried out at the same time: "Why that is just what we need to sew a garment for the moon!" They all agreed that they must obtain that wonderful material so that the sun could fulfill its promise and the moon could keep warm on cold winter nights. But how were they to obtain it? They discussed this among themselves, and decided that the poor tailor who had heard of this fabric must set out on a journey to this land, find it and bring it back. They collected a few kopeks among themselves with which to purchase the fabric, and they each wished their fellow tailor good luck.

The tailor, whose name was Yankel, packed a few clothes in a sack and took along a few loaves of bread, and set out on his journey. But how was he to begin to search for that distant land? He stopped wherever he went and asked the people if they knew where that kingdom was, but when the people heard that Yankel was searching for a cloth made out of light so that he and his brother tailors could sew a garment for the moon, they always broke out laughing and assumed Yankel was just a fool.

Yankel travelled like this for many months, sleeping under the stars, until the nights began to grow colder. As he lay on the ground at night and looked up at the moon, Yankel thought he saw the moon shiver, and he was determined to keep going until he found that material so that the moon could have a garment of her own.

Then it happened one day that Yankel arrived at a great river, and took the ferry across to the other side. And since the river was so wide, it took quite a while to get across, so Yankel decided to ask the old ferryman if he knew the location of the kingdom in which that fabric could be found. The ferryman did not laugh as had so many others, but told him he would find what he was seeking on the other side of that very river. And when Yankel heard this, he could hardly believe his ears, for in his heart of hearts he too had begun to wonder if that kingdom truly existed.

Then Yankel asked the ferryman if this fabric was easy to acquire, or if it was very dear. And the ferryman told him that it was very dear indeed, for only the queen of that land possessed a gown woven of that wonderful material. When Yankel heard this his heart sank, for how was he, a poor man, to obtain this material if only a queen could afford to own it? Still, he had travelled so far, and he did not intend to abandon his quest just when he had finally reached that faraway kingdom. He consoled himself by hoping that the queen might assist him when she heard why he was seeking that fabric.

Now when he entered that city, Yankel was surprised to see everyone walking around with a sad face. He wondered about this, and at last he stopped someone and asked why this was. The man replied, "You must be a stranger here, for everyone knows the reason. We are sad because our beloved queen is sad." Now Yankel was sorry to hear this, since he had hoped the queen might help him, but what chance would there be if she were so unhappy? Then Yankel himself began to grow sad, so that his face resembled the faces of the inhabitants of that city. At last he asked someone, "Why is it that the queen is so sad?" The man replied, "Because her royal garment, which is woven out of light, has become unravelled. Now she has nothing to wear to the wedding of her daughter, the princess. And since she has nothing to wear, the wedding has been delayed, who knows for how long?"

When Yankel heard this, his heart leaped. For after all, was he not a tailor? And did he not make his living—a meager one, it is true—by repairing garments, as well as sewing new ones? In fact, Yankel spent most of his time restoring old garments, for his customers were the poor folk who could not afford new ones. But Yankel wondered if there were no tailors in that land who might repair the queen's gown themselves. He asked the man about this, and the man said, "Of course we have tailors here. But none of them know a thing about working with cloth woven out of light.

For the royal garment was made long ago, and handed down from one generation to the next. And since the material stretched or shrank as needed, it has fit every queen to perfection. But now that the garment has become unwoven, there is no one who knows how to repair it, for this secret was lost long ago."

Now when Yankel heard this, he remained hopeful, but he was also afraid, for if none of the tailors of that kingdom knew what to do, how would he? Still, he had not given up hope when the great tailors of his own kingdom failed, nor would he give up hope now.

Then Yankel told the stranger he was a tailor, and that he was willing to try his hand at repairing the garment for the queen. The stranger was delighted to hear this, and told Yankel that the queen had announced some time ago that any tailors who entered that kingdom were to be brought to the palace, to attempt to repair the royal gown, since all of the tailors of that kingdom had already tried and failed. So he led Yankel to the palace, and when the guards heard he was a tailor, they quickly gave him an audience with the queen.

Now when Yankel found himself, a poor tailor, standing in the splendor of that court, before a great and powerful queen, he was overcome with fear, for it was only then that he realized he had forgotten to ask what would happen if he failed. Now, though, it was too late, and with a quivering voice Yankel told the queen he was willing to try to repair her royal gown.

The queen nodded sadly and said, "I wish that repairing it was all that was needed. But the problem is more serious than that. You see, the fabric of the gown has begun to unravel, and because it is woven out of light, when it unravels it simply turns to light again and disappears. Therefore it is not only a matter of repair, for it is first necessary to create some new material. But the secret of how to weave cloth out of light has long been lost."

Now Yankel realized that if he could discover that secret, he would be able to produce the fabric needed to weave a garment for the moon. So he told the queen that although he did not know how such miraculous material could be made, he was willing to search for the secret, no matter how long it would take for him to find. The queen was very impressed with his determination, for the tailors of that kingdom had quickly abandoned all hope of accomplishing this task. She told him she would gladly help him any way she could and certainly wished him luck, for she longed to attend the wedding of her daughter, the princess, but could not until she was able to wear the royal gown woven out of light as had been the custom in that kingdom for so many centuries.

Then Yankel asked to see the garment that had become unravelled, for that seemed like a reasonable way to start. And the queen had the garment brought at once, and gave him a room in which to examine it.

Now when Yankel sat down to study that royal gown he was amazed at its beauty, for the fabric was like moonlight, exquisitely woven and without any sign of stitches or seams. He also marvelled at how supple it was—it would stretch as far as he pulled it, but when released would shrink back to its original shape. So too did the sleeve fit snugly around his arm when he placed it inside, only to grow back to its natural size when he took his arm out. And the more he studied it, the more Yankel thought that this material would make a fine garment for the moon.

Then Yankel examined the hem of the garment, where the unravelling had begun. He searched for the loose end of the thread of light, and when at last he found it, he saw that as soon as the thread unravelled it turned to light and disappeared, just as the queen had said. Meanwhile Yankel had become so absorbed in the task of studying that wonderful garment he did not notice that many hours had passed, and night had fallen. And while he worked, the full moon rose up in the sky until it was framed in the window of the chamber in which Yankel sat, and cast its light inside. And when the light of the moon struck that garment, a remarkable change took place—the gown began to glow with a wonderful, pale light. This change startled Yankel, and he jumped back, for it seemed as if the garment had come to life. It was then that a miracle took place—the hem of the garment, which had been unravelling and growing shorter, began to grow larger again in the light of the moon. Yankel was astounded, for the weaving of light which had seemed so impossible was taking place right before his eyes. And suddenly, in a moment of true inspiration, Yankel snipped off a tiny piece of the garment and held it up in the moonlight. And as he watched, the swatch began to grow, little by little, as if it were being woven in the light, until it was ten times larger than it had been at first. And Yankel knew that he had stumbled upon the secret of that precious material, woven out of moonlight.

Meanwhile, the light of the moon had continued to restore the queen's gown, and by the time the sun came up, the dress had been completely repaired. Yankel proudly showed it to the queen, who was amazed at his skill, for the garment was as good as new. Then the queen tried it on, and the garment shrank until it fit her perfectly. And when she looked into the mirror and saw how beautiful she looked in it, her sadness turned to joy, for now she could make plans for the wedding of the princess. But before she did, she asked Yankel how she might reward him, and told him he could have anything his heart desired. Then Yankel took out the tiny piece of cloth he had snipped from the hem of the garment, and asked the queen if he might keep it as a momento. The queen readily granted this request, and saw to it that Yankel received a bag of gold coins as well. Then she thanked him once more from the bottom of her heart and hurried off to make preparations for the wedding. And Yankel took his leave and made his way back to the city from which he had come.

Now since Yankel had travelled very far to reach that kingdom, it took him many months to return. During that time there were many full moons, and while the full moon shone in the sky, Yankel would take out the small piece of material and hold it up to the light of the moon. And on each night of the full moon the size of the cloth would multiply ten fold, until by the time Yankel returned home it was so immense, that it was large enough to fit the moon.

When Yankel finally reached his town and all the simple tailors saw the magnificent fabric he had brought with him, their hearts leaped for joy, and they all joined together to sew a garment for the moon. So it was that the sun was finally able to keep its promise, and give the moon a wonderful garment to keep her warm on cold nights. And that garment fit perfectly, expanding when the moon grew larger and shrinking when it grew small. And the moon has kept that garment to this very day, wearing it with pride and joy since, after all, it was created out of its own light.

Eastern Europe: Nineteenth Century
A Tale of Rabbi Nachman of Bratslav

The Treasure

Once there was a poor woodcutter who lived with his family at the outskirts of the forest and sold firewood to the other poor people who lived there. This man worked very hard and his rewards were few. But he had faith in God and he loved his family dearly, so he was never bitter about his lot. One night this man had a dream in which he travelled down a path until he came to a bridge. A soldier was stationed upon the bridge, who crossed over it back and forth. Led by a strange certainty, the man went beneath the bridge and began to dig in a certain place. Before long he struck something, and when he had uncovered it he found it was a chest. And when he opened the chest, he found a treasure inside it. The treasure was so precious that he gasped when he saw it. Just then the man awoke and realized he was dreaming. He sighed, for in the dream he had been overjoyed at having discovered that treasure, and now it had all vanished into thin air.

During the day, though, as he worked cutting wood in the forest, the man daydreamed a bit about that treasure, and the thought crossed his mind that he could search for it. But he dismissed this thought as foolish—after all, it was only a dream. So he went about his work and forgot all about it.

That night, however, the man again dreamed about the bridge beneath which he found a treasure. And this time the dream was even more vivid, for now the man could see the face of the guard who paced back and forth on the bridge. When he awoke he found his desire for that treasure was even stronger, and he was unable to fall back to sleep, for now that he had dreamed the same dream twice, he began to wonder if it was a sign that he really should seek out the treasure. But in the morning he laughed at himself for taking the dream so seriously. For how would he ever know where to begin to search? After all, there were a great many bridges in the world and he could not dig beneath every one of them.

But when the dream recurred for a third night, the man realized that his destiny was calling to him, and he vowed to find that treasure no matter how difficult it might be. His wife tried to dissuade him, but when she saw he was determined to go, she wished him well and prayed that his dream might come true. And so the man set out into the world to search for a bridge he had only seen in a dream.

But where does one find such a bridge? The woodcutter decided to walk into the town, to see if someone there knew where it might be found. Once he reached town he tried to ask people about it, but when he was unable to say which bridge it was or what river it crossed, they just shrugged their shoulders and walked on. Thus the man realized that he had to recall some detail about it that would make it recognizable. He thought for a long time, and then he remembered that the guard on the bridge had worn a helmet with a feather in it, unlike any helmet he had ever seen. So the next time he asked someone, he mentioned that helmet, and soon he learned that the guards of the king wore helmets like that in the capital of that country. Now the capital was a great distance from there, but when this detail of his dream turned out to be real, the woodcutter decided he must go there at once. For he had become confident that his dream might be true after all.

After many months and many hardships, the woodcutter reached the capital at last. Before he had walked very far from the gates of the city he saw a river. He decided to follow that river, hoping it might lead him to the bridge he was searching for. And sure enough, before he had walked a mile he reached the very bridge he had seen in his dream. Not only that, but there was a guard pacing up and down upon it—the very same guard he had glimpsed in his dream! A chill went down the woodcutter's spine as he approached the bridge. He greeted the soldier, and asked him if he might dig beneath the bridge. When the soldier heard this, he seemed startled, and he asked the man why he would want to do such a thing. With no other choice, the woodcutter told the guard about his dream. When he heard it, the man laughed heartily and said, "If you have come all this way just because of a dream, you are indeed foolish. And your dream is merely a common one. Why, I have just dreamed three nights in a row of a treasure beneath an old oak tree at the entrance of a forest." And the soldier went on to describe the tree and the place he had found the treasure. And as he did, the man suddenly realized that the guard was describing the woodcutter's own home in a distant province of that land. It suddenly dawned on the woodcutter that the dream had led him to that bridge not to dig beneath it, but to hear the dream of that guard. And as if to confirm this, the guard suddenly became stern and said, "As to your request to dig here, why that is out of the question. This bridge belongs to the king, and if I permitted the ground beneath it to be dug up, I would soon be deprived of my head. Go now, and if I see you here again I will not hesitate to arrest you!" And he angrily chased the wood-cutter from there, and frightened him out of his wits.

So it was that the woodcutter traveled back to where he had come from, to his family and home. And when his wife saw that he had returned empty-handed, she was not even sorry, so happy was she to have him back. But no sooner had he kissed his wife and children than he hurried out to the giant oak tree at the entrance to the forest, and dug beneath it. And before he had dug very far, he struck something, which turned out to be the very treasure he had seen in his dream, buried behind his very own house.

Eastern Europe: Nineteenth Century
A Tale of Rabbi Nachman of Bratslav

The Prince and the Slave

Once a queen and her slave each gave birth at the same time. And the midwife, who was actually an evil witch, switched the two infants, and gave the prince to the slave, and the son of the slave to the queen. In this way the two were raised by the wrong parents, and the prince grew up thinking that he was a slave, and the slave grew up believing that he was the prince.

The witch was very proud of herself, for in this way she had confused the destinies of these children and added confusion to the world. She was so proud, in fact, that she had the overwhelming desire to tell someone about her accomplishment. But of course she had to keep her evil deed a secret; if the king and queen were to find out, they would take back their child, the true prince. Yet the witch could not bear to keep this secret to herself, and one day she went over to the open window and whispered it there, in the certainty that no one would hear her. And it is true that no human being heard those words, but the wind caught them, and carried them until they reached the birds, and the birds spoke of the exchanged children among themselves. And in the forest there lived an old man who knew the language of the birds.

He heard what they had to say, and he whispered what he heard to many another, until the rumor of the exchange was known throughout the kingdom, although no one dared to bring this rumor to the attention of the king or queen.

So it was that the true prince was raised as a slave and taught how to serve. And the true son of the slave was raised as a prince and taught how to rule. But in time the rumor that they had been exchanged reached them both. Now the false prince did not mention this rumor to the king and queen, of course, and while the true prince knew that he resembled the king as do two drops of water, he had no other proof of his origin. In due time, the slave came to inherit the throne, and was crowned king.

As king, the son of the slave immediately ordered the exile of the true prince. In truth he would have preferred to have had him killed, but he was afraid that this might somehow cause him to be overthrown. For he believed that he would remain the ruler as long as the true prince remained a slave. Thus the prince was sent into exile far from the country of his birth. This new misfortune was unexpected, and he could not understand why he was so cursed with bad luck, for not only had he been deprived of his kingdom, but he had even been exiled from it.

As for the slave who had become king, even though he wielded great power he was not happy, for the thought that he was actually the son of a slave gnawed away at him. So too did he feel guilty for sending the true prince into exile. Once it happened that the false king was hunting in the forest with the royal ministers. They were pursuing a deer but could not catch it. Hours passed, but the king would not abandon the chase. At last the royal ministers caught up with him and told him it was time to turn back, since night was falling. But the false king was by now obsessed with that deer, and refused to turn back. When he saw that the others were terrified of being in the forest at night, he ordered them to return without him, and since they could not disobey his order, they did so. In this way the false king continued to chase after that deer for many days, until the days turned into weeks, and still he could not catch it. But by this time he found himself lost in a deep forest, far from the kingdom he ruled.

Now shortly after he was sent into exile, the true prince dreamed that he came to a city where a fair was taking place. In the dream he was told to go to the fair and to take the first job he was offered, whatever it was. The prince remembered this dream when he woke, but he paid it little heed. Yet when he dreamed it a second and then a third time, he realized that the dream was bringing him a message and therefore he decided to obey it. He walked until he came to a large road, and he followed that road until he reached a city, and just as in his dream, there was a fair taking place. Shortly after he arrived he met a merchant, who asked him if he wanted to work. He needed some men to help him drive home the cattle he had purchased at the fair. And the prince agreed to work for him, as he had been told to do in the dream.

Now it happened that this merchant was a vicious, hateful man, who drove his workers as hard as he drove the cattle. And one morning, when three cattle suddenly ran off into the forest, the merchant shouted at the prince to chase after them, and not to return without all three. So the prince went dashing off into the forest, trying to catch up with the cattle. But each time he approached them, they would run off, each in another direction, and in this way they led him further and further into the forest, until he was quite lost.

By that time the sun was about to set, and the prince realized that the forest could be very dangerous at night. He looked around and saw a large tree nearby and climbed into it just as the forest grew dark. And as soon as darkness fell, a terrible laughter rang through the forest, which made the prince's blood grow cold, and he gave thanks that he had found refuge in that tree. Just then the prince heard a cough nearby, and discovered another man huddled in that tree. "What are you doing here?" The prince asked. The other replied, "I can ask the same of you." Then the prince said, "I was chasing after cattle that ran away." And the man in the tree said, "I was following a deer on the hunt, and it led me to this forsaken forest." For the other man in that tree was none other than the son of the slave who had been made a king.

Meanwhile the terrible laughter would ring out from time to time, causing both men to shudder with fear. The prince told the other that to pass the time they should speak, and so the slave told of his life as king, and the prince came to realize he was in that tree with the very one who had usurped his throne. Then he decided to conceal his true identity for the time being, lest the other try to kill him, since he had already sent him into exile.

Now the false king had not eaten for several days, and he was truly famished. And it happened that the prince had been carrying some bread with him when he had run off into the forest. So the false king wasted no time in asking if the other had any food. But the prince realized that while he was lost in the forest, food was of great value, more valuable than gold. And at that moment he saw a way for him to take back what was truly his. So he said, "I have only enough bread to sustain myself until I get out of his terrible forest." The false king could not accept this, and he offered to pay any price the other would ask. The prince told him that in that forest nothing was more precious than bread, and asked what the king would offer for it. Then the false king said, "I would give everything for some of that bread. I would even give up my kingdom." "Let us agree, then," said the prince, "that this is what shall be done. I will divide the bread I have with you, and you will become my slave, and all of your property will become mine." "Yes, yes," said the son of the slave, and at that moment he became the slave it was his destiny to be, and the prince was restored to his true place as the son of a king.

At daybreak the prince looked down from the tree and saw the three cattle grazing nearby. And the slave looked up and saw the deer he had chased for so long. But the prince realized that he did not have to chase after the cattle, for he was no longer a slave. And the slave realized he was no longer hunting that deer for sport, for he was no longer king. Nor could he run after that deer without the permission of the other, since he was now his slave. And the changes that had taken place in that tree overnight amazed and overwhelmed both the prince and the slave, for their roles had truly been reversed.

The prince saw that the slave still longed to chase after that deer. So he said, "It is not in my nature to expect someone to be my slave, for I have served as a slave for too long to want that. Instead, I ask that you sign a statement that all you possess now belongs to me. And after that you shall be free to chase that deer to the ends of the earth, should you so desire." Then the slave broke off a piece of the bark of that tree, and on the smooth side of it he wrote with the pen that he had once used as king that he was giving everything to the prince. Then he climbed down from that tree and began to chase after the deer again, but it only led him still further into the woods. And he never emerged from that forest again.

As for the prince, he cared nothing for the chase any longer. He abandoned those cattle as if they had been sins left behind after repentence. Then he set off to find his way out of that forest, and by following the signs he had left when he had entered there, he found his way to a path, and that path led him to a road, and that road led him to a kingdom. He came to the gate of that kingdom and sought to be allowed in. The gatekeeper, however, refused to open the gate. When the prince asked why, the gatekeeper told him that he had come to a kingdom that had lost its name. Only those who were prepared to restore the lost name were permitted to enter those gates. And the gatekeeper asked the prince if he were willing to undertake such a task. The prince had not expected this, and he did not know how to reply. So he said, "This is a matter for deep consideration. I will come back when I am able to give you an answer." And he left and went back into the forest.

But now he was in a different part of the forest, far from the shrill and terrifying laughter. Instead, that night a wondrous music, the most beautiful the prince had ever heard, came drifting in the darkness. All night long his heart sailed on that music, filled with longing. And in the morning he understood that the music had filled him with the desire to restore the kingdom's lost name. He climbed down from the tree and all day he thought about that music, wondering what might be its unearthly source and hoping that it might return that night. And by the time three stars could be seen, the music drifted again throughout the forest.

Then the prince found that he was unafraid of the dark and climbed down from the tree to seek out the source of that music. He let the music lead him, for it grew louder as he drew closer to its source. In this way he was led to another tree, in whose branches the full moon could be seen. When the prince came closer, he saw that in the place where the full moon rested, some kind of vessel was glowing in the dark. He did not know if it was the light of the moon that shone on it, or if the light came from within. And he climbed up into that tree and stared at that glowing source all that night and fell into a deep trance.

At dawn, just as the sun rose, the prince came out of the trance. He realized it had been brought on by the unearthly music and the glowing light. And he discovered, as well, that he felt strengthened and refreshed as he had not felt in years. Then the prince looked up into the place where that light had been and from which the music had come. And there he saw a wooden vessel, which he realized must be some kind of musical instrument. So he climbed up into the branches until the vessel was within his reach, and he took it from a hollow place in the trunk.

Perched in that tree, the prince examined the instrument, turning it over and over. It had been carved from a very rich wood, and engraved with intricate designs and various signs and symbols. They were not in any language the prince had ever seen, and when he discovered that he could read them, he was most astonished. He surmised that listening to that music during the trance had somehow made it possible for him to read those symbols. And by reading them he learned the secret of that strange instrument and knew he was ready to restore the lost name of the kingdom.

Taking the precious instrument with him, the prince returned to the gate. This time, when the gatekeeper asked his question, the prince replied that he was indeed prepared to restore the kingdom's lost name, and the gate was opened to him. In that kingdom there was a garden, and it was said that whoever could enter that garden and come out of it in peace would restore the lost name. But until then, all of those who had entered there had soon come running out, terrified. For they had been greeted by a horrible screaming, which had frightened them out of their wits. The prince, too, was greeted by these cries, but they did not sound like screaming to him. Instead he understood the meaning of these sounds, for since he had fallen into the trance, he also understood this language. And so he heard the cries of the spirits who pleaded for him to restore the lost name. And from listening to these cries, he learned that everything in that garden had an order, which had been lost over time. Now everything was out of place. If only he could restore everything to its proper place, the name of the kingdom would be restored at last.

Following the guidance of the spirits, who were more than happy to help him, the prince did whatever they told him to do to restore the old order in the garden. He moved the statue of the king who had established that garden to the center, and when he did a fountain that had been dry for a long, long time sprang up around it. And when he had done everything that needed to be done, the spirits led him to the throne in that garden. There the prince discovered that it was carved out of the same wood as was the enchanted instrument. He took out the instrument and placed it on the throne. And all at once a music emerged from that instrument that carried the true name of that kingdom to every corner of the land, so that everyone knew that the lost name had been restored at last, and each and every inhabitant knew what it was. For that was the Kingdom of Music, which had been ruled by silence for so long. And now the true ruler, music, took its place. And even though music is invisible, still everyone who can hear knows of its existence. Only the deaf are deprived of its beauty. And when the inhabitants heard that unearthly, enchanting music, they realized how empty their lives had been without it, and how heavily the silence had weighed upon them.

So it was that when he emerged from that garden in peace, the prince was met by the elders of the kingdom, and each one thanked him with all his heart for restoring the music to the kingdom, and thus restoring its name. And they invited him to become their king, for they had always known that whoever could restore the lost name was the one who should serve as their king as well. The prince agreed to become their king and served for many years to come. And in the end he even found a way to unite that Kingdom of Music with his own, which he had been born to rule in the first place. And that was a joyous day indeed.

Eastern Europe: Nineteenth Century
A Tale of Rabbi Nachman of Bratslav

The Enchanted Tree

There once was a wise man who had three sons. Before his death, this man called together his sons and said, "There is a mystery I wish to reveal to you before I take my leave of this world. Know that there exists a certain tree with ten branches, and each branch of that tree bears a different fruit, and each kind of fruit has its own special power. One has the power to provide children to the childless, while another can cure any illness; one can provide the wisdom of Solomon, while another can reveal the secrets of heaven. If that tree is watered, its blessing descend upon the world. But if it is not, the absence of its blessings haunts us all. Recently I have learned that for many years the tree has not been watered, and it thirsts. But demons have dug a deep pit all around it, so that no water can reach it. For when the tree flourishes in all its glory, the demons will be destroyed, and they know this; that is why they guard the tree, and prevent it from being watered.

"You, my sons, must go out into the world and find this tree, and somehow see that it is watered. That is my dying wish to you." And with that the old man passed away. His sons greatly grieved

/307/

over his loss, but after the period of mourning, the eldest son came to the others and said, "Since I am the eldest, it is my duty to search for the enchanted tree of which our father spoke." His brothers wished him luck, and he set off on his quest.

Now he searched for many years, but nowhere did he find this miraculous tree. And at last he returned defeated, for he had come to believe that it was nowhere to be found in the world of men. After this the second brother took it upon himself to try to fulfill the dying wish of his father. He too searched everywhere, but nowhere was the tree to be found. When he returned home at last, empty handed and dejected, the youngest brother announced that he too wished to undertake the quest. But his older brothers did not take him seriously because he was quite lame, hardly able to take a single step on his own. How, they asked, could he search throughout the world as they had?

But the youngest brother, in spite of his lameness, refused to give up the idea. He insisted that he could travel in a wagon, with a wagon driver. Together they could search for the tree as well as his brothers, who had travelled on horseback. At last his brothers agreed to let him go, if he so desired, and they hired a wagon and driver to take him wherever he asked to go. They paid the wagon driver well for his services, and he and the youngest brother set out on the quest to find the tree that was the source of so many blessings.

On the third day of their journey, while they were riding through the forest, the wagon was attacked by a band of thieves. When he saw them coming, the wagon driver jumped down and ran away as fast as he could. But the youngest brother, being crippled, could not move from his place. The thieves, who had a terrible reputation for being ruthless, were surprised to see the young man still seated, for all those who could run for their lives did so whenever they attacked. They asked him why he did not flee, and he told them that he was crippled and could not. Then the robbers laughed and proceeded to strip the wagon bare. They left him nothing to eat or drink and abandoned him in that forsaken place.

When the band of thieves had gone, the young man realized

that he could not stay in the wagon, for he might die of starvation if he did not find something to eat. So he cast himself down from the wagon, and pulled himself along the ground. In this way he came upon various herbs and berries that were growing there, and sustained himself on these. Whenever he had eaten all the herbs and berries in one place, he would crawl to another likely spot, and search for more. Soon he came upon a new kind of herb and plucked it, root and all. To his amazement he found a diamond in the cluster of its roots. He pulled that diamond out and marveled at it, for it was square and there was writing on every side.

The young man was astonished at his good fortune at finding such a precious object, and he read one side of the diamond. On it was written that whoever grasped that side of the diamond would be brought to the place where the sun and moon meet. Now this greatly interested the young man, for perhaps in that place he could find out something about the enchanted tree. So he took hold of the diamond from that side, and in the blink of an eye he found himself at the end of the world, in the place where the sun and moon meet. And lo and behold, before him he saw both sun and moon, and they were speaking together. And perhaps because he held that magic jewel in his hand, the young man understood every word they spoke.

The sun was complaining to the moon. He said that demons were constantly enlarging the ditch they had dug around the life-giving tree, and the tree had been cut off from all water, and so all the world had been cut off from its blessings. And the moon replied that it too suffered from the evil demons, who sought for ways to dim its light. Those demons made their home in the Mountains of Darkness, where the light of neither the sun nor the moon ever penetrated.

Naturally the young man was amazed to hear this conversation, for it gave him the first clues in his quest. He listened very carefully to see if he could learn anything else. Then the sun asked the moon if there was any way these demons could be defeated. The moon replied, "I know how it could be done. There is a crossroads at which ten paths meet. Each of the paths branching from there has a miraculous dust of its own. One of those paths is that of the righteous. Whoever steps on the dust from that path will become righteous at once. Another path is that of the insane. Whoever walks on that dust will surely lose his mind. And there are eight other paths, each distinct from the others. If only someone would take the dust of the path of the righteous and cause the demons to walk over it, the pit they have dug around the life-giving tree would soon be gone."

Now when the youngest brother heard this, a shiver passed through his body, and he knew that he would not give up until he had succeeded in defeating the demons in just that way. Then he took out the diamond and looked at another side of it. And there it was written that whoever took hold of that side would be delivered to the crossroads where the ten paths meet. The young man did so, and in an instant he found himself at that very crossroads. There each of those ten roads had been marked with a sign that identified it. These signs were not in words, but since he held the diamond he understood them. And among those roads there was one whose dust could cure any cripple. The young man crawled out that road, and he no sooner touched that dust than he was no longer crippled but could stand and walk and run as well as any other. A boundless joy filled his heart, and he gave thanks to the Holy One, blessed be He, for granting him the great blessing of a cure. And he vowed that he would never rest a moment until he had succeeded in watering that thirsty tree.

Then he very carefully took samples of dust from each of the roads, tying them in packets. And he wrote down the proper name on every bundle. After that the young man took out the diamond once more, and turned to its third side. There he read that whoever took hold there would be brought back to the place where the diamond had been found. This seemed like a good idea to the young man, so he grasped the diamond from that side, and at once he was back in the very forest where he had first been robbed.

Now the young man recalled very well the path the robbers had taken after they had abandoned him. He followed that path, and before long he found that he was very close to their camp. Then he took out the dust from the path of the righteous and sprinkled it on the road that the robbers passed over every day, but he also mixed it with a little dust from the road of the insane.

The next day all of the robbers set out on that path except for their leader, who remained behind. And the instant they set foot on that miraculous dust, they became righteous, and recognized that they had been leading a life of great evil, and that their sins were beyond measure. Then they grieved terribly over what they had done, and because the young man had thrown in a bit of the dust of the insane, they began to accuse each other of leading them into evil, and before long they grew so angry they began to fight with each other. In no time at all, none of them remained living.

After a while the leader began to wonder what had happened to his band and he set out to look for them. And when the robber chief came to the path on which the magic dust had been sprinkled, he too became one of the righteous, and was filled with remorse for all the sins he had committed. And because of the pinch of the dust of insanity, he beat his breast and tore his clothes and cried out that all he wanted was a way to repent. Then the young man climbed down from the tree in which he had hidden himself, and he said to the robber chief, "You can perform your first act of repentance by giving back to me all that you stole." The robber was amazed to see him, and astonished to see that he was no longer a cripple. But he did not dwell on this, for he was so happy to have a way to repent. He returned to their den at once to get the chest he and the other robbers had stolen from the young man, and brought all their other treasures as well, for he was prepared to give up everything if in that way he could repent.

So it was that the young man received back all he had lost and much more besides. And the young man led the robber chief to the nearest city, where the repentant robber gave himself up to be punished. But in the end the people recognized that he had truly repented of his crimes, and at last he was forgiven. As for the young man, he gave back the stolen treasure to everyone who had suffered a loss, and all that was left over he gave to the poor of that city, keeping for himself only that which had originally belonged to him.

The young man was very gratified to know that the evil band of thieves had been stopped, but now he recalled that his true quest was to find the enchanted tree, and he wondered how he might continue. So he took out the diamond and looked at its last side, which he had never before examined. There he read, to his great delight, that whoever took hold of that side would shortly be taken into the presence of the very life-giving tree he had been seeking. This he did without delay, and an instant later he saw with his very own eyes the magnificent tree with its ten branches and its precious fruit. But he saw as well the huge pit that had been dug around the tree, preventing anyone from coming close enough to the tree to water it. And surrounding that pit was an army of demons, each demon armed with a spear, guarding the way to the tree of life.

At first the young man was frightened by the sight of those terrible looking demons, but then he remembered all of the miraculous dust he had brought with him. He took out the dust of the righteous, waited for the wind to blow in the right direction, and cast a handful that way. The wind carried it to the feet of the demons, who scurried around in great confusion at first—and then one by one they simply vanished. For when the demons became righteous, they recognized how evil they were, and in that moment of supreme contradiction they ceased to exist. And the young man saw with joy in his heart that only the ditch around the tree now prevented him from reaching it. He approached that great pit, which he saw was a great abyss. Then he took out another handful of dust from the path of the righteous, and he cast it into that abyss. And in an instant the pit disappeared, for in truth it was only an illusion, and the way to the enchanted tree was freed of obstacles at last.

As he stepped up to the tree and stood in its sacred shelter, the young man suddenly heard a sound like that of running water. And from where he stood he saw nearby a stone from which a fountain sprang forth. Water from that fountain had not been flowing for many generations, but now that the way to the tree was clear, the water began to flow once more. And the young man saw how in a short time the water from the rock formed a stream that

". . . but then he remembered all of the miraculous dust he had brought with him."

flowed directly to the tree, and watered it, so that its fruit could grow ripe and give the world its abundant blessings. And all this took place in the presence of the young man, who knew that the purpose of his life had been fulfilled at last.

Eastern Europe: Nineteenth Century
A Tale of Rabbi Nachman of Bratslav

The Palace Beneath the Sea

There once was a king who possessed a price-less treasure. This was a miraculous golden lamp in which was set a stone that glowed with a wonderful light. What the source of the stone's light was nobody knew—the light simply shone from within. And although the king did not know it, the stone had a wondrous history. For in that stone was preserved the last of the primordial light. When the Holy One, blessed be He, decided to withdraw the primordial light from the world, He preserved some of it inside that stone. That is why it shone still with such a radiant light. For many generations after the Fall, the stone was hidden in one of the treasuries of heaven, and not even the angels shared in the blessing of its light. It was only when Enoch proved himself to be perfect in his righteousness that the Holy One permitted the stone to be revealed in the celestial realm, and to cast its light throughout the upper world. And when Enoch ascended into Paradise in a fiery chariot, this jewel was presented to him as a sign that his pure soul had been accepted on high.

When Enoch returned to earth for thirty days to share the secrets he had learned on high, he gave the wondrous stone to his son, Methuselah, who hung it above his bed and slept in its radiance every night, and thus lived longer than any other man. The stone, called the *Tzohar*, was inherited by Lamech, Methuselah's son, and thus it came into the possession of Noah, Lamech's son. Having been raised in the presence of the light cast from that stone, Noah was the most righteous man of his generation, and thus it was he who was chosen to preserve the human race at the time of the Flood. Noah hung the stone inside the ark, and thus illumined the deck during the long darkness brought on by the Flood.

But Noah proved to be a less than perfect man, and no sooner did the ark come to rest on Mount Ararat, than the *Tzohar* fell from where it was hung and sank into the sea. It was then carried by the currents until it became lodged in the crevice of a cave that was then still underwater. But the waters soon receded and the cave re-emerged in an Egyptian valley. As fate would have it, it was to this cave that Emetel brought her infant son Abraham. And although Abraham was left alone in that cave, the radiant glow of the *Tzohar* not only turned the darkness into light, but preserved the infant, and even caused him to flourish, so that in a short time he could walk and speak as well as a grown child. This was the miracle Emetel discovered when she returned to that cave, and from then on she knew that her child bore a great blessing. Abraham took the stone with him when he left the cave and hung it around his neck, and before long he discovered that it was both an astrolabe, in which the secrets of the stars could be read, and a healing stone as well. For any sick person who came into the presence of that stone was healed. In fact, some say that the stone possessed the power of bringing the dead to life, and that Abraham discovered this when the stone touched a bird he was about to cook over a fire, which came to life and flew away.

Abraham bestowed the stone on his son Isaac, who gave it to his son Jacob, rather than Esau, at the time Isaac was deceived into blessing him. Jacob secretly gave it to Joseph, whom he loved more than his eleven other sons. And so the stone, hanging around his neck, was the one possession Joseph clung to when his brothers took his coat-of-many-colors and cast him into the pit. It lighted the darkness and frightened off the snakes and scorpions, until he was found by a passing caravan. When Joseph reached Egypt he set the stone inside a golden cup, and used it to divine the future and interpret dreams. Later, the cup was buried in Joseph's coffin, and the coffin was sunk to the bottom of the Nile. But before the children of Israel departed from Egypt, Moses came to the banks of the Nile and called out to Joseph for him to join them, and soon the coffin rose up from the bottom as if it consisted of the lightest wood, while in fact it was made of solid gold.

Moses recognized how precious was the stone, and he had Bezalel set it inside a golden lamp, which hung inside the Tabernacle the children of Israel carried through the wilderness beside Joseph's coffin. This is how the *Ner Tamid*, the eternal light, came into being, a spark of which burns in the flame we been before the Ark at all times. The sacred lamp remained in the possession of the Jews for many generations, and eventually took its rightful place inside the Holy of Holies of the Temple in Jerusalem. When the Temple was destroyed, the lamp and the illuminating stone fell into the hands of pagans for many generations. Eventually it came into the possession of a king who ruled a great kingdom, and who recognized at once that it was a priceless treasure.

Now since this king, who lived in a palace by the shore of the sea, did not know the true history of the golden lamp, he assumed it to be enchanted and wondered if it had any other powers. He showed the lamp to the palace soothsayer, who sought to discover its powers by reading the stars. And because he was a master at this art, he was able to discern one very important truth about the lamp, although many other mysteries remained unrevealed to him. He revealed to the king that the lamp endowed the king with great blessings merely by its presence. For as long as the king kept the golden lamp in the palace, and passed it on to his descendents, his kingdom would flourish. But if he were to lose it, or if it was taken away, then his kingdom would surely be lost. And if his heirs should ever be unmindful of its importance, its power would cease to protect them.

When the king heard this, he grew terrified that the golden

lamp might somehow be stolen, and he made the soothsayer vow never to reveal even the existence of the lamp, much less its great powers. But even after this the king did not feel secure. So he decided to conceal the lamp in a place so well hidden no one would ever find it. Yet this place could not be beyond the palace, or the blessings of the lamp would be lost. Faced with this dilemma, the king decided to construct a labyrinthine cave beneath the palace, at the end of which the golden lamp would be hidden. In this way it would continue to protect him while remaining well concealed.

Now the king kept the purpose of the cave and labyrinth secret even from the builders. They were even forbidden to reveal their work to their wives. And when the labyrinth was complete, the king had a heavy metal door placed at the opening of the cave, locked with seven locks and sealed with seven seals. After he had completed the labyrinth, the king called in the astrologer and told him to inquire of the stars if he had hidden it well enough, and if his destiny was now secure. The soothsayer sought to discern these matters, and succeeded in divining answer to both questions, for the replies were interwined: If the king wished to remain safe, he had to have engraved on the metal door the secret of how to open the gate and pass through the labyrinth, or the golden lamp would be lost for all time. For otherwise, the action of the king would be regarded by heaven as selfish, and the blessings of the lamp would be withdrawn. But at the same time the king was free to conceal the key to the gate and the labyrinth in a code, using any symbols he wished. For it was understood that the king needed at least that much protection to prevent the lamp from being stolen during his lifetime.

When the king heard this, he commanded that the soothsayer devise a code which no one could penetrate. And the king told him that he would test it by giving it to ten of the wisest men in the kingdom. And if even one of them deciphered even a single symbol, the soothsayer's life would be lost. The soothsayer left the royal chamber terrified, for although he was skilled at deciphering codes himself, he had no experience in creating them.

And he feared that there would be nothing he could create which one of the wisest could not decipher.

Now the soothsayer had been taught his skills by an old sorcerer, and he recalled that the old man had often consulted a book of signs and symbols whose meaning he had not revealed even to his apprentice. The soothsayer thought to himself that perhaps the old man could help him write this message in those obscure symbols, for surely no one else could decipher them.

When the old sorcerer heard the plea of his former student, he did not refuse him, but took down the secrets which were to be conveyed and expressed them in the mysterious symbols of the Kabbalah, in which he was well versed. For he suspected at once from the description of the golden lamp that it might be the eternal light of the Tabernacle, which had been lost for so long, and he discerned the hand of fate in the astrologer coming to him for help. And by using those symbols and their powers he hoped to transmit the secret of how the lamp could be retrieved sometime in the future by a sage, like himself, steeped in those supernal mysteries. In that way the eternal light might come into the possession of the Jews once more. The old man did not consider taking the lamp for himself, using the knowledge he had of its location, for he knew that to do so would be to sign a death warrant for the king.

The soothsayer himself was greatly mystified by the signs and symbols the sorcerer wrote down, which were to be engraved on the cavern door. But that was all for the better as far as he was concerned; he hoped, above all, that the code remain unbroken. And it did. None of the ten wise men to whom the king showed the symbols could decipher even a single one. The king was greatly pleased at this and gave the order to engrave the symbols on the metal door, and considered the matter closed. The soothsayer was rewarded for his good work and became the closest adviser to the king. Thus their lives and the kingdom flourished, while the golden lamp continued to glow in the depths of the labyrinthine cave constructed beneath the palace.

This king ruled for many years, and he was succeeded by his

son, and the dynasty lasted for many generations. But a time came when his descendents came to doubt not only the importance, but even the existence of the hidden lamp. So it was that before long the waters of the sea rose up and covered the palace and the city beside it, and no trace of their existence remained. Meanwhile, as the generations passed, the underwater palace was covered over with fine particles of sand and earth, which mixed together until it became a pure, white clay. So it was that for hundreds of years the kingdom was covered with waters, and no record of it remained in the world. Yet the time also came when the waters began to recede, and little by little the land appeared, but still no trace of the palace or the kingdom was to be seen, for they were buried beneath many layers of clay.

Now when that land emerged from under the waters, it became part of the kingdom of another king, who decided it should be settled and a city built there, for he did not know that there was a city buried beneath it. He had it announced that all of the Jews of his kingdom were commanded to leave their homes and resettle in that land, which had been underwater so long. Since the power of the king was very great, the Jews obeyed him, and travelled there to make their homes.

Among those who settled in that new city there was a potter who was the Hasid of a great master. All who owned the pots and vessels made by this potter found them to be almost indestructible, even when heated on a fire, yet they were also unusually light. Now the secret of this potter's wonderful pots was the clay that he used, which came from a particular pit. The potter was aware of the remarkable qualities of this clay and he continued to dig far down in that one place rather than dig in another, for that clay was unique. After years of such digging, his shovel one day struck metal, far down at the bottom of the pit. He could not imagine what could be buried there, for at that time the people still did not know of the city beneath them, on which their own had been built.

The potter carefully scraped away the clay, and found himself confronted with the metal door that was the entranceway to the labyrinth in which the golden lamp had been hidden. The potter saw that the door was locked with seven locks and sealed with seven seals, and when he tried to read the symbols engraved on it, he could not make out a single word. Nevertheless he suspected it might prove to be of great value, and thereupon the potter went directly to his Rebbe, and told about the discovery in the bottom of the clay pit. When the Rebbe had the potter draw some of the symbols he had seen on the door, he recognized them at once as symbols of the Kabbalah. Therefore he agreed to accompany the potter to the door, and soon was climbing down with him into the pit.

When they reached the metal door, the Rebbe studied the symbols and soon recognized that they had been written by a master of the Kabbalah. Because he was well versed in these symbols and knew how to read them, he was confident he could decipher the secret of how to unlock and unseal the door. But more importantly, he recognized that the potter had been guided to that place by the Holy One, blessed be He, so that he could bring him, his Rebbe, there.

By deciphering those symbols, the Rebbe discovered that it was necessary to pronounce the Ineffable Name in order to release the locks and seals of that door. Now in every generation there is only one Tzaddik who knows how to pronounce the Name. Just as the sorcerer who had created the code had been the chosen Tzaddik of his generation, acquainted with the mystery of the Name, so too was this Rebbe the very one who knew the secret; even thus does fate make it possible to thread a needle while our eyes are closed. And no sooner had the Tzaddik spoken the sacred Name, than the locks fell away and dropped to the floor and the doors swung open. The entrance to an underground cave was revealed, but the Rebbe was quick to notice that the cave was not pitch black like most caves, but was instead filled with a crystalline light, which had the cast of a pale aura. And when the Rebbe stepped inside the entrance of that cave, he felt as if a change had taken place, as if he were standing upon sacred ground. The potter followed after him, rapt by all that had occured, and wondering greatly at what they would find.

Before they had walked more than a few steps, a sweet

fragrance reached them, fresh and ripe. It was the scent of fresh fruit, and the two men both wondered how any such fruit could grow in that cave, which had been closed up for so long. It was then that they reached the first of the carob trees that flourished in that underground cave. The presence of these trees, filled with ripe fruit which no man had ever seen or tasted, filled them with a strange sensation. At last the Rebbe broke off two carobs, and gave one of them to the potter. They said the blessings together and when they tasted them, they were astonished at how sweet they were, and how ripe. They would have been even more amazed had they known that the cave had been barren when it had been closed up years and years ago, and that over the ages the primordial light which shone from the wondrous stone in the golden lamp had fertilized every passageway in that labyrinth, and carob trees had grown up, even though not a single carob seed had been left in that place.

Soon after they had tasted the carobs, both the Rebbe and the potter heard a low murmur, which sounded like the sea from a great distance, or a barely audible song. The Rebbe said, "Do you hear a distant song, like that of the sea?" And the potter nodded, for he had just been trying to make out what the sound was. And the Rebbe said, "I am certain that the taste of the carob has made it possible for this sound to reach our ears. Now we must follow that distant music, for it is the guide which will lead us through this labyrinth."

And that is what they did. They followed the voice of the waters, and if they made a wrong turn, the voice faded away, and thus they were guided through the labyrinth, the sound becoming clearer and clearer, the song more unearthly and intriguing, until at last they reached the source of the underground stream which ran through those passages (a stream which had also not existed when the king had the caves dug out beneath the palace). And the source of the wonderful music was a waterfall which cascaded down one side of the cave. The Rebbe and the potter listened to that voice, wrapped in the glowing light that shone so strongly there, and it seemed as if they were in the presence of another being, its limbs woven by the tender waters as they poured down from the top of the rock from which they arose. For a while it seemed to hypnotize them, but then the Rebbe shook himself free and climbed behind that rock. There, in a deep crevice, he found the golden lamp from which had come the flowing light that filled every passageway. He reached in and took out that lamp, and held it so that he could see the glowing stone. And when he looked into that source of the light, a vision took form before the Rebbe's eyes, and he found himself in the presence of the *Shekhinah*, and saw that the true source of that light, was the reflection of her robe, which was woven out of light. And in the presence of the *Shekhinah*, the Rebbe bowed his head, and the potter followed suit. Then the Rebbe wept tears of joy, for he knew that the miraculous light that had been lost for so long had been restored at last in his generation.

Eastern Europe: Nineteenth Century
A Tale of Rabbi Nachman of Bratslav

The Wishing Ring

In a village near a small town lived a poor Jew
with his wife and young son. The man made his living by collecting twigs and branches in the forest, and selling them in town for
kindling. But what he earned was only enough to buy kasha for
his wife and son.

One day, when the man went into the forest to collect wood
as usual, he suddenly grew tired and lay down to take a nap under
a tree. While he was sleeping he had a dream in which a stranger
came to him and said, "On the other side of the forest there is a
goat, from whose neck hangs a golden ring on a chain. You should
take this ring and keep it for yourself, for it is priceless. With it you
can obtain anything in the world you want. All you need to do is
put the ring on your finger, make your wish, and then say: 'Ring,
ring, I long for this—it is for you to give me what I wish.' Then
whatever you have wished for, even the moon, will be yours. But
do not tell anyone else of your luck, even your wife. Nor should
you ride over any water with it, lest it be lost."

It was then that the woodgatherer woke up. After he was
awake he debated with himself about whether to go to the other

side of the forest, as the stranger in the dream had told him to. At last he decided to go. After he walked for some distance he came upon a goat with a golden ring on a chain that hung around its neck. He approached the goat slowly, taking care not to frighten it away, and when he reached it he quickly unclasped the ring, and put it in his pocket. Then he took the wood he had collected to town and sold it for kindling, as he always did, and with the money he earned he bought kasha for his wife and son. He said nothing about the wishing ring when he reached home, but kept it secret even from his wife.

Then one day, when he had carried his bundle of kindling wood into town, he saw a crowd gathered for an auction. From the midst of the crowd he heard a voice call out, "Who will give me ten thousand rubles for this fine, fine house? Truly a mansion!" Then the woodgatherer called out from the back of the crowd, "I will pay you fifteen thousand rubles." At this there was a murmuring among the people, who said to themselves, "How will such a poor man get so much money?" Then the auctioneer said to the woodgatherer, "If you bring the money to me within three days, the house will be yours. If not, you will be thrown into the dungeon!"

Leaving the auction, the man went off behind a tree, took out the wishing ring, and wished for fifteen thousand rubles, so that he could pay for the house. Then he said: "Ring, ring, I long for this—it is for you to give me what I wish." No sooner had he spoken these words, than the money lay in a bag at his feet. He gave the money to the auctioneer, and in return he received the deed to the house. This he folded and put away in his pocket, and then went back to gathering wood, so that he could buy kasha for his family. He did not tell them of his purchase that day, nor for many months thereafter.

Then one day the woodgatherer decided it was time to do something with the house he had purchased in town. So he said to his wife, "Pack up our bags and all of our possessions, for we are moving from here." So his wife packed their belongings, and his son went to bring the village driver. When the driver arrived they loaded their few possessions onto the wagon, and rode into town.

But as the darkness fell the wagon driver lost his way and the wagon became stuck in the mud, and could not go any further. Then the woodgatherer and his family continued on foot, until they arrived at their new house. The wife and son were amazed when they saw how beautiful it was, and were speechless when servants came out to greet them and welcome them to their new home. The woodgatherer sent some of the servants to unload the wagon, while the others prepared a meal of the finest foods, far more delicious than anything they had ever tasted. The Jew and his son ate the food with great relish, but his wife refused to take more than a single bite, for she was not used to eating such fine food. The servants could not understand why she did not like it, but the man said to them, "For my wife, it is enough to cook plain kasha."

That night they slept in soft, canopied beds, as might belong to a grand duke. The father and son fell asleep at once, and their sleep was filled with the sweetest dreams. But the man's wife found she could not sleep on such a soft bed, and lay awake until she decided to sleep on the floor, as she had always done.

Early in the morning there was a knock at the door. The servants informed them that it was an old Jew who wished to speak to them. They had him invited in, and the old Jew said, "Peace be with you. I know that you have just moved into this house. Perhaps you would like me to teach your son to study Torah and be a scholar?" The father was delighted, for until then his son had not learned even to read or write.

So it was that they lived many years in that fine house, where the servants took care of their every need. The father and son took the change in their lives in stride, and spent their time in study of the sacred books. But the mother was at a loss as to how to occupy her time, nor was she ever comfortable with the splendor in which they lived.

Time passed, and the boy became a man. So too did his father age, and when it seemed to him that he might not live much longer, he called in his son, and told him about the source of his riches. Then he gave his son the golden ring, and taught him how to make a wish. He made him promise to keep the existence of the ring a secret even from his wife, when he married, and to be careful not to carry the ring over water, lest it be lost. It was not long after that that the old man became sick and breathed his last.

Now the young man who had inherited the wishing ring did not wait long before deciding what it was he wanted to wish for, for shortly afterward he was standing in a crowd while the daughter of the king passed in a grand carriage. He was so taken with her beauty that he could not think of anything else. So it was that he soon put on the wishing ring, made his wish, and said, "Ring, ring, I long for this—it is for you to give me what I wish." And no sooner had he spoken these words than he found himself standing by the bed in which the king's daughter slept. Amazed at this good fortune, the young man filled his gaze with her beauty all night, and before leaving at dawn he placed a diamond bracelet around her wrist.

Now the princess was astonished when she woke up and found the diamond bracelet on her wrist. She went to her father, the king, and showed it to him and told him how she had found it. But the king said, "You have so many diamond bracelets. Surely this is one of them, and you merely forgot to take it off when you went to sleep." The princess nodded in agreement, although she was far from certain that this had been the case.

The next night the young man again desired to stand by the bed of the princess. He took out the wishing ring, made his wish and in less than an instant found himself standing next to her bed again. This time he gazed at her all night again, and before dawn clasped a diamond necklace around her neck. In the morning, when the princess awoke, she was amazed to find the necklace there, and hurried to show it to her father. This time the Emperor decided to place a guard in her bedroom, and capture whosoever dared to enter the bedroom of the princess. But the young man had expected the guard, so he added to his wish that he be invisible, and again he was able to stand all night by the bed of the princess. And before leaving at dawn he slipped a golden ring on the finger of the sleeping princess, who found it when she awoke. Then the king became frightened at the power of his daughter's nightly visitor, and so he announced that whoever could capture the intruder would receive a great reward. As soon as the young man heard this announcement, he decided to turn himself in. After all, he still possessed the wishing ring—why should he be afraid? If the king was unkind, he would simply make a wish and disappear.

So it was that he came before the king and said, "I am the one who has been standing at night by your daughter's bed. The truth is that I want her for my wife." The eyes of the king grew narrow when he heard these words, but he restrained his anger, and he said, "If you are so powerful, I shall declare war with another king, and place you in charge of the troops. If you win the war, you will receive my daughter for your wife." To this the young man said, "I will fight this war and win it. All that I ask is that you give me a hundred strong iron chains." The king ordered that the chains be brought, and they were given to the young man. Then the king sent messengers declaring war on the neighboring kingdom, and the young man left for battle.

When he reached the battlefield, he put on the wishing ring and said, "As soon as the fighting begins, these chains shall be thrown at the enemy, and as each one lands I want it to burn with full force until the enemy is destroyed." And as soon as the battle started and the chains were thrown, they burst into flames, and destroyed the other army—the young man had won the war for the king. When he returned from the war, the king gave him his daughter in marriage, and also gave them half of his kingdom as a wedding gift.

Meanwhile the king had instructed his daughter to try to find the source of her husband's power, and whence he got his strength. She begged him to tell her how it was possible for him to accomplish such wonders, but he remembered the warning of his father, and refused to reveal his secret. In this way several years passed, and the young man and the princess became the parents of three beautiful children. Still the princess would not give up trying to discover the source of his power, and at last he told her the truth—that his power came from the wishing ring, which he wore on his finger at all times. Then the princess hurried to the king, and told him all that she had learned. When he heard this, the king smiled and said to her, "You must steal the ring from him when he is asleep." This she did that very night, and then she brought the ring to her father.

The next day the king said to his son-in-law, "Come, let us declare another war." Then the young man touched his hand, and discovered that the wishing ring was missing. All at once he turned pale, and his legs grew weak. And he whispered to the king: "Now I cannot accomplish anything." The king laughed a wicked laugh, and said to him, "What shall we do with you now?" And the man replied, "Do what you will with me." Then the king and his advisers decided to hang him at the end of thirty days, and then they threw him into the dungeon to await his fate.

That night, while the man was asleep in his cell, his father came to him in a dream, and said, "My son, do not fear. I will save you from all danger." His father then disappeared and the man suddenly woke up.

Soon afterward the spirit of his father appeared in the form of a mouse, and went into the king's chamber, where he stole the wishing ring from its hiding place and brought it back to his son. He left him the ring, and said, "Here, my son, is the wishing ring. Ask, and you will have anything you wish." And then he disappeared.

At the end of thirty days they took the man from the dungeon, and brought him to the place where he was to be hanged. Before they put his head in the noose they asked him if he had a final request. He said, "Before I die, I would like to speak to the king." The king came at his request, and the man said, "I would like to bid farewell to my wife and family. I would also like you to have three things brought here: a scarf, a rope, and a dog." Now the king could not imagine what it was that the man wanted with these things, but since there is a tradition that a condemned man's last wishes shall be fulfilled, the king gave the order, and everything was brought as the man had asked. And when they were given to him, the man put his hand in his pocket and put on the wishing ring and said, "Let this scarf become a saddle; let this rope become a bridle; let this dog become a horse. Ring, ring, I long for this—it is for you to give me what I wish." And in a flash the scarf became the finest saddle, the rope became a leather bridle, and the dog became a great-limbed horse. And all those who witnessed this were so astounded that they stood there speechless as the man quickly leaped on the horse and told his wife and children to mount behind him. And when they had done this, he said to the wishing ring, "Let us fly away from here, to another country. Ring, ring, I long for this—it is for you to give me what I wish." As soon as he said this, the horse flew into the sky, and took them far away from there. And that is how he saved himself and kept his family together.

Eastern Europe: Oral Tradition

The Man Who
Escaped Misfortune

Thereonce was a poor man who seemed to be plagued with misfortune, and he never knew whence it came. Every venture he undertook led to failure, and he and his family met with bad luck no matter how hard they tried to avoid it. One day this man was walking in the forest, searching for the dry wood he sold for a pittance. Suddenly he noticed a big black raven flying above him which perched high in the branches of a nearby tree. The raven followed behind the man everywhere he went, as if it were another shadow, and little by little, as he continued to see the raven wherever he turned, the man grew fearful. What raven was this, and what did it want of him? Then the thought crossed his mind that perhaps it was the Angel of Death, who was following him on his last day.

This thought frightened the man even more, and at that moment he looked up and saw that the raven had perched on a branch just above his head, rather than at the top of the tree. The man felt that this, too, was a sign of danger. After a moment, he drew on some unexpected source of strength, turned to the raven and said, "Who are you, and what do you want of me?"

Now the man was not overly surprised when the raven replied, for he was right in thinking that it was surely no ordinary bird. And the raven said, "I am your misfortune. I have followed you in many forms, and this time I have taken the shape of a raven. And next time it will be something else, so you will never know how to recognize me. But I will be there. Of that you can be certain."

Then the man cried out, "Yes, I am certain that you have been following me, for I have known nothing but bad luck. But is there any way to get rid of you, so that you will no longer shadow my every step?"

"Yes," said the raven, "there is one way to free yourself from me." "Then tell me, please, what it is," said the man. "You and your family must pack up all your belongings into a wagon and follow the road wherever it leads you. If you go now, before the full moon wanes, you will be free. But for every day you wait after the moon has started to wane, you will bring a little part of me with you. And if you wait until the new moon, I will follow you with full force for the rest of your days, as I have until now. Know, too, that once you set out, you cannot turn back. If you turn back, for any reason, you will never see the last of me for as long as you live."

Then the raven took wing and vanished from the man's sight, although he imagined that it was still following him, perhaps already in some new and unexpected form. The man took to his heels and ran back to his house as fast as he could. And when he told his wife what had happened, she agreed that they should go at once, before the moon, which was becoming full that night, had started to wane.

So it was that before the third and last day of the full moon they had set out in their wagon. But before they had gone one mile, the boy asked for something to drink, and they discovered that they had forgotten their water jug. The wife insisted that they return for it, although the man begged her to leave it behind. Finally the man gave in and took them back to the house. He went in to get the jug, and when he picked it up a voice said, "Here we are, back together again." The man jumped when he heard this, and a chill went down his spine. "Who are you?" said the man. But he was afraid that he already knew. "I am one and the same misfortune that has accompanied you for so long" the jug replied. "I thought we were going to have a parting of the ways, but I see that I was wrong. Now we shall stay together for all time."

With trembling knees the man turned and ran back to the wagon. But when he climbed inside he found that the jug was already there. Then he realized that he could not escape it, that the curse had been renewed. With sagging heart he continued on his way, and his wife asked him what was wrong. At last the man told her, and when she heard this, his wife picked up the jug and threw it into the forest as hard as she could. But in less than the blink of an eye it was there again, right beside her, as if she had never thrown it away at all. That is how she found out that the jug was truly possessed by that dreadful spirit.

Now both man and wife were dejected, as they drove together in the wagon. At that time they were passing over a bridge, which ran above a river, and the wife had an idea. She said to her husband, "Stop the wagon here." "But why?" he asked. "Just do as I say," she said, not wanting to reveal her plan to the spirit in the jug. So they stopped there, and the wife picked up many pebbles from the side of the road and filled the jug with them. And without any hesitation she tossed the jug from the bridge into the river, where it soon sank to the bottom. And lo and behold, when they returned to the wagon, the jug was not to be seen, nor did it reappear at all. And the man embraced his wife and thanked her with all his heart for finding a way to rid them of his misfortune.

Soon afterward they reached a town, and settled in a hut near the river, where the man fished for a living. From the very first day, he was remarkably lucky, and caught more fish and finer fish than any other fisherman in that town. And his life was happy and content for the first time.

Then one day the fisherman caught a white fish that was so beautiful he decided not to sell it, but to share it with his family, as a sign of their new found luck. And when his wife cut the fish open, she found something shining inside it. She reached in and pulled the object out, and saw it was a stone. She showed it to her husband, and he too noticed that the stone seemed to give off a reflection of some kind. That night, when the sun had set, they saw that the stone was truly glowing, as if it were somehow burning from within.

The man decided that the stone could serve them well if he set it inside a lamp, so that all the hut would be lit, as well as the ground outside the window, on which the light also shone. Then it happened on the third night after the stone had been set inside the lamp, that the shoots of a young tree suddenly sprang up outside that window. The tree flourished in that light, until it was full grown after only ten days. And it turned out to be a carob tree, whose fruits were so ripe and sweet that everyone who tasted one felt that they had tasted a fruit from the Garden of Eden. These carobs were widely sought after, and within a short time the man found that he no longer had any need to fish, but could spend his time in study of the Torah. And so it was that for many years to come this man and his family were sustained by the wonderful fruit that grew from that tree, and he spent his time studying the words of the Torah by the light of that enchanted lamp, a light which sustained his soul.

Eastern Europe: Oral Tradition

"... and he made certain that many armed guards stood between
him and the monk."

The Black Monk and the
Master of the Name

Not so many generations ago there was a Black Monk, a sorcerer of great power, who was an enemy of the Jews. This monk was very important in the eyes of his people; only the king was held in greater esteem. The Black Monk derived his power from an evil demon he had conjured up, who remained with him at all times, supplying his vast powers for whatever evil purpose the Black Monk had in mind. No one, of course, knew about the demon, and the monk made certain that all believed the powers were his own. Using the black magic of the demon, it was possible for the monk to snatch a man's soul merely by touching his finger to the man's forehead. This the Black Monk sought to do to every Jew he encountered, spreading terror among the people, who knew that his touch was just as fatal as the kiss of death.

In appearance the Black Monk was awesome. He stood head and shoulders above all other men, and his eyes were fierce. No one knew his history, but it was rumored by some that he was a demon himself. In any case, his hatred of the Jews was boundless, and should any poor Jew cross his path, the Black Monk did not hesitate to touch his forehead. In his mad lust against the Jews, the Black Monk haunted the marketplace, trying to see how many Jews he could serve as the Angel of Death. So too did he purchase a house next to the entrance of the Jewish cemetery. There he threatened all those who sought to enter to attend a funeral or to visit a grave, reaching his long arm out the window to touch them as they passed. The situation became so dangerous that it became impossible to go to the market or the cemetery, and at last the Elders of the Jews went to the king, and pleaded for his mercy in protecting them from the mad monk.

The king summoned the Black Monk before him, and ordered the Elders of the Jews to come to the palace at the same time. While the elders waited in another room, the king said to the Black Monk, "Is it your intention to destroy the Jews?" The monk said, "Let them make this accusation in my presence." The king had the three Elders brought into the room, and the moment they entered, the Black Monk, who stood by the door, touched them on the forehead. Dazed by the evil force that had suddenly torn out their souls, the elders remained silent, unable to speak. The king ordered them to repeat what they had said, but they could not. The king became angry and sent them away, and the Black Monk left, laughing to himself.

That night each of the Elders took ill, and by the second night they had all lost consciousness, and on the third night, at midnight, they all passed away. And when this disaster became known among the people, a tremor of terror passed through them, for those three Elders were the pillars of the community, and now they were gone. Now the terrible intentions of the Black Monk were clearer than ever, and all of them feared that the worst had not yet begun. Again the Jews sent three rabbis of the Council of the Elders to plea for help from the king. These Elders asked the king if the Black Monk had touched the foreheads of their predecessors in his presence. The king said yes, and then the eldest of the three, Rabbi Meir, said, "The Black Monk is an evil wizard, my lord king. Merely by touching his finger to a man's forehead, he can steal his soul. If I were you, your majesty, I would not get too close to him. Who knows if he does not desire to usurp your throne? All that he would need to do would be to reach out and touch you on the forehead once."

These words astonished and frightened the king, who suddenly realized the incredible danger posed by the Black Monk. He decided then and there that he would never again let the monk come close enough to touch him. And at the same time he came to realize the terror of the Jews in the face of such an enemy. Then the king called the Black Monk back to his palace, this time without the Jews, and he made certain that many armed guards stood between him and the monk. And he said, "I am well aware that it was you who silenced the three Jews who came to accuse you, and brought their lives to an end. What is it that you want from the Jews? Leave them alone!"

Then the Black Monk replied coldly, without any sign of fear, "If the Jews wish to continue to accuse me, let them face me in combat and decide the matter once and for all. Let them chose one of their own to meet me. If he triumphs, the Jews can do what they like with me. And if they refuse to duel with me, or if the one they send is defeated, then I will leave no trace of them at all!" The king saw that only in this way would the bloodlust of the Black Monk be satisfied. But at the same time he wanted to find a way to stop him, and all at once the king thought of a plan. He said, "I will convey your challenge to the Jews if you will agree to restore the lives of the three Elders." Now the king assumed that this was impossible, and that he had caught the Black Monk in a trap. He was awestruck when the wizard replied, "That is not a difficult matter for me. The three Jews will get their miserable lives back today, and when they do, a date for the duel will be set." The king could not believe his ears, and he was afraid that a great tragedy was about to take place. So he made one last attempt to delay the duel, and said, "Go now, and do as you say. And if the three Jews come into my presence tomorrow, I will announce the challenge to them, and tell them that the duel will take place in one year. For surely they will need the time to find a worthy opponent." These last words appealed to the vanity of the Black Monk, and he accepted those terms, bowed, and took his leave.

Now the funerals of the three Elders who had lost their lives to the Black Monk were all held at the same time. All of the Jewish community trembled for their lives as they passed the house of the Black Monk, outside of the gate of the cemetery. Yet none was singled out by the deadly monk, and a faint hope began to grow among them that the king might have called him to task. Imagine how frightened the people were when the Black Monk himself strode into the cemetery and approached the coffins of the Elders. The people scattered in terror, fearing the Black Monk's touch. Only Rabbi Meir remained to guard the coffins, but he too moved aside when the Black Monk scowled so fiercely that the rabbi felt his blood turn cold. Then the Black Monk threw open the coffins of the elders, and reached out and touched each one on the forehead as before, saying some magic words. And all at once, to the amazement of all, the corpses stirred, and the rabbis came back to life. First one sat up, dazed, then the others. The people slowly crept back, and they heard the Black Monk say to the revived Elders, "The king has ordered that you come before him tomorrow. He has something to tell you." Then the Black Monk stalked out of the cemetery, and the people did not know whether to laugh or cry, for the beloved rabbis were alive once more.

Now the three rabbis had no memory at all of having died, and they were astounded to find themselves in their coffins, before a great funeral gathering. And they were so staggered by this turn of events that their hearts almost stopped beating. Then their loved ones rushed up to them and helped them out of the coffins, and everyone cried tears of joy. And yet they greatly wondered why the Black Monk had done this, and what it was that the king would say.

The next day, when the three elders stood before the king, he realized at last what a powerful adversary the Black Monk was. Not only could he bring death by a mere touch of his hand, but he could restore life as well. (Actually, the three rabbis were not really dead. The spell of the Black Monk's demon had only made them appear so. Thus the people proceeded with the funeral. To bring the sages back to life, the monk merely had the demon remove the spell. In fact, all those who seemed to have lost their lives to him were actually buried alive! Then the Black Monk would secretly return to the cemetery in the middle of the night and have the demon restore them to life, and they would find themselves locked in a coffin, buried beneath the earth, and would cry and struggle in vain to free themselves until they died a truly horrible death. But all this was not known until much later, when the secret journal of the Black Monk was found, in which he recounted his terrible deeds.) It was then the king told the Elders of the Black Monk's challenge, and when they heard it, they wished they had not been restored to life, for they knew that the worst had come to pass. For there was none among them who could match the Black Monk either in strength or in magic, much less defeat him.

The frightened Elders led the people in fasting and prayer to find a way to meet this terrible challenge. Then it happened that on one night the three Elders who had been restored to life dreamed the same dream, in which they learned that their only hope lay in the Jews who lived on the other side of the river Sambatyon. And when they discovered that this prophetic dream had come to them all, they knew that they must not wait, but send a messenger at once to those Jews, begging for their help.

The sages of the Council of the Elders cast lots, and Rabbi Meir was chosen for the mission to the ten tribes, who lived on the far side of the river Sambatyon. Those Jews had been separated from their brothers for centuries, without any communication between them. Why was this so? Not by choice, but because of the nature of the river Sambatyon itself. For this river threw up rocks as big as a house six days of the week, making it impossible to cross. And on the Sabbath the waters would subside, until all that remained was white sand—and the river rested. Then it was possible to cross, of course, but the Jews who lived there could not, because it was the Sabbath. For centuries it had been said among them that their exile would not end until the river stopped running on a day when they were permitted to come across. And they had awaited that day for very long, but it had not yet come.

Now that Rabbi Meir had been chosen to set out to the river Sambatyon, the question was raised in the Council of the Elders, how could he cross the river once he reached it? For a while there was silence, as the sages contemplated the matter, for they knew that he must somehow convey the message to them; it was a matter of life and death. Then the eldest sage among them, one of those who had been spared the grave at the last moment, said: "This is a matter of *Piku'ach Nefesh,* the saving of a life—all our lives—and that takes precedence over all other matters of the Law. Let Rabbi Meir cross the river Sambatyon on the Sabbath. The three of us, who have had this sudden restoration to life, will write a letter to our brothers among the ten lost tribes, and explain why this desecration of the Sabbath has been necessary. But I am afraid that Rabbi Meir may not return. For only the one who is sent to save us, to combat the evil monk, will be permitted to come back across the river—and he will be forced to remain among us, for neither will he be permitted to return to his home." All of those present agreed that the ruling of the sage was the right one, and Rabbi Meir hung his head, for he realized that he was being sent into exile, away from his family, although it would be an exile among fellow Jews.

But one other matter remained to be settled and it was Rabbi Meir who was the first to recognize it. He said, "If it is the will of heaven that I undertake this quest, I accept it, just as I long ago accepted the yoke of the Law. Let us pray that this new burden will become as light as that one, for in truth it uplifts me and is not a burden at all. But there remains one matter that must not be ignored—that of time. For everyone knows that it takes at least six months to travel to the Holy Land, and the distance to the River Sambayton is even further. Even if the winds are with me, how is it possible for the one who is sent to return in time?" The three sages contemplated this matter, which they had somehow overlooked. They consulted among themselves for a long time, and at last one of them said: "If it is the will of heaven that we should be saved in this way, then heaven will provide a means for him to come to us in time."

Thus was the matter settled, and Rabbi Meir took a tearful leave of his family and set out on the quest, accompanied by three young rabbis, the sons of the three Elders. It was they who would accompany the savior from the other side of the river Sambatyon, should Rabbi Meir succeed in reaching that distant kingdom and letting their dire need be known.

Now the journey to the river Sambatyon was not a simple one. The rabbis had to reach the port of the Black Sea, and from there sail to Istanbul, and from there take another ship to the Holy Land. Once they reached the port of Jaffa, and kissed the holy ground and gave thanks for arriving there, six months had already passed. After that the only way to reach the river Sambatyon, in the desert of Sinai, was by caravan, and it was in such a caravan that the four rabbis traveled. But the place to which they were going could not be reached by a single caravan, and at last they traveled to a remote oasis, where a few tents were cast, and from which no other caravans set out further into the Sinai. Here the four rabbis had no choice but to continue on their own, without the benefit of any map. Nor were they able to find anyone who knew precisely where the river Sambatyon ran.

But the rabbis had brought with them the accounts of those daring travelers who had sought out the River Sambatyon and the Ten Lost Tribes, among them Benjamin of Tudela and David Reubeni. Every evening, after they set up their tent and said the evening prayers, they studied these accounts with the kind of intensity that they normally brought only to the sacred texts. And as they traveled through the desert they sought out these landmarks—a particular oasis; a peculiar rock formation, a rare tree. And lo and behold, they found that they never had to travel more than three days between these landmarks, and in this way they were able to guide themselves to the river Sambatyon.

The rabbis heard the distant roaring of the river long before they reached it. At first it sounded like the gentle voice of a waterfall, but as they came closer and closer, it began to sound like distant thunder. At last the day came when they were able to glimpse the river from several miles away, appearing first as a great mist, like a cloud that had descended to earth, but as they came near they saw how the mist was really huge rocks being cast into the air. For the river was anything but peaceful—it was more like a never-ending landslide in reverse, with boulders being cast upward instead of falling down. Nor were they able to come within a mile of it, so dangerous was it to approach the river while its waters were flowing. The rabbis arrived on a Tuesday, and they pitched camp there and waited until the Sabbath. During that week they fasted and prayed and repeated the Psalms night and day. For even though they had no choice in the matter, still they regretted that Rabbi Meir would be breaking the Sabbath. He, especially, was weighed down by the thought, for he had never before broken the sanctity of the Sabbath. And once he crossed that river they thought sadly, he could never return, and his exile among the Ten Lost Tribes would be permanent.

It was to free himself of these thoughts that Rabbi Meir immersed himself in fasting and prayer, and thus by the eve of the Sabbath he had succeeded in purifying his body and soul, and had put all fears and regrets behind him. It was precisely as the Sabbath arrived that the waters of the river Sambatyon first slowed down and then came completely to a halt. At that moment, since there was no time to spare, Rabbi Meir embraced the sons of the three Elders, whom he had come to love as if they had been his own sons, and set out across the great river.

Now the river Sambatyon was far wider than most rivers. For its spring flowed from the rock that Moses had struck with his staff in the wilderness, and the waters had continued to pour forth ever since, until the great river had been formed. And Rabbi Meir knew, from the writings of the explorers who had gone before him, that if he did not hurry the Sabbath could end before he had reached the other side, and if that should happen, then his life was as good as lost. It was not for himself that Rabbi Meir feared, but for the lives of his family and friends and his fellow Jews he had left behind. It was this fear that inspired him to cross the river quickly, so that he reached the other side several hours before sunset on the Sabbath. Yet no sooner did Rabbi Meir step on shore, than he found himself met by grim and imposing guards, who told him that he was under arrest for having broken the sanctity of the Sabbath. Rabbi Meir tried to tell the guards the reason for his visit, and to show them the letter he had brought from the Council of the Elders, but they said they could not read anything that he carried on the Sabbath. And they took him to the rabbinical court. Here Rabbi Meir found himself face to face with a *Beit Din* of nine rabbis, who informed him that he was on trial for his life, having broken the primary law of that land— crossing the River Sambatyon on the Sabbath. For such an act did not only desecrate the Sabbath, it also defiled the purity of the Sambayton, which itself was a sacred river.

It was then that Rabbi Meir pleaded with the rabbinical court to hear him out, and they agreed to listen to all that he had to say. Then Rabbi Meir told them of the Black Monk and the terrible danger facing the Jews of his land, and how their only hope lay in finding a savior from among the inhabitants of the land of the Ten Lost Tribes, as the three Elders had dreamed. And he explained how the Council of the Elders had ruled that crossing the river was thus permitted, since it was a matter of life and death. Finally, since it was clearly a matter of *Pikuach Nefesh*, Rabbi Meir asked the *Beit Din* to read the letter he had brought from the council, so that they could realize that what he told them was true.

Now the rabbis of that *Beit Din* recognized at once the extraordinary reasons Rabbi Meir had broken the Sabbath, for under those circumstances it was not only permitted, it was required. So they read the letter Rabbi Meir had brought, and then they understood that the lives of all of the Jews of that city were truly at stake. They agreed unanimously that they would see to it that someone would indeed cross the river Sambatyon, and accompany the rabbis waiting on the other side back to the city, to face the Black Monk. And when Rabbi Meir heard this decision, he cried tears of joy, for he knew that he had accomplished his quest to the best of his ability, and that hope remained to save the Jews of his city.

Now the Jews who live on the other side of the river Sambatyon were exceptional in every way. For all of them observed the Law with joy, and the level of wisdom of the average man was equal to that of the wisest sages among the Jews elsewhere. As for the sages among the Jews of the Ten Lost Tribes, they were familiar with the most obscure mysteries of the Torah, and there were a dozen among them who knew the pronounciation of God's most secret name, known as the Tetragrammaton, while among the rest of the Jews there was never more than one such sage in each generation. It was this circle of extraordinary sages that the rabbinic council assembled and revealed the pressing need among the Jews across the Sambatyon for their help. Even though going on such a mission meant never returning to their home, still all twelve sages expressed a willingness to go. The rabbinc court, recognizing their wisdom, left it to them to select the one who would undertake the quest, and the twelve sages made their decision by consulting the *Urim ve-Thummim*, which was based on the twelve stones of the breastplate of the High Priest. The secret of how to use this oracle had long been lost among the rest of the Jews, but it had been preserved here, along with the very breastplate worn by Aaron the High Priest. And when they inquired of the *Urim ve-Thummim*, it led them to the oldest among them, a wizened old man who was also lame.

Now Rabbi Meir was somewhat startled when he saw whom the twelve sages had chosen, but he kept his doubts to himself, for he knew that the choice had not been theirs, but had come from on High. And he reminded himself that just as it had been his destiny to seek out the Jews on the other side of the River Sambatyon, so too was it the destiny of that sage, old and lame though he may be, to save the Jews of his city from the terrible Black Monk.

Now ever since Rabbi Meir and his companions had reached the station of the last caravan and set off on their search for the River Sambatyon, they had lost track of time. Only now did Rabbi Meir realize that he did not know how much time remained before the year ended. He quickly asked to know the date, and found that his wanderings in the desert had lasted for so many months, that but a single day remained before the duel was to take place. This news devastated Rabbi Meir. The sages of the court, seeing this, asked him what was wrong, but when they found out they did not seem to despair, but smiled. Rabbi Meir could not understand this at all—it appeared certain that all his effort had been in vain. But one of the rabbis said, "To one of the Masters of the Name, such as he who has undertaken this quest, distance is a trifling matter. Know that the master and those who accompany him are already in your city, and that the time of the reign of the evil monk is about to come to an end."

And it was true. Just before the Sabbath was about to end and the waters of the river grow wild, the master finished crossing the River Sambatyon without ever touching his feet to the ground, so that he alone, and not the river, should suffer the desecration of the Sabbath. There the old master had met the three young rabbis, had them hold hands so that they formed a chain, and had pronounced the Ineffable Name that makes all things possible. And an instant later they had found themselves back in the city, outside the synagogue where all of the inhabitants had been gathered for two days, fasting and praying for rescuer's arrival. And when they entered together, a great cheer rang through the people, for they knew that the Holy One, blessed be He, had not forgotten them. But when they saw how old the inhabitant from beyond the river Sambatyon was, they became terrified again. Was this the man who would defend them against the Black Monk?

It was only the words of the three young rabbis who had accompanied him that set their mind at rest. For when the people learned that only moments before they had been at the shore of the River Sambatyon, they understood that the powers of the Master of the Name were very great indeed. Their hearts grew calm, and their faith was restored.

The next day all of the people of the city, including the Jews, gathered in the town square. The first to enter was the Black Monk, who drew many cheers from his supporters. He appeared much larger than the Jews of the city had remembered, and he looked much fiercer as well. A gasp passed through the crowd when they saw that his opponent was a lame and bent old man. As for the Black Monk, he roared with mocking laughter, and pointed derisively at the old man. Suddenly the old master mumbled something to himself and from the finger that pointed at him a branch of a tree sprouted forth. This branch sprang up, and other branches grew up out of it, which bore blossoms and then fruit. And all at once, where a moment before he had been pointing, the Black Monk had a tree growing out of his finger, the very finger with which he had terrorized the Jews, who feared his touch more than anything in the world.

This occurred so suddenly that a wave of terror washed over the Black Monk, for then he realized that his opponent, despite his appearance, was a great sorcerer, far greater than any with whom he had contested before. The evil monk knew that he must act quickly, or else his supporters would lose faith in him. So he pronounced a spell and turned the tree into a flaming lion, which leaped from his hand and rushed toward the master from the other side of the Sambatyon. The master no more than lifted his hands, and in an instant the sky grew dark and rain began to pour down, which quickly put out the fiery lion. And as soon as it was out, the rain stopped and the sky cleared up, so that not a single cloud was to be seen. Then all the spectators, both the Jews and Gentiles, stood in stunned silence, for it was clear that the old, lame man truly had great powers, far greater than any mortal had ever seen.

The Black Monk knew that he must do something, so he pronounced a spell and a massive millstone appeared out of nowhere. And the Black Monk picked up with one hand what twenty men could not have lifted and threw it so that it rolled toward the Master of the Name with great speed, and appeared as if it would crush him. Yet the master stood calmly, and spoke for the first time only when the millstone was within an arm's reach. Then it stopped suddenly, as if it had struck a stone wall, and the master but extended a finger, lifted up the millstone as if it weighed less than a feather, and threw it up into the sky, high above them, causing the Black Monk to panic out of fear that it would fall and crush him. The terrified monk threw his hands over his head, and at that moment the demon jumped out of his pocket and ran away. The people were absolutely amazed to see the demon, for they had not known that it was the source of the monk's power. As for the monk, he cried out for the demon to come back, but by then it was long gone.

Trembling, the panic-stricken monk looked up and saw the

great millstone still hovering above him, ready to crush him at any instant. Then, in his desperation, he ran over to a giant tree on the side of the square and pushed the tree over with his hand, using his brute strength, the only power he had left. He hoped in this way to divert the crowd and somehow escape, using the tree as a bow to shoot him far away from there. But the Master of the Name understood this perfectly well, and as the monk held the tree down, the master spoke a holy name, and the tree suddenly straightened itself, so swifly that the Black Monk was shot into the air as if he were an arrow, and he soared upward until he landed on top of the millstone, still hovering in the sky. All the people laughed hysterically when they saw this, even the enemies of the Jews, for the truth was that everyone was relieved to see the defeat of the Black Monk.

The Black Monk, who was terrified of heights, pleaded from the top of the millstone for the master to bring him down, and a moment later he and the millstone fell from the sky with such force that it felt as if an earthquake had taken place. The weight of the millstone caused the earth to crack open, and it sank within. And the Black Monk, still on top of it, suddenly found himself up to his waist in the earth, which seemed to grow hard around him. The Black Monk struggled to pull himself out, but he could not. In his fury he cursed the Master of the Name and the Jews and demanded to be set free, refusing to face his defeat. While he continued to rant and rave, the master asked that a hammer and nail be brought to him. This was done, and the old man pushed the nail into earth, about half way in. Then he hammered once on the nail, and at the very instant he did, the Black Monk sank deeper into the earth, up to his shoulders.

Now the furious monk could not move at all, but he continued to spew out hatred like a mad man, vowing to bring the most horrible deaths to each and every Jew, deaths that would only come after long and terrible torture. Hearing this, the master tapped lightly on the nail again, and the Black Monk found himself in the earth up to his chin. Even then he did not stop screaming in hatred, and the old man turned to the king, who had observed everything, and asked what he should do. The king replied, "The contest will not be over until one or the other has met complete defeat."

Understanding very well what the king meant by this, the master from beyond the Sambatyon hammered once more on the nail, driving it into the ground. And at that instant the head of the Black Monk vanished under the earth, never to be seen again. And at the same instant a great rainbow emerged in the heavens, reaching from one end of the earth to the other, a rainbow such as had not been seen since the days of Noah. It was visible throughout the world, and thus it could be seen in the far off land on the other side of the Sambatyon. And when Rabbi Meir saw that wonderful rainbow he knew that the miracle had indeed taken place, and that the rainbow was the sign of the new Covenant. His sacrifice had saved his people, and he knew that they would never forget him. And when the supporters of the evil monk saw how complete was his defeat, they ran off in terror, and feared the Jews and did not attempt to harm them in any way. For they had heard that the old master would now make his home among the Jews of that city, and serve, along with the three Elders who had once been the victims of the mad monk, on the Council of the Elders.

As for the Jews, it was a time of great joy and relief. The king, having witnessed the miracle of the Black Monk's defeat, declared that he wished to become a Jew, and in time he did, devoting himself every day both to the Torah and to the law of the land. So too did he choose his closest advisors from among the Jews, and foremost among these was the old master who had miraculously defeated the Black Monk. So it was that ever after Rabbi Meir became known as Rabbi Meir Baal ha-Nes, which means Rabbi Meir the Miracle Worker. And from that time on the Jews of that land became honored citizens, and they never again lost faith in the Holy One, blessed be He, and his servants, especially those who lived on the other side of the river Sambatyon.

Eastern Europe: Seventeenth Century

Sources and Commentary

There are two primary kinds of sources represented in this collection: written and oral. The written sources were derived from texts of the Apocrypha, Talmud, Midrash, medieval folklore and Hasidic lore. The oral sources include those collected in Yiddish by Y.L. Cahan in Eastern Europe and those collected in Israel from various ethnic groups, especially those tales gathered by the Israel Folktale Archives (IFA), under the direction of Professor Dov Noy of Hebrew University. Tales collected in Israel by others, such as Zevulun Qort and Nissim Binyamin Gamlieli, are also represented.

The work of the Israel Folktale Archives is of vast importance because it represents an effort to preserve a rich oral tradition on the verge of extinction due to the upheavals involved in the destruction of European Jewish civilization, and in the creation of a Jewish state and the consequent change of languages involved. These tales include variants of earlier Jewish folk and rabbinic lore, as well as many tales for which no earlier written parallels are to be found—the latter tending to be the "universal" type of fairy tale less likely to be preserved by the rabbis, the primary guardians of the tradition. In all cases, every effort has be made to identify the names of the tellers and collectors of these oral tales, along with the IFA number where appropriate.

The dating of these tales often poses difficult problems, and is generally linked to the date of the earliest known manuscript or publication. There is no way of knowing how long they may have existed orally before they were written down. Likewise, the country of origin is generally linked to the place of publication. Tales deriving from the Babylonian Talmud have been identified as coming from Babylon, although they may date from well before the Babylonian exile. Unless it was possible to pinpoint a particular tale as coming from one of the countries of Eastern Europe, such as Rumania in the case of "The Staff of Elijah," no country has been specified. The shifting boundaries of Poland, in particular, make the country of origin for tales deriving from there particularly hard to specify. In the case of the oral tales collected in this century, dating is even more difficult, as there is no way of knowing how long the tales have circulated. These tales have been identified as "Oral Tradition" and their country of origin has been derived from that of the teller.

All of the folktales collected here are based on either Hebrew, Aramaic or Yiddish sources, except for "Daniel and the Dragon," which exists in a Greek version, and "King Solomon's Ring," which is only known in the Arabic version found in *The Arabian Nights*. Some of the stories, such as "The Black Monk and the Master of the Name" are found in both Hebrew and Yiddish variants. In such cases, elements of these variants have often been combined into one archetypal version of the tale. The original languages are noted in the following source notes, along with the texts in which they were found. A few of the IFA tales, such as "Romana" and "The Palace of Tears," were unpublished even in Hebrew. Comments intended to supplement the Introduction follow for each tale. These include background information, discussion of variants, and moral and psychological implications.

One of the primary influences on Jewish folklore, especially for those tales of oral origin deriving from the Middle East, is, strange as it may seem, *The Arabian Nights*. Knowledge of this massive and largely uncodified collection of folktales permeated the Middle East, and it is therefore not surprising that variants of these tales were told in the Jewish communities as well as in the Arab ones. In addition, it seems certain that at least some of the tales in *The Arabian Nights* were drawn from Jewish sources. The famous folklorist Joseph Jacobs has identified a Jewish text, *Kitab al-Isra'iuliyyat*, edited by Wahb ibn Munabbib in the 7th Century, as one of the four primary texts that provided sufficient tales to fit into the framework of a thousand and one nights. Among the tales Jacobs identifies as coming from this manuscript are a number from the Talmud and other Jewish sources. One such tale, "King Solomon's Ring," has been included here. While not extant in other Jewish sources, many elements of the tale suggests it is of Jewish origin, from the fact that the king is identified as the king of the Israelites, to the fact that the books his son, Bulikiya, finds, are said to be taken from the Torah and other "Books of Abraham." Although King Solomon is also an important figure in Arabic folklore, many other details such as the quest to find the Messiah, earmark this as a Jewish tale.

In addition to "King Solomon's Ring," there are four tales included here that are variants of tales found in *The Arabian Nights*. These are "A Voyage to the Ends of the Earth" from Babylon, a variant of "The Voyages of Sindbad the Sailor," "The Tale of the Magic Horse" from Afghanistan, and "The Stork Princess" from Persian Kurdistan. The other tale, "The Magic Lamp of Rabbi Adam," is easily recognizable as a variant of "Aladdin and the Magic Lamp."

"A Voyage to the Ends of the Earth," the fanciful sea tales of the sage Rabbah bar bar Hannah, which derives from the Talmud, is a special case. Since the Talmud was codified in the 5th Century, these tales were not likely influenced by the tales about Sindbad; in fact, the reverse is possible. More likely, however, is that the kind of sea fantasies found in both tales are typical of the folklore of ancient sailors, upon which both traditions surely drew.

"The Tale of the Magic Horse" and "The Stork Princess," on the other hand, are very likely oral variants based directly on the versions of these tales found in *The Arabian Nights*. If so, these

/351/

provide additional examples of the ways in which written folklore can later give birth to additional oral variants, a process that has been documented as occurring quite often by the Israel Folktale Archives, where such variants of written sources are not infrequent. "The Donkey Girl," included here, is based on an oral retelling deriving from Iraq, does not appear to exist prior to its inclusion in the book *Oseh Pele,* published in the nineteenth century. It is one of ten tales in that collection that may have been the creation of the editor, Joseph Farhi. But so wisespread and well-known did the tales in that collection become that they entered the oral tradition and came to exist in oral variants.

Most of the following tales have been grouped according to the Aarne-Thompson (AT) system, found in *The Types of the Folktale* by Antti Aarne, translated and enlarged by Stith Thompson (Helsinki: 1961). Specific Jewish additions to these types are listed according to the type-index of Heda Jason, found in *Fabula,* volume 7, 1965 (pp. 115-224) and in *Types of Oral Tales in Israel: Part 2* (Jerusalem: 1975). Reference to these tale types will be of use to those seeking both Jewish and non-Jewish variants of the tales included in this collection. The editor's volume of Jewish fairy tales, *Elijah's Violin & Other Jewish Fairy Tales* (New York: Harper & Row, 1983) is abbreviated here as *EV.*

Miriam's Tambourine (Eastern Europe) • Pages 1–7

From *Maaseh me-ha-Hayyat* (Yiddish) (Vilna 1908). AT 465C.

This tale is an outgrowth of the midrash about Miriam's well. According to this legend, this well followed the Children of Israel during their forty years of desert wanderings, supplying them with fresh water. The legend finds its origin in Number 21:16: *That is the well whereof the Lord said unto Moses: 'Gather the people together, and I will give them water.'* The subsequent list of places through which the Israelites traveled is the likely source for the legend of the traveling well. Since for the rabbis the fact that one passage follows another in the Torah indicates that the two are linked, they assumed that the places listed were among those where Miriam's Well came to a rest, so that the people could drink from it. According to the Talmud the well was one of the ten things created on the eve of the Sabbath at twilight during the days of Creation

(B. Pesachim 54a). Since this means that the well existed long before the time of the Exodus, other rabbinic legends suggest that it not only followed the Israelites at that time, but that "Every place where our forefathers went, the well went before them" (*Pirke de-Rabbi Eliezer* 35). "Miriam's Tambourine" offers a final resting place of the well: the Garden of Eden. In another version of the legend, Miriam's Well reached the Holy Land with the Israelites and was hidden in the Sea of Galilee (B. Shabbat 35a). The theme of the book that can be opened by only one in each generation is a varient of the legend of the Book of Raziel, which the angel Raziel delivered to Adam to reveal the future to him. This book was passed down to the primary figure in each subsequent generation until it was destroyed along with the Temple (*Sefer Noah 150*).

A Plague of Ravens (Persia) • Pages 8–14

From Hebrew manuscript Codex Gaster 66, number 14, in John Rylands University Library of Manchester. A variant is found in Hebrew manuscript Codex Gaster 185, number 58, Oxford manuscript 1466. Summaries found in *Exempla of the Rabbis* edited by Moses Gaster, numbers 335 and 352. (London: 1924). An oral variant is found in *Hodesh Hodesh ve-Sippuro: 1974-1975*, edited and annotated by Dov Noy (Jerusalem: Israel Folktale Archives, 1978). IFA 10635, collected by Tamar Fleishman from Jacob Ben-Yishay of Algeria. AT 517 * A.

Moses Gaster identifies the source of the first variant of this tale as a French manuscript of the Twelfth Century. This version is based primarily on the second variant, which Gaster identifies as deriving from Persia in the Sixteenth Century, but it combines elements of both. In each version the young man first acquires vast knowledge, and then uses it to resolve the king's dilemma. A legend is found in the Nidrasty (*Pirke de-Rabbi Eliezer* 26) about how the child Abraham was hidden under the earth for 13 years without seeing the sun or moon. After 13 years, he went forth from the earth speaking the holy tongue. This brief legend was likely the inspiration for the present tale. Likewise, the story of Jonah and the whale no doubt inspired the episode in which the boy is swallowed by a great fish. The ability to master the language of the birds is first attributed to King Solomon in Jewish folklore. The role of the ravens as the reincarnation of murdered Jews is an expression of the concept of *Gilgul* or transmigration of souls. This theme first becomes popular in such late kabbalistic texts as the tales of the Ari found in *Shivhei ha-Ari*, which date from the same period as the second variant of this tale, where the notion of reincarnation first appears.

Daniel and the Dragon (Babylon) • Pages 15–19

From Bel and the Dragon (Greek) of the Additions to Daniel. AT 300.

This tale combines two episodes, each presenting a lesson intended to demonstrate the failings of idolatry. The first shows how the king (and, by association, the people) are tricked by the priests into believing that an idol devours great quantities of food. In this it echoes the famous midrash about the child Abraham, who destroyed all but the largest idol in his father's idol shop, then attributed the destruction to that idol. When his father protested that it was impossible for an idol to destroy other idols, Abraham pointed out that it was therefore useless to worship such idols (Genesis Rabbah 38:13). The second episode is one of the earliest dragon tales. Such tales are a staple of later folklore, especially that concerning medieval Christian quests. Here the dragon is at least real, but in permitting itself to be tricked so easily and destroyed, the tale demonstrates that the dragon too is unworthy of worship.

Miraculous Dust (Babylon) • Pages 20–22

From the Babylonian Talmud (Aramaic), tractate Ta'anith 21a. AT 50G * C, AT * 730.

This is one of the earliest prototypical Elijah tales, in which the prophet appears to save the Jews in a time of distress. Such tales proliferate in later Jewish folklore. Elijah, of course, derives his powers from God. That is why the miraculous transformation of the dust into invincible weapons takes place for him, but utterly fails for the evil innkeepers. The character of Nachum Ish Gam Zu is unique, combining naive innocence and optimism which is based on an unshakable faith in God, that is inevitably justified. This character serves as the model of the holy fool though Nachum himself is counted among the sages of the Talmud which is often echoed in later folklore and literature. Elements of it may be found in the tales of the wise men of Helm, and in I.B. Singer's story "Gimpel the Fool." Underlying the tale is the sense of impotence in the face of a mighty power such as that of Rome, and the Jewish dependence on the miraculous in order to protect themselves, which finds its echo in the later tales of the medieval sorcerer Rabbi Adam and in the tales of the Maharal of Prague, among others.

A Voyage to the Ends of the Earth (Babylon) • Pages 23–34

From the Babylonian Talmud (Aramaic), tractate Baba Bathra 73a-74a. A variant of "The Voyages of Sindbad the Sailor" in *The Arabian Nights*. AT 1930.

The several talmudic tales of Rabbah bar bar Hannah, which have been combined here to form a single narrative, have long constituted an enigma. They are characteristically so willfully exaggerated that they fit the criteria for tall tales. Yet they are reported in the Talmud in a consistently serious fashion. Those who doubt the veracity of the talmudic legends have long singled out these tales as evidence. In response, the rabbis, also recognizing that the tales should not be taken literally, have sought allegorical readings in them. These have usually been of a political nature—as commentaries about the oppression of Rome, which could not be safely stated in a more forthright manner. But some of these commentaries have also been of a religious allegorical nature. In *Likkutei Moharan* (Ostrog:1806). Rabbi Nachman of Bratslav made extensive commentaries along these lines about all fifteen of the Rabbah bar bar Hannah tales found in the Talmud. In his readings, "giant waves" are identified as the evil inclination, "sailors" as guardian angels, "sailing on a boat" as gathering in a the House of Study, and "a bird standing in the water up to its ankles" as coming to understand the Torah's deepest secrets. Thus, although the tales were originally probably simply tall tales such as were so common among the ancient sailors (of the type that are found in the series of tales about Sinbad in *The Arabian Nights*), their presence in the Talmud, whose teachings are regarded as the next most sacred after those of the Bible, could not be easily dismissed, giving rise to various kinds of allegorical readings. Though these may not reflect the original intention of the tale-tellers, they did provide excellent opportunities to establish elaborate systems of allegorical interpretation, which no doubt influenced later rabbinic developments such as the mystical allegories found in the various kabbalistic texts.

Rabbi Joshua and the Witch (Palestine) • Pages 35–38

From the Jerusalem Talmud (Aramaic), tractate Sanhedrin 7:25d. AT 307.

This tale exemplifies the rabbinic ambivalence about the use of magic. Although forbidden by the biblical injunction, *Suffer not a witch to live* (Exodus 22:17), Jewish lore is filled with tales in which Jewish figures such as King Solomon, Rabbi Adam, and the Baal Shem Tov make use of supernatural powers for purposes of good. Several such tales, including this one, involve talmudic sages. In tractate Sanhedrin, where the primary rabbinic discussion of witchcraft and magic is to be found, Abaye attempts to make a distinction between magic that is forbidden and that which is permitted: "If one actually performs magic, he is stoned; if he merely creates an illusion, he is exempt." In this same tractate there is a tale in which Rabbi Jannai diverts a witch who attempts to turn him into a donkey, and causes her to be transformed into this beast herself. Later he rides the donkey down the streets, when a fellow witch recognizes her transformed sister and releases her from the spell, so that Rabbi Jannai is seen riding on the back of a woman (B. Sanhedrin 67b). In both of these cases the rabbis demonstrate a mastery of the supernatural that permits them to overcome the adversary—but on their own terms. Whether this meets Abaye's distinction between magic and illusion is unclear, although it is true that the flax seeds in this tale of Rabbi Joshua which appear to grow magically, afterwards return to their original state, suggesting that all that occurred was, in fact, an illusion. The conjuring up of Rahab, the Prince of the Sea, in order to recover the amulet on which the spell was written, is a further demonstration of the mythic elements in Judaism and of their attraction even to the talmudic sages. This story also provides the legendary circumstances surrounding the birth of Rabbi Judah ben Bathyra, who studied under Rabbis Eliezer ben Hyrcanus and Judah ben Hananiah (B. Pes. 3:3).

The Sword of Moses (Iraqi Kurdistan) • Pages 39–47

From *Sippurim mi-Pi Yehude Kurdistan* (Hebrew) edited by Dov Noy (Jerusalem: Israel Folktale Archives, 1966). IFA 6602. Collected by Zvi Chaimovitz from Zion Sayda. Also, from Codex Gaster 178, "The Sword of Moses," in *Studies and Texts in Folklore, Magic, Medievel Romance, hebrew Apocrypha and Samaritan Archeology*, collected and reprinted by Moses Gaster (New York: Ktav Publishing House, 1971). AT 550, AT 551.

For Jews scattered in various countries, almost always an oppressed minority, the longing for a Jewish state and the belief in the coming of the Messianic age fused into a single dream, as this tale clearly demonstrates. Here "the sword of Moses" (Deut. 34:29) invokes the past—Moses serves as the model for a Messiah more than any other figure—and also the coming redemption of the future. Over the centuries the Jews gave allegiance to several false messiahs, most prominently Shabbatai Zevi, and the temptation to do so is suggested here in the trick played on the young Jews searching for the sword of Moses, who find instead the rusty sword, which in turn can be seen to symbolize such false messiahs. Unlike some of the followers of Shabbatai Zevi, however, who when disillusioned, ended their search for the Messiah, the young men continue their quest, and come to an understanding that what they are seeking may not be an actual object, but something more elusive and symbolic, though equally potent. Such a conclusion is harmonious with the objectives of kabbalah, where the transformation of the literal meaning into its symbolic counterpart is one of the primary goals.

The Maiden in the Tree (Eastern Europe) • Pages 49–55

From *Rosinkess mit Mandlen: Aus der Volkliteratur der Ostjuden* (Yiddish), edited by Emmanuel Olsvanger (Basel: Schweizerische Kommission für Jüdischen Volkskunde, 1931). AT 930*A.

This tale is clearly a disguised variant of Rapunzel. Here, instead of being imprisoned in a tower, the heroine is imprisoned in a tree trunk. In fact, this tale is a direct variant of "The Princess in the Tower" (found in *EV*), which itself is probably the earliest version of Rapunzel. Like "The Princess in the Tower," the intention here is to foil fate by isolating the princess on a remote island. In fact, the attribution of her imprisonment to a whim of the Queen of Sheba makes the linkage to the other tale even more apparent. And as in the earlier tale, the inevitable arrival on the island of the one destined to marry the princess takes place despite all efforts to the contrary. According to Ephraim E. Urbach, in an article entitled "The Fable of the Three and the Four of H. N. Bialik" (*Ariel*, No. 28, 1975), this Eastern European version of the tale inspired Bialik's epic retelling entitled "The Princess of Aram," found in his book *Vayehi ha-Yom* (Tel Aviv: 1934). It is interesting to note that this late Eastern European reworking of an Eighth Century tale turns almost entirely to the earlier Jewish source of its inspiration, omitting other elements of the Rapunzel tale (beside the imprisonment of the heroine) which was no doubt well-known by the time of its appearance. This is further evidence of the direct line of descent of Jewish lore and literature, which constantly turns to its own past for inspiration.

The Three Tasks of Elijah (Tunisia) • Pages 56–63

From *Hibbur Yafeh me-ha-Yeshu'ah* (Hebrew) compiled by Nissim ben Yaakov, edited by H.Z. Hirschberg, 1953. With episodes from the Babylonian Talmud (Aramaic), tractate Baba Mezi'a, and from *Pesikta de-Rav Kahana* 18:5 (Hebrew), edited by Solomon Buber (Lyck: 1860). AT 503.

The folkloristic role of Elijah the Prophet was formed as early as the talmudic erà. It is characteristic of Elijah in this role that he is unsparing in his efforts to assist poor Jews in their time of trial, often making use of supernatural powers in order to accomplish this. Here Elijah goes as far as to sell himself as a slave, and having done so, remains a slave until he has fulfilled the king's requirements to set himself free. Of course Elijah could have freed himself at any time, but his character is such an honest one that any deception is unthinkable. Instead Elijah fulfills his tasks, then resumes his role as benefactor of the Jews. This tale derives from the oldest non-sacred Jewish anthology, and has no earlier source extant, although many of the tales in the collection were drawn from the Talmud. In order to expand the tale into the standard three-part fairy tale narrative, two additional tasks have been drawn from the tales of Elijah found in the legends of the Talmud and Midrash.

The Staff of Elijah (Rumania) • Pages 64–66

From *Hailan Shesafag Demaot* (Hebrew) collected by Yaakov Avitsuk, edited by Dov Noy (Haifa: Israel Folktale Archives, 1965). IFA 258, told by Azriel Zaid. AT 304 *.

This story, drawn from the orally collected material of the Israel Folktale Archives, is evidence that miraculous tales about Elijah the Prophet have continued to be told up to the present. The symbol of the staff naturally echoes the staff of Moses, which possessed supernatural powers, turning into a serpent in Pharoah's court and releasing water from the rock that Moses struck in the wilderness. But the purposes for which this staff is used are more characteristic of those associated with Elijah—to protect against the enemies of Israel and to provide for poor Jews in need. However, the role of Moses is suggested in the final episode, in which the old man travels to the Holy Land and is led, as if by accident, but in fact by fate, to the tree from which the staff was taken, where it once again becomes a branch. This suggests that the ultimate destiny of every Jew is to return to the Holy Land, where Moses sought to lead Israel, and that returning there restores the branch that, in the Diaspora, was cut off from the living tree of Israel. That the staff was taken from a tree on Mount Carmel is natural, since that was the site of Elijah's defeat of the priests of Baal (I Kings 18:19ff.).

Romana (Egypt) • Pages 67–78

IFA 6273. (Hebrew) Collected by Ilana Cohen from Flora Cohen. Previously unpublished. A variant of Snow White from *Grimm's Fairy Tales*. A variant is IFA 6, collected by Elisheva Schoenfeld from Mordecai Litsig of Greece. AT 709.

The body of Jewish folklore is unique in that it is possible to trace the evolution of individual tales and motifs over many generations. Such tales were retold even after they were set down, and often exist in several versions, sometimes recorded centuries apart. However, no such dating is possible for tales collected orally, such as those of the Israel Folktale Archives. All that is certain is that these tales continued to be told into the present. But as to when they were first told, this is simply unknown. In a case such as this, then, where there is a variant of one of the most famous fairy tales, "Snow White," it is impossible to state with any finality whether this version of the tale preceded the famous one found in *Grimm's Fairy Tales* or whether this is a variant based on the version of the Grimm brothers. In such cases the best that can be done is to examine the internal evidence. In some of the tales found in the IFA there is evidence of the tale having been based on the knowledge of some famous collection, often of Jewish origin, such as *Oseh Peleh*, but also including collections known around the world, such as *Grimm's Fairy Tales*. In one such case (IFA 3615, "Amsha the Giant," from Iraq) it is apparent that the tale is a combination of "Hansel and Gretel" and "Jack the Giant Killer." Even such obvious cases indicate that the living process of folklore continues, but otherwise such tales are of little importance. In the case of "Romana," however, the internal evidence suggests that the tale may, indeed, be an *earlier* rather than later variant of Snow White. Most important is the fact that Romana comes to the house of forty thieves, rather than the famous seven dwarfs of "Snow White." If "Romana" were based on "Snow White," it is unlikely that this number would have changed, as it is one of the constant numbers, along with three, repeated in all fairy tales. So too is it unlikely that the kindly dwarfs would have been replaced by hardened thieves. As it is, "Romana" hints at the kind of situation that gave birth to this tale in the first place: a young girl forced to leave her home, finding refuge among those who were truly outcasts—a den of thieves. It would seem more likely that further evolution of the tale would lead to a smaller number of less intimidating figures, rather than the opposite. In addition, one detail omitted in this retelling has the thieves making sexual overtures to Romana, before accepting her as their sister. The almost complete absence of sexual suggestion in the role of the dwarfs further suggests a reworking of the German folktale along lines more appealing to young readers. It is possible, then, that in "Romana" we have a much earlier version of the tale of "Snow White," of Middle-Eastern origin, which only evolved into its now famous version at a much later date.

The Princess Who Became the Morning Star (Germany) • Pages 79–84

From *Yalkut Shimoni* (Hebrew) compiled by Shimon Ashkenazi (Frankfort: 1678). An oral variant is found in *Hodesh Hodesh ve-Sippuro 1976-1977* (Hebrew) edited by Dov Noy (Jerusalem: Israel Folktale Archives, 1979). IFA 10856, collected by Ahuva Baner from Shmuel Nohi of Persian Kurdistan. AT 468.

This tale is based on a midrash which itself grew directly out of a brief and obscure biblical passage referring to the sons of God and daughters of men (Genesis 6:1-4): *And it came to pass, when men began to multiply on the face of the earth, and daughters were born unto them, that the sons of God saw the daughters of men that they were fair; and they took them wives, whomsoever they chose.* In archetypal midrashic fashion, this story is expanded in the midrashic text *Yalkut Shimoni*, focusing on two angels, Shemhazai and Azazel, who were identified as the sons of God, and on two maidens, Istahar and Naamah, the daughters of men. Note that none of these was named in the biblical account. The tale, then, concerns a bargain struck between God and the two angels, to test whether they could resist the force of the Evil Inclination *(Yetzer Hara)* if they lived on earth. The angels insisted that they could easily resist, God that they could not. As such it probably finds its model in the Prologue to Job, where God strikes a bargain with Satan to test the devotion of Job (Job 1:6-12). The starting point of the debate between God and the angels echoes the famous midrash (found in Genesis Rabbah 8:6) in which the angels question the propriety of creating man by quoting a passage from the Psalms: *What is man, that Thou art mindful of him, and the son of man, that Thou shinkest of him?* (Psalms 8:5). Also echoed is the legend of the Fall of Lucifer (Isaiah 14:12-15 and 2 Enoch 29:4-5), for in their descent to earth the angels do become, in a sense, "fallen angels."

The Secrets of Azazel (Holland) • Pages 85–90

From *Emet ha-Melech* (Hebrew) compiled by Naftali Hirsh ben Elhanan (Amersterdam: 1653). AT 803.

It is characteristic of rabbinic legends that once a character has come into being, his or her story will continue to be ellaborated until it has reached a final conclusion. The story of Lilith certainly follows this pattern, proposing her first as the wife of Adam, before Eve, and later as the mother of demons, the incarnation of lust and a child-destroying witch. The story of Azazel also follows this pattern. Azazel was one of the two angels who descended to earth to demonstrate their capacity to resist evil, unlike men. Instead Azazel and his companion, Shemhazai, immediately succumb to the ways of evil, in a manner that suggests premeditation. Shemhazai ultimately repents and is hung upside-down from heaven to earth as a punishment, becoming identified with a constellation. Azazel refuses to repent, and becomes a figure closely identified with the other key manifestations of evil: Lucifer, Samael, and Satan. As a punishment for his revolt against heaven Azazel is punished by being hung upside-down in a dark canyon, but even here he continues to plot against the forces of good. Azazel's name almost certainly derives from the passage in Leviticus *And Aaron shall cast lots upon the two goats; one lot for the Lord, and the other for Azazel* (16:8). The derivation of the legend of the punishment of Azazel, which is the central focus of this tale, comes from the Book of Enoch (10:4-5), where the angel Raphael is commanded to "bind the hands and feet of Azazel and cast him into the darkness. Make an opening to the wilderness which is in Dudael and cast him there." The present tale, a sequel to the previous one, considers the question of the legendary history of Azazel once he has been cast into the canyon in Dudael. Its primary assumption, of course, is that the wicked angel who refused to repent at having proven himself unworthy of God's trust, would certainly refuse to repent even after his ultimate punishment in Dudael, and would continue to plot evil. And that is exactly what he does.

The Wise Old Woman of the Forest (Morocco) • Pages 91–95

From *Shivim Sipurim Vesipur* (Hebrew), edited by Dov Noy (Jerusalem: Israel Folktale Archives, 1964). IFA 3598, collected by Menashe Razi from Shalom Yitah. A variant is found in *Shishim Sippurei-am mi pi Mesa prim b'Ashkelon*, edited by Zalman Barhav (Haifa: Israel Folktale Archives, 1964). Collected by Zalman Barhav from Ovadia Yonasian (Persia). IFA 3947. Another variant is found in *Hodesh Hodesh ve-Sippuro: 1968-1969* (Hebrew), edited by Edna Cheichel. (Jerusalem: Israel Folktale Archives, 1970). IFA 8214, collected by Deboraha Dadon-Wilk from her mother, Heftsibah Dadon of Morocco. In still another variant, the poor brother is told to "Go to Gehenna," Jewish Hell, and sets out in search of it. This is IFA 1161, collected by Heda Yizon from Yefet Shvili of Yemen. A variant of this general tale type is also found in "The Eagle's Treasure," included here. AT 460B, AT 461A.

In later Jewish legend the tradition of the scapegoat sent to Azazel on Yom Kippur found in Leviticus 16:10—*The goat, on which the lot fell for Azazel, shall be set alive before the Lord, to make atonement over him, to send him away for Azazela into the wilderness*—was combined with the fate of Azazel as recorded in the Book of Enoch (see the previous note) to be associated with a place of punishment, not unlike Gehenna or Hell. This gave birth to the insult "Lech le-Azazel!"—"Go to Azazel!"—which is still used today in Israel in precisely the way as the phrase "Go to Hell!" This expression is the starting point of this almost satirical tale, in which the naive poor brother is sent on a non-existent quest by his selfish, rich brother and, in the tradition of Nachum Ish Gam Zu (see "Miraculous Dust"), reaches his goal anyway. In these three stories ("The Princess Who Became the Morning Star," "The Secrets of Azazel" and the present tale) it is possible to see the evolution of a legend from a brief, enigmatic biblical passage into a fully developed tradition, echoed in the everyday language of the people. It should be noted that this tale type, of a quest undertaken to supply answers to riddles, is very common, especially in the oral folktales of the Mideast, and exists in many variants. See "The Princess and the Slave" in *EV* for another variant.

The Palace of Tears (Morocco) • Pages 96–104

IFA 6282 (Hebrew), collected by Zehava Peretz from her mother, Rachel Peretz. Previously unpublished. AT 303. A variant (on the theme of the demon in the chest) is found in *Sippure Baale-Hayim Befdot Yisrael* (Hebrew), IFA 107, collected by Heda Yazon from Yeffet Shivili (Haifa: Israel Folktale Archives, 1978).

This is an excellent example of the typical Middle-eastern fairy tale, especially of those drawn from oral sources. Note that this type of exotic fantasy has much in common with the same tale type found in *The Arabian Nights.* The tale also lends itself to psychological readings, in that both the husband and the lover might be seen as two sides of the same man—the king. In such a reading the long sleep of the wounded lover suggests that the aspect of the king that the queen had once loved had become wounded and inaccessible. It is to this part that the queen clings, rejecting the king as he has become, for whom she has nothing but hatred. In such a fashion could a love-hate relationship be presented in mythical terms, where each figure symbolizes one side of a single personality. The duel figures of Lilith and Eve operate in a similiar fashion, where Lilith has come to symbolize everything assertive, lustful and contrary, from the rabbinic point of view, while Eve represents the woman that can be trusted. Fairy tales, which give every indication of being spontaneous creations of the unconscious, manifest these mythic elements in the same fashion.

The Disguised Princess (Tunisia) • Pages 105–111

From *Shivim Sipurim ve-Sipur mi-Pi Yehedey Tunisya* (Hebrew), edited by Dov Noy (Jerusalem: World Zionest Organization, 1966). IFA 2043. Collected by Rachel Seri from Rivka Brami. AT 506.

The two polar roles of the princess in this tale—that of princess and slave—suggests, as does the preceeding tale, an expression of the two sides of the same person. This princess has to give up all the trappings of royalty in order to undertake the quest to find the prince who left her the golden amulet. There are various ways to interpret this sacrifice: that she becomes a slave to love; that she must discover her true self, her unconscious self, so that she will be worthy of the prince; that she must sacrifice herself in order to save the prince. All of these are true to some extent. Note that the tale is of the type in which a princess saves a wounded prince, rather than the more common tale type of prince saving an imprisoned princess, such as in "Rapunzel" and its many variants.

The Boy in the Cave (Italy) • Pages 112–117

From *Sefer ha-Yashar* (Hebrew) (Venice: 1544). Also, *Masseh Abraham* (Hebrew) in Jellinek, *Beth-Hamidrash*, Vol. 1. Also *Pirke de-Rabbi Eliezer* (Hebrew) (Lemburg: 1857). AT 2031B.

This tale provides a childhood for Abraham in pure midrashic fashion, as nothing of this is recorded in the Bible. The midrashic method is to seek out parallels in the biblical text, in this case the childhood of Moses. The tale is virtually retold here, with a few variations. Both begin with the decree that all male infants of Jewish descent be slain and the attempt on the part of the parents to save them by hiding them away from their home. Moses was hidden in a basket that floated on the water, as Miriam, his sister, watched; Abraham, in this midrashic tale, was left in a cave and miraculously saved by the angel Gabriel. Abraham and Moses are, of course, the two central figures of Judaism: Abraham because he was the first Jew, Moses because he not only redeemed the Jews from Egyptian slavery, but received the Torah from God at Sinai. From a midrashic perspective, then, it would be natural for their childhoods to be parallel.

Alexander Descends into the Sea (Italy) • Pages 118–121

From *Sefer Alexander Mokdon* (Hebrew), edited by Israel Levi in *Tehillah le-Mosheh: Festschrift Moritz Steinschneider* (Leipsiz: 1896). AT 465A.

Strange as it may seem, Alexander the Great is a major figure in Jewish folklore. His kind treatment of the Jews, including support of them against the Samaritans, and his role as the greatest conquerer made him a unique exception to the rule that such heroes be Jewish. (There are also Talmudic traditions in which Alexander shows great respect for Jewish learning and the High Priest. See B. Yoma 69a.) Among the Jewish chronicles of Alexander, of which there are several of medieval origin, this is the most fantastic, describing a descent into the sea. Such an undertaking is typical of the daring of Alexander, who also takes flight, carried aloft by four eagles bound together, in the following tale, "The Waters of Eternal Life." Alexander, whose ambition is portrayed as boundless, has a great lust for knowledge; he is the very archetype of the inquiring intellect. The figure out of Jewish folklore closest to this model is King Solomon, who, like Alexander, is also portrayed as somewhat reckless. Alexander and Solomon represent the heroic in Jewish lore just as Moses and Elijah are the primary examples of the prophetic. The unidentified old man Alexander meets in the cave is an Elijah-type figure, with great and mysterious powers, who uses them for the benefit of the Jews. Note that this tale provides a reason for Alexander's considerable support of the Jews in his empire by placing him in the debt of the Jews. Note also the motif of the glowing stone, which derives from the description of the *Tzohar*, the glowing stone Noah used to illuminate the ark. This motif recurs in several tales collected here, including "A Garment for the Moon" and "The Man Who Escaped Misfortune." (See the note to "A Garment for the Moon.") For the legend of the lion of the forest Ilai, see B. Hullin 596.

The Waters of Eternal Life (Italy) • Pages 122–134

From *Sefer Alexander Mokdon* (Hebrew), edited by Israel Levi in *Tehillah le-Mosheh: Festschrift Moritz Steinschneider* (Leipsiz: 1896). Also, *Toldot Alexander* (Hebrew) in *Kovets 'al Yad* (Berlin: 1886). AT 550.

The quest to find the waters of eternal life is one of the oldest motifs in all of world folklore. That it is here attributed to Alexander the Great befits the role he plays in Jewish folklore. (See previous note.) The fact that Alexander finds himself a prisoner in the kingdom of demons, and finds respect from Asmodeus, their king, is no doubt an echo of the talmudic tale (in B. Gittin 68b) of Solomon and Asmodeus, in which Solomon has the demon king captured and brought to him in chains—and treats him with such respect. (See "King Solomon and Asmodeus" in EV). The speaking tree is also a common motif in world folklore. Here it serves as an oracle, not unlike that at Delphi, whose replies were said to be equally perplexing. In entering the Garden of Eden Alexander accomplishes what very few others have. But here, again, it is an earlier legend, that of Rabbi Joshua ben Levi and the Angel of Death, re-counted in the Talmud, which serves as the model here. Rabbi Joshua convinced the angel to take him to the wall of the Garden, and there he leaped inside, taking the angel's deadly sword with him (B. Ketubot 77a). Here we have additional evidence that the midrashic influence on Jewish folklore is considerable, and that these two great rivers of Jewish lore flowed together more than has generally been acknowledged. (See "Miriam's Tambourine" for another example of a folktale having grown out of a midrashic legend.)

The Princess Who Became a Garland of Flowers (Afghanistan) • Pages 135–140

From *Bat ha-Melech Shehafcha L'ezer Prachim* (Hebrew), edited by Zevulun Qort (Tel Aviv: Yehudit: 1967). IFA 3984, collected by Zevulun Qort from Sarah Gad. AT 407.

This tale, about a princess and an evil usurper, is a transformation tale, in which the princess, rather than drowning, is magically transformed into a garland of flowers. In this way she is preserved and ultimately saved. Note that the theme is parallel to that of "The Disguised Princess." Such polar themes of duality are quite common in all folklore, but have a particularly central place in Jewish folklore in the polarity of Lilith and Eve. In the case of Lilith and Eve it is not difficult to see how the rabbinic response to the threatening qualities that they perceived in women were all projected into Lilith, while Eve—flawed though she is—was seen as the incarnation of the positive qualities admired in women. All women, then, manifest, to some extent, these two poles. From this example it is possible to recognize a similar dualism in this tale, even though it is an even more extreme example. It is also worth noting that the most extreme negative portrayal of Lilith is found in the Kabbalah, where she is described in completely destructive and demonic terms, as well as those of sexual abasement. From the Kabbalistic perspective the polarity is not between Lilith and Eve, but Lilith and the *Shekhinah*, the Bride of God. In fact, there is a kabbalistic legend (Zohar 3:69a) that is virtually parallel to the plot of this tale, where Lilith, aware that the *Shekhinah* has chosen Exile with her children, Israel, offers herself to God as his paramour until her return. In one version of this myth, God accepts her offer, while in another God rejects it in great anger. Shocking as is the former ending, it fits the kabbalistic belief that whenever the sacred is exiled, evil always fills the void, usurping its place. Ultimately, then, the present tale from Afghanistan may be viewed as the struggle between good and evil, in which good is defeated but not destroyed, and ultimately is able to overcome the forces of evil and reestablish itself. This is the very theme of many crucial Jewish myths, especially those of the coming of the Messiah and the myths of the Shattering of the Vessels and the Gathering of the Sparks of the Ari, Rabbi Isaac Luria.

The Tale of the Magic Horse (Afghanistan) • Pages 141–149

From *Bat ha-Melech Shehafcha L'ezer Prachim* (Hebrew), edited by Zevulun Qort (Tel Aviv: Yehudit: 1967). IFA 2470. Collected by Zevulun

Qort from Reuben Menashe. A variant of "The Story of the Magic Horse" from *The Arabian Nights*. AT 314.

The oral tales collected in the Israel Folktale Archives include tales that have no specific parallel in earlier Jewish lore, and many others that are variants of tales found in the rabbinic texts and in earlier written collections of Jewish folklore. In the cases where the earlier written versions are known, it is likely that the oral version is based on it, although there may have been many retellings in the process. This is the case because the oral recounting of tales was characteristic of one element of Jewish culture, especially of the poor and less educated, while the knowledge and transmission of the written texts was the task of the rabbis, and was largely overseen by them. For those for whom the tale itself was central, regardless of its source, the folklore of surrounding cultures was often found to be as vital as their own. In any case, the boundaries of folklore are no more defined than those of the waves of the sea, and exchange of such lore is the rule. It seems likely that this telling is based on that found in *The Arabian Nights*. At the same time, this version differs in several respects, which suggest its adaptation to the harsh deserts of Afghanistan.

The Enchanted Well (Spain) • Pages 150–155

From *Meshal ha-Kadmoni* (Hebrew) by Issac Ibn Sahula, edited by Yisrael Zemor (Tel Aviv: 1952). AT 681 * A.

The central narrative device here, that of the moment suspended in time so that it appears that years have past, is repeated in later medieval Jewish folklore. This is one of the earliest versions, although some of the variants of the tale of King Solomon being overthrown by Asmodeus, which are difficult to date, also make use of this motif. Later this same device is found in the tales about Rabbi Isaac Luria, as well as in tales of the medieval sorcerer Rabbi Adam and the Baal Shem Tov. This tale identifies the lure of the mystical with the longing of the young man to be initiated into the ways of magic. The sorcerer forces him to experience its effects firsthand. In this he is not unlike the kabbalistic or especially the hasidic model of the master, especially Shimon bar Yoahai and the Baal Shem Tov. Thus although the mysteries sought out by the young man are not specifically of a Jewish nature, the tale takes place in the same period and setting out of which the Zohar, the primary expression of Jewish mysticism, emerged, and thus its parallels to kabbalistic themes should not be overlooked. Note also the primacy of the symbol of the well. The primary rabbinic echo of the well is found in the midrash about Miriam's Well. (See the note to "Miriam's Tambourine.") The use of the well in another tale included here, "The Magic Lamp of Rabbi Adam," is more typical of its general role in folklore. In any case, it is a primary symbol in all of world folklore, where a descent into a well often signifies, from a psychological perspective, the descent into the unconscious. In the tale at hand, the well signifies the transition between this world and the enchanted world that exists outside of time, where the young man finds himself. And even though the sorcerer insists that it was all an illusion, the young man knows that it was not; in the same way the world portayed in these tales is more than a mere fantasy, but contains strong elements of truth.

The Golden Amulet (Palestine) • Pages 156–162

From *Pirke de-Rabbi Eliezer*, chapter 38 (Hebrew). With episodes and passages from Pentateuch-Tosafot in *Hadar-Zekenim* (Hebrew) and *Kodex Sachau* no. 70 (Hebrew, with Latin translation) of the Berlin Library, published in *Fabula Josephi et Assenethae Apocrypha*, edited by G. Oppenheim.

In the Bible Joseph weds Asenath, who is described as the daughter of Potiphar, the priest of the Egyptian god On (Genesis 41:45). This troubled the rabbis, since this was the first time that one of the patriarchs did not marry one of their own. Thus was the history of Asenath revised in the rabbinic texts, beginning with *Pirke de-Rabbi Eliezer* in the eighth century (first published in Constanitinople in 1514), and she came to be identified as the daughter of Dinah, whose father was Jacob and whose sister was Joseph. This child, Asenath, was said to be fathered by Shechem, in the rape (or seduction) of Dinah recounted in the Torah (Genesis 34). According to the midrash, this illegitimate child was cast out by the tribes despite the protests of Jacob. He made a golden amulet for the infant girl to wear, which identified her as the granddaughter of Jacob. The infant, like Joseph, was abandoned in a pit, where a giant eagle found her and carried her to Egypt, to the home of the High priest of On, the Egyptian god of the sun. He raised her as his daughter, thus returning to the line of the biblical text. Notice how the sufferings of Joseph serve as the model for the childhood of Asenath, for since their fates were parallel the rabbis turned to the narrative about Joseph as a model for the revised history of Asenath. Note as well how in this version Asenath is reunited with her family and Joseph is wed to one of his own. It is not difficult to see how for the rabbis this was a far more gratifying explanation. Another version of the legend of Asenath is found in a first or second century Greek text, *Joseph and Asenath*, which is something of an early novel. This version of the legend resolves the problem of Jacob marrying a non-Jew by having Asenath convert. See *Joseph and Asenath* in *The Old Testament Pseudepigrapha* edited by James H. Charlesworth, volume 2, pp. 177-247. For an exceptionally thorough article on the legendary history of Asenath, see "Asenath, the Wife of Joseph: A Haggadic Literary-Historical Study" by V. Aptowitzer, in *Hebrew Union College Annual*, volume 1, 1924, pp. 239-306.

David's Harp (Palestine) • Pages 163–167

From *Aggodot Le-Yamin Noraim* (Hebrew) by S.Z. Kahana. (Jerusalem: Brit Ivrit Olamit, 1970). Based on the sources found in the Babylonian Talmud (Aramaic), tractate Berachot 3b and Sanhedrin 16a. AT 465B.

This tale grows directly out of the talmudic legends about David's harp: "A harp hung over David's bed, and as soon as midnight arrived, a northerly wind blew upon its strings and caused it to play of its own accord. Immediately David arose and studied the Torah until the break of dawn." In setting out on a quest to find the harp, the old man Shabbatai fulfills the midrashic tendency to complete the history of any particularly sacred object. Thus there is a chain of legends about the staff of Moses, which traces it backward in time to Adam, and links it to every major figure in between. So too for the precious jewel said to illumine Noah's ark, known as the *Tzohar*. Abraham, for example, was said to have worn this jewel around his neck as a healing stone. A long midrashic chain also concerns the legendary Book of Raziel, said to have been given to Adam by the angel Raziel, whose history lasts until the book was said to have been destroyed in the Temple. According to one midrash, David made the strings of the harp out of the sinews of the ram that Abraham sacrificed on Mount Moriah, thus linking the king to the patriarch. The midrashic consideration of the harp includes a debate as to whether it had seven or ten strings. Both numbers are of seminal importance—the seven days of creation and the later emergence of the ten sefirot as an alternate myth of creation in the Zohar. The messianic harp was said to have eight strings, suggesting David's link with a messianic role, a link also noted in Christian lore. The music of the harp is also said to have induced a state of ecstasy for David, in which he composed the Psalms with Divine inspriation. Shabbatai's certainty that the harp still exists is not unlike that of the three young men in "The Sword of Moses." This suggests that for some, at least, the sacred objects of Jewish legends, especially those of the Midrash, were presumed to have a literal existence. The biblical passage quoted in the story is from Psalm 137:1–4.

The Eagle's Treasure (India) • Pages 168–172

From *Shomrim Neemanim* (Hebrew), collected by Zvi Moshe Haimovits, edited and annotated by Dov Noy (Haifa: Israel Folktale Archives, 1976). IFA 5205. Told by Yitzhak Sassoon. Among the many variants of this tale is IFA 2308, collected by Yehuda Mzuz from Masuda Mazuz of Tunisia. In this variant a poor man finds that a large pot filled with water is empty every morning. He hides in it to see what happens, and finds that a large eagle carries it to a tree of diamonds, to water it. After that he hides on a regular basis, and collects diamonds in this way. Another variant is IFA 1637, recorded by Menashe Razi from his aunt, L. Gribi of Iraq. AT 676 * A.

In its theme this tale is parallel to "The Wise Old Woman of the Forest," included here. In both, a poor brother is denied help by a wealthy brother and as a result are led into unexpected riches of his own, which provokes jealousy and greed in the wealthy brother, leading him to destruction, an appropriate punishment for his selfishness. In fact, this theme is found in an astonishing number of variants, especially those collected orally by the Israel Folktale Archives. This suggests that these tales mirror the real life situation in which poor Jews generally found themselves, namely, in desperate need of help, which was not forthcoming. It is always at the point where no alternative is left for the poor brother that the tale moves into the realm of fantasy. This is the same pattern found in the tales of Jewish oppression, when no relief can be found in the real world, giving birth to fantasies of salvation by miraculous rabbis, as in the tales of Rabbi Judah Loew and the Golem. (See "The Golem," included here.) The fantasy also includes revenge at the one who denies help in a desperate time. This pattern suggests something of the way folklore comes into being, and why this happens. It also demonstrates that such tales do provide a kind of succor to the poor, holding out, at least in fantasy, the hope of one day achieving great wealth.

The Prince of Coucy (France) • Pages 173–185

From *Notser Te'enah* (Hebrew), Tarnow, 1900. Also, found in *Sefer Maaysiot* edited by Mordecai Ben Yezekel (Tel Aviv: Dvir, 1971). A variant is found in *Sefer Sipurim Noraim* (Hebrew) (Jerusalem: 1952). AT 610. An oral variant is IPA 5854, collected by Ben Zion Yehousha from his father, Rafael Yehousha of Afghanistan.

The central symbol in this epic tale is the apple from the Tree of Life, with its miraculous powers. As such the tale might be regarded as a midrash on the mysterious Tree of Life mentioned in Genesis, which existed in the Garden of Eden along with the Tree of the Knowledge of Good and Evil. The conclusion of the narrative of the Fall suggests that the role of the Tree of Life was far more important than is apparent at first, because "He placed at the east of the Garden of Eden the cherubim, and the flaming sword which turned every way, to keep the way to the Tree of Life (Genesis. 3:24)." Moses Gaster, in *The Folklore of the Old Testament*, suggests that in the original myth there was a Tree of Life and a Tree of Death, and that if Adam and Eve had eaten from the Tree of Life, they would have received eternal life. Instead they ate from the Tree of Death and became mortal. Here too the apple seems capable of conferring life-giving powers, so much so that Rabbi Samson decides to cast it into the ocean rather than give it to a mortal king, who might misuse its power. It should be noted that the theme of such a miraculous apple or other fruit is common in world folklore, but that this is one of the only cases in which it is directly identified with the Tree of Life. It is in such a manner that universal folklore is transformed into a folklore that has specific Jewish characteristics. Such a fusion of the Jewish and universal almost always takes place by natural links between the two lores, as in this case, making the transformation seem not only natural, but inevitable. Although this tale is certainly legendary, Samson ben Samson was a famous Tosafist who lived in Coucy in the 13th Century and was known as the Prince of Coucy. This title was problably intended to denote the level of accomplishment of his learning, but this legend probably arose in order to explain the title in a more literal fashion. Similiar legends have grown up about other major figures in places where they were rumored to have lived for some time. Many such legends are to be found about Maimonides, including "The Healing Waters" from Turkey, included here.

The Eagle Prince (Persian Kurdistan) • Pages 186–195

From *Ha-Na'ara ha-Yefefiya u-Sheloshet Beney ha-Melekh* (Hebrew), edited by Dov Noy (Tel Aviv: Am Oved, 1965). IFA 3863, collected by Dov Noy from David Eliyahu. A variant of Rapunzel from *Grimm's Fairy Tales*. AT 310.

This tale and the two that follow all concern human transformation into bird and beast. In this tale, the prince is transformed into an eagle once a month, while in the next, the princess becomes a stork. The third concerns a young woman born with the head of a donkey. The critical issue in all three is to find a way to free them from this transformation, and this occurs in every case. In becoming an eagle, the prince loses his will-power to resist the witch. In finally breaking the spell, he finds a way to regain control over himself. The issue here may well be that of the struggle between the conscious and unconscious self for control. When transformed into an eagle, the prince is ruled by the unconscious self, which is here portrayed in a negative light. The witch's spell backfires, however, when the prince is united with the beautiful princess rather than the toothless old hag. Both prince and princess are quickly bonded to one another with a love that will always last. And it is the princess, taking great risks for his sake, who finds a way to free him from the witch's spell. This is another example of the resourceful princess who is able to save the prince, as that found in "The Disguised Princess," or in the tale "The Pirate Princess" in *EV*.

The Stork Princess (Persian Kurdistan) • Pages 196–201

From *Min ha-Mabua* (Hebrew) edited and annotated by Eliezer Marcus (Haifa: Israel Folktale Archives, 1966). IFA 6961. Collected by Hannah Sabbah from Itzak Sabbah. A variant of "The Tale of Hasan of Bassorah" from *The Arabian Nights*. AT 432.

The early episodes of this tale strongly echo the beginning of "Aladdin and the Magic Lamp," which, of course, is also from *The Arabian Nights*. The charge that the young man is given not to open one particular door of the house is parallel to the central theme of "Bluebeard," where Bluebeard's wife is told not to unlock one particular door. It is also the theme of the Greek legend of Pandora. Naturally the young man opens the door, but unlike the parallel tales, the discovery is not a terrible one, for there he sees the stork princess to whom he loses his heart, suffering all the pangs of lovesickness. The motif of stealing the feathers from the princess when she sheds them and resumes her human shape, compelling her to remain a woman, is found as well in "The Princess Who Became a Garland of Flowers." Variants of this motif are to be found in world folklore. Here the loss of the ability to transform into the stork seems to symbolize the loss of freedom that is a natural consequence of marriage. The girl is no longer free to fly off as she pleases and go anywhere she wishes. The final episode of the tale returns to the Aladdin motif, and aportions out proper reward and punishment.

The Donkey Girl (Iraq) • Pages 202–208

From *Oseh Peleh* (Hebrew) compiled by U.S. Farhi (Leghorn, Italy: 1902). This version is based on the retelling of Simcha Abed of Iraq, collected by Dov Noy, IFA 60, from *Ha-Na'ara ha Yefefiya u-Sheloshet Beney ha-Melech* (Hebrew), edited by Dov Noy (Tel Aviv: Am Oved, 1965). AT 873 * A.

This tale has not been found in written versions earlier than *Oseh Peleh*. This has led some folklorists to conclude the tale was the creation of Farhi, and entered the oral tradition because the collection became very widely known, especially in the Middle East. The version included here is based on one of these oral retellings, which remains close to the original storyline, but is presented in a much simpler narrative fashion. However, the motif of humans transformed into donkeys is widely found in sources as early as the Talmud. There Rabbi Janai prevents a witch from turning him into a donkey, and turns her into one himself (B. Sanhedrin 67b). Here, however, it is only the head of the girl that is that of a donkey, suggesting that the tale is a metaphor for some kind of severe disability. The tale reflects the longing of the rejected wife to be freed of the curse, and in fairy tale fashion accomplishes this, with the help of Elijah the Prophet, who here appears only in a dream. The true moving force of the tale, though, is her son, whose longing to have his mother and father reunited is also fulfilled. Thus does the tale resolve their dilemmas through fantasy, offering an imaginary kind of relief. This, certainly, is one important function of the fairy tale.

The Healing Waters (Turkey) • Pages 209–216

From *Hodesh Hodesh Ve-sippuro: 1962*, (Hebrew) edited and annotated by Dov Noy (Haifa: Israel Folktale Archives, 1963). IFA 977, told by Abraham Daniel Farhi. A variant is found in *Hodesh Hodesh ve-Sippuro: 1965*, edited and annotated by Dov Noy. (Hebrew). (Jerusalem:

Israel Folktale Archives, 1966). IFA 6502, collected by Sarah Abraham from Esther Cohen of Tunisia. AT 908 * - * A.

There are an astonishing number of legends about Maimonides, many, such as this one, placing him in countries that he may not have even visited. Thus does Maimonides become a universal figure in Jewish legend, not unlike Elijah. Here Maimonides saves the Jews of Turkey on two occasions, functioning as a sorcerer in a manner parallel to tales of King Solomon, Rabbi Adam and Rabbi Judah Loew. The bath of King Solomon referred to is one of the magical objects Jewish folklore attributes to the Temple, along with other enchanted creations, such as a golden bird that Solomon could command to fly. So it is that this tale recalls the tales about King Solomon in several respects, suggesting that these tales served as the model for it. The descent to the Palace of Leviathan beneath the sea strongly recalls the same episode of another folktale from *The Alphabet of Ben Sira* (no. 7) and is likely derived from there. This suggests that later Jewish folktales turned to earlier ones (which themselves turned to the midrash for their models, while the midrash, in turn, turned to the Bible) for inspiration.

The Reincarnation of a Tzaddik (Egypt) • Pages 217–220

From *Hodesh ve-Sippuro: 1961* (Hebrew), edited by Dov Noy (Haifa: Israel Folktale Archives, 1962). IFA 2937, collected by Ilana Cohen from her mother, Flora Cohen. AT 759, AT 750B.

One of the primary kabbalistic principles is that of *Gilgul*, or reincarnation. The wandering of the soul from one body was a common belief among the Sephardim, the Jews of the Middle East. One reason for this wandering was that a soul had not fulfilled its destiny in its lifetime, and that is why the Tzaddik is reincarnated in this tale. The strange actions of the boy recall a famous tale from *Hibbur Yafeh me-hay Yesuah*, chapter 2, in which Elijah lets a sage accompany him, and shocks him by his unpredictable behavior which turns out in the end, as it does here, to have been for the good. This tale also echoes the talmudic tale (B. Giffin 68b) of the strange acts of Asmodeus. See "King Solomon and Asmodeus" in *EV*.

King Solomon's Ring (Egypt) • Pages 221–229

From *The Arabian Nights* (Arabic). Originally derived from *Kitab al-Isra'iliyyat* (Arabic) compiled by Wahb ibn Munabbih. Found in *The Book of the Thousand Nights and a Night*, translated by Richard F. Burton, edition of 1885, as "The Adventures of Bulukiya." AT 456A, AT 465C.

The central theme of this tale, a quest for King Solomon's ring, is similiar to that in "The Sword of Moses" and "David's Harp." In all three stories a precious, legendary object is sought out, but the purpose of the quest is not merely to find the object, but has messianic overtones. Here Bulukiya intends to use King Solomon's ring to assist him in finding the Messiah, whose existence he has learned of from the Torah and the "Books of Abraham." His companion, Affan, however, intends to use the power of the ring for his own selfish purposes, which parallels the intention of the evil head of the village, who plans to let the three youths find the sword of Moses and then steal it from them. Neither Bulukiya nor the three youths find the object of their quest, but both are rewarded for their efforts and gain knowledge that is invaluable to them. These tales are a testament to the power of the midrashic legends that trace the history of such sacred objects, those found in these tales and others such as the Book of Raziel, the staff of Moses, and the garments of Adam and Eve. The many legends that report the history of these sacred objects are so convincing that they raise the desire and expectation that they may be sought out for another generation—at least in tales such as these.

The Magic Lamp of Rabbi Adam (Egypt) • Pages 230–237

IFA 3676 (Hebrew). Collected by Abraham Bachar from his parents. Previously unpublished. AT 561.

This tale is easily recognized as a variant of "Aladdin and the Magic Lamp," from *The Arabian Nights*. Here the witch hopes to obtain the magic lamp from the well and abandon Rabbi Adam there, exactly as did the sorcerer in Aladdin hope to recover the lamp from a cave and leave him behind. The primary difference comes from the fact that Rabbi Adam himself is a great sorcerer, whose magic is able to match and ultimately defeat that of the witch. The echo of Aladdin no doubt reflects the Egyptian origin of this tale, while most of the Rabbi Adam tales derive from Eastern Europe. These tales, including this one and the three that follow (as well as the three included in *EV*, "The Magic Mirror of Rabbi Adam," "The Enchanted Journey" and "The King's Dream"), generally follow the pattern established here. That is because Rabbi Adam was a fantasy creation of medieval Jewry whose piety and mystical knowledge enabled him to protect the Jews from the irrational and vicious persecutions to which they were so often subject. These tales, then, bring an imaginary sense of justice to bear on situations where no actual justice was to be found. An historical model for such a figure of fantasy is Rabbi Judah Loew, around who grew a cluster of miracle tales, including that involving the creation of the Golem. (See "The Golem," following.) In fact, a number of tales about Rabbi Adam are also attributed to Rabbi Loew, including "The Enchanted Palace."

Rabbi Adam and the Star-Gazing King (Greece) • Pages 238–244

From *Notzat ha-Zahav* (Hebrew), edited and annotated by Dov Noy (Haifa: Israel Folktale Archives, 1976). IFA 10086, collected by Moshe Attias from Aharon Avraham Mizrahi. AT 325 * *.

This tale is a variant of "The Magic Mirror of Rabbi Adam," found in *EV*, and the magic mirror plays an identical role in both, informing the Jew in the former tale and the king in this one of the unfaithfulness of their wives, who were also plotting against them. Such variations on a similiar theme are the rule, rather than the exception, in all folklore, not only that of the Jews. The life of the Jew is saved in "The Magic Mirror of Rabbi Adam" when he obeys Rabbi Adam and is saved from the magic arrows shot at him by the sorcerer who was his wife's lover. Here the vizier loses his life in a similiar manner, when the king blows out the flame of a candle while looking into the magic mirror. From this point on, the tale follows the standard format of the Blood Libel tale, in which the Jews are accused of a crime they did not commit, and are saved at the last moment by the magical intervention of figures such as Rabbi Adam or Rabbi Loew. Most of the tales about Rabbi Loew and the evil priest Thaddeus and other enemies of the Jews follow this same pattern. Note that the king saved by Rabbi Adam is himself a soothsayer, who finds Rabbi Adam by searching for one born on the same day as himself. This underscores the role of destiny in these tales, in which Rabbi Adam serves as the vessel of fate. This dominant role of destiny serves to emphasize that the role of Rabbi Adam in these tales is primarily as the servant of God, fulfilling His will, rather than being credited for the miracles he accomplishes himself. For as Rabbi Adam himself often notes, he derives all of his power from God. Such statements, quite common in Jewish legend, maintain the proper perspective about the powers demonstrated by these heroic figures, from Moses to King Solomon to Rabbi Adam and Rabbi Loew to the Baal Shem Tov.

The Enchanted Palace (Eastern Europe) • Pages 245–249

From *Eretz ha-Hayim* (Hebrew) collected by Hayim Liebersohn (Przemysl, Polland: 1926). A variant is found in *Shivhei ha-Besht*

(Hebrew), compiled by Dov Baer ben Samuel, edited by Samuel A. Horodezky (Berlin: 1922). An early Yiddish variant was published in Prague, and is listed as Steinschneider catalogue no. 3911, Bodleian Library, Oxford, no. Opp. 8 1120. Another version was printed by H. Shmeruk in *Zion*, volume 28, 1963, pp. 86-105. Shmeruk concludes that the original language of the earliest version of this tale was Yiddish. AT 561.

This is an early and important medieval folk legend which establishes the pattern in which the Jewish sorcerer, here Rabbi Adam, defeats an evil vizier, often a sorcerer himself, who intends to bring great harm to the Jews. Shmeruk dates it from the second half of the 16th Century. A retelling of this same tale, about Rabbi Judah Loew rather than Rabbi Adam, dates from the 19th Century. An abridged version of this tale, with Rabbi Adam as the central figure, is included in *Shivhei ha-Besht*, the first and most important collection of legends about the Baal Shem Tov. Here Rabbi Adam is presented as the Baal Shem, or Master of the Name, who passes on the necessary secret knowledge to the boy Israel ben Eliezer, who will later become known as the Baal Shem Tov. This legend linking the Baal Shem Tov to Rabbi Adam is an attempt to place the Baal Shem Tov in the chain of great sages. Gershom Scholem, in his *Major Trends in Jewish Mysticism* (pp. 331-334), suggests that the Rabbi Adam of the legends of the Baal Shem Tov might have been a pseudonym for the Sabbatian kabbalist Rabbi Hershel Zoref, in order to disguise the influence of the Sabbatian movement on Hasidism. In any case, the legendary role of Rabbi Adam as an adversary of gentile sorcerers and enemies of the Jews was well established by the time the legends in *Shivhei ha-Besht* were recorded.

The King Descended from Haman (Eastern Europe) • Pages 250-254

From *Mifalot ha-Tzaddikim* (Hebrew) (Lemberg: 1897). A variant of the biblical Book of Esther. AT * 730A.

This is a fascinating example of the biblical imprint on later Jewish folklore. In all respects the model for this tale is the Book of Esther, a link that is made apparent by the fact that the evil king is descended from Haman and that the Jew whose life is at stake is named Mordecai. Here, though, the intervention comes not from Esther, interceding with the king, but from Rabbi Adam, portrayed in this tale as a beggar who stands outside the walls of a city. There is also a legendary parallel for this transformation of Rabbi Adam's role, namely an account of the Messiah at the gates of Rome found in the Talmud (B. Sanhedrin 98a). Here the Messiah is said to be a lepper who stands before the gates of Rome, winding and unwinding his bandages, so that he will be ready if the time arrives for him to come. This subtle link of Rabbi Adam with a messianic figure suggests the importance of his role, albeit a fantasy one, in the medieval Jewish imagination. The importance of the link to the biblical tale of Esther demonstrates not only the enduring power of the biblical narratives on later generations, but, even more importantly, the fact that those generations found themselves in a situation they regarded as virtually identical to that recounted in the Bible.

The Demon's Tail (Eastern Europe) • Pages 255–261

From *Ma'aselech un Mesholim* (Yiddish), edited by Naftali Gross (New York: 1955). See also *Studies in Jewish and World Folklore* by Haim Schwarzbaum (Berlin: Walter de Gruyter, 1968), #288, p. 246. AT 1173A.

The brave but reckless poor man who is the hero of this tale is a familiar figure in Yiddish folklore. He consistently disregards the warnings he is given and puts himself at great risk, but always manages to escape by the skin of his teeth. This character combines the opposing roles of the good and bad brothers in most fairy tales. There the bad brothers discount the advice they are given and come to some inglorious end, while the good brother follows it to the letter and succeeds in his quest. Here the poor man, who is the only hero of the tale, behaves like the bad brothers but, in the end, is rewarded like the good one. This seems to stand the traditional moral of the fairy tale on its ear, but in fact it suggests another kind of moral: that the poor Jews of Eastern Europe had to take great risks in order to advance themselves in a hostile environment. This implicit moral explains the apparent empathy with the poor man and his elevation to the role of hero in this tale. The tale also has the structure of a joke: on one hand the giant insists on deluging the man with wishes, in such quick succession that he does not have the opportunity to enjoy his sudden abundance; on the other hand the man finds a way of giving the giant his own medicine, by assigning him an impossible task, to make the water of the river flow backward. This keeps the giant busy and frees the man to wallow in his new riches. The implicit black humor here suggests that with Jews it is either drought or flood, and that their lives are never out of danger.

The Grateful Dead (Eastern Europe) • Pages 262–264

From *Sha'are Yerushalayim* (Hebrew), edited by Jacob ben Joseph Reischer (Warsaw: 1873). AT 506.

There are many tales to be found with this motif of the spirits of the dead returning to reward those who have somehow honored their memory or assisted their descendants. In fact, it is one of the primary tale types in all of world folklore as noted by Aarne and Thompson. However, it is particularly appropriate to Jewish lore because of the reverence paid to ancestors. Indeed, such reverence, especially of the ancient prophets and sages, is the primary themes of all Jewish teachings. And since honor is given to ancestors, both far and near, it is possible to assume that the caring is mutual, and that the spirits of the dead continue to look out for the living. In this tale, then, such a spirit takes an active role in the rescue of the young man who gave up his inheritance in order to preserve the dead man's honor after his death. This is the direct cause of his life being saved by the magical eagle—the form taken by the spirit of the deceased—when the young man's ship has sunk. Note that the motif of a giant eagle that carries a man, such as King Solomon, is often found in Jewish folklore. See "The Princess in the Tower" and "The Flight of the Eagle" in *EV.*

The Golem (Eastern Europe) • Pages 265–270

From *Niflaot Maharal* (Hebrew), edited by Yudel Rosenberg. (Piotrkow: 1909). AT *730E.

Almost no legend has captured the popular imagination as has that of the Golem, the creature-man out of clay by Rabbi Judah Loew of Prague (Known as the Maharal) and brought to life by the use of various magical incantations, including the use of holy names. This creature, according to the legend, protected the Jews of Prague from various dangers, especially that of the Blood Libel accusation—that is, of using the blood of Christian children to bake unleavened bread for Passover— with its disastrous consequences. Here the Golem discovers the body of a murdered Christian child who has been carried into the Jewish ghetto, and carries it back through underground tunnels into the basement of the actual murderer, the priest Thadeus, thus staving off a pogrom. Knowledge of this legend is primarily derived from *Niflaot Maharal*, a collection of tales about Rabbi Loew and the Golem, published in 1909 by Rabbi Yudel Rosenberg, who claimed that they had been compiled in the 16th century by a relative of Rabbi Loew. Recent scholars, including Dov Sadan and Gershom Scholem, have insisted, however, that Rabbi Rosenberg himself was the author of the book, which he based loosely on the existing legends. (Such legends certainly existed. In 1808 Jacob Grimm published a description of the legend in *Journal for Hermits*. For a translation see "The Idea of the Golem" by Gershom Scholem in *On the Kabbalah and Its Symbolism*, (New York: Schocken Books, 1969, p. 159.) The issue here is whether these are authentic 16th century legends, deriving from the period in which Rabbi Judah Loew lived in Prague or immediately afterward, or if they were in fact largely drawn from 19th Century folklore, embellished in this century by Rabbi Rosenberg. The earliest published legends about Rabbi Loew are those found in the first volume of the *Sippurim* series, edited by Wolf Pascheles, first published in Prague in 1847. There are a number of precedents for the creation of the Golem in earlier Jewish literature, including the description of a calf that was created magically found in the Talmud: "Rabbi Hanina and Rabbi Oshaia spent every Sabbath eve in studying the Laws of creation, by means of which they created a third-grown calf and ate it" (B. Sanhedrin 67b). There is also a legend about Solomon Ibn Gabirol, in which he is described as having created a female golem, for allegedly sexual purposes: "They say that Rabbi Solomon Ibn Gabirol created a woman who served him. When he was denounced to the authorities, he showed them that she was not a full or complete creature. And he restored her to the pieces of wood of which she had been constructed" (*Ma'aseh Ta'atulim*, edited by S. Rubin, Vienna: 1887). Certainly, part of the popularity of the Golem legend is due to the fact that it prefigures the modern myth of Frankenstein, brought to life not with the magic of God's Name, but with the new magic of science. The influence, if any, of the Golem legend on Mary Shelley's novel, *Frankenstein*, has yet to be established, although several studies have attempted to find a link between the two.

The Demon in the Jug (Eastern Europe) • Pages 271–276

From *Shivhei ha-Besht* (Hebrew), compiled by Dov Baer ben Samuel, edited by Samuel A. Horodezky (Berlin: 1922). AT 926A.

This tale is a sequel to "The Boy Israel and the Witch," found in *EV.* There the young Israel ben Eliezer, who later became the Baal Shem Tov, foils a witch who causes a drought by breaking the spell she cast. This provokes her anger, leading to a confrontation in which the boy

Israel, emerges victorious, destroys the witch, and transforms the demon slave she had invoked into a little fish, which he closes up in a jug. This is the jug that the man opens in this tale, releasing the evil demon once more, only to wreak havoc until the Baal Shem Tov, now fully grown, defeats him again. This tale, then, can be recognized as a variant of the prior tale. The motif of imprisoning demons in bottles is often encountered in Jewish folklore and in *The Arabian Nights*. The most famous version of this tale, which is found in written versions and in oral variants collected by the Israel Folktale Archives, involves Asmodeus, king of Demons, who was said to have been imprisoned in such a bottle by King Solomon. One such oral variant is found in *Sippure Baale-Hayim Befdot Yisrael* (Hebrew) (Haifa: Israel Folktale Archives, 1978). IFA 107, collected by Hada Yazon from Yeffet Shvili.) Here the account of how Asmodeus got into the bottle is itself a variant of the talmudic tale about King Solomon and Asmodeus found in tractate Gittin 68b. There Asmodeus throws the ring of King Solomon into the sea, and here Solomon traps Asmodeus in the bottle, and throws *him* into the sea. Such reversals of earlier themes are commonly found in Jewish folklore.

The Princess and the Baal Shem Tov (Eastern Europe) • Pages 277–281

From *Sippure Tzaddikim* (Hebrew) (Cracow: 1886). AT 610, AT 467.

This is one of the few tales about the Baal Shem Tov in the classic form of the fairy tale. Here the Baal Shem plays the role of the one who finds the enchanted flower the princess longs for. This is the role given both to princes and to poor but ingenious youths in a multitude of fairy tales. The rabbi who obtains the apple from the Tree of Life in "The Prince of Coucy," included here, fulfills a similiar quest, as does the Jewish slave Samuel in the tale of "The Princess and the Slave" in *EV.* The reason such tales are so rare in Hasidic folklore is that the primary model for the Hasidic tale is the rabbinic legend, such as those found in the Talmud and Midrash. Echoing these tales enables the Hasidic master to be seen as a part of the chain of tradition that includes the patriarchs, prophets and ancient sages. In this context the various types of the folktale, including the fairy tale, are a less attractive model. The one major exception to this rule are the tales of Rabbi Nachman of Bratslav, most of which are drawn from folk models, although they incorporate a great deal of aggadic and kabbalistic elements. Five of Rabbi Nachman's tales are included here, beginning with "A Garment for the Moon."

The Demon and the Baal Shem Tov (Eastern Europe) • Pages 282–286

From *Adat Tzaddikim* (Hebrew) edited by M.L. Frumkin (Lemberg: 1877). With an episode from *Shivhei ha-Besht* (Hebrew) compiled by Dov Baer ben Samuel, edited by Samuel A Horodezky (Berlin: 1922). An oral variant is found in *Hodesh Hodesh ve-Sippuro: 1973* (Hebrew), edited by Aliza Shenhar. IFA 9958, collected by Irit Amit from Zion Eliyahu of Palestine (Haifa: Israel Folktale Archives, 1974). AT 797 *.

The greatest desire of the Baal Shem Tov was to travel to the Holy Land, but every attempt he made to get there was frustrated. In time, he concluded that it was not the will of God that he reach the Land. This matter became embellished by the disciples of the Baal Shem Tov, who concluded that the reason he was barred from going there was that his soul was so pure that its power combined with that of the Land would force the coming of the Messiah. Therefore heaven hindered him from completing the journey. The two episodes of this tale describe such attempts to reach the Holy Land, one in which the Baal Shem Tov is lured by a demon into a cave that led directly to the Land of Israel. Folklore held that such cases existed, and in another tale, found in *Shivhei ha-Besht*, the earliest collection of tales about the Baal Shem Tov, he was shown such a cave by robbers, but had a vision of a flaming sword in the entrance which indicated that he was not to enter there (See Genesis 3:24). Such caves had been created so that the bodies of the resurrected could roll through them at the time of the coming of the Messiah and in this way reach Jerusalem. This legend is recounted in the Talmud (B. Ketubot IIIa): "Rabbi Abba Sala the Great demurred: 'Will not rolling be painful to the righteous?' Abaye replied: "Caves will be made for them underground.'" This tale, then, is one more example of how the legends initiated in earlier rabbinic texts are resurrected and embellished in later Jewish literature. For the Hasidim, this method enabled them to link their masters with the earlier prophets and sages of ancient times, who they considered to be of an equal stature. See "The City of Lyz" in *EV* for another tale in which these enchanted caves can be found, and also "Fable of the Goat" by S.Y. Agnon in *Twenty-One Stories*.

A Garment for the Moon (Eastern Europe) • Pages 287–293

From *Sippurim Niflaim* (Hebrew), compiled by Samuel Horowitz (Jerusalem: 1935). AT 298.

This tale is an attempt to complete a fragmentary tale of Rabbi Nachman's. In the original the tale ends with the offer of the poor tailors to help the great tailors in sewing a garment for the moon, which the great tailors refuse. Such fragmentary and incomplete tales were often told by Rabbi Nachman and were dutifully recorded by his scribe, Rabbi Nathan of Nemirov. The fact that the great tailors have the last word here is a clear indication that the tale was unfinished, as Rabbi Nachman's sympathies in such cases were always with the "little" people. In fact, a passage from Bereshith Rabba (6:3) strongly suggests the identification of the poor tailors with the Jews: "Rabbi Levi said in the same of Rabbi Jose ben Lai: 'It is but natural that the great should count by the great, and the small by the small. Esau counts time by the sun, which is large, and Jacob by the moon, which is small.'" The discussion is continued by a sage whose name also happens to be Rabbi Nachman: "Said Rabbi Nachman: 'That is a happy augury. Esau counts by the sun, which is large: just as the sun rules by day but not by night, so does Esau enjoy this world, but has nought in the World to Come. Jacob counts by the moon, which is small: just as the moon rules by day and by night, so has Jacob a portion in this world and the World to Come." The present dependent condition of the moon on the sun echoes a talmudic myth (B. Hullin 60b) about competition between the sun and the moon, which is a commentary on the passage *And God made the two great lights* (Genesis 1:16): "The moon said to the Holy One, blessed be He, 'Master of the Universe, is it possible for two kings to wear one crown?' God replied: 'Go then and make thyself smaller.'" Thus the rebellion of the moon brought about its decrease. This talmudic legend is echoed in a dialogue, closely resembling that in Rabbi Nachman's tale, found in *Pirqe de-Rabbi Eliezer*, chapter 6: "Rivalry ensued between the sun and the moon, and one said to the other, 'I am bigger than you are.' The other rejoined, 'I am bigger than you are.' What did the Holy One, blessed be He, do, so that there should be peace betwen them? He made the one larger and the other smaller, as it is written, *The greater light to rule by the day, and the lesser light to rule the night and the stars* (Genesis 1:16)." It seems certain that Rabbi Nachman had these rabbinic myths in mind when he told his enticing, fragmentary tale. It is also possible to read this tale as an allegory in which Israel is the moon, God is the sun, and the garment is the Torah, which protects Israel against the winters of Exile.

The Treasure (Eastern Europe) • Pages 295–298

From *Maasiot U'Meshalim* in *Kokhevey Or* (Hebrew) (Jerusalem: 1896), edited by Rabbi Abraham ben Nachman of Tulchin. AT 1645.

This well-known tale has been attributed to Rabbi Nachman of Bratslav, and is included as one of his tales in several collections. But it is most likely a folktale of medieval origin. Its attribution to Rabbi Nachman is, however, appropriate as far as the content of the tale is concerned, and it also seems likely that he told the tale to his Hasidim. Its faith in dreams and destiny, and the moral drawn, which suggests it is necessary to travel to the Tzaddik in order to discover the treasure within, is certainly characteristic of Rabbi Nachman's vision. The thirteen primary tales told by Rabbi Nachman, which are collected in *Sippurey Ma'asiyot*, are generally acknowledged as original creations, although they often echo themes and motifs common in folklore. But Rabbi Nachman also selected from the abundant pool of Jewish Eastern European folklore some tales to which he was particularly drawn, such as this one and "The Wooden Sword," included in *EV*. He no doubt told these to his Hasidim with the same fervor with which he told his own.

The Prince and the Slave (Eastern Europe) • Pages 299–306

From *Sippurey Ma'asiyot* (Hebrew), by Rabbi Nachman of Bratslav, edited by Rabbi Nathan Sternhartz of Nemirov (Ostrog: 1816). AT 920, 975*.

This is a tale not only about exchanged children, but, from a kabbalistic perspective, about exchanged souls. The biblical model for it is clearly the story of Jacob and Esau, which is strongly echoed in many places. From a rabbinic perspective, Jacob was justified in taking the blessing of the firstborn since he had purchased his brother's birthright (Genesis 25:33). But even so, the story leaves a nagging feeling since Esau was indeed the firstborn. The idea of the exchange thus suggests the resolution to the problem. Rabbi Nachman is quoted as having said about Napolean, shortly before having told this story: "Who knows what sort of soul he has? It is possible that it was exchanged. There is a Chamber of Exchanges, where souls are sometimes exchanged' (*Chayay Moharan*, Lemberg: 1874). According to Rabbi Aryeh Kaplan, good and evil are confused in the Chamber of Exchanges, which is therefore a place of evil. Rabbi Nachman's scribe, Rabbi Nathan of Nemirov, offers a midrash about the way in which this chamber came into existence. He links it to the Fall, saying that it came into existence at the time Adam ate from the fruit of the Tree of Knowledge. He also associates it with *the flaming sword which turned every way, to keep the way to the Tree of Life* (Genesis 3:24), which the cherubim swung at the gate of the Garden of Eden. This reinterprets the Hebrew for "the revolving sword" into "the transforming sword," or "the sword of reversals." He also linked the Chamber of Exchanges with the staff of Moses, which was transformed into a serpent in Pharoah's court, and then back into its original form. Rabbi Nathan also suggests that the tale is an allegory of an inner dualism, in which the slave represents the body, and the prince, the soul. (This is a remarkably modern psychological view of the story, consistent with the theories of C.G. Jung.) This reading of the tale, which rings true, indicates the extent to which Rabbi Nachman's tales were interpreted in an allegorical manner, consistent with kabbalistic teachings. And there is no doubt that Rabbi Nachman himself encouraged and often even provided such readings of his tales, which for him were another aspect of his teachings. This theme of exchanged children is also found in a story of Rabbi Judah Loew, the tale of Black Beryl and Red Beryl, in Yudl Rosenberg's *Niflaot Maharal*. Since this collection is held by many scholars to be a 19th century creation, it is possible that his version was influenced by Rabbi Nachman's tale.

The Enchanted Tree (Eastern Europe) • Pages 307–314

From *Sippurey Ma'asiyot* (Hebrew) by Rabbi Nachman of Bratslav, edited by Rabbi Nathan Sternhartz of Nemirov (Ostrog: 1816). AT 610.

This tale is a complex kabbalistic allegory. The enchanted tree in the story is itself the most complex and resonant symbol. It represents, first of all, the Torah, about which it is written, *The Torah is a Tree of Life to all who hold on to it* (Proverbs 3:18). It also symbolizes the enigmatic Tree of Life described in the Genesis narrative as being located in the Garden of Eden. After Adam and Eve had eaten of the Tree of Knowledge and were expelled from the Garden, *He placed at the east of the Garden of Eden the cherubim, and the flaming sword which turned every way, to keep the way to the Tree of Life* (Genesis 3:24). Above all, the enchanted tree in this tale represents the kabbalistic Tree of Life, as the mystical system of ten emanations, called the efirot, is known. The forces of evil that prevent the watering of the tree are known as the *Kleippot*, which means "husks" or "shells." In this tale, the crippled son goes through a great struggle to reach the tree, and this is equivalent of breaking through the *Kelippot* in order to achieve his goal. In his tales, Rabbi Nachman often uses physical impairments in a symbolic fashion. The role of the crippled son here is similiar to that of the cripple in his epic tale of "The Seven Beggars." The transformation that takes place when the crippled son reaches the enchanted tree is thus intended to be more of a spiritual than physical one. The diamond, with its four sides, may represent the four-tiered system of interpretation known by the acronym *PaRDeS*, in which the same text may be interpreted in four different ways, literal *(Peshat)*, symbolic *(Remez)*, allegorical *(Drash)* and mystical *(Sod)*. The crippled son is able to reach the enchanted tree by turning to the side of the diamond symbolized by *Sod*; i.e. by delving into the mystical meaning he is able to achieve a spiritual healing of himself. Note that the tale within the tale about the sun complaining to the moon strongly echoes Rabbi Nachman's tale "A Garment of the Moon," and is evidence of his reworking of similiar motifs in various tales. (See the note to that tale for the midrashic background of this motif.) The instrument the true prince finds in the forest resembles the mythical *magreifah*, a ten-holed instrument said to exist in the days of the Temple, which could play a thousand notes (Mishnah Tamid 3:8; 5:6).

The Palace Beneath the Sea (Eastern Europe) • Pages 315–323

From *Sippurey Ma'asiyot Hadashim* (Hebrew), attributed to Rabbi Nachman of Bratslav (Warsaw: 1909). AT 467.

Certain objects and motifs of a uniquely Jewish origin are also found in general folklore. One such legendary object is the glowing stone, which is widely found both in general and Jewish lore. Rabbi Nachman was attracted to such convergent themes, for they enabled his tales to have a foot in both worlds. Thus his tale "The Lost Princess," found in *EV*, works both as a fairy tale about the quest to find a lost princess and as a kabbalistic allegory about the myth of the Exile of the *Shekhinah*. Here the whole midrashic history of the glowing stone, identified as the *Tzohar*, is given, which grows out of the biblical contradiction of the light that was created on the first day and that cast by the sun and the moon, which were not created until the fourth day. This contradiction is resolved by the rabbis by identifying the earlier light as a special light known as the primordial light, by which it was possible to see from one end of the world to the other, all of which was lost at the time of the Fall—except for that small amount preserved in a jewel—the *Tzohar*. Identifying the glowing jewel by this name also resolves another biblical problem, the nature of the object identified as the *Tzohar* in the account of Noah and the ark, which somehow provides light in the ark. Some rabbis identified it as a window in the ark, while others observed that since the skies were covered by dark clouds for forty days and nights, the only light that could have illuminated the ark must have come from this object, thus the formulation of the glowing stone and the link to the legend of the primordial light. Such ingenious exegesis of the biblical text, which quite often gives birth to new legends, is the very essence of the midrashic method. The powers attributed to the light of the jewel, such as causing the carob trees in the cave beneath the palace to grow, are consistent with its magical nature and midrashic origin. The theme of the glowing jewel is also found in several other tales collected here. For a list of these tales see the note to "Alexander Descends into the Sea."

The Wishing Ring (Eastern Europe) • Pages 324–330

From *Yiddishe Folksmayses* (Yiddish), edited by Yehuda L. Cahan (Vilna: 1931). AT 560.

This is one of the most famous of all Eastern European Jewish fairy tales. It serves as the inspriation of the Yiddish novella by Mendele Moker-Seforim of the same title. The fantasy is a simple one, commonly found in all folklore: a magic ring provides riches in abundance to a poor man in dire straits. In the case of Jewish folklore it is important to observe, however, that this theme has a rich legendary history, linked to the magic ring of King Solomon, on which the Name of God was inscribed and which was the source of his vast powers. It is this ring which Asmodeus, King of Demons, throws into the sea, rendering Solomon powerless (B. Gittin 68b). The tale of "King Solomon's Ring," included here, recounts a quest to recover the ring. The magic found in this Yiddish folktale is never linked to King Solomon, but such a link could never be far from the mind of those who heard it—it was recounted orally, and was collected from an oral source by the pioneering Yiddish folklorist Y.L. Cahan. But unlike Solomon's ring, which clearly derived its power from God, the ring in this Yiddish tale is simply magic, and the only Jewish elements are to be found in the context of the tale. The importance of this tale, then, is not to be found in its rabbinic echoes, of which there are few, but in what is revealed about the fantasies and longings of the poor Jews of Eastern Europe. For a Middle Eastern variant of this tale see "The Magic Flute of Asmodeus" in *EV*.

The Man Who Escaped Misfortune (Eastern Europe) • Pages 331–334

From *Yiddisher Folklor* (Yiddish), edited by Yehuda L. Cahan (Vilna: 1938). Also in *Sippurey 'Am mi-Sanok* (Hebrew), collected by Samuel Zanvel Pipe. (Haifa: Israel Folktale Archives, 1967.) IFA 7334. AT 947.

Belief in the concept of *mazel* or luck—both good and bad—was widespread among the Jews of Eastern Europe. In this tale the concept of bad luck is personified, and although it appears in a different form—first as a raven and then as a voice coming from a water jug—the man finds it impossible to rid himself of it. The episode of the water jug derives from a superstition that when leaving a place, one should not return for something left behind. The man's wife insists that he return and despite his reluctance, he does, only to discover that he has recovered the bad luck he had hoped to escape. This time his misfortune is more persistent than ever, and resists every attempt to free himself of it, until his wife finally comes up with a clever solution. The role of the wife in this tale reflects the kind of rabbinic ambiguity toward women that goes back to Eve, who brought about Adam's fall from grace, but still remained his loyal and faithful wife and the mother of his children. Here the wife provokes the problem in the first place by insisting that they turn back, but once they are saddled with misfortune again, it is she who finds the ingenious way of freeing them from it. The man himself is seen as a passive actor in the world of fate. When the wind of ill luck blows his way, there is no escaping it, but once his luck turns, good fortune comes to him in great abundance. This tale, then, reveals as well the pervasive Jewish sense of helplessness in the face of an array of forces, both natural and supernatural, largely beyond their control, although the action of the wife seems to suggest that there is still room for human ingenuity to shift the balance of fortune one way or another.

The Black Monk and the Master of the Name (Eastern Europe) • Pages 335–348

From Paris Hebrew manuscript 157 number 7, translated from the Yiddish by Yisrael Cohen in 1630. Published by Eli Yassif in *Bikoret Ufashanut*, volume 9-10, 1976. The Yiddish original was published in

Fyorda in 1694 and reprinted by Yitzhak Rivkind in *Yivo Filologische Schriften* 3 (Vilna: 1929). A second Yiddish variant is found in the Bodeian library. Another variant is found in *Haggadot Ketu'ot* (Hebrew) published by Louis Ginzberg in *Ha-Tzayyad Veha-of* in *Ha-Goren* 9, Berlin: 1923. Another variant is found in codex Gaster, folio 37a. One of the earliest versions of this tale was presented as an actual incident in an early Yiddish travel book, *Gelilot Erez Yisroel* by Gershom ben Eliezer ha-Levi Judels (Lublin: 1634). An oral version is found in *Notzat ha-Zahav* (Hebrew), edited and annotated by Dov Noy. (Haifa: Israel Folktale Archives, 1976). IFA 10103, told by Moshe Attias of Greece. An oral variant about Rabbi Shalem Shabazi of Yemen is found in *Hadre Teman* (Hebrew) (Tel Aviv: Afikim, 1978), edited by Nissim Binyamin Gamlieli. Collected by Gemlieli from Shlomo Ben-Yaakov of Yemen. AT * 730A.

Knowledge of this elaborate tale of the rescue of a Jewish community by an emissary from the Ten Lost Tribes on the other side of the river Sambatyon was wide-spread in Eastern Europe, and exists in many variants, ranging from a page or two to novella length. The longest and most complete version is that published in Yiddish by Yitzhak Rivkind. Elements of several variants have been combined here. The hero in this tale is usually identified as Rabbi Meir Baal ha-Nes, although this attribution is purely legendary. The tale is closely associated with the "*Akdamut Millin*," an Aramaic poem composed by Rabbi Meir ben Isaac Nehorai, which is recited in the synagogue on Shavuoth. The origin of the poem is connected to the legend recounted in this tale. The legend of the river Sambatyon is first noted by Josephus (*Wars*, Volume VII, 5:1, although he reverses it, describing the river as running only on the Sabbath.) The correct legend, that the river runs six days a week and rests on the Sabbath, is clearly stated in the Talmud (B. Sanhedrin 65b) and the Midrash (Genesis Rabbath 11:5 and 73:6), and in the latter the Ten Lost Tribes are identified as being on the other side of the river. The legend of the river Sambatyon is also found in *Sefer ha-Zichronot*. See the *Chronicles of Jerahmeel*, edited by Moses Gaster, chapter 61. In this way the river supplies a reason for the lost tribes remaining in exile—the river is impossible to cross when it is running, and they are forbidden to cross on the Sabbath. A multitude of legends about the Ten Lost Tribes are to be found, as well as accounts of visitors who claimed to have reached them, including Benjamin of Tudela and David Reubeni. In most of these legends they are described as being exceedingly pious and observant. In some folktales, however, they are described as "little red Jews from the other side of the river Sambatyon." The Black Monk is a legendary figure who combines all of the elements of the anti-Semetic hostility that so plagued the Jews of Eastern Europe. His defeat at the hands of the old man from the other side of the river Sambatyon is parallel to the same tale type told about Rabbi Adam, Rabbi Judah Loew and the Baal Shem Tov, among others, who vanquished dangerous enemies of the Jews using supernatural powers based on kabbalistic incantations and holy names; i.e. powers deriving from God. The fact that the Jews in this tale had to turn to their brethern on the other side of the river Sambatyon indicates the desperation felt by Eastern European Jews in the face of the persecution they suffered, and their inability to find any other solution to the problem. At the same time, the tale is a reaffirmation of faith in God, and it is this aspect of it that is recalled in conjunction with the song of Akdamut. In fact, this story is generally known as *"Maaseh Akdamut,"* the tale of Akdamut.

Glossary

All of the following terms are Hebrew unless otherwise noted.

Agunah   A woman who is forbidden to remarry because her husband either has abandoned her without a divorce or has possibly died, but without leaving any proof that this has occurred.

Beit Din   A rabbinic court convened to decide issues relating to the *Halakhah*, the Law.

Brit   Lit. "Covenant." The circumcision given to every male Jewish child on the eighth day after birth.

Drash   An interpretation of a passage of the Torah. Also the third level of *Pardes*, the system of interpretation of sacred texts, representing allegory.

Emet   Truth.

Gehenna   The place where the souls of the wicked are punished and purified: the equivalent in Jewish legend of Hell.

Gilgul   The transmigration of souls; the kabbalistic equivalent of the belief in reincarnation.

Golem   Lit. "shapeless mass." A creature, usually in human form, created by magical means, especially by use of the Tetragrammaton, the four-letter secret Name of God, YHVH. The best-known legends are connected with the Golem created by Rabbi Judah Loew of Prague to protect the Jewish community against blood-libel accusations.

Kabbalah Lit. "to receive." The term designating the study and texts of Jewish mysticism. A Kabbalist is one who devotes himself to the study of those texts.

Kelippot A kabbalistic concept referring to the empty shells which represent the concentrated forces of evil and obstruction.

"Lech le Azazel" A phrase used to mean "Go to the Devil!" or "Go to Hell."

Maharal Acronym for Rabbi Judah Loew of Prague.

Mazel Luck.

Midrash A method of exegesis of the biblical text. Also refers to post-Talmudic Jewish legends as a whole.

Mikvah The ritual bath in which women immerse themselves after menstruation has ended. It is also used occasionally by men for purposes of ritual purification.

Mitzvot The divine commandments. Ther are 613 *mitzvot* listed in the Torah.

Moshe Rabeinu Lit. "Moses our teacher."

Ner Tamid The eternal light that burned in the Tabernacle and The Temple, represented today in every synagogue as a continuous light burning before the Ark.

Pardes, PaRDes Lit. "orchard," and also a root term for "Paradise." Also an acronym of a system of textual exegesis, based on four levels of interpretation; *peshat* (literal), *remez* (symbolical), *drash* (allegorical), and *sod* (mystical).

Peshat A literal kind of textural exegesis. Also the first level of interpretation in the system known as *Pardes*.

Piku'ach Nefesh Lit. "regard for human life." The rabbinical term for the duty to save an endangered life, which temporarily overrides the other commandments.

Rambam Acronym for Moses ben Maimon, or Maimonides.

Rebbe (Yiddish). The term used for Hasidic leaders and masters; a Yiddish form of "rabbi."

Remez Lit. "a hint." The second level of interpretation in the system known by the acronym *Pardes*. It implies the perception that the meaning has moved from the literal to the symbolic level.

Sefirot Emanations, ten in all, through which the world came into existence, according to kabbalistic theory.

Shekhinah Lit. "to dwell." The Divine Presence, usually identified as a feminine aspect of the divinity, which evolved into an idependent mythic figure in the kabbalistic period. Also identified as the Bride of God and the Sabbath Queen.

Sod The fourth, mystical level of the four-level system of interpretation represented by the acronym *Pardes*.

Tallis A four-cornered prayer shawl with fringers at the corners, worn by men during the morning prayer services. It is worn throughout the day on Yom Kippur. (*Tallit* in modern Hebrew.)

Talmud The second most sacred Jewish text, after the Bible. The term "Talmud" is the comprehensive designation for the *Mishnah* and the *Gemara* as a single unit. There are Babylonian and Jerusalem Talmuds, which have different Gemaras commenting on the same Mishnah. The material in the Talmud consists of both Halakhah (law) and Aggadah (legend); in addition there are discussions on philosophy, medicine, agriculture, astronomy, and hygiene.

Tefillin Phylacteries worn at the morning services (except on the Sabbath) by men and by boys over the age of thirteen.

Torah The Five Books of Moses. In a broader sense the term refers to the whole Bible and the Oral Law. And in the broadest sense it refers to all of Jewish culture and teaching.

Tzaddik (pl. **Tzaddikim**) An unusually righteous and spiritually pure person. Hasidim believed their rebbes to be *tzaddikim*.

Tzohar The legendary gem which was hung by Noah in the ark to light it in the darkness during the forty days of the Flood.

Urim ve-Thummim The breastplate worn by the High Priest, which was believed capable of divination.